HYBRID IDENTITIES

Studies in Critical Social Sciences Book Series

The Studies in Critical Social Sciences book series, through the publication of original manuscripts and edited volumes, offers insights into the current reality by exploring the content and consequence of power relationships under capitalism, by considering the spaces of opposition and resistance to these changes, and by articulating capitalism with other systems of power and domination—for example race, gender, culture—that have been defining our new age.

Haymarket Books is pleased to be working with Brill Academic Publishers (http://www.brill.nl) to republish the Studies in Critical Social Sciences book series in paperback editions. Titles in this series include:

Culture, Power, and History: Studies in Critical Sociology
Edited by Stephen Pfohl, Aimee Van Wagenen, Patricia Arend,
Abigail Brooks, and Denise Leckenby

Dialectic of Solidarity: Labor, Antisemitism, and the Frankfurt School
Mark P. Worrell

The Future of Religion: Toward a Reconciled Society
Edited by Michael R. Ott

Globalization and the Environment
Edited by Andrew Jorgenson and Edward Kick

Hybrid Identities: Theoretical and Empirical Examinations
Edited by Keri E. Iyall Smith and Patricia Leavy

Imperialism, Neoliberalism, and Social Struggles in Latin America
Edited by Richard A. Dello Buono and José Bell Lara

Liberal Modernity and Its Adversaries: Freedom, Liberalism,
and Anti-Liberalism in the Twenty-first Century
Milan Zafirovski

Marx, Critical Theory, and Religion: A Critique of Rational Choice
Edited by Warren S. Goldstein

Marx's Scientific Dialectics: A Methodological Treatise for a New Century
Paul Paolucci

Race and Ethnicity: Across Time, Space, and Discipline
Rodney D. Coates

Transforming Globalization: Challenges and Opportunities in the Post 9/11 Era
Edited by Bruce Podobnik and Thomas Reifer

Series Editor: David Fasenfest, Wayne State University

Editorial Board: Chris Chase-Dunn, University of California-Riverside; G. William Domhoff, University of California-Santa Cruz; Colette Fagan, Manchester University; Matha Gimenez, University of Colorado, Boulder; Heidi Gottfried, Wayne State University; Karin Gottschall, University of Bremen; Bob Jessop, Lancaster University; Rhonda Levine, Colgate University, Jacqueline O'Reilly, University of Brighton; Mary Romero, Arizona State University; Chizuko Ueno, University of Tokyo

HYBRID IDENTITIES
THEORETICAL AND EMPIRICAL EXAMINATIONS

EDITED BY KERI E. IYALL SMITH
AND PATRICIA LEAVY

Haymarket Books
Chicago, Illinois

First published in 2008 by Brill Academic Publishers, The Netherlands
© 2008 Koninklijke Brill NV, Leiden, The Netherlands

Published in paperback in 2009 by
Haymarket Books
P.O. Box 180165
Chicago, IL 60618
773-583-7884
www.haymarketbooks.org

ISBN: 978-1-608460-35-9

Trade distribution:
In the U.S., Consortium Book Sales, www.cbsd.com
In the UK, Turnaround Publisher Services, www.turnaround-psl.com
In Australia, Palgrave Macmillan, www.palgravemacmillan.com.au
In all other countries, Publishers Group Worldwide, www.pgw.com

Cover design by Ragina Johnson.

This book was published with the generous support of the Wallace Global Fund.

Printed in the United States on recycled paper containing 100 percent post-consumer
waste, in accordance with the guidelines of the Green Press Initiative,
www.greenpressinitiative.org.

10 9 8 7 6 5 4 3 2 1

Library of Congress Cataloging-in-Publication Data is available.

Keri E. Iyall Smith dedicates her work on this book to people who live in between borders, across borders, or through borders, particularly her family.

Patricia Leavy dedicates her work on this book to Dr. Stephen Pfohl in recognition of his mentorship.

Contents

List of Figures

Acknowledgements

Without the support of others, books would not exist. We especially want to thank Ashley Garland, Laura MacFee, and Paul Sacco for research assistance at Stonehill College. Financial support from Katie Conboy and Karen Talentino, also at Stonehill, contributed to our ability to produce a polished book. We have also had the opportunity to work with topnotch professionals who assisted in the production of this book. We gratefully thank series editor David Fasenfast, who provided us with invaluable guidance and assistance in the process of assembling and producing this book. We are also thankful for the generous assistance from our copyeditor, Julia Maranan. Finally, we thank the authors, both those who contributed and those who were unable to contribute to the project. Many of the authors experienced personal loss and struggles, and still gave so much to this book. We thank you all; it was a pleasure to work with you.

Part I. Theoretical Study of Hybridity

Chapter One
Hybrid Identities: Theoretical Examinations
Keri E. Iyall Smith

Globalization is an historical, dialectical process. Cultural globalization tends to produce one of three outcomes: differentiation, assimilation, or hybridization. There are multiple historical layers of hybridity, which span the longue duree (Pieterse 2004). The study of the processes and outcomes of hybridization of cultures will be essential to allow for a deeper understanding of globalization (Ang 2003, Canclini 2000, and Hannerz 1996). Cultural hybridization refers to "the ways in which forms become separated from existing practices and recombine with new forms in new practices" (Pieterse 2004: 64). A reflexive relationship between the local and global produces the hybrid. The identities are not assimilated or altered independently, but instead elements of cultures are incorporated to create a new hybrid culture. The creation of a hybrid identity is a "twofold process involving *the interpenetration of the universalization of particularism and the particularization of universalism*" (Robertson 1992: 100). The local and the global interact to create a new identity that is distinct in each context. As the two interact, the local influences the global and the global influences the local. The local is universalized and the universal is localized. The result is a form of hybridity that "signifies the encounter, conflict, and/or blending of two ethnic or cultural categories which, while by no means pure and distinct in nature, tend to be understood and experienced as meaningful identity labels by members of these categories" (Lo 2002: 199). Power and hierarchy influence the process of globalization, resulting in the uneven integration of human life and contributing to the emergence of diasporas and migration (Pieterse 2004).

For example, Simmel's (1950) "The Stranger" occupies a hybrid identity space. The stranger arrives today and has the *potential* to leave tomorrow (Simmel 1950). Strangers are simultaneously members of the community and not members of the community. The stranger is one new identity that might emerge by combining two identities that were previously discrete and now overlap. They are not seen as individuals, but as a particular type that is a combination of the stranger's identity and the local identity. One resolution to the problem of having two identities, or being identified by types and labels, is to create a new identity. It is the hybrid identity that includes a local and global identity form, merged to create the hybrid identity.

It is common to find hybridity in the context of a colonized culture that has been destabilized (Gandhi 1998). When cultures take in elements of global influence, they are doing so within the context of their local lives and creating a new hybrid. Individuals occupying a hybrid space simultaneously experience a doubleness and cultural intermixture (Gilroy 1993). Initially a term of derision, the meaning of hybridity is changing in the globalized world. Given a compressed world and a constrained state, identities for all individuals and collective selves are becoming more complex. With globalization and increasing modernization, being a hybrid is now a benefit. The ability to negotiate across barriers – language, cultural, spiritual, racial, and physical – is an asset. Although the hybrid contains elements of the local and the global, the intermixture makes it unique. Those who occupy hybrid spaces benefit from having an understanding of both local knowledge and global cosmopolitanism. Those who can easily cross barriers in a world of amorphous borders have an advantage.

The hybrid concept has roots in the hard sciences (e.g., botany or biology), as well as in the social sciences. Young's (1995) review of the genealogy of the term "hybrid" illustrates this. In the more literal interpretation, the hybrid is the product of "pure" or "distinct" categories. Notions of purity cannot be as easily linked to cultural identities, which consist of constructed and imagined elements. In this interpretation, cultures are not sealed off from each other (Gilroy 1993), which renders it nearly impossible to assert that there are "pure" cultures that could produce a hybrid. In the plant world, purity can be maintained with plastic bags and controlled pollination by a gardener. The same gardener can engineer hybrids, as Mendel illustrated with his peas, using planned cross-pollinating. However, even the most isolated culture cannot be so carefully maintained or manipulated. Instead of using the more literal biological model, we choose to follow recent scholarship in postcolonial studies. Biology is an excellent inspiration for the idea of the hybrid, but it does not properly reflect the process of cultural production.

Although hybridity was initially an outcome of oppression, a way of negotiating stability for a fragile dual identity (DuBois 1996 [1903], Gandhi 1998), the expansion of globalization brings hybridity to the privileged and the disadvantaged. Universalizing processes are acting simultaneously with localizing processes. A global culture is spreading, and as it comes in contact with various localities a hybrid identity develops. Hybridity is about creativity and cultural imagination (Lo 2002). Those who occupy hybrid spaces benefit from having an understanding of both local knowledge and global cosmopolitanism.

Hybridity encompasses partial identities, multiple roles, and pluralistic selves. The individual or community with a hybrid identity mimics the squeezing of the world community with a simultaneous expansion of the world community. Exposure to global communication and culture plant the seeds for the formation of a hybrid culture. The hybrid identity might allow the globe to unite in its differences, to be a truly multicultural society that is able to recognize and reconcile diversity. This blending of multiple cultural categories is happening around the world, and hybrid identities are emerging. Hybridity is also a cross-category process and a subversion of hierarchy (Pieterse 2004).

Globalization and localization are two contradictory processes operating simultaneously. As a global culture, economy, and society are spreading, local communities continue efforts to maintain their particular cultural, economic, and societal customs. Hybridity has become one way to re-create and re-vision a local community, while incorporating elements of outside groups, such as the global culture. The hybrid allows for the perpetuation of the local in the context of the global – using the global selectively while continuing essential elements of the local.

The sociological analysis of hybridity investigates the range of types of hybrid identities that are explored theoretically and empirically in the literature on identity. Multiple forms of hybridity are analyzed: identities that exist across borders, duality, gender (a false dichotomy), new identities, the diaspora (borderless), and the internal colony hybrid (formed within boundaries). A hybrid identity might form as a result of a false dichotomy, where an identity that seemingly only has the capacity to occupy two forms is actually shown to encompass another form. Physical borders of states assume discrete identities, people who experience double consciousness also experience a "two-ness" that is distinct from either single identity contributing to the duality, and, finally, the dichotomized sex and gender identities do not encompass the full range of sexed or gendered identities. Alternatively, it is possible for a hybrid identity to emerge as a category that defies borders. This type of hybrid exists simultaneously in multiple contexts. Hybrid identities that occupy the third space, or that emerge as a result of a diasporized population are two examples of hybrid identities that are borderless. Finally, hybrid identities form when multiple categories exist within borders and fuse to create a new form of identity. The hybrid identity that is born among internally colonized populations is a hybrid identity that is formed within boundaries.

Hybridity on the Borders

The creation of a hybrid identity crosses borders, as the local and the global interact to create a new identity that is distinct. It also challenges existing borders, particularly those of political and ethnic communities. Yet, hybridity can only exist in a world with borders. The creation of hybrid identities is evidence that borders are shifting, reforming, and being created. This chapter will survey developments in the study of boundaries and boundary crossing in a breadth of contexts. Patrick Gun Cunginghame explores the economic and political aspects of bordered hybridity, critiquing the "bordered" construct as he explores the identity formation that is emerging in this distinct context. Cuninghame also explores the distinction between hybridity and transnationalism, using the maquiladoras to apply his theoretical ideas empirically.

Double Consciousness

DuBois (1996 [1903]) describes hybridity as resulting in a double consciousness. Double consciousness is distinct because it explicitly embodies multiple identities instead of crossing identity group boundaries. Groups or individuals that occupy this space experience a kind of "two-ness," as two identities trying to exist within one person (DuBois 1996 [1903]). Expanding this idea to all blacks in the West, Gilroy describes the position as "between (at least) two great cultural assemblages" (Gilroy 1993:1). The individual occupying a hybrid space navigates between two cultural groups and occupies space within both cultural groups. This space holds a challenge and a privilege. Two-ness can be a hindrance. Yet, Judith R. Blau and Eric S. Brown explore how it is possible to create a reflexive perspective on two-ness, allowing African-Americans to achieve synthetic emancipation in their chapter. The African-American is described as having a veil, and a second sight (DuBois 1996 [1903]). Blau and Brown suggest that the veiled individual is able to see others better than they can be seen. The veil creates distance, but the second sight affords a way of seeing the self in the view of others.

Gender and the Hybrid Identity

Examination of the hybrid identity applied to gender is less common than many of the other classifications identified in this book. Fabienne Darling-Wolf's chapter examines the dichotomized expressions of gender in our society, identifying a hybrid form of gendered identity that occupies both maleness and femaleness. Alternatively, it is also possible to interrogate the categories of man and woman by looking at gender hybridity. The result of this work might be a reshaping of definitions of maleness and femaleness. Studies of gender hybridity allude to the false dichotomy of sex and gender identities, suggesting that maleness and femaleness do not adequately represent the range of sex and gendered identities. Salvador Vidal-Ortiz further interrogates the dichotomy of sex and gender, exploring the process of what he calls passing through. With passing through, Vidal-Ortiz explores transgenderism and transsexuality in a society that conceives of sex and gender as dichotomous.

Globally, there are also multiple definitions of gendered identity: Maleness and femaleness are not expressed in the same ways in all societies. Mobile men and women and place-less cultures are redefining the meanings of male and female as well, adopting elements of multiple cultures to create new conceptions of masculinity and femininity. Studies of immigrant women analyze attire to see how women choose to express their gender and their culture. Darling-Wolf explores the impact of globalization on gender in her chapter, identifying the importance of the transnational influence, cultural identity formation, and nationalism on gendered identities.

The Third Space

Where communication, negotiation, and translation bridge societies, a new space emerges (Bhabha 1994). The third space is a product of the negotiations, interface, and exchange across cultural boundaries. The third space is the in-between position, and it is also a newly crafted position. It did not exist prior to the merging of identities. This is one type of hybrid identity that arises as cultural boundaries meet and blur. Identifying this space allows for the recognition of identity groups and the creation of institutions that recognize and can speak to people who occupy this particular type of hybrid position. Alex Frame and Paul Meredith explore the third space (see Chapter 16), suggesting that the third space is not new, but has been in existence and is applicable to customary law, language, and culture. The co-existence of cultures, Frame and Meredith suggest, can be particularly useful in the legal system. David L. Brunsma and Daniel J. Delgado's empirical analysis of the third space also considers the theoretical construct (see Chapter 17). They argue that the third space does not adequately represent the experiences of multi-racial individuals, and instead Brunsma and Delgado recommend applying an identity matrix to show the range of identity experienced by multiracial people.

The Diasporized Hybrid Indentity

Although the term diaspora was initially only applied to cases of historical dispersion, it is now more widely used to apply to any population that has spread beyond its borders (Ang 2003). Diasporas become divorced from the homeland as they spread to new lands. Yet the diaspora remains tied to a border via their shared national identity. Simultaneously, diasporized populations are borderless, as members of the diaspora might live anywhere beyond the borders of the homeland. The result is a dissolving of the territorially bounded nation and the diminishing of the possibility of the cosmopolitan imagination of "one world" (Ang 2003). As members of diasporized groups attempt to fit in within their new homeland, they might be more likely to adopt a hybrid identity. Alternatively, they might be less likely to adopt a hybrid identity as they attempt to cling to their identity that is tied to the homeland. Or, more likely, they become different from those who remain in the homeland as they adopt elements of the society they now live within.

Using immigration literature to inform their study of the diaspora, Melissa F. Weiner and Bedelia Nicola Richards explore the experience of diasporized populations and their adoption of hybrid identities. They explore the history of immigration in the Untied States, looking at how the waves of immigrants interact differently with American society, resulting in different forms of diasporized hybrid identities. Keith Nurse explores the diasporized culture and hybrid identity, focusing his lens on the carnivals of the Americas. Nurse uses the idea of geocultures to examine the role of diasporization on identity formation, using these ideas to question the constructs of empire, nation, and race. Carnivals, a cultural product of the diasporized peoples, allow peoples to negotiate their cultural identity and practice, and they are also a site of contestation of value and meaning. Nurse also recognizes the ways that carnivals reflect a hybridized identity type, adopting localized elements even as they are part of a broader American cultural festival.

The Internal Colony Hybrid

An internal colony exists within the boundaries of another identity group. This hybrid identity bridges the space between colonizer and colonized within a distinct context. The idea of internal colonialism comes from the power-conflict school of theory, which emphasizes the role of stratification and power. Internal colonialism debunks the salt-water thesis, which suggests that colonies can only exist overseas. An internal colony is a colony within the boundaries of the state that colonized it. This concept is significant because "by defining inter-regional relationships as 'colonial,' nationalist leaders have tried to inspire popular support for movements designed to promote greater autonomy, if not outright secession" (Stone 1996 [1979]:279). The internal colony is subjected to oppression from the outside government, questions of legitimacy, and forced assimilation. The colonizing government legitimates their expropriations by transposing them into "customs," but the internal colony can appeal to the same customs they resist.

As internal colonies, these hybrid groups are a society living within another society. They live under legal rules and cultural norms of the external society most of the time, simultaneously seeking to maintain cultural and legal independence and integrity. The internal colony creates an opportunity to maintain the integrity of its culture while learning to exist within the outsider culture. The internal colony is used to explain the social, economic, and political experiences of hybrid identities: Mexican-Americans, black Americans, Appalachian-Americans, Arab-Israelis, and many others. Roderick Bush focuses on the structural aspects of colonialism in his critical analysis of internal colonialism and hybrid identities, looking at how this positioning might allow them to become change agents within their societies. Bush explores the history of internal colonialism, along with its origins, and then he charts the critique and the decline of this concept. Yet Bush argues that internal colonialism continues to be relevant, pointing out that the structural relations of colonial oppression persist, and that these relations are important in the formation of identity and culture.

Conclusion

Culture is our general human software, and none of the world's institutions can function without software (Pieterse 2004). Cultural traits are programmed into society and individuals through processes of socialization across the life course. As people cross arbitrary institutionalized categories of identity, a synthesis occurs and a hybrid identity emerges.

In the theoretical chapters that follow, the authors analyze multiple types of hybrid identities to build more accurate theories of identity in a globalizing world. The authors pose critiques to existing theoretical constructs, seeking to develop more accurate concepts with which to examine the empirical world. Alternatively, they build upon previous research to create more relevant models of identity. The resulting texts present an array of identity constructs for analyzing the processes that produce the fusion of identities where once only two identities existed, across borders, and within borders. In response to diverse contexts, hybrid identities emerge: when a false dichotomy fails to represent identity fully, when identities merge across bordered spaces to span the previously established boundaries, and when cultures fuse within boundaries.

Chapter Two

Hybridity, Transnationalism, and Identity in the US-Mexican Borderlands

Patrick Gun Cuninghame

"We," the Other people
We, the migrants, exiles, nomads & wetbacks
in permanent process of voluntary deportation
We, the transient orphans of dying nation-
states
la otra America; l'autre Europe y anexas
We, the citizens of the outer limits and cre-
vasses
of "Western civilization"
We, who have no government;
no flag or national anthem
We, the New Barbarians
We, fingerprinted, imprisoned, under surveillance
We, interracial lovers,
children of interracial lovers, ad infinitum
We, in constant flux,
from Patagonia to Alaska,
from Juarez to Ramalla,
We millions abound,
defying your fraudulent polls & statistics
We continue to talk back. (Guillermo Gomez-
Peña, date unknown)

> Doing is converted into being: this is the core of power-over. Whereas
> doing means that we are and are not, the breaking of doing means that
> the 'and are not' is torn away. We are left just with 'we are' identification.
> 'We are not' is either forgotten or treated as mere dreaming. Possibility is
> torn from us. Time is homogenized. The future is now the extension of the
> present, the past the preparation for the present. All doing, all movement,
> is contained within the extension of what is. It might be nice to dream of a
> world worthy of humanity, but that is just a dream: This is the way things
> are. The rule of power-over is the rule of 'that is the way things are', the
> rule of identity. (Holloway 2002)

The above quotations represent two possible extremes of the contemporary
debate around identity, hybridity, transnationalism, and borderlands. The
Mexican-American performance artist Gomez Peña makes the "we" of hybrid
identity the centerpiece of his rant against racist "Western Civilization" and
one of its mains points of separation from non-Western (or not quite Western
enough) civilization, the US-Mexican border. The Mexico-based heterodox
"open Marxist" Holloway claims that all identities, hybrid or singular, are
mere equivalents of passive "being" as opposed to active "doing." He equates
them with the contemporary, seemingly fatalistic, acceptance of neoliberal
capitalism and implies that the adoption of "non-identity," the negation of all
identity, as argued for by Adorno (1966), is a precondition for the exit from
capitalism. In between are various intermediary positions, including those,
such as Anzualda (1987), who celebrate the resistance of hybrid "border
crossers" against the oppressive structure that is the US-Mexico border. There
are also those, like Vila (2001, 2003), who reject such idealized, essentialized,
and epistemologically privileged hybrid identities, observing instead messily
ambiguous, contradictory interactions between "border crossers" and "border
reinforcers," both of whom have hybrid identities.

The debate over hybrid identities at the border calls for an analysis of the
relationship between economic and cultural globalization in the construction
of social identities, whether hybrid, transnational, national, regional, or local.
Identities have probably always tended toward hybridity in the borderlands,
and the impacts of globalized circuits of production, homogenized consumer
patterns, media images, mass migration, and incessant travel have intensified and accelerated a process as old as the bordered nation-state itself, but

often with unforeseen consequences. In tracing contemporary debates about hybrid identities and borderlands, this chapter will also make a distinction between more culturally orientated hybrid identities and more politically related transnational identities. It will also focus on the question of the US-Mexico border itself and the conflicts rotating around it.

As well as distinguishing between hybridity and transnationalism, two separate but related processes produced by globalization, this chapter endeavors to theorize the effects on both sides of the border, no matter how asymmetric the embedded power relationship that the border itself represents. Its theoretical perspective is influenced by the ongoing debate between poststructuralist Marxist, postcolonialist, and cultural studies-based border theorists over the emancipatory potential of hybrid, transnational, or indeed any type of "identity," individual or collective, to overcome the present global rigidification of borders between the "advanced" capitalist North and the "emerging" capitalist South. Methodologically, the chapter is informed by four years of research work in Ciudad Juarez, the capital of the Mexican maquiladora industry and twin city of El Paso, Texas, on the relationship between globalization, the maquiladora export industry, and the hypothetical emergence of transnational identities in those borderlands.

The chapter begins with an investigation of identity itself as a sociological concept through a discussion of the differences between individual and collective identities. There follows a comparison of hybrid and transnational identities and their historical roots as categories, in which it is argued that hybrid identities do not have the liberatory potential with which some postcolonial and postmodern theorists have endowed them, while transnational identities seem to offer more hope for the emergence of a genuinely transborder society. The perpetually shifting nature of contemporary borders, both symbolic and real, is discussed before examining the effects of globalization and glocalization on identity construction in the US-Mexican borderlands, as debated by American border theorists who either pit hybrid "border crossers" against hybrid "border reinforcers" or fuse both together. It is argued, however, that the central locus of hybridization, at least on the Mexican side of the border, is in the workplace, specifically in the maquiladora export industry, the site of an ongoing clash of work cultures. This conflictual process produces first hybrid and possibly later transnational identities among those workers, trade unionists, and transborder activists who build solidarity networks with the hyper-exploited Mexican maquiladora workers and on other related human rights and environmental issues. The chapter concludes by agreeing that, while hybrid identities are characteristic of the borderlands, they can also be both border-crossing and border-reinforcing and are, therefore, not necessarily emancipatory. In any case, a new form of emerging global sovereignty, "Empire," as opposed to the old form of sovereignty based on the nation-state, arguably has already recuperated and thus nullified the liberatory potential of both hybrid identities and the politics of difference. Nonetheless, an admittedly minoritarian transborder civil society, tentatively based on transnational and even postnational[1] identities, continues to mobilize itself around the social and political conflicts present in the borderlands, building on the experience of previous cross-border social movements and consolidating and expanding existing transborder networks.

Individual and Collective Identity

Identity is currently a vogue term, often used but seldom fully explained by a contemporary social science struggling to keep pace with globalizing cultures and societies. Originally, identity was thought of as being primordial and embedded in territory, language, kinship, and blood lines. Although the primordial conception of identity continues to be powerful both in the popular imagination and among policy makers ("You cannot be Mexican if you don't want to live in Mexico," "You cannot be from the US unless you can speak English," etc.), the idea of identity as a construct rather than a primordial given has become prevalent in the social sciences. Castells (1997: 7) agrees that "from a sociological perspective, all identities are constructed" and defines it thus:

> Identity is people's source of meaning and experience...By identity, as it refers to social actors, I understand the process of construction of meaning on the basis of a cultural attribute, or related set of cultural attributes, that is/are given priority over other sources of meaning...[M]eaning is organized

---

[1] Based on the rejection of any type of regional or national identity, and widespread among the alterglobal and anti-capitalist movements.

around a primary identity (that is an identity that frames the others), that is self-sustaining across time and space. (idem:6–7)

Constructed from the building blocks of history, geography, biology, religion, language, collective memory, and personal fantasies, among others, Castells has identified three forms and origins of identity building: legitimizing, resistance, and project identities. Legitimizing identity is "introduced by the dominant institutions of society to extend and rationalize their domination vis-à-vis social actors." It is an "over-imposed, undifferentiated, normalizing identity" that "generates a civil society" and is linked above all to nationalism (idem:8–9). Resistance identity is "generated by those actors that are in positions/conditions devalued and/or stigmatized by the logic of domination." It is linked to identity politics and leads to the formation of communes or communities, which may in reality be little more than fragmented "tribes" (*ibid.*). A project identity happens "when social actors…build a new identity that redefines their position in society and…seek the transformation of the overall social structure." It produces desiring subjects who are not individuals as such, but who are more like "collective social actors," such as new social movements (idem:8–10).

The concept of social identity has been defined in sociology as the manner in which individuals label themselves as members of particular groups, so producing national, gender, and work identities, among others. Based on the writings of the American pragmatists, Symbolic Interactionism has shown how identity can both influence and be influenced by social reality. The symbolic interactionists of the Chicago School argued that social reality is emergent and is constructed from the process of impression management, that is, from personal, situated interaction. Another important sociological source for identity theory has been Durkheim's theories of mass *anomie* and how this social phenomenon relates to identity formation strategies. This is of particular relevance to the study of US-Mexican borderland identities, as Zermeño (2005) and others have attempted to use the concept of *anomie* to explain the particularly harsh social environment found in border cities like Ciudad Juarez and the resulting high levels of sexual, social, and intrafamiliar violence.

Regarding the study of social identity from the perspective of social and historical change, some postmodernists view identity as a function of historical and cultural circumstances. For instance, Berger and Luckmann (1966) emphasize the changeability of identity and the possibility of negotiated multiplicity and, by implication, hybridity, by claiming that theories of identity are included in a more general interpretation of reality in that they are built into the symbolic universe with their theoretical legitimations, and they change together with the nature of the latter. Moreover, Berger (2001: 425) highlights how global processes have led to the decrease in the unifying power of the nation-state; the revival of local identities and forms of social interaction as ethnic, religious, and cultural communities; and of regional and transnational alliances that have redefined the "cultural frontiers of religion," a key element of individual identities in both Mexico and the southern "Bible belt" states of the US.

Analyzing the construction of social identities in the transnational context of the Mexico-United States borderlands of Ciudad Juarez (Chihuahua)-El Paso (Texas), Vila (2003a) concludes that people create their own "narrative identities" through the use of social categories, tropes, and/or by narrating stories about themselves and others. Most of the time, however, social actors use all these linguistic resources in a complex interplay of narrations, interpellations, and categories where it is not always clear which mechanism precedes the other, since all have a similar ability to order reality. On the question of the differences between narrative identities and Foucauldian "discursive identities," Vila (*ibid.*) underlines the importance of the overlapping of narrative and categorical systems in the self-construction of social identities, so that narratives are always needed to understand their relational and sequential character. It is also very common for social actors to use narratives to support the connotations of the categories they use to describe the reality surrounding them, especially when those categories are used to explain "others" in a context of symbolic struggle for meaning. As a result, it is impossible to know and interact with the real "other," since we can only know the "other" through descriptions. Vila (2001) notes that we use narratives to understand the reality that surrounds us and this indicates their importance in what Berger and Luckman (1966) call the "social construction of reality," or the way identity, together with all aspects of social reality, is a construct created by historical facts, which, nonetheless, have direct consequences on human behavior.

Thus, identity is seen in this chapter as a narrated, multiple, negotiated construct dependent on external markers and signs, and above all on the presence of "others," who both mirror and delimit private-individual and public-collective boundaries. Moving on to the question at hand, we now examine how hybrid and transnational identities differ from each other and how they can interact in the borderlands.

The Hybrid and the Transnational

Having identified various types of identity, their definitions, and some of the discussions around their construction, we will now explore the question of the hybrid and the transnational before looking at the state of contemporary American border theory and then applying the concepts of hybridity and transnationalism to the issue of identity at the US-Mexican border. Papastergiadis (2000) reminds us that the concept of the hybrid did not always enjoy its present positive connotation. In fact, it has a very dark and disturbing past, originating in the attempts by the late 19th century pseudo-scientific eugenics movement and social Darwinism to justify the intensification of European imperialism (and of the North American genocide of indigenous peoples) at that time as the preordained "civilizing mission" of the racially "pure" and, therefore, "superior" western nations over "inferior" and therefore enslaveable and expropriable races in Africa, Asia, and the Americas. However, imperialism had an unforeseen consequence, that of interracial sexual relations and the reproduction of hybrid offspring, such as the part-African, part-European "mulatoes" of Latin America, not to mention the ethnically, if not politically, dominant part-indigenous, part-African,[2] part-European

---

[2] This part of the *mestizo* (meaning "mixed") ethnic group is usually deliberately overlooked by official Mexican culture. For example, no stamp was issued in 1992, as part of the 500th anniversary of Columbus' "discovery" of the Americas, to celebrate the African presence in Mexico, while stamps were issued to celebrate the European and indigenous elements of *mestizaje*. African-Mexicans are mainly concentrated in the coastal states of Veracruz and Guerrero (particularly around Acapulco, although many have migrated to Mexico City and other urban centers) and are also often "invisibilized" by popular culture. Often, people in Mexico City assume that black Mexicans are either Cubans or Dominicans. In 2006, we saw two examples of the inherent racism of white (as opposed to *mestizo* or indigenous) Mexican culture, both right and left:

mestizo in Mexico. Thus imperialist pseudo-science turned to the problem of the hybrid, the "half-breed" of European and non-European extraction, and how to discourage such dangerous liaisons by depicting its offspring as weak, sickly, inferior idiots. The concomitant search for European racial "purity," the avoidance of hybridity, and the extermination of the eternal "internal enemy" that threatened white, Western, European, Christian, Greco-Roman "purity" – above all the Jew, but also the Gypsy, the Negro, the Slav, the communist, the homosexual, the mentally and physically disabled, and the racial hybrid – led to the ultimate evil of Auschwitz and the Shoah. But not even that unshiftable stain on human history and consciousness dispatched eugenics to oblivion, and elements of eugenics-influenced genetic determinism continue intermittently to raise their ugly heads.

Nevertheless, the negativity surrounding the word "hybrid" began to disperse due to the discrediting of social Darwinism and pseudo-scientific racism following the Shoah, postwar decolonialization, and the national liberation struggles. The anti-imperialist, "anti-racist racism," and postcolonial discourse produced by Franz Fanon and others in relation to those struggles also helped to instigate a positive recuperation of the term. By the 1970s its present generally positive nuance had emerged in anthropology, ethnography, and sociology with their increasing interest in the emerging multicultural societies of Western Europe, the rights of ethnic minorities and indigenous peoples slowly emerging from centuries of invisibilization, and the massive migratory flows that have increasingly come to characterize the post-1945, post-imperialist, neocolonial, globalized world.

The principal postcolonial theoretician of hybridity has been Homi Bhabha, who, according to Papastergiadis:

---

the furor produced by then-President Fox's public statement that Mexican migrants in the US had to do the jobs that "not even blacks want to do," which led to a lightening visit by Jesse Jackson to educate the reluctant Fox, who still refused to apologize for his racist remarks; and the scandal over the evidently racist "Memín Pinguín" cartoon character of popular magazines, which presented a distorted portrayal of the supposed dominant facial attributes of an African-Mexican boy with exaggeratedly large lips and curly hair, while the European and *mestizo* Mexicans are drawn in a much more realistic and respectful way, saw the usually politically correct, center-left *La Jornada* daily newspaper weighing in to defend those who denied it was racist.

[C]learly differentiates his use of the term 'hybrid' from earlier evocations which defined it as the diabolical stain or the harmonic transcendence between races. Bhabha has divorced the term hybridity from the context of miscegenation by placing it at once in both the semiotic field of discursive reconfiguration and in the socio-political domain of deterritorialized subjectivity. The exilic drives that underline our understanding of language and identity in modernity are thus made available to highlight the complex structures of agency. (193)

Bhabha (1994) argues that cultures interact with and transform each other in a much more complex manner than the traditional binary oppositions of Western thought (center/margin, civilized/savage, and enlightened/ignorant) permit. Accordingly, hybridity and what he terms "linguistic multivocality" have the potential to dislocate the process of colonization through the reinterpretation of political discourse. How this applies to the context of the US-Mexican border is open to debate. However, the political and cultural subalternity of Mexican identities before those of the United States – a condition intensified by globalization – is certainly comparable to the processes of cultural colonialization. Among those with problems with the idea that the operation of contemporary Western power can be reduced to opposing hierarchical binary structures are Hardt and Negri (2000). Certainly as Marxists, even if highly poststructuralized ones, they are bound to defend the binary nature of historical dialectical materialism. Nevertheless, while they too celebrate the apparent liberatory potential of hybridity as the basis of a new politics of difference, they perceive the same weakness at the base of postmodernist and postcolonial discourses: the insistence on attacking a target – modern Western sovereignty and its hierarchical monological identities – that has already shape-shifted and is not only already in the process of reinventing itself as postmodern global "empire," but also re-founds its new identity sets on recuperated difference and hybridity:

Hybridity itself is a realized politics of difference, setting differences to play across boundaries. This is where the postcolonial and the postmodern most powerfully meet: in the united attack on the dialectics of modern sovereignty and the proposition of liberation as a politics of difference... Like postmodernists too, however, postcolonial theorists in general give a very confused view of this passage [from modern national to postmodern, postnational-'imperial' sovereignty] because they remain fixated on attacking an old form of power and propose a strategy of liberation that could be effective only on that old terrain. The postcolonial perspective remains primarily concerned with colonial sovereignty. (Hardt and Negri 2000:145–146)

Nevertheless, the question remains as to the applicability of Bhabha's rather abstract discourse of hybridity to the identities of the Mexican-US borderlands and the immediate social conditions from which they arise and to which they return. Most, if not all the authors in *Ethnography at the Border* (2003) would contest the idealized notions of "hybrid identities" and the hypothetical emergence of a third, liminal, space that is both/neither the US nor Mexico, as presented by the postcolonial theory–influenced mainstream border theory that emerged in the mid-90s:

> This characterization of those living on borders, the hybrids, as having a kind of privileged ontological status (in terms of gender, class, ethnicity, nationality, etc.) is not only mainstream in border studies and theory but also part and parcel of…current mainstream cultural studies in general…The privileged position of those living on the US-Mexico border to understand and change reality arises precisely from the hybrid character of their identity, the complex mixture of Indian, Mexican, black, and Anglo[3] that characterizes the border. (Vila 2003c:323–324)

As Vila reiterates, locally based border analysts have trouble in recognizing so-called "Amexica," particularly in the (para-)militarized-post 9/11-Minuteman militia-border wall extension context, when crossing the border, both legally and without documents, has become increasingly problematic, and identities on both sides of the border, let alone across it, tend increasingly toward "border reinforcement" (hostility, fragmentation, and division) rather than "border crossing" (solidarity, synthesis, and hybridization):

---

[3] The term "Anglo" in the context of the border is, in fact, inherently dissatisfactory since it does not exclusively refer to English-Americans, but really to all white Caucasian Americans, some of whom still have strong cultural differences with each other and experienced racism and discrimination (not unlike that now being suffered by Latino immigrants) from the English-Americans and other whites when they first arrived as mass immigrant cheap labor in the US in the late 19th and early 20th centuries. See Bourne, 1916.

[Border] studies identify a subject who is clearly and undoubtedly 'resisting,' and a structure of power that, without contradictions is always 'oppressing.' This makes us lose sight of the much more complicated picture of the actual border, where people constantly move from positions of 'resistance' to positions of 'oppression'; when…a native Juarense who is 'oppressed' by American discursive formations that treat him or her as the 'other' applies the same treatment to his or her Southern Mexican 'other'…asking…for a Northern Mexico 'frontier' to the South, to 'stop' new migrants coming from Southern Mexico. Or when Juarenses…harshly 'other' Mexican Americans as pochos (highly Americanized Mexican-Americans, or, even worse, 'sell-outs') or as malinchistas (traitors). (idem:325)

Having outlined some of the debates around hybrid identities, we now pass onto the questions of transnationalism and transnational identities, which supposedly are more related to the economic and political spheres than the hybrid is. Another important difference between the transnational and the hybrid is that the former tends to refer more to collective identity and the latter more to individual identity. As a theory, transnationalism dates back to Randolph Bourne's classic Atlantic Monthly article of 1916, "Trans-national America," in which he attempted to overcome the limits of the assimilationist "melting pot" as the most effective way to "Americanize" the waves of migrants then arriving from Southern and Eastern Europe. Bourne denounces assimilationism as a counterproductive cultural model imposed by the English-American elite, based on creating "hyphenated Americans" (Irish-Americans, Italian-Americans, etc., although "negroes," "coloreds," and "Hispanics" did not become African-Americans and Mexican-Americans until the 60s), while the English-American elite assumed that their version of "Americanism" was the paradigm to which all other migrants should aspire and conform. The result was a "bastardized culture" in which neither did a strong, unifying "American" national identity emerge, nor were the strengths of each migrant culture really appreciated and incorporated into this collective American identity. In this sense, Bourne's discourse unconsciously (there is no specific reference in the text to Social Darwinism) echoes his contemporaries' denunciations of any kind of racial hybridity. Bourne's inherent racism is also evinced by his failure to even mention African-Americans or Mexican-Americans as part of the North American "nation of nations." However, in calling for the end of the assimilationist "melting pot" and its replacement by a transnationalization of the North American peoples to create a new national identity that appreciates the ability of all ethnic and cultural groups to be simultaneously both North American and their own original identity, Bourne may perhaps have given us a means for overcoming or, at least, mitigating the pessimism and skepticism that seems to characterize present discussions on hybridity at the border:

> America is coming to be, not a nationality but transnationality, a weaving back and forth, with the other lands, of many threads of all sizes and colors. Any movement which attempts to thwart this weaving, or to dye the fabric any one color, or disentangle the threads of the strands, is false to this cosmopolitan vision. (1916:96)

Of course, what is missing here is a cogent analysis of why and how English-Americanism continues to impose its version of American national identity and the power relations based on entrenched economic and social divisions that enforce and maintain this imposition. Nevertheless, Bourne's vision of a "transnational America" points toward the postnational "transnational world," to which contemporary alter-globalist and anticapitalist global social movements aspire when they claim that "another world is possible." An integral part of these movements are the growing number of "no border" movements, particularly against the exclusionist immigration policies of the US and European Union governments, whose basic slogan is that "no human being is illegal," and whose founding principle is that if goods, services, and currency transactions are free to cross borders under the present neoliberal version of globalization, then so too must human labor.

Transnationalism at the US-Mexican border takes the form on one hand of the domineering presence of the mainly US-based transnational corporations and their maquiladoras and industrial parks. Further on, we shall discuss the extent to which their economic presence translates culturally and socially into the construction of new transnational identities, particularly on the Mexican side of the border. However, another form of transnationalism, often overlooked by both economists celebrating the dynamism of the maquiladora-based border economy and sociologists fascinated by the processes of hybridization and identity construction, have been the various transborder social movements of recent decades (see the conclusion of this chapter).

A more sociological interpretation of transnationalism is presented by Beck (2000), who claims that the nation-state vision of society breaks down completely once the theory of the container of society, of separate social worlds contained within the national state, is substituted by third forms of life transnationally integrated by spaces of social action that cross frontiers. Thus, "transnational" means the emergence of ways of life and action whose internal logic is explained by the inventive capacity of humans to create and maintain social worlds and relations of exchange without measuring distances. It is clear that in these often illegal transnational social landscapes, with their "impure" forms of life and action, something is happening that the nation state, with its need for order, finds repugnant and seeks to control. The form this control takes historically has been the border, or internationally recognized and sanctioned boundaries between independent nation-states, and the juridical and military control of migration across those borders.

Shifting Borders, Symbolic and Real

Borders are the margins of the modern nation-state, simultaneously artificial, permeable, and militarized. They represent spaces where centralized power's struggle to control and maintain the "purity" of national identity, language, and culture begins to break down. For the modern nation-state, as Butler (1990) and Vila (2003a) have argued, borders represent potential pollution and fragmentation, dangerous spaces for the exercise of power, while offering new opportunities for identity experimentation and mutation for those who seek to cross them, physically, culturally, and sexually. Borders, while increasingly rigidified in the geo-physical plane with ever higher barriers, military patrols, and hi-tech surveillance as the nation-state struggles to reverse its decline in the face of global mobility, are in fact constantly shifting and re-forming in the symbolic dimension. The state seeks to filter and accommodate new hybridities by building new borders, sometimes internal, sometimes beyond its own margins. This can be seen in the new anti-terrorist security arrangements between Mexico and the US, where Mexico is obliged to adopt the same extreme measures but ultimately for use against its own population and Central American migrants passing through on their way to the States, rather than against Al Qaeda or even narco-traffickers, the main source of anti-state violence in Mexico since the 1980s. On the other hand, in some states like Arizona, employers are now obliged by law to verify the migratory status of their employees and report any undocumented migrant to the authorities on pain of imprisonment and heavy fines. Thus, every workplace in Arizona has become both a real and symbolic border post.

Furthermore, the border itself is a confusing place, where national identities are at once reinforced and undermined, as the state paradoxically inflicts identity crisis on its own citizens by over-asserting itself. For example, when crossing southwards from El Paso into Ciudad Juarez there is virtually no control either on traffic or pedestrians, one could almost miss the border itself. However, the real border with customs controls and so on, is to be found both in the small international airport and a few miles outside the city itself on the Pan-American Highway, going south to Chihuahua City, where much more rigorous checks are carried out, but mainly on Mexican citizens (few foreign tourists pass through) presumably suspected of smuggling cheaper goods from El Paso for which they should have paid import duties. Applying this confusing aspect of the borderlands to her research on how identities are affected by the border itself, Chapin concludes that:

> [T]hings are not as they seem; there is more to it, a dangerous difference, a loss of ground that defines the other. Elaine [a middle-class Anglo-American informant] and Juana [a working-class Mexican national informant] are both border crossers and border reinforcers, and at the same time they are both neither. Each narrative contains a dialectic of the two, subverting and reinforcing the border at the same time. Thus the border, the borderlands, and its hybrid populations and their identities are in a state of constant flux, despite the appearance of rigid control and territorial fixity. Even though power relations appear to be overwhelming and identities clearly demarcated, yet subtle divisions and fusions permeate the populations on both sides of and across the frontier. (2003:9)

The processes of hybridization and transnationalism finally seem to affect those who live on either side of the border almost to an equal extent. However, borders, always considered to be the porous edges of the nation-state, have recently been overwhelmed by the effects of both globalization and glocalization. The following section looks at how this interaction between globalization, glocalization, and borders affects the forms of hybrid and transnational identity in the US-Mexican borderlands.

Globalization, Transnationalism, and Hybrid Identities

Having discussed some interpretations of the principle variables at play, our attention now turns to the analysis of the relationship between globalization and the construction of social identities, whether transnational or hybrid, before passing to the question of the role of the economically hegemonic Maquiladora Export Industry (MEI) in this process of identity formation. A further objective is to discern the interaction of these transnational and hybrid identities as products or consequences of globalization, with more established types of identity such as national, regional, gender, and social class.

While most postcolonialists and some postmodernists emphasize the role of hybridity in the long-term decline of the nation-state, Hardt and Negri (2000) have a more ambivalent stance. In their book on "Empire" as the emerging form of postnational, global sovereignty, they recognize hybrid identities as part of its structure, along with "flexible hierarchies and plural exchanges [managed] through modulating networks of command" (2000:xii). In fact:

> [T]he sovereignty of Empire itself is realized at the margins, where borders are flexible and identities are hybrid and fluid. It would be difficult to say which is more important for Empire, the center or the margins. (2000:39)

However, while both postmodernism and postcolonial theory have tended to champion hybridity as the potential basis of a new oppositional politics, especially at the US-Mexico border,[4] Hardt and Negri counter-claim that, as with difference, hybridity has already been incorporated into the structures, norms, and practices of Empire, and that as a result, neither hybridity nor difference can of themselves form a new negative dialectic and anti-imperial antagonism:

> The affirmation of hybridities and the free play of differences across boundaries...are liberatory only in a context where power poses hierarchy exclusively through essential identities, binary divisions, and stable oppositions. The structures and logics powering the contemporary world are entirely immune to the 'liberatory' weapons of the postmodernist politics of difference. In fact, Empire too is bent on doing away with those modern

---

[4] See what Vila (2003c) calls the "new mainstream border theory of the 1990s," and in particular Anzualda (1987).

forms of sovereignty and on setting differences to play across boundaries. (2000:142)

Regarding the local-global debate as it refers to identity construction, the same authors also criticize the false dichotomy between the global and the local, since it is often assumed that:

[T]he global entails homogenization and undifferentiated identity, whereas the local preserves heterogeneity and difference...Implicit in such arguments is the assumption that the differences of the local are...natural, or...that their origin remains beyond question. Local differences pre-exist to the present scene and must be...protected...against the intrusion of globalization. This view can easily devolve into a kind of primordialism that fixes and romanticizes social relationships and identities. (idem:44–45)

As a result, it is necessary to analyze the production of localism and globalism and how both local and global identities and differences are created and reproduced:

Globalization, like localization, should be understood...as a regime of the production of identity and difference, or really of homogenization and heterogenization. (idem:45)

According to Hardt and Negri, who depend in this part of their theory on the poststructuralist concepts of "deterritorialization" and "reterritorialization," the best way to distinguish between the global and the local is to:

...refer to different networks of flows and obstacles in which the local moment or perspective gives priority to the reterritorializing barriers or boundaries, and the global moment privileges the mobility of deterritorializing flows. It is false, in any case, to claim that we can (re)establish local identities that are in some sense outside and protected against the global flows of capital and Empire. (*ibid.*)

Consequently, Hardt and Negri criticize, for example, the orthodox international leftist strategy of resistance against globalization and defense of the local and national as:

...damaging because in many cases what appear as local identities are not autonomous or self determining [since] globalization or deterritorialization operated by the imperial machine is not in fact opposed to localization or reterritorialization, but rather sets in play mobile and modulating circuits of differentiation and identification. (*ibid.*)

Returning to the specificity of the Mexican-US borderlands, particularly those of El Paso-Ciudad Juarez, Vila (2003c), in his attempt to recast border theory, outlines three definitions of hybridity in relation to identity: the border crosser, liminality, and "third space," a concept introduced by Bhabha (1994) that is explored elsewhere in this volume, but which also has a direct application to border theory. Hybrids crisscross borders (geo-political, cultural, sexual, and symbolic), as the local and the global interact to create a new identity that is distinct. However, where Garcia Canclini, Anzualda, Bhabha, Gomez Peña, and Hardt and Negri see the power of hybrids to cross borders, with and above all without documents; physically as migrants; culturally as bilinguals and biculturals; and symbolically as human beings who have outgrown the nation state's project for racial, cultural, and political "purity," with its array of national, regional, and local identities, Vila rejects such mainstream border theory as empty abstractions, produced by academics and thinkers who do not have direct experience of the borderlands (with the massive exceptions of Gomez Peña and Anzualda). For Vila, their excessively optimistic vision of the hybrid "border crossers" is ultimately divorced from the reality of those who actually live there and have to cross the border, whether they want to or not, to make a living. Instead, while recognizing and accepting the existence of an inevitable level of hybridity at the border, Vila firmly emphasizes the power of the border to divide and to reproduce identities that reinforce the border, often even while being apparently hybrid. The classic example of this phenomenon is the Mexican-American *pocho*, the second- or third-genera-tion Border Patrol agent with a Hispanic name, who is maybe still speaking Spanish as his or her first language, but who often has a racist disdain for his former countrymen south of the border. However, this identity, often stereotyped by Mexican nationals as that of the overwhelming majority of Mexican-Americans in general and particularly of those in El Paso, is only one extreme of a broad array of both contradictory and complementary hybrid identities, mainly north but also to some extent south of the border.

With reference to the latter, Lasso (2005) presents an arguably idealized portrayal of intercultural society in Ciudad Juarez and the variety of identity positions so produced and reproduced. His argument is that the locally rooted population of *Juarenses* (people from Ciudad Juarez) and more generally the *fronterizos* (borderlanders), particularly those of working-class origin, tend to resist better the "homogenizing"[5] processes of cultural globalization at the border, namely Americanization. They therefore retain traditional Mexican national identities and values better than the recently arrived internal migrants from the south and center of Mexico – the *foráneos* (outsiders), who are more susceptible to the processes of cultural and identity hybridization since they are not rooted to the border and wish, in the most cases, to cross it as quickly as possible to integrate themselves into US society as Mexican-American immigrants. The working class *Juarenses* tend to resist better than the middle classes because they have less opportunity to cross the border, often cannot afford to consume iconic US imports such as the McDonald's quarter-pounder, and are more deeply embedded in traditional Mexican culture, particularly "revolutionary nationalism" and Guadalupan Catholicism. On the other hand, they experience most directly the impositions of US and globalized neoliberal work culture – sharply different from traditional Mexican work cultures – as the vast majority either work, have worked, or have close relatives who work in the maquiladoras. Meanwhile the *Juarense* middle classes, with the exception of intellectuals and artists, are more prone to cultural hybridization through their constant exposure to and contact with US culture, particularly through their regular shopping and family visits (many middle-class and some working-class *Juarense* families have members in both Ciudad Juarez and El Paso, who usually keep in close contact), and their constant exposure to and use of the English language through the mass media and professional contacts with US citizens. Intellectuals and artists, according to Lasso, while sharing the same levels of exposure, are better equipped to resist cultural globalization and thus defend Mexican national culture, identity, and values because they are more conscious of the power imbalances involved in the processes of globalization and have the means to actively expose and redress these imbalances through their art, writing, or political activism. On the other hand, Lasso points out that cultural globalization is not a one-track process and that, in fact, Mexican-based cultural hybridization is also spreading throughout the southern US and cities like Chicago and New York, which have large Mexican immigrant populations. As

---

[5] Accepting that cultural globalization is homogenizing, which glocalization theory doesn't.

a result, the use of Spanglish (or *espanglés*) has increased, as has the popularity of reggaeton, ranchero, and Latino rap music, as well as the iconography of Guadalupan Catholicism (above all, the Guadalupan Virgin, which is now one of the principle identifying symbols of the Mexican and Latino communities in the US) among, but not exclusively, the more recently arrived sections of the deeply divided Mexican-American community. Nevertheless, strong differences of opinion exist over the ultimate benefits of these hybrid Mexican and Latino cultural products, some of which provoke as strong a rejection by Mexican and Hispanic traditionalists as they do from racist Anglos. However, apart from the essentializations and contradictions[6] involved in some of these claims, Lasso's essay describes the suspicion, which in other contexts has transformed into racist rejection,[7] of the *foráneos* by some *Juarenses*. These cultural divisions on the Mexican side of the border, which map onto class and ethnic divisions, have also been strongly emphasized by Vila (2003b), as previously mentioned.

Arguably the most important site for hybridization in the Mexican-US borderlands remains the maquiladoras, the principal source of jobs and income for the population on the Mexican side of the border and increasingly important for the economy of the US side, which continues to provide most of the investment and senior management and where the twin plants have almost all closed down and moved to the much cheaper Mexican side since the implementation of NAFTA in 1994. Since the MEI dominates

---

[6] For example, traveling on the ramshackle buses and taxies of Ciudad Juarez, driven by both working class *Juarenses* and *foráneo* migrants, you are just as likely to hear US rock and rap as Mexican ranchero music playing loudly on the radio. Mexican frontier intellectuals and artists are increasingly dependent on the globalization of the academy and the publishing and entertainment industries, not to mention their symbiotic relationship with the globalized and globalizing mass media.

[7] Two examples suffice here: the "chilangophobia" (hatred of people from Mexico City, derisively called chilangos because of their supposed penchance for eating chilies) of the mid- to late 1980s when many migrants arrived in the borderlands from Mexico City following the massive earthquake of September 1985, resulting in their violent rejection by some Juarenses, assaults, and even murders, and the coining of the now infamous chilangophobic slogan "Haz patria, mata un chilango" (Be patriotic, kill a chilango). The second example is that of the 450 or so "femicides" since 1993 in Ciudad Juarez and Chihuahua City, the vast majority of which remain unsolved due to the institutionalized indifference and probable collusion of the authorities and arguably to the fact that the majority of the victims are working-class internal migrant women or *foráneas*, while strong suspicion has fallen on the powerful narco traffickers of the Juarez Cartel, the police, and the "juniors" of the richest families for conducting women-killing "safaris." See Zermeño, 2005.

the borderlands economy in the twin cities along the border, almost to the exclusion of any other significant economic activity, barring tourism, the sex industry, smuggling, drug trafficking, and second-hand car importing, it is necessary to examine closely its impact on changes in both the work culture and worker identity and more generally on the rest of border society.

Hybridity in the Bordered Workplace: Maquiladoras and the Clash of Work Cultures

We can hypothesize here that the maquiladora mode of production and organization of work, as an expression of the economic and cultural globalization that dominates the US-Mexico borderlands, help to promote the formation of hybrid identities (from which could eventually emerge transnational identities) among men and women workers, particularly in Mexico, given that the "twin plant" is fast disappearing from the US side of the border. That being so, we need to identify how the imposition of new work practices and values, in other words a new work culture, by the Maquiladora Export Industry is leading to hybridization in the bordered workplace and how this type of hybridization may lead to the emergence of hybrid and eventually transnational identities among maquiladora workers and their communities. We are interested here in the "bordered" workplace, as the MEI first emerged in Ciudad Juarez and Tijuana in the mid-1960s as the keystone of the National Frontier Program, the Mexican government's attempt to resolve the problems caused by the ending of the Bracero Program in 1965, which led to the "dumping" of hundreds of thousands of unemployed ex-braceros in the border region, and to reactivate the until-then dormant economy of the borderlands, thereby attracting new populations to a dangerously underpopulated frontier. The MEI rapidly expanded during the 70s and particularly during the 80s and 90s, giving employment above all to very young internal migrant women, who were considered by the US management that initially ran the maquiladoras as more docile, responsible, and skillful workers, and less likely to unionize than locally based men. However, levels of sometimes autonomously self-organized industrial conflict, notably *tortuguismo* (go slows and working to rule), were actually higher during the 1970s and 1980s when the vast majority of line workers were young women, than since 1990 as the gender imbalance has gradually disappeared.

According to some sociologists (Zermeño 2005) the gender imbalance in maquiladora recruitment has provoked a crisis in the traditional extended Mexican family, generally accepted as the backbone of Mexican society, given the poor quality of education, the weakness of the Mexican social state, and the strength of the Catholic Church,[8] which promotes above all "family values" as part of its campaign, in alliance with the PAN (*Partido de Acción Nacional*/National Action Party) governing party, against abortion, birth control, the use of condoms against the spread of HIV/AIDS, gay marriage, and women's and gays' rights in general. Zermeño goes so far as to claim that the resulting *anomie* created by the crisis of the extended family in the borderlands may well explain the femicides as a "male backlash" copycat phenomenon. However, he fails to acknowledge that the younger women maquiladora workers, most of whom are *foráneas* and stigmatized in a racist-sexist fashion as *maquilocas* ("loose" women from the maquiladoras), seem to prefer actively the marginal benefits of having their own income and relative economic independence from their male partners, despite being extremely low-paid and even if some of the results are significantly higher rates of divorce, single-parent and female-headed families, and intrafamily violence than the rest of Mexico.

It can be said that three generations of maquiladoras now co-exist at the border. The first generation is one of simple assembly and packaging for export, present since the 1960s, where the labor skill level is low, pay is very low, and the conditions are poor, but the work culture is not particularly alien in that many such maquiladoras are owned and run by Mexican industrialists and corporatist trade unions linked to the PRI (*Partido Revolucionario Institucional*/Revolutionary Institutional Party) political party may be tolerated. This type of maquiladora has spread throughout Mexico, Central America, and the Caribbean since the 1960s – the textiles "sweatshop" is a typical example. A second generation came into being during the 1980s and is typified by its manufacturing capacity, although still exclusively oriented toward the exporting of the finished product to the US or European markets, and with

---

[8] Mexico is the world's largest Roman Catholic country and, despite the global crisis of the scandal-ridden Roman Catholic Church, the majority of its population, particularly women, continues to describe themselves as "practicing Catholics," as in the *Instituto Nacional de Estadística, Geografía e Informática* (INEGI, National Institute of Statistics, Geography and Informatics) 2000 census.

a minimum or total absence of coordination with Mexican suppliers or other local ancillary services. The administrative style has shifted from the North American "peripheral Fordism" of the first generation to the post-Fordist and Toyotist "just in time" and "total quality management" of Japanese origin. Management is no longer almost exclusively North American and is increasingly Mexican, at least at junior and middle levels. Skill levels increase, and there are more technical positions, which are the almost exclusive preserve of men, while women continue to be the majority of *operadoras* (line workers). Salaries and work conditions improve marginally, although they continue to be extremely low compared to equivalent jobs in the US. The globalized Japanese work culture, typical of the second generation of the MEI, is significantly more alien than the first generation to Mexican workers, who respond by "tropicalizing" it, although this process of industrial hybridization can be conflictual depending on the flexibility, cultural sensitivity, and communication skills of management. The typical products are white goods for the US domestic market. Only after 2000 has a third generation of maquiladoras emerged, which now has research and development capacities and employs a large number of highly skilled workers who are significantly better paid and more secure than workers in the other two generations. In reality, there are only two such establishments in Mexico: Delphi in Ciudad Juarez, which tests and produces parts for the US car industry, and Samsung, the South Korean electronics transnational corporation, in Tijuana. Their work culture is much less rigid and disciplined than that of the previous two generations, and there is much greater room for creativity and improvisation. However, employment here requires a high degree of cultural adaptation and integration of the employee into globalized Western work culture, advanced English language and computer skills, and, increasingly, a university degree. Aspects of both Mexican general and work culture are accepted on condition that they are integrated into productive creativity. Industrial hybridization is much more advanced than in the other two generations and is practically a prerequisite for employment and integration into the transnational corporate culture. There are also opportunities for transnational identities to emerge as there are frequent contacts between Mexican line workers and managers from a variety of national, ethnic, and religious backgrounds (not just Mexican or North American), and global corporate identification is strongly encouraged, as in the second generation. Respect for Mexican traditions such as in-company shrines for the worship of the *Virgen de Guadalupe* and holidays on Mexican Independence, Revolution, and Labor Days are carefully recognized. Nevertheless, it must be underlined that there are only two such plants in Mexico, and the third generation of maquiladoras, which can only be called so in that they continue to be tax-exempt export-oriented platforms with little interaction with other sectors of the local or national Mexican economy, is only in its early stages. It could signal a shift toward high-skill but still relatively low-paid work at the US-Mexico border and the opening of a new "silicon valley" from Albuquerque to Chihuahua City.[9] While the first generation of maquiladoras was characterized by conflictual industrial relations, the levels of industrial conflict are much lower in the second generation and virtually absent in the third. However, recent surveys have shown that line workers remain dissatisfied with their much lower wages (compared to the US labor market), although they seem reluctant to take industrial action, mainly because job security is minimal given the prevalence of flexible, precarious, short-term contracts, and employment turnover is high, because access to the informal sector of the US labor market is still available (if increasingly less so), even if as an undocumented migrant.

Regarding the creation of hybrid and transnational identities in the workplace and their diffusion throughout working class communities, through the imposition of globalized work cultures, Reygadas (2002) has compared the role of maquiladoras in Ciudad Juarez, Chihuahua City, and Guatemala in the construction of new work cultures through their relationship with diversity and conflict within the processes of globalization. He analyzes the cultural dimension of the transnational experiences of industrialization in Latin America in which the global factory does not automatically produce a global labor culture. In assembling these cultures, a homogeneous mixture does not occur, but rather singularities persist, misunderstandings arise, discrepancies are generated and, sometimes, consensus is built as hybridization occurs in the maquiladora. The formation of global factory networks, value chains, and clusters causes new problems and challenges for intercultural dialogue among the actors involved. In the maquiladora, whether in Chihuahua or

---

[9] This claim is based on a formal proposal made at the "US-Mexico Collaborative Research Workshop, 'El Porque y El How Not To,'" New Mexico State University, Las Cruces, February 3, 2005.

in Guatemala, there is permanent conflict among these different work cultures (that of the North American, South Korean, or Mexican managers and that of the Mexican or Guatemalan workers) as an intrinsic element of class struggle. These cultures influence each other mutually, although not equally since there is always a power relation at play, but their conflictual interaction has certainly changed identities, values, and lifestyles in the frontier region. Reygadas describes the work regime in the assembly plants as one of authoritarian flexibility, with an exclusive coexistence among Mexicans and North Americans, particularly in the first- and some second-generation maquiladoras. In general, the maquiladora assembly plants are a sign of two-speed globalization, multiple transnationalism, and glocalization in that they straddle the US-Mexican border in a localized fashion, while being integrated into the global division of labor and networks of production. Ultimately, they represent the most radical expression and one of the main causes of the extreme disparities in power, wealth, and opportunity that characterize the US-Mexican borderlands:

> [T]he new work cultures in maquiladora plants are not just a reaction to the present conditions of the world market, technology, or the social situation; they also demonstrate and model the confrontation of classes, social groups, and organisms that seek to control work processes in the maquiladora according to their interests. For this reason, the construction of new work cultures is inscribed in power relations... [T]he globalization of industry has not led to the generation of a single homogenous work culture, but rather to the reconstruction of the diversity of work cultures in new scenarios, in which the differences between companies, countries, and social groups in processes of conflict and negotiation are, at the same time, both local and global. (Reygadas 2002:302–305)[10]

Thus, on one hand, the constant exposure to neoliberal and globalized work practices and cultures in the maquiladora workplace, and on the other the industrial hybridization produced through the mostly cultural-individual and sometimes political-collective resistance of the Mexican workers and technicians, together produce hybrid identities. However, this does not necessarily result in transnational worker identities, where Mexican maquiladora workers

---

[10] My translation.

actively identify with workers from the US or other countries in order to build networks of mutual solidarity that could help to improve radically their work conditions and bargaining strength vis-à-vis their transnational employers. Various factors intervene, particularly on the Mexican side to prevent this, namely the individualist attitude promoted by the maquiladoras through their suppression of independent trade unions and promotion of short-term individualized contracts, both of which tend to undermine collective workplace solidarity. Secondly, the dominance of "revolutionary nationalism"[11] and Guadalupan Catholicism within Mexican national identities, which both promote suspicion of and diffidence toward "gringos" in general, including twin-plant workers and Mexican-Americans, on the grounds that they are all in some way responsible for the historical oppression of and continuing racism against the Mexican peoples by US neo-imperialism and that most of them belong to the "heretical" Protestant faith.[12] On the US side of the border, the growing racism toward Mexican undocumented emigrants in particular and the Latino communities in general is shown by the official tolerance of the extreme-right, anti-immigrant Minuteman militia in Arizona, New Mexico, and Texas. The construction of an "iron curtain"-style, three-meter-high, twin wall along most of the 3,000 km border, and the failure of the US Congress and Presidency to alleviate or even to clarify the situation of some 11 million Mexican undocumented migrants have also exacerbated the historical tensions between the two nations.

There have been cases of cross-border cooperation between MEI and twin plant workers as part of civil society networks. Usually these are initiated from the US side in the form of solidarity campaigns to denounce the excessive exploitation of Mexican workers by transnational corporations, the lack of properly enforced health and safety measures to report transparently and effectively reduce the number of industrial accidents and injuries in

---

[11] The official ideology of the PRI, which dominated Mexican politics as a state party from approximately 1930 to 2000, and which infused itself throughout the population through close control of education and the media. It is still present in different forms in the ideologies of all political parties and most social movements, including the pro-US government, neoliberal-Catholic right PAN governing party.

[12] Many Mexican Guadalupan Catholics refer to Protestants as "Christians," inferring that Catholicism and Protestantism are not two sects within the same religion but are, in fact, two separate religions.

maquiladoras,[13] and the uncontrolled and unregulated pollution of the borderlands by the maquiladoras, which also affects US border communities.[14] They aim to promote the improvement of workers rights and conditions in Mexico, so that wages and conditions become at least closer to those in the US, thus helping to lower unemployment in the US by making it less attractive to US corporations to shift production south of the border. Unfortunately, these efforts are not always fully reciprocated on the Mexican side of the border, mainly because Mexican civil society has much fewer resources to draw on and has to operate in a much more hostile and even dangerous political environment than does US civil society. For example, the majority of the participants at the first Border Social Forum in Ciudad Juarez in October 2006 were from US trade unions and NGOs. Even the 1,000 or so who marched through the center of Ciudad Juarez to denounce the femicides and the proposed construction of the "Wall of Shame" were mainly from the US. Very few independent maquiladora trade unionists, let alone workers, participated.

Although these transnational social movements tend to be more resource-mobilized from the US side, nevertheless they do represent real instances of cross-border cooperation, which in turn help to create new and consolidate already existing transnational and transborder identities. That being said, however, it has to be underlined that the majority of the Mexican participants in such movements still probably cling to some form of "left nationalist" identity that views all North Americans (including Mexican-Americans) with a certain amount of wariness, including those who are openly opposed to their government's policies in general and toward Mexico in particular. Perhaps

---

[13] A senior IMSS (*Instituto Mexicano de Seguridad Social*/Mexican Institute of Social Security) manager, who regularly inspects the health and safety conditions of maquiladoras, informed me in 2006 that various tricks are used by both the transnational corporations and the Mexican authorities to massage down the real numbers of industrial accidents and injuries. For instance when a worker is injured, s/he is immediately sent home and put on long-term sick leave, allowing the company to "lose" the accident statistically.

[14] On the other hand, examples of Mexican-initiated transborder campaigns have been those against the ASARCO smelting plant in El Paso, suspected of being the cause of the abnormally high level of infant cancer rates in Anapra, the poorest district of Ciudad Juarez and very close to the ASARCO plant, which was temporarily closed in 1999 but will soon be reopened. There was also an important and successful transborder social movement in the mid-1990s against the proposal to construct a nuclear waste dump next to the New Mexico-Chihuahua border.

this diffident attitude can also be explained by the economic dominance of the US social movements, which also tend to initiate and control the organizational processes of cross-border mobilization.[15]

Thus, despite the hybridization taking place within maquiladoras, this has not yet translated into fully hybrid, border-crossing identities, let alone the transnational identities necessary for the construction of effective cross-border working-class solidarity to improve radically the working and living conditions of men, and particularly women, maquiladora workers in Mexico. However, does this mean that transnational identities do not really exist yet in the borderlands?

Conclusion

One aspect of border life that tends to be overlooked or ignored by contemporary cultural and postcolonial studies-influenced border identity theorists, who tend to privilege the "everyday" over all other aspects of life, is both the victimization and protagonism of mainly working-class women in the borderlands. They are the both the most hybridized section of the population, often employed in the globalized working culture of the maquiladoras or as domestic servants in El Paso, many of whom have to cross the border "illegally" in the morning and cross back in the evening because they cannot afford the cost of a passport and visa, or as the mothers and supporters of femicide victims, forced to cross borders so that their voices can be heard. They are often the most transnational too, as transnational civil society networks are feminized because the issues they deal with are increasingly related to the victimization and exploitation of women as maquiladora, sex, and/or domestic workers, obliged to have two or three jobs to hold their

---

[15] These observations are based on my own participation in the cross-border "Other Campaign" (initiated both nationally and internationally by the EZLN in 2005) in Ciudad Juarez and its principal campaign to denounce the grave human rights abuses taking place in Colonia Granjas Lomas de Poleo in Ciudad Juarez, where a group of "colonos" are resisting illegal and violent attempts by the powerful Zaragoza family to drive them off their land, while the Mexican state simply refuses to intervene to protect their lives, property, or rights. The campaign recently made common cause with a similar one in El Paso, Texas, where the mainly ex-bracero population of the Segundo Barrio in downtown El Paso are resisting the gentrification of their barrio and the expulsion of its working-class population. For more information on both campaigns, see the Paso del Sur website, www.pasodelsur.com.

fragmenting families and lives together in a brutalized, deregulated, and poorly planned urban environment.

Recently, a new network of both men and women transnational activists has emerged to oppose, firstly, the construction of the planned San Jeron-imo–Sunland Park transborder twin city that will rival Ciudad Juarez-El Paso (sometimes referred to collectively with its pre-1847 and pre-border collec-tive name of "Paso del Norte") and reduce access to significant resources for Juarez, above all the already diminishing access to water of a city that daily receives several hundred new internal migrants; secondly, the attempt by the oligarchical Zaragoza family to terrorize an entire community in Lomas de Poleo, one of the poorest *colonias* (neighborhoods) of Juarez and close to the proposed San Jeronimo development, to force them off their land and allow the Zaragozas to speculate over its fast-rising value; and thirdly, the neoliberal gentrification plans for the Segundo Barrio, the historical heart-land of the bracero-Chicano community in downtown El Paso, promoted by the same transborder business, media, and political interests at work in San Jeronimo-Sunland Park.

Thus, it can be argued that transnational identities do exist in the Ciudad Juarez-El Paso-Las Cruces (New Mexico) borderlands, even if they are limited to a small section of the civil society of that region, sufficiently well-edu-cated, informed, and politically experienced to challenge and overcome the stereotypes, suspicions, and "othering" narratives and regional racisms that hybridized communities on both sides of the border tend to harbor against each other and, according to some sociologists, perhaps even more so against the "others" on their own side of the border. Of course, transnational and "border crossing" (as opposed to "border reinforcing") hybrid identities exist throughout the borderlands and in all sections of society, not just in the more illuminated sections of civil society, but so far in a much more diffused and not so visible or aggregated way.

Chapter Three

DuBois and Diasporic Identity:
The *Veil* and the *Unveiling* Project[1]

Judith R. Blau and Eric S. Brown

Lemert (1994) points out that although DuBois's *Souls of Black Folk* ([1903] 1965) is a powerful theoretical masterpiece, it was never incorporated into the sociological canon. His explanation for its neglect is the "occluded vision" of those on the dominant side and their structured inability to see those in the racially Other position (Lemert 1994:387). An important point to make is that although this neglect may have been due to racial prejudice, it also might be traced to the particular way in which DuBois theorized racial differences.

Most social scientists in the early decades of the twentieth century considered races as distinct groups with given origins forming a natural hierarchy (Sanjeck 1996). In striking contrast, DuBois viewed race and racial differences as historically contingent social constructions that ought to be vitally preserved as a

[1] We acknowledge the support of the Andrew W. Mellon Foundation and the National Science Foundation for undergraduate student support under its REU program. We thank Stacey Janine Hoffler, Kitty Mahmoud, Mignon Moore, and Susannah Paletz for their contributions to the empirical work incorporated into this paper and the faculty and students who participated in the 1998 Minority Undergraduate Research Program, University of North Carolina, Chapel Hill. The suggestions of Eduardo Bonilla-Silva, Lewis Coser, and two anonymous reviewers were extremely useful. Address correspondence to: Judith R. Blau, Department of Sociology, University of North Carolina, Chapel Hill, NC 27599-3210, USA; e-mail: jrblau@email.unc.edu.

basis of social pluralism. Defending the preservation of black culture, DuBois wrote in 1897: "As such, it is our duty to conserve our physical powers, our intellectual endowments, our spiritual ideals; as a race we must strive by race organization, by race solidarity, by race unity to the realization of that broader humanity which freely recognizes differences in men, but sternly deprecates inequality in their opportunities of development" ([1897] 1971:183). In this essay, DuBois states clearly that he appeals to a larger "human brotherhood" and "common humanity" ([1897] 1971:177, 181). We draw on Outlaw's (1996) and Boxill's (1996) interpretation of DuBois's views on race to argue three preliminary points. These are as follows: First, that oppression of blacks by whites in the United States was achieved through slavery and deterritorialization; second, that deterritorialization – which was central in creating a black diaspora – is also, paradoxically, a source of group identity and strength; and, third, black culture compensates for deficits in white culture, such as individualism, status striving, and materialism.

DuBois's work was rooted in a philosophical tradition that was very distinct from the one that dominated early U.S. sociology. At least for the first three decades of the century, the approach developed by Park and Burgess at the University of Chicago defined what sociology was in the United States, and they drew heavily from Comte's positivism and Spencer's evolutionary theory in laying out an agenda for a U.S. sociology (see Park and Burgess [1921] 1969). In contrast, as a student of William James and George Santayana, at Harvard, and Adolph Wagner and Gustav van Schmoller, at Berlin, DuBois drew from quite different traditions, namely, Hegelian phenomenology and neo-Kantian idealism (Zamir 1995:68–112; Broderick 1958; Lewis 1993:140– 47).

Thus, while it is likely that DuBois's theoretical work was ignored because of his race, we suggest that another reason may have been that his understanding of race was not acceptable at the time and that in a very general way his interpretation of social life was rooted in philosophical premises not widely shared in sociology. However, DuBois's writings, especially *Souls*, are particularly germane for contemporary sociology. We suggest that DuBois's conceptions of Self and community are relevant for issues now being raised in conjunction with global migration. The Self is now theorized in terms of cosmopolitanism and hybridity (e.g., Clifford 1992; Appadurai 1996), which is quite consistent with DuBois's conceptions in *Souls*. We also indicate that DuBois's works are relevant for how sociologists pose questions about social justice.

DuBois, as activist-scholar and public intellectual, was engaged in the national black community as he helped to represent it (Banks 1998:236–37), and one way of examining this is by indicating similarities between DuBois's conceptions and the way in which black journalists interpreted and organized experiences for their readers. DuBois clarified in *Souls* that the black experience in the United States is fragmented and contingent, while he stressed there were options for choice. Black journalists writing in the early decades of the century, during the Great Migration from the South to North, likewise communicated these messages to their readers while clarifying how local cultural grammars must and could be bridged to achieve racial solidarity across regional and class lines.

A central theme in both *Souls* and black newspapers was the expansion of community through black migration and through the increasing diversity of black culture. DuBois was neither a strict separatist nor an assimilationist but wished to preserve a positive black identity in a white society (Lewis 1993:281). His vision for the active construction of Self and community rested on this dialectical tension between participation in the white world and in the black world. As Zamir (1995) suggests, it was DuBois's view that all blacks participate in the black experience, shaping a shared community, but all blacks also participate in the American experience, and they do so as individuals. This dialect of consciousness, under favorable circumstances, fosters creativity and personal freedom, while it also enhances an understanding of collective experiences that in turn inform an enlightened perspective on the ethics of living. We conclude our paper with a section from *Souls* that we believe clarifies how DuBois universalizes oppression but amplifies its particular aspects through accounts of the experiencing of it. His contemporaries – white academics – may have missed this powerful point or taken offense at it. He indicates in *Souls* (esp. pp. 186–203)[2] that racism is comprised of many varied, particular, and discrete events and actions and that it is from this perspective, rather than from sociologists' abstractions,[3] that we ought to address questions of racial justice.

---

[2] Page numbers in *Souls* refer to the Penguin edition, listed in the References.
[3] Race prejudice is traced by Park and Burgess ([1921] 1969:240–41) to "instinct" and racial conflict to the "struggle for status."

Preliminary Considerations

Souls, we argue, anticipates the current debates about cosmopolitan conscious-ness as fostered within globally dispersed racial and ethnic groups under postnational, globalizing conditions (Bauman 2000; Augé 1999; Appadurai 1996; Soysal 1994; see also Werlen 1993; Urry 2000). Our interpretation of DuBois is that he rejected the modernist convention that race is a social or biological category and instead proposed a conception that anticipated the current formulation that imagined worlds simultaneously unite and trans-form a diasporic community (see esp. Appadurai 1996). It is also important to indicate that DuBois's theoretical assumptions are somewhat different from those of multiculturalist theorists, who advocate group autonomy (esp. Kymlicka 1995:181–85), and from those of communitarian theorists (see Etzioni 1995; MacIntyre 1984), who stress the importance of shared values. For both multiculturalists and communitarians group unity is paramount, whereas for DuBois individual identity tricks group boundaries and finesses group memberships.

DuBois's Axiomatic Concepts

Along the lines of Lemert's (1994:386) interpretation, we understand DuBois's term, *Veil*, as the color line that divides and separates and as an essential aspect of perceptions and communications between those divided. DuBois also posits that the Self is complexly constituted as are the groups that are composed of Selves (Lemert 1994:389–90). For blacks, the Self is divided – as the objectified and excluded Other and as the subjective and agential Self – and experience *Twoness* as divided lives. *Twoness* is, most centrally, being "an American, a Negro" ([1903] 1965:5) but is rooted in a more complex sensibility, namely, *Double Consciousness*. DuBois's term suggests, as it did in nineteenth-century dialectical philosophy, a tension between bodily and spiritual selves, or a ten-sion between rationality and emotions (see Zamir 1995:153–54). DuBois used the term to indicate that between the white world and the black world, U.S. blacks must not internalize whites' attitudes but instead cultivate a reflexive perspective on *Twoness*. That is, blacks can embrace their *Twoness* but need to maintain a critical perspective on the moral impoverishment of racism and the hypocrisy of racist practices. *Twoness*, in this sense, potentially either is debilitating or is the key to synthetic emancipation.

Subversive too is the voice of DuBois. He writes *Souls*, as he states in "The Forethought" (pp. 1–2), from several perspectives: From a white perspective – "without the *Veil*" – from a black perspective – "within the *Veil*" – and, then, remarkably, "within the *Veil*, raising it," to allow whites to view "faintly" the culture's "recesses, – the meaning of its religion, the passion of its human sorrow, and the struggle of its greater souls." In other words, whites do not have the burdens associated with the *Veil*, but neither do they possess the agency blacks do in taking it on and off. Our interpretation is that DuBois is suggesting that whites have limited understanding of black people, whereas the latter have a profound understanding of the cultural frameworks and the institutions that whites employ to oppress them. blacks bear the burden of *Twoness*, but whites are deluded by how they position themselves in their invented hierarchy. The underlying logic is clear enough: Privilege constricts perceptions and social conscience.

Narrating the Great Migration

DuBois's advocacy for a pan-African American identity ([1897] 1971; [1903] 1965:esp.165–68) became, we contend, a practical and narrative possibility only when the Great Migration was fully under way. If DuBois provides us with a framework for understanding diasporic identity in *Souls*, the black press was the vehicle for narratizing practices and helping to shape an expanding community consciousness. Accounts in the black press help to clarify DuBois's conceptions, but we can also consider that journalists advanced these conceptions as praxis. The Great Migration refers to the South to North migration in the early decades of this century, when an estimated 1.5 to 2 million blacks left the South for homes and jobs in northern cities (Marks 1989; Gottlieb 1991). The predominant emphasis in contemporary study of this period is on the demographic and economic aspects of migration, and a major conclusion is that European immigrants arriving in northern cities during these decades fared far better than did blacks.[4]

---

[4] There are many reasons that help to account for why African Americans did not share benefits in the expanding economy: Timing of their migration (Lieberson 1980); labor skills (Marks 1989); the coincidence of the Great Depression with migration (Logan 1965); a disadvantageous sex ratio among migrants (Johnson and Campbell

Our focus is not on this migration per se but rather on the development of a diasporic identity that could not have emerged prior to sustained high migration rates and prior to the expansion of the black community. We will indicate how narratives in print media provide reinforcement of the vision articulated in *Souls*. Accounts embraced northern and southern communities and did so in terms of the practicalities of pluralism and in terms of the ideals of a unified moral community. The black diaspora is comparable in many respects to Anderson's (1983) "imagined community." However, it was not, as Anderson's concept indicates, a nationalizing project but rather anticipates Appadurai's (1996; also see Anderson 1998) argument that contemporary diaspora can be independent of nation building and, indeed, can subvert nationalizing projects.

Metagrammars of Community

The analysis is based on the study of eight black newspapers published in six cities (Chicago, Pittsburgh, New York, Boston, Washington, and Atlanta) during the early decades of the century, 1900 to 1935.[5] We (the senior author and four undergraduate students) plumbed the pages of papers to learn how

---

1981); and, perhaps, the vulnerability of southern black institutions in the urban North (Johnson 1934; Lemann 1991; but see Tolnay 1997; Price-Spatlen 1999). Regardless of the role of these various factors, there is agreement that racism and discrimination largely account for blacks' incomplete incorporation into northern communities and for their continuing marginality in the South (see Drake and Cayton [1945] 1962; Frazier 1957; Pinkney 1969; Henri 1975; Kornweibel 1981; Lieberson 1980; Wilson 1987; Grossman 1989; Marks 1985, 1989; Trotter 1991).

[5] We are not interested in how newspapers changed over this time, from 1900 to 1935, but we wanted to ensure that the study spanned a period of rapid social change and included the Great Depression, which had a devastating effect on urban black communities. Many issues of eight newspapers for the time period considered were skimmed and some read in their entirety. Students copied and distributed articles at project meetings and discussed their interpretations. Each student wrote summaries about topics he or she repeatedly encountered. The papers are the following: *New York Age, Pittsburgh Courier, Atlanta Daily World, Negro World, Chicago Defender, Atlanta Independent, Washington Bee,* and *Chicago Broad Axe.* Other newspapers consulted for the purpose of comparison were the *New York Times, Washington Post,* and *Chicago Tribune.* DuBois's own magazine, the *Crisis,* was not included because it was a journal of political opinion rather than a newspaper. The interpretations in this article bear little resemblance to the project objectives and student summaries (which focused on concrete topics, such as lifestyle, religion, art, etc.), but the project provided the opportunity for immersion in the newspapers and amassing a large collection of microfiche copy. It was possible to return to this collection while preparing this article.

journalists framed their own and readers' understandings about family, work, class, politics, religion, race relations, and other spheres of life.[6] According to Drake and Cayton ([1945] 1962:398–429), black papers had an extraordinarily broad readership and were a major focus of community life, as they were shared and discussed at neighborhood gatherings and in churches, barbershops, and clubs. Prominent papers were circulated in the North and South, and their links with one another were established through the Negro Associated Press and through referencing one another's editorials.

In spite of worsening legal and economic conditions in the South and largely unfilled expectations of northern migrants, journalistic accounts often stressed the great vitality and social strength of communities. Religious devotion, family strength, and educational progress were praised, and black arts – poetry and literature as well as rural crafts and religious music – were described with pride. In contrast with the sociological accounts of pathological conditions in urban ghettos by Park, Burgess, Wirth, Reckless, and others from the University of Chicago, journalists of urban papers described northern black communities in positive terms. Their accounts document how residents were involved in churches, political associations, and unions and in their jobs. Ghettos, when mentioned, referred to housing owned by slumlords, not to residents.

The black press is interestingly different from the immigrant press of the same historical period. The immigrant (or ethnic) press did not particularly affirm transspatial connections and a multifold identity for new residents but provided immigrants with support to ease the burdens of settlement and to help them become incorporated into U.S. society (Dinnerstein and Reimers 1988). Instead, the black press in the early decades of the twentieth century can be compared with contemporary diasporic media in that it framed collective subjectivity in transspatial and broadly integrative ways (Appadurai 1996).

We highlight narrative framing strategies – not content – to anticipate our later discussion that elaborates DuBois's concepts of *Veil*, *Twoness*, and

---

[6] The development of the black press is described by, among others, Tinney and Rector (1980); Oak (1948); and Danky (1999). Yet, similar to Kinshasa (1988), who focuses on the themes in the nineteenth-century African American press, our own study is not about African American newspapers and journalists per se, but rather we use their accounts to help answer questions about community and identity. Questions about how representative these accounts are or the relative frequency of given topics are not relevant for these purposes.

Double Consciousness. These framing strategies included "differencing and uniting," "leveraging," and "identification and disidentification." We term these strategic framing devices "metagrammars." They help to organize many accounts, events, and people's experiences by providing continuities over time and across differences of locale and region. We assume that these framing strategies operated like cultural maps for readers.[7]

Differencing and Uniting

Expanding community while recognizing differences within it was a concrete objective in the black press. Because many urban papers had a wide and sometimes national circulation,[8] and because the experience of spatial uprootedness was so widely shared, journalists sustained themes that would bridge language, conditions, and culture for a broad audience. Circumstances in the North and South were sharply different. Racism, for example, took different forms: Jim Crow, disenfranchisement, and mob lynching incidents in the South and widespread bigotry and discrimination in the North. No single objective could encompass the experiences of all blacks during this period, and journalists used language that bridged difference and created common bonds. They praised the work habits of the urban working classes and the perseverance of rural southerners who toiled on poor land and used northerners' educational achievements as an object lesson for southerners and southerners' religiosity as an object lesson for northerners. Biblical parables were piously drawn upon for moral guidance. So was humor, and its self-deprecatory tone could have a critical bite.

In contrast with newspapers that served social movement objectives – trade union and party papers and, earlier, abolitionist papers – black papers in the first decades of the twentieth century presented heterodox views, and while all stressed the burdens of racism, the dominant theme was that the strengths of the black community would ultimately prevail. Journalists denied what

---

[7] We do not intend to suggest that these "framing strategies" were used by journalists to manipulate opinion (see Iyengar 1996; Gans 1979); black journalists were strongly identified with their readers.

[8] Northern papers were widely distributed in the South because employers placed notices in them to recruit workers and migrants sent clippings and entire papers to relatives in the South (see Henri 1975:49–80).

Drake and Cayton ([1945] 1962) later termed "fixed status" and stressed instead that members of the race were making progress as entrepreneurs and professionals and also in education, literature, and the arts.

Accounts drew on collective understandings for mobilization around particular issues, such as a boycott, improving educational opportunities, and support of women's franchise. The great differences in conditions faced by readers in the South and North posed challenges for journalists, and they equivocated on those things for which a given position may have created or heightened divisions between their northern and southern readers. For example, nationally circulated northern papers used stilted language in their descriptions of city night life and entertainment, mindful, one might assume, of the high general levels of religiosity and traditionalism in the South. Parody about particularizing identities modulated difference across regional and class lines and deflected the intention behind white epithets. "Sambo" referred to rural people, "lily white black" or "black carriage trade" referred to pretentious northerners, and "Tom" referred to being ingratiating; "good Niger" (or "nigger") was used to describe blacks who toiled for whites. These expressions are inserted into journalistic text for the purpose, we infer, to highlight equality among blacks, whether rural or urban, middle class or poor, educated or not. Recoding whites' epithets, such barbs became satire that deflected the vicious intentions that whites had and fostered solidarity across class and regional divisions.

Most contemporary accounts emphasize the differences among Booker T. Washington, Marcus Garvey, and W. E. B. DuBois (e.g., Franklin and Meier 1982). Interestingly, however, such differences were not especially stressed in the black press, not even in the papers owned or edited by them, namely, The *Crisis* (edited by DuBois), *New York Age* (acquired by Washington in 1907), *Negro World* (Garvey's paper), and the *Boston Guardian* (edited by William Monroe Trotter, a vocal opponent of Booker T. Washington). The reason for this, apparently, was the recognition that the problems faced in the North and the South were so different. A 1914 editorial in the *Chicago Defender*, no supporter of Washington, maintains that Washington's strategy "represents a line of thought essential to the masses living under the conditions from which he arose." And the *Chicago Broad Axe* reported on September 7, 1912, that "both radical and conservative strategies are necessary to complete the armament of this oppressed race." The *Atlantic Independent* was loyal to Booker

T. Washington but sometimes undercut its loyalty rhetorically by substituting for his preferred term *Negro*, the coinage *Raceman*. Journalists, no doubt, could expand their readers' knowledge and emotional frameworks by such word play, even if they were not especially hopeful for major changes in the immediate future.

For southern journalists, covering racist incidents posed complex problems. An editorial in the *Atlanta Independent* in 1912 turns adversity into a means of racial resolve: "it will take the white man's discrimination and his segregation to build up in the Negro that faith in his own possibilities necessary to make a more helpful and useful citizen." Throughout these years, editorials in the *Atlanta Independent* urged blacks not to oppose segregation, but the phrasing can have implications that are just as potent as those embraced by Garvey and more radical than most northern black papers. One 1917 editorial from the *Atlanta Independent* states: "[the Negro] does not want to place himself in the position of opposing segregation *because* he wants to mix with white folks" (emphasis added). The implication is that blacks should not *want* to engage in mixing with whites.

Far more than any northern paper, the southern *Atlanta Independent* praised black fraternal organizations, schools, churches, military divisions, insurance companies, retirement homes, and YMCAs (see Blau et al. 1996; Blau and Heying 1996). In contrast, most northern papers expressed impatience with such arrangements, and editorials often disparaged organizations that were exclusively for "the race."[9]

Increasingly during this period, conditions in the South deteriorated, and northern blacks contended with crowded housing conditions, discrimination in employment, and lack of political influence. In the South, the accommodationist views of Booker T. Washington prevailed, whereas in the North there was more support for an activist and reform agenda. Yet both southern and northern papers covered the problems faced in the other region, often playing off the merits and implications of particular visions – integrationist, separatist, and accommodationist – for different regions. In this way the

---

[9] Yet it might be added that by the time the courts finally did pursue the implications of *Brown v. Board of Education*, many northern black papers endorsed the view that black institutions could better serve their communities than could integrated or predominantly white ones.

construction of a collective identity was based on a medley of possibilities without privileging one over others.

Leveraging

Journalists obliquely downplayed adversity by using very specific events as a means of countering economic exploitation or racism for their stated purpose of advancing an agenda for social change. The worst brutalities after the end of slavery were lynchings, and during the period between 1900 and 1935 there were an estimated 1,374 (Johnson 1999). Strangely, a lynching was often reported with austere crispness, and it was seemingly trivialized by its appearance in a small column on the front page or relegated to a back page. With some exceptions, especially in the early years, a lynching received little prominent attention in the metropolitan papers we examined. Our interpretation is that little rhetorical gain – other than infuriating black readers – could be achieved through dramatic coverage of violent murders of blacks. With some degree of disingenuousness, the source that was often given was a wire report from one of the white associated presses, when in fact the black press association, the National Negro Press, had the capability of transmitting such news and no doubt did.[10] However, it became clear to us that such violent incidents were often expected to "speak for themselves" and thereby could be used to leverage extended critical analyses that could then be used to press for reforms and new policies.

For example, discussing a lynching in a lengthy editorial in 1920, a journalist for the *Atlantic World* in 1920 states that "it is not the role of the Negro press to describe the suffering of blacks." Writers frequently suggest that the fight for civil rights and equality "must not," as one put it, "be clouded by issues about the black victim, since doing so belabors and elevates the language of racism." Journalists and editors did not blame all whites for these atrocities but did blame all whites for conditions and attitudes that allowed such atrocities to occur.

The racial violence that broke out in Chicago during the summer of 1919 provided another opening for newspapers to leverage on events for other

---

[10] The motive for attribution, we suspect, was to reward white editors and journalists for their reporting of white violence. This also sent a message to black readers that the struggle for justice was reaching a broad audience.

purposes. The riots started when white youths attacked a black youngster for swimming in "white" water at a Chicago beach. The initial accounts published in the *Chicago Daily Tribune* and the *Daily Defender* differ little in detail, for it was obvious that whites were guilty. However, the attribution of the underlying problem was quite different. White newspapers emphasized the attitudes of residents, focusing on the apathy in the white community and the "uppity" attitudes of blacks. But black papers instead took the opportunity to document the political, economic, and social conditions in Chicago that precipitated the beach incident for the specific purpose of advocating thoroughgoing changes.

The virtually exclusive focus of articles published in northern black papers (see *Broad Axe*, August 2, 9, 16, 1919; *Pittsburgh Courier*, August 24, 1919; *Washington Bee*, August 19, 23, 1919) about the Chicago murder was the urgency of the need for sweeping changes in all cities. This included reform of police departments, changes in the justice system, implementation of fair employment policies, and improving schools and housing. Long excerpts from comments by state officials, including the state's attorney general, were printed in Chicago's black papers, providing evidence of city corruption as well as discriminatory practices in housing, government, and employment. White citizens, interestingly, were less the target of attacks by Chicago black papers than the municipal government. One editorial summed up a series of earlier articles: "There is no dispute of the colored man's plea for justice and equality. The question is as to the disposition of the fact. Public policy has first call" (*Chicago Defender*, July 29, 1919). In contrast, white pressmen wrung their hands over whites' prejudice and blacks' provocative behavior, with some speculation about the possibility of a black conspiracy (*Washington Post*, July 28, 1919).

Full and detailed reporting about the murder and the ensuing riots – just as complete disclosures of the horror of a lynching – may have provoked a militant response and, therefore, may have been perceived as risky. The metropolitan dailies that covered the Chicago (and Washington, DC) race riots spoke with one voice, and the message can be interpreted as follows: As slavery was abolished by laws, not by appeals to people's attitudes, so should law and policies end segregation and discrimination.

When racism was the specific focus of an article, journalists drew for authority on articles in the foreign press, such as *L'Homme Libre* or *L'Avenir*.

The message was that in the civilized nations of the world there was widespread disbelief about the extent of segregation and discrimination in the United States. A series of editorials in the *Chicago Defender* and the *Pittsburgh Courier* provides a detailed and sophisticated analysis of the consequences of massive migration of southern blacks to northern cities. They drew attention to the coincidence of European and black migration and the impact of this on blacks' worsening conditions and their relative disadvantage with respect to housing, employment, and schools. Journalists documented how job possibilities for blacks plummeted after World War I, leaving blacks at the bottom of an extremely competitive labor pool. This became only worse during the depression.

Identification and Disidentification

Just as a prime metagrammar in the black press was leveraging an agenda for social change using very particular events to pose generic solutions, another was to show how blacks ought to identify – or not – with other groups. For example, journalists advocated working class solidarity by describing economic injustices faced by both whites and blacks. It is "industrial jobs," an article in the *Pittsburgh Courier* (May 6, 1925) states, "that will unite all working people," and Garvey's paper, the *Negro World*, often contended that the enemy of both white and black workers was the capitalist. Class solidarity was used in another rhetorical way, namely, to distinguish what the *Washington Bee* termed "the lower order" from law-abiding and respectable black and white citizens. A mob attack on several blacks in 1925 is described in the following way by the *Washington Bee* (May 31): "prosperous, respected, family members" were attacked by "illiterate, worthless whites." Similarly, the *Bee* (January 24, 1903) reports, "If a law were passed allowing railroad companies to discriminate between the bad and the good of both races, there would be no objections to the passage of such a law. Certainly these dirty and filthy white people are equally objectionable to respectable colored people as similar characters are objectionable to the white people." Thus, behavior and attitudes were color coded and switched around for effective narrative and storytelling.

The exposure of the Russian pogroms in 1911 provided a vehicle for sustaining an argument about gross injustices in the U.S. South. "It might not be a bad plan, now that the American people have been so recently wrought over the treatment of Jews in Russia, to appeal to the great American public to look around at home and take notice of the outrageous acts being perpetrated on black American citizens" (*Broad Axe*, December 30, 1911). At the end of World War I, the *Washington Bee* (May 31, 1919) makes the point that the KKK could be compared with the Huns, a syllogism that referenced stories about black soldiers who fought the Germans and returned home to face white racism.

Advocacy for women's right to vote was often linked with advocacy for racial equality. For example, the *Chicago Defender* (July 31, 1909) noted that millions of women worked out of the home and yet did not vote. "A vote for women is a vote for equality, and thus for blacks." Papers updated their readers on women's progress around the world. Along these same lines, black papers condemned anti-Semitic and anti-Asian practices, while forging bonds of solidarity with Jews, Asians, and other white ethnics. Articles on immigrants described their ordeals, sacrifices, and hard work. Also stressed were the good feelings in multiple-ethnic communities. *New York Age* had a series of articles in 1905 about New York neighborhoods. One offered accounts of congeniality and neighborliness within a midtown community of "African-Americans and natives of South America, France, England, Haiti, Mexico, Cuba, British and Danish West Indies." Solidaristic identities generally subvert the taken-for-granted hierarchies and antagonisms. Class solidarity with "all working people" is a theme that runs through the pages of the northern press, and this often is made concrete in terms of immigrant groups: "as Jews are persecuted, so are Blacks"; "the Chinese share the same despicable housing that we do."

No other minority group is discussed as much in the pages of black papers as the Jews, and this with a tone of both ambivalence and familiarity. In 1915, the *Atlanta Independent* denounces Jews for their business practices but in the same article criticizes educated blacks for their "Tomism." Living in the same neighborhoods and observing Jews' rapid social and economic ascent meant that Jews were often resented but also often praised, sometimes for their work ethic, sometimes for strong families, and also, interestingly, for being proud of their ancestry and ancient descent. The *Broad Axe* notes in 1909 that "tests which made the Jew great have only served to drive the Negro to the extreme of denying his own race whenever and wherever his color and circumstances would permit him to do so."

In short, forging bonds of solidarity within a stigmatized group requires a discourse of subtle complexity. Journalists went to some lengths to educate readers about their rights as workers, citizens, soldiers, and residents, and they did so by stressing the similarities among all workers, all citizens, all soldiers, all homeowners, and all residents. At the same time, the consequences of being blocked at every turn in having access to these commonplace roles were always present in the pages of African American newspapers. There were no solutions posed in newspapers, but the conundrum was stated again and again in terms of consciousness. For example, an article in the September 1914 issue of the *Atlanta Independent* states, "the race...must depend on itself and less on others." And later in the same article the author states, "the Negro must awaken to race consciousness." Yet, "race pride" and "race consciousness" were viewed suspiciously, since white racism could unleash hatred and furor against blacks. A long editorial in the *Broad Axe* in 1909 defines race pride as "the exaggerated love and esteem of one's own race exhibited by whites...a dangerous attitude not to be adopted by blacks."

Herein lies an important connection between the narratives of the black press and DuBois's analysis of consciousness and identity. The metagrammars reveal a multifaceted group identity but also a pan-identity of the diasporic community. For U.S. blacks the diaspora does not have a single origin but is pluralistically constituted, originating as much in the United States as in Africa. Given dispersion and varied experiences, for blacks to essentialize race is a denial of pluralistic identities and experiences, although such essentialization is at the same time a mechanism for cultural and social survival and linked to prospects of economic advance. As DuBois noted in an editorial published in the *Crisis*, racial solidarity is essential for such advance:

> It is the race conscious black man cooperating together in his own institutions and movements who will eventually emancipate the colored race, and the great step ahead today is for the American Negro to accomplish his economic emancipation through voluntary determined effort. (*Crisis*, January 1934, p. 20)

DuBois could mount any one of very many different platforms to convey the nuance of possibilities for black Americans: He was a teacher, wrote for scholarly journals, was a magazine editor, wrote books, was a leader in the NAACP, was a delegate to the Universal Races Congress and the Pan-African Congress, and so forth. Black journalists and editors had only a single platform, so they relied instead on expanding a dialogical space (Bakhtin 1981). It was in this space that they constructed conversations involving all segments of the community, attempting to achieve a broad and shared consciousness. This pan-black consciousness involved northerners and southerners, unionists and farmers, the faithful and the secularists, and the activists and the traditionalists.

Language and Perspectives in the Black Press

Newspapers played off a prism of experiences through language. Drake and Cayton ([1945] 1962:718) noted that black city dwellers and southern black rural people expressed their frustrations in the same way, by "taking it out in talk" – that is, in stories, songs, performances, parables, sermons, and riddles. Such talk, as Drake and Cayton indicate, essentially allows for expressing distance and closeness (to people and to social roles embedded in a divided society). African American culture has fostered playful and complicated language that we interpret as objectifying the experience of oppression, as DuBois implies by his terms *Twoness* and *Double Consciousness*. "Code-switching," in contemporary times, involves the skills of talking and acting differently in various settings (Heath 1983), and adolescents refer to "acting white but being black" (Fordham 1996; Ogbu 1978; Gibson 1988). These linguistic and behavioral skills require adept observations of selves and others, a detachment from personal identity, and a certain ironical attitude about the world. One might consider "code-switching" and "acting white but being black" in a chain of cultural development to which newspapers early contributed.

Newspapers nurtured a collective recognition of diversity among blacks, which is to say that they created and capitalized on a discourse that stressed difference, varied circumstances, and alternative views. A leading indicator of this is the varied appellations used in the pages of newspapers, which were not only negative, as already noted, but also constructive of identity, such as "African Americans," "blacks," "Blacks," "the race," "race-men," "Negroes," "Afro-Americans," "sisters and brothers," "colored," and "coloured." Aesthetically and often wittily, language is embellished in contemporary black culture – signifyin', playing the dozens, rap, and hip hop – and subverts whites' paternalism while promoting democratically hared styles and experiences (e.g., see Mercer 1997).

As Byerman (1994:17) emphasizes, DuBois's own style in *Souls* is to contextualize the black experience so that it makes *blackness* a cultural and historical term, rather than a scientific or moral one. Telling stories to blacks about themselves and about whites, and telling stories to whites about blacks, DuBois writes about individuals – as preachers, scholars, farmers, shopkeepers, and laborers – and creates backdrops for the people he describes – schools, churches, communities, villages, and farms. This is also a striking feature of the black press. At a time when the mainstream white press was doing the bidding of advertisers and simplifying stories to attract white immigrants as readers by emphasizing assimilationist, homogenizing, and patriotic perspectives (Emery and Emery 1992:95–118)[11] the black press strove to affirm difference and diversity, not homogeneity and assimilation.

DuBois Reconsidered

It is in this context that we reconsider DuBois's (1897, [1903] 1965) conceptions of *Veil*, *Twoness*, and *Double Consciousness*. An initial starting point is to consider DuBois's own statements about his racial identity – both autobiographically and as author – and his intended audience for *Souls*.

Born in Great Barrington, DuBois grew up with whites and describes in his autobiography that only with his university experience at Fisk did he "become black" (DuBois 1968:110). Then later rejected while in Harvard from the university glee club because of his color, he chose being "encased in a completely colored world" (DuBois 1968:136); still later, DuBois was the only black officer of the NAACP (Lester 1971:56–57). In similar ways, *Souls* is written from different perspectives and for different audiences. In "The Forethought," he informs the reader that he enters the black world ("leaving, then, the world of the white man") to step within the *Veil* but "raising it that you may view faintly its deeper recesses." Other sections, he states, are written more conventionally to describe the struggles of blacks and the relations of the "sons of master and man." As journalists encouraged their readers to shift their perspectives, so does DuBois. In *Souls* he elaborates many

---

[11] The immigrant press for the period under consideration is different from both the commercial press and the black press; compared with the latter it was more focused on readers' practical adjustment needs (see Blau et al. 1998).

possibilities – scholar, sharecropper, preacher, factory worker, northerner, southerner – as helping to comprise a black identity.

The synthetic conception underlying *Double Consciousness, Veil,* and *Twoness* DuBois states thus:

> After the Egyptian and Indian, the Greek and Roman, the Teuton and Mongolian, the Negro is a sort of seventh son, born with a veil, and gifted with second sight in this American world – a world which yields him no true self-consciousness, but only lets him see himself through the revelation of the other world. It is a peculiar sensation, this double-consciousness, this sense of always looking at one's Self through the eyes of others, of measuring one's soul by the tape of a world that looks on in amused contempt and pity. One ever feels his twoness – an American, a Negro, two souls, two thoughts, two unreconciled strivings, two warring ideals in one dark body, whose dogged strength alone keeps it from being torn asunder. ([1903] 1965:5).

There is general consensus that *Veil* is a metaphor for racial division (Bell et al. 1996; Marable 1986; Bruce 1992; Byerman 1994), and Lemert (1994:386) stresses that the *Veil* represents a barrier to communications. We do not argue with this but suggest that those who are *veiled* see others better than they are seen themselves.[12]

It is on this basis that we argue that *Souls* is a more subversive theoretical statement than it is generally considered. Moreover, DuBois emphasizes choice, both autobiographically and as an author. The *Veil* may be a symbol for exclusion and racism, but those who wear it can understand that it is a mere reification. This interpretation of *Veil* is quite consistent with journalists' objectifications of whites and blacks as sometimes united and often distinct and, therefore, of the complexity of blacks' conditions and identities. The danger, stressed by DuBois (and by journalists), is that the *Veil* is not only the consequence of racism but continues to divide and to exclude. It denies black people the "right to share modern culture" ([1903] 1965:167) and the right to "real thoughts" and "real aspirations" (p. 166) and instills "deep religious fatalism" (p. 162) and "moral hesitancy" (p. 164).

Also important, the *Veil* is something that hides a vital culture ([1903] 1965:204–16), a deep social consciousness (pp. 67, 180–85), and a tradition of

---

[12] This is how veiled women experience the world.

ideals and idealism (pp. 2, 240, 265). He states that being aware of the contradictions of *Twoness* can have positive consequences – "longing for peace" (p. 213) and "ethical ferment" (p. 165) – and can engender "creative inquiry" (p. 165). Thus, the *Veil* represents a reified social construction; *Twoness*, the divided sociological Self; and *Double Consciousness*, the divided phenomenological Self. Together they capture the experiences and feelings of exclusion in white America, but they also clarify the complexity of black consciousness. It is useful to briefly suggest that DuBois's ideas are evident throughout the canonical tradition without full recognition of his importance.

DuBois's Contributions to the Canon

Souls, compared with other theoretical contributions of the first quarter of the century, is more pointedly a work that sustains utopian and ideological themes. Yet it is nonetheless interesting to highlight how DuBois anticipated subsequent sociological conceptions. There are evident parallels between *Souls* and George Herbert Mead's account of the development of the self, published in 1934, and Cooley's (1964:184) "looking glass self" and, most especially, with Simmel's writings. In particular, there are striking similarities between, on the one hand, *Twoness* and *Double Consciousness* with Simmel's account that the person "is determined sociologically in the sense that the groups 'intersect' in his person by virtue of his affiliation with them" ([1922] 1955:159; also see Simmel 1950:58–59) and his writings on the stranger (Simmel 1950:402–08).[13] We do not attempt to trace the diffusion of ideas here, although Coser (1971:326–27, 346) suggests that intellectual bonds may have been forged between Mead, Simmel, and DuBois through their contact with Weber between 1892 and 1894. Weber thought very highly of DuBois, published a paper by him in *Archiv für Sozialwissenschaft und Sozialpolitik*, and arranged to visit DuBois when he was in the United States (Marable 1986). A

---

[13] We suggest that DuBois's ([1903] 1965) idea of the pluralistic Self, first published six years earlier (DuBois 1897), is strikingly similar to Simmel's ([1922] 1955) later account of how multiplicity and fragmentation of consciousness develop in the context of multiple relationships. Simmel (1950:58–59) considered the dialectical relations among the "parts" of individuals and between the parts and the whole; he described the "stranger," who is both near and far at the same time (Simmel 1950:402–08) and also examined the consequences of multiple viewpoints for the modern personality (Simmel 1950:409–24; see esp. Simmel [1922] 1955:125–95).

central point here is that the theoretical premises in *Souls* were absorbed into the canon although with little recognition of the source and devoid of their original significance. Like Mead's self and Cooley's looking glass Self, *Twon-ess* is complexly reflective, and with striking similarity to Simmel's writings, DuBois conceptualized the group as constituted through pluralistic intersections with other groups and the Self as the intersection of groups. However, DuBois problematized exclusion and diversity in ways that resonate more with contemporary theory on global migration and cosmopolitanism than do those of Mead, Cooley, and Simmel.

Conclusions

The imagined worlds constituted within and by diasporic communities involve the creation of cosmopolitan identities that partially overlap with official cultures but also contest and subvert them (Appadurai 1996:33; Thompson 1998; Anderson 1998). We conclude that one of DuBois's purposes in *Souls* was to show that it was through the sharing of diasporic experiences that hegemonic racism could be *unveiled*. Likewise, journalists, by telling stories about lived, particular experiences, also clarified the contradictions of racism and racist practices, thereby contributing to this *unveiling* project.

DuBois points us to this conclusion in the last lines of chapter 13, "Of the Coming of John." The background is that John has returned to teach school in Altamaha, Georgia, the place he was born, after his college studies and after living briefly in New York. At the end of the chapter, DuBois describes John's musings while sitting on a tree stump by the ocean. John is aware that a lynch mob is closing in on him.

> Amid the trees in the dim morning twilight he watched their shadows dancing and heard their horses thundering toward him, until at last they came sweeping like a storm, and he saw in front that haggard white-haired man whose eyes flashed red with fury. Oh, how he pitied him, – pitied him, – and wondered if he had the coiling twisted rope. Then, as the storm burst around him, he rose slowly to his feet and turned his closed eyes toward the Sea.
>
> And the world whistled in his ears. ([1903] 1965).

In this epitasis, DuBois leaves the identity of the haggard white man confusingly obscure. It could be the white judge ("Judge") in Altamaha (who has family ties with Princeton University), or it could be the "tall and fair-haired man" whom John stoned as he was in the act of raping his sister. The most evident interpretation unquestionably relates to racial justice, and in the context of his account of John's travels, DuBois suggests that the foundations for generalized racial justice are laid only through understanding myriad forms of racial injustice. Such understanding informs choice and responsibility. It was John's choice, in keeping with his responsibility, to stone his sister's rapist. DuBois also clarifies that even though different unjust acts might appear to take different forms, they may be systemically related. Note here DuBois's contrived ambiguity as to the real identity of the "haggard white-haired man." The subversive DuBois states twice, for emphasis, that it is the white man who is to be pitied.

Chapter Four

Disturbingly Hybrid or Distressingly Patriarchal? Gender Hybridity in a Global Environment

Fabienne Darling-Wolf

Few studies have considered gender as a central axis on which hybrid representations and identities are constructed and negotiated. Despite the recognition that "racial, gender, class, sexual, and national identities, among others, should be thought through together, as mutually constitutive and defining," (Kondo 1997:6), analyses of hybridity have tended to remain focused on its racial dimensions and transcultural manifestations. How gender might influence definitions of hybridity at both the local and global levels and determine individuals' experiences of its construction has, thus, so far been relatively ignored.

This chapter investigates the gendered dimensions of hybridity manifested both locally – through acts of gender-bending and expressions of androgyny, and globally – through transcultural exchange, transnational influence, and globalization. Drawing from feminist theory, it starts with an examination of how gendered identities are constructed in society and culture through processes of socialization. It then explores how gender hybridity might serve to destabilize essentializing categories of "man" and "woman," and consequently challenge patriarchal definitions of what these categories mean. The second part of the chapter links these local acts of resistance to the global environment, where gender hybridity must be negotiated in relationship to broader processes of transnational influence, cultural identity formation, and nationalism.

These diverse issues are considered in an effort to address the following questions: How do individuals negotiate gender when defining their hybrid identities? Is hybridity defined differently for men and women? What are the socio-political consequences of hybridity for individuals of different genders? How does gender hybridity intersect with other elements of hybrid identities? What are the implications of hybridity for gender equality in the context of 21st century global capitalism?

The Personal Is Political: the Socio-cultural Nature of Gendered Identities

One of the most-often cited statements of feminist theory is Simone De Beauvoir's assertion that "one is not born, but rather becomes, a woman" ([1949] 1989:267). By this, De Beauvoir means that rather than being biologically based, differences between the sexes are, by and large, culturally and socially constructed. This crucial distinction between sex (the biological differences between men and women) and gender (the socially constructed differences resulting from this biology) remains a central tenet of contemporary feminist thought. As feminist scholar Teresa De Lauretis explains, "[G]ender is not sex, a state of nature, but the representation of each individual in terms of a particular social relation which preexists that individual and is predicated on the conceptual and rigid (structural) opposition of two biological sexes" (1987:5).

The fact that notions of masculinity and femininity are, at least to some extent, social constructs predicated on a binary opposition is difficult to deny. One only needs to take a stroll down the baby isle or the toy section of a major department store to get a sense of how this "representation of each individual in terms of a particular social relation" happens. The products targeted at children are unequivocally coded (through color, graphics, placement, illustrations) as intended for boys *or* girls. This gendering of even what might otherwise be considered "(gender) neutral" items, such as bicycles, roller blades, or video games, results in children's ability to determine at a young age whether these items are "for them" or not, and it encourages them to "pick a side" in the gender dichotomy.[1] This process, which sociologists Candace West and Don Zimmerman call "doing gender," creates "differences between girls and boys and women and men, differences that are not natural, essential, or biological" (1987:137). These differences are then "used to reinforce the 'essentialness' of gender."

The extreme nature of the efforts to differentiate between individuals who have yet to develop clear exterior signs of sexual identification (such as breasts, facial hair, or height), points to the importance of the process of gendering in contemporary society. While what is considered appropriate clothing, attitude, or behavior within each category of gender might evolve over time – girls can now play soccer – the fact that the genders remain strictly *differentiated* is incontrovertible – soccer cleats now come in shades of pink and purple. According to feminist scholars, this early gender differentiation ultimately results in profound psychological, behavioral, and sociological issues as it (over)emphasizes the differences between biological males and females and works to construct the socio-cultural order in which it takes place as natural and justified. As feminist theorist Marilyn Frye explains, "The redundancy of sex-marking and sex-announcing serves not only to make the topic seem transcendently important, but to make the sex-duality it advertises seem transcendently and unquestionably *true*" (1983:29).

This process of naturalization of a "sex-duality" only tenuously linked to the actual performance of physical bodies (at least until they reach puberty) is thus perceived by feminist scholars as a building block of patriarchy, a process through which women have historically been kept in subordinated roles through exclusion from activities deemed only appropriate for men, and which garner significant socio-cultural power – property ownership, public speaking, voting, politics, higher education, scientific investigation, etc. In order to justify such exclusion, a particularly difficult task in

---

[1] It should be noted that at least until a certain age, children might decide to identify with the "wrong" category. Boys and girls, unless otherwise instructed will often interchangeably play with toys targeted at either gender – my four-year-old daughter recently fell in love with a red "boy bicycle" (anything not pink or purple seems to fall in that category). The fact that children are aware of this "crossing over," however, is what is significant. In addition, the pressure to align with the gender that matches their biological sex increases as children grow older. (When my oldest daughter was five, one of her male friends started refusing to drink from pink straws).

post-enlightenment democracies predicated on the central notion that "all men [sic] are created equal," men and women must be constructed as *naturally* very different from each other and, hence, *biologically destined* or *naturally inclined* to perform very different roles. Early gender differentiation does just that: "Things are the way they are by virtue of the fact that men are men and women are women – a division perceived to be natural and rooted in biology... *The structural arrangements of a society are presumed to be responsive to these differences*" (West and Zimmerman 1987:128, emphasis mine). In other words, as Frye concludes, "The forces which make us mark and announce our sexes are among the forces which constitute the oppression of women" (1983:33).

Scholars have pointed to the role of language, culture, and social institutions in constructing and perpetuating dichotomized notions of gender. The media, the schools, the courts, the family, the Church, the arts, the universities, the economic and medical systems – what theorist Louis Althusser calls "ideological state apparati" – all contribute to this construction. While the specific meaning attributed to each category may vary in different cultures and societies, "[t]he cultural conception of male and female as two complementary yet mutually exclusive categories into which all human beings are placed" happens cross-culturally (De Lauretis 1987:5). Considering the problematic nature of socio-cultural constructions of gender, one goal of feminist theory has been to deconstruct and "de-naturalize" these dichotomized categories. To work, in other words, toward a more hybrid understanding of gender. This, however, has not been an easy task.

Hybridity and the Deconstruction of Gender Differentiation

In her seminal text, Judith Butler proposes to make "gender trouble" by "subverting and displacing those naturalized and reified notions of gender that support masculine hegemony and heterosexist power" ([1990] 1999:44). She offers to do so through "the mobilization, subversive confusion, and proliferation of those constitutive categories that seek to keep gender in its place." Gender hybridity offers one possible avenue for creating this confusion by helping to blur the boundaries between notions of appropriate "masculinity" and "femininity." I choose to define gender hybridity here as a broad set of acts, behaviors, and attitudes that do not conform to the socio-culturally constructed meaning assigned to each gender in a particular society or culture at a particular point in time. Individuals who enact gender hybridity by engaging in such acts, those whose gender identities "fail to conform to those norms of cultural intelligibility" (Butler 1990/1999:24) – homosexuals, transsexuals, bisexuals, cross-dressers, and those who, in any way, shape, or form, refuse to conform to a gender-stereotyped view of how they should look, act, or think – can help destabilize the system of oppression by exposing the constructed nature of gender.

The level of controversy surrounding current debates over gay marriage and adoption or the intensity of society's reaction to "second-wave feminists" who refused to shave their legs (to this day, feminism is frequently reduced in popular culture to a mere capillary pronouncement), points to how hybridity can unsettle hegemonic constructions of gender. Again, these individual acts of rebellion against culturally established normative definitions of what it means to be male or female are disruptive because they expose gender as a construct – as something that individuals do not naturally possess, but must perform (most often unconsciously) if they are to function in the broader socio-cultural context. Thus, as Frye concludes, "Perhaps the difference between heterosexuals and queers is that when queers go forth in drag, *they know they are engaged in theater – they are playing and they know they are playing*" (1983:29, emphasis mine).

Beyond the individual level, it should be noted that the meaning of gender might be explored within some of the very "ideological state apparati" responsible for its social-cultural construction. Because cultural productions and mass-mediated texts are a significant terrain on which gender is represented and negotiated, they also occasionally serve as a terrain on which gender hybridity is explored. The cross-dressing performances of Japanese theater – from the *onnagata* (male actor playing a female role) of Kabuki Theater to the *otokoyaku* (female actor playing a male role) of the Takarazuka Revue – provide opportunities to challenge the stability of a sex-gender system premised on a male (masculine)/female (feminine) dichotomy (Robertson 1998). The fact, for instance, that *otokoyaku* are often deemed "more feminine" than their female counterparts powerfully disconnects gender from its biological origin. *Yaoi manga* featuring androgynous male characters in homoerotic situations have likewise been interpreted as a site through which their young female readers can fantasize about and identify with characters located outside the boundaries of limiting cultural discourses of gender and sex roles (Russ, 1985). More recent American texts featuring gay characters have also been praised for their attempts at deconstructing the masculine/feminine binary. For instance, in her analysis of the Showtime drama *Queer as Folk*, Margaret Johnson argues that Stuart Jones' character exists in a conflicted liminal space between traditional gender constructions as he "pushes beyond our expectations and manages to manipulate the feminine and masculine behavior into a new hybrid sexuality" (2004:293).

Virtual spaces and new communication technologies may offer additional positive opportunities for the deconstruction of gender binaries and the establishment of hybrid identities freed of the biological constraints of the body. Donna Haraway's image of the cyborg, offered as a "way out of the maze of dualisms," suggests a utopian vision of hybrid technologically mediated identities that construct embodiment as fluid and fragmented (1991:181). Similarly, the anonymity of cyberspace was initially heralded as a possible foundation for the development of virtual selves liberated from gender (and race) dynamics, as a space where sexless avatars would dominate, and gender would become irrelevant.

Unfortunately, gendered dichotomies are not that easy to sidestep. Because of the lack of other possible identifications, the categories of man (masculine)/woman (feminine) can never be completely escaped in the daily realities of individuals' lives. In contrast to the gender-hybrid utopia imagined in early theorizing, cyberspace has developed into a highly gendered domain where pornographic and dating sites abound, where games are dominated by male players and male avatars, and where women often feel uncomfortable (Balsamo 1995, Clerc 2000). Likewise, while technology may be used to free women from the constraints of biology – as when it aims at extending women's reproductive choices (birth control, abortion, in-vitro fertilization) – it may also be employed to further inscribe gender onto male and female bodies rather than to free them from it. The proliferation of cosmetic surgical techniques aimed at helping individuals fit normative constructions of femininity and masculinity illustrate this process. Feminist theorist Kathryn Morgan (1991) warns, for instance, against the increased pressure to seek technological remedies to fit culturally ascribed standards of attractiveness. Medical anthropologist Emily Martin (1992) notes that reproductive technologies increasingly alienate women from the process of reproduction by conceptualizing the body as the mere raw material on which doctors intervene. Or consider the fact that imaging technologies that reveal the sex of embryos now allow for sexual differentiation to start taking place even before birth, as evident in the color-coded nature of contemporary baby showers. Gender hybridity, even in a technologically advanced virtual reality, is not that easy to produce.

This is due in part to the fact that, at least in Western cultures, conceptualizations of the world have long been dominated by dichotomized thinking – nature vs. culture, brain vs. body, good vs. evil. Thus, even those who challenge socio-culturally imposed gender constructions through "hybrid" social and/or sexual identities often continue to do so through the framework of binary oppositions – top/bottom, femme/butch. In other words, while challenging the stability of the male/female dichotomy through its "scrambling of gender markers," androgyny also "retains the components of that dichotomy" (Robertson 1998:47). Even feminist thought, in its efforts to elaborate practices, discourses, and social spaces in opposition/reaction to patriarchy, was initially built "within a conceptual frame of a universal sex opposition" (De Lauretis 1987:2). The next step was to not only deconstruct binary opposition between male (man)/female (woman), but also to recognize the essentializing nature of each category, that is, to deconstruct the category "woman" as a label that can be understood to have the same meaning for individuals around the globe. As Butler explains,

> If one 'is' a woman, that is surely not all one is; the term fails to be exhaustive, not because a pregendered 'person' transcends the specific paraphernalia of its gender, but because gender is not always constituted coherently or consistently in different historical contexts, and because gender intersects with racial, class, ethnic, sexual, and regional modalities of discursively constituted identities (1990/1999:6).

This recognition of the "political problem that feminism encounters in the assumption that the term *women* denotes a common identity" (Butler 1990:6, emphasis in original) has been one of the most significant contributions of feminist theory in the last few decades. This is also where feminism most significantly intersects with theories of hybridity developed to describe broad processes of transcultural influence and adaptation.

Hybridity in a Global Context

Hybridity theory, as it is currently employed by scholars studying processes of transcultural and transnational influence, developed in reaction to dystopic scenarios of global cultural influence emphasizing the homogenizing effect of American power (see, for example, Schiller 1993). As the fact that international flows of goods, information, and popular culture have become increasingly multilateral and decentralized became incontrovertible in the latter part of the 20th century, scholars started to question scenarios of "cultural imperialism" for their tendency to portray poorer nations as passive victims of their more powerful counterparts' ideological propaganda. Hybridity theorists contend that one problem with such characterizations is that they fail to account for the complex negotiation of transcultural influence taking place at the local level in the lived realities of individuals' lives. They argue that rather than being "thoroughly penetrated" by the global (Giddens 1999:19), local agents might actively engage in a complex process of transcultural reinterpretation through which they translate, mutate, and "indigenize" cultural imports (Tomlinson 1999:84). As local identities and hybrid cultural forms are fashioned in relationship – and even opposition – to the global, the global-local nexus becomes a site of simultaneous resistance and domination.

However, as international communication theorist Marwan Kraidy posits, hybridity in such a broad context is a "risky notion" that "comes without guarantees" (2005:vi). Uncritical celebrations of transnational cultural hybridity run the risk of justifying, or at least excusing, the spread of commodified cultural forms from powerful nations by giving too much credit to consumer power and by, basically, "endorsing the cultural claims of transnational capital itself" (Ahmad 1995:12). Emphasizing the material realities of a global environment, Kraidy underscores the importance of "grounding hybridity contextually and theoretically" to more assertively take into account both global inequalities and the potential for local resistance (2002:323). This process of contextualization demands that we consider hybridity in relationship to the significant power dynamics of race, gender, and class as they are enacted at both the local and global levels. Unfortunately, as noted above, while hybridity's racial subtext has been addressed in studies elucidating the political nature of such concepts as *mestizaje, creolization*, or *negritude*, and while neo-Marxist scholars have pointed to class as a crucial element of its analysis, hybridity's gendered dimensions have remained relatively unexamined.

Gender in a Global Context

We know that gender is a significant subtext of international and intercultural relations (see, for example, Enloe 2004). Indeed, international intervention and/or transnational influence has often been justified on the grounds that it is necessary to protect women from patriarchal oppression. In other words, Western nations have often justified their imperialist aggression by defining themselves as liberators of non-Western women from the particularly severe oppression of "their" men. For instance, when Americans opposed themselves to Japan at the turn of the century, they opposed Christianity to paganism, and respect for women to polygamy. In their minds, one thing that implicitly needed to be changed if Japan was to become Westernized was the status of Japanese women (Iriye 1967).

The pictures of "liberated" Afghan women returning to work or school shortly after the American intervention are a contemporary example of the continuation of this discourse in the US media, where much coverage of non-Western women serves to position them as archetypal victims of their culture. Thus, "The issue of representing non-Western cultures in media discourse of the West brings up certain problems that need to be addressed: exoticizing, producing essentialist notions of a culture, homogenizing diverse and specific experiences, and rendering non-Western people as passive, among others" (Parameswaran 1996:90). Conversely, global media producers often rationalize their poor representation of females and minorities by claiming that progressive messages about gender and race do not resonate with international audiences. In this case, "The assumption that foreign audiences are racist and misogynist...exonerates exclusionary casting practices" (Kraidy 2005:81).

White middle-class Western feminist scholars have similarly been charged with constructing women in other parts of the globe as particularly oppressed and in need of "saving," and for tending to impose Western standards of evaluation on non-Western women while showing little interest in exploring indigenous constructions of gender and sexuality. As Chandra Talpade

Mohanty puts it, "[A]ssumptions of privilege and ethnocentric universality, on the one hand, and inadequate self-consciousness about the effect of Western scholarship on the Third World in the context of a world system dominated by the West, on the other, characterize a sizable extent of Western feminist work on women in the Third World" (2003:19). Even well-intentioned and self-conscious attempts to give women "a voice" have often turned into essentializing searches for indigenous tradition and authentic cultural forms resulting in "a fetishization of women of color that once again reconstitutes them as other caught in the gaze of white feminist desire" (Friedman 1995:11). Placed in the difficult position of "accurately" representing their culture, non-Western feminist scholars have been faced with the difficult task of "navigating between the excommunication as 'traitor to the nation' and 'betraying of the race' by patriarchal nationalism, and the imperial rescue fantasies of cliteridectomized and veiled women proffered by Eurocentric feminism" (Shohat 1996:184).

These criticisms point to the failure on the part of some scholars to fully come to terms with the fact that individuals construct their identities on multiple planes – race, culture, nation, class, sexual orientation – and in an increasingly interconnected global environment. As Mohanty continues, "Western feminist scholarship cannot avoid the challenge of situating itself and examining its role in...a global economic and political framework" (2003:20). Mohanty's critique resonates with scholars' calls for the development of a critical hybridity theory that "considers hybridity as a space where intercultural and international communication practices are continuously negotiated in interactions of differential powers" (Kraidy 2002:317). Such a theory would require feminist scholars to more honestly acknowledge and more assertively address the influence of the local framework(s) in which discourses about global gendered identities are produced and disseminated.

Gender, the Nation, and Culture

Theorists have explored the link between femininity and culture in different historical moments to conclude that cultural identities and ideologies are frequently inscribed on ideal representations of the female body (see, for example, Bordo 1993). Up until the early 20th century, the well-fed bourgeois woman was a symbol of material prosperity and success. Today, it is the thin body that represents the upper class. Cultural theorist Stuart Ewen (1988) ties such changes in cultural representations of Western femininity to the advance of modernity, characterized by the development of speculative capitalism and the increased reliance on science and technology that followed the Industrial Revolution. He argues that as the dominant system of profitability came to be based on financial speculation rather than more materially grounded land ownership, the female body followed suit. He identifies an increased emphasis on slenderness as an emblem of changing ideology, which he parallels to similar changes in architecture – symbolized by the slick skyscraper – and the development of increasingly minimalist design. Like buildings and designs, the female body, Ewen argues, became an icon of the new order. Inscriptions of culture onto female bodies in a number of other cultural contexts have been hotly discussed and are too numerous to address here. They point to the interconnection between definitions of gender, culture, ethnic, and national identity.

Women have, more generally, historically been cast in the role of keepers of tradition and/or representatives of the nation – positions that have rendered their local negotiation of transcultural influence particularly complex. Numerous scholars have discussed, for instance, how constructions of femininity intersect with the aggressive negotiation of national/global/racial identities on the stages of global beauty pageants, as well as in cultural discussions about these events (see, for example, Borland 1996, Cohen 1996, Parameswaran 2001). Locating these contests within the broader context of the spread of Western-style consumerism, Radhika Parameswaran concludes in an analysis of their media representation in India:

> [N]ewspaper and magazine stories celebrate global beauty queens' material accomplishments, but also strive to ensure that readers are aware of these women's loyalty to their own cultural traditions and family values... Using the language of nationalism, some media reports idolize the Indian beauty queen for setting innovative global standards for ideal femininity (2005:424–425).

In a global context, gender constructions may thus be negotiated simultaneously as acts of resistance against foreign influence (nationalism), means to safeguard "indigenous" elements of culture (own cultural tradition), and as claims of membership in global geopolitics (innovative global standards).

I have observed a similar intersection between national, cultural, global, and gender identity in my own research on Japanese magazines. Like the Indian media Parameswaran describes, Japanese consumer magazines supported by advertisements for a broad collection of globally distributed products and targeted at a young urban cosmopolitan audience strategically locate the men and women they portray as active participants in the global economy. Fashion shoots in Tokyo streets are juxtaposed with similarly designed spreads in London, Paris, or Milan, young Tokyoites are shown enjoying a wide array of foreign products, and the global reach of Japanese art, fashion, or animation is enthusiastically celebrated. Additionally, the magazines' ideals of female attractiveness tend to privilege "Westernized" facial features and body types initially based on a Caucasian ideal and often achieved through plastic surgery and skin whitening.

The gender identity of female models portrayed as Japanese in the magazines is, however, also clearly constructed in opposition to that of "non-Japanese" women – typically Caucasian or African-American models assumed to be either American or European. "Western" models are portrayed as more sexually aggressive and more mature than their Japanese counterparts and, ultimately, as "exotic" and distant (Darling-Wolf 2000, 2006). As Japan expert Millie Creighton cogently observes, the inclusion of Western models in the Japanese media thus serves to create "visual quotations of what Japan and Japanese are not" (1995:136).

This contrast is accentuated by the fact that Japanese women are frequently shown in women's magazines in traditional settings and wearing traditional garb – shown, in other words, in the process of enjoying their own traditions. Again, while such representations may be interpreted in part as acts of resistance against Western global hegemony, they also feed an Orientalist, or self-Orientalizing, discourse problematically resting on constructions of ideal femininity (Yegenoglu 1998). As social anthropologist Brian McVeigh says of the nostalgic and political process of defining tradition: "[D]esignating certain objects of material culture as 'traditional' is a very modern project in itself whose effect is to establish national identity-building binaries: *our* cultural heritage/*your* practical things; past/present; we/them; self/other; Japan/the West; and the Japanese/the rest" (2000:4, emphasis in original). Or, as sociologist Immanuel Wallerstein explained in a seminal essay on the modern world-system, "there seems to be nothing which emerges and evolves as quickly as 'tradition' when the need presents itself" (1974:356).

In the case of Japan, these representations can also be located within a larger nostalgic popular cultural discourse in which Japanese "tradition" is exoticized through the vehicle of young urban women portrayed as reconnecting with an idealized evanescent past (Ivy 1995). Thus, while encouraging readers to engage in globalized consumption, Japanese women's magazines' representations of gender also resonate with discourses that problematically link femininity to nostalgic definitions of Japanese cultural and national identity. The implications of the fact that Japanese magazines targeted at men offer a very different version of gender and national and global identities will be addressed below.

Constructing the Ideal Hybrid Woman

Hybridity is a significant subtext of the local negotiation of gender constructions in relationship to the global, as illustrated in the examples above. Offered as alternatives to globally dominant ideals of Western/white femininity and to pre-modern local understandings of gender, these mediated representations construct feminine ideals as a fusion of East and West, of trendy global consumption and ancient local tradition. As Parameswaran concludes, "Media representations of middle-class identity in India deploy 'hybridity,' a mutually interactive combination of global and national cultural images, values, and symbols" (2005:424). Keeping in mind the role of the media as an influential "technology of gender" (De Lauretis 1987:1) contributing to restrictive characterizations of what it means to be male or female, it is important to critically consider this specific characterization of hybridity. What, for instance, might this hybridity mean for the women being represented and, more generally, for global understandings of gender dynamics? How might this construction of "female" hybridity differ from that of "male" hybridity? What are its possible consequences on the lived experience of women and men around the globe?

First, as noted above, while media representations celebrate female bodies as hybrid canvases on which global multiculturalism and local practice are skillfully fused, these representations, by constantly re-inscribing femininity within the framework of tradition, ultimately offer female consumers a narrower range of possible identifications than is offered to their male counterparts. The study of Japanese magazines described above revealed, for instance, that portrayals of ideal masculinity in magazines targeted at a male audience were actually much more racially and culturally hybrid than those found in similar women's magazines (Darling-Wolf 2006). In other words, because women negotiate their national, cultural, racial, and gendered identities in relationship to each other, those who embrace too "globalized" an identity through dress or behavior interpreted as "foreign-influenced" might be regarded as "unfeminine." Those who, inversely, pay close attention to gender dynamics expose themselves to the risk of seeing their feminism interpreted as an act of national, cultural, or ethnic betrayal (see, for example, Bow 1995, Fujieda and Fujimura-Fanselow 1995). Men, on the other hand, are rarely portrayed as in danger of losing their virility through their engagement with the global. While men's transcultural hybridity might be considered unpatriotic or racially problematic, it is hardly considered "unmanly."

More importantly, if women are encouraged to adopt a hybrid cultural and/or racial identity, the mediated celebration of hybridity does not extend to gender and sexuality. Androgyny is still approached with much suspicion, and hybrid representations of femininity rest on a problematic equation between a discourse of global female empowerment and an increased hyper-sexualization and objectification of female bodies. Thus, as Parameswaran concludes, "The cross-cultural process of classifying women's 'othered' bodies as sexualized icons of consumerist euphoria...is ultimately a form of powerful objectification that silences the interests of women" (2004:387). While restrictive constructions of ideal masculinity still abound in the media, gender hybridity enacted by male bodies is starting to be explored in popular culture.

Japanese men's magazines, for instance, play with gender hybridity as much as they do with cultural and racial identifications. In a phenomenon familiar to scholars of Japanese popular culture, they powerfully complicate gender distinctions in their pages by featuring highly androgynous male (and occasionally female) models, and by playfully encouraging male readers to experiment with signifiers traditionally assigned to the opposite sex – skirts, makeup, elaborate hairstyles, purses, pink fur – in their fashion choices. No such blurring occurs, however, in magazines targeted at a female audience, which strictly adhere to a culturally omnipresent ideal of female sexuality based on a mixture of cuteness, youth, thinness, and subtle sexual shrewdness (Darling-Wolf 2006). Similarly, while representations of hybrid sexuality have started to appear in texts featuring gay males in the United States (as in the example of *Queer as Folk* mentioned above) representations of lesbians are still more strictly confined to heteronormative conceptualizations of sexuality. Lesbian characters are either portrayed as un-feminine (i.e., not truly female) or, in a relatively more recent development, as over-sexual and objectified – as in Showtime's *The L-Word*, which features a cast of lesbian and bisexual characters who closely fit stereotypical constructions of ideal North-American female beauty – ultra-thin, long-haired, carefully groomed – and who were posed nude as a group in the show's promotional posters (Kern 2005).

Finally, it is important to keep in mind that the kind of hybridity offered to global media audiences, and often encouraged at the local level, is one that is typically achieved through active engagement in upper class capitalist consumption. Theorists have warned against celebratory accounts of such hybridity in elite global media (and some academic circles), which they have charged with glossing over the "complex hierarchies of power" through which hybridity is constituted and contested (Coombes and Brah 2000:2). This mediated "corporate transculturalism" (Kraidy 2005:90) fails to account for the unequal distribution of wealth brought about by globalization as it constructs narratives of prosperity and progress based on transnational hyper-consumption and "uses hybridity strategically to highlight certain aspects of the global order...while at the same time discarding other elements that do not fit its strategic vision" (Kraidy 2005:95–96). As I have argued elsewhere (Darling-Wolf 2004), class-specific ideals of hybrid upwardly mobile femininity developed as a means to spur domestic as well as global consumption are ultimately more likely to serve national and international capitalist interests than the women they allegedly represent. We clearly need to approach the concept of hybridity with a healthy dose of cynicism and persist in exploring its multiple connections and intersections with various forms of oppression for individuals around the globe.

Hybridity without Guarantees

The construction and negotiation of hybridity in relationship to gender and other aspects of individuals' lives is particularly complex, and the resistance hybridity offers against hegemonic practices is often fragile at best. In our efforts to critically consider hybridity's emancipatory potential, we must thus continue to include gender as a significant constitutive element of transcultural and transnational relations. Failing to do so would lead not only to an incomplete understanding of the specific "technologies of gender" women in varied environments and situations must contend with, but also to an inadequate assessment of the nature of power relations in 21st century global capitalism. As political scientist Cynthia Enloe warns, "[I]f we miss patriarchy when it is in fact operating as a major structure of power, then our explanations about how the world works will be unreliable" (2004:4).

In particular, we need to continue to assess how individuals might negotiate hybridity at the local level in relationship to the global along the significant axes of gender, race, class, sexuality, national/cultural identity, and all other relevant aspects of their daily lives. We need, in other words, to assertively (re)insert gender into our examinations of the "global-local articulations" (Murphy & Kraidy, 2003:310) of transnational cultural dynamics, as well as in our own personal understanding and performance of hybridity. Because "[t]he interwoven processes of sexism, racism, misogyny, and heterosexism are an integral part of our social fabric *wherever in the world we might be*" and because "[w]e need to be aware that these ideologies, in conjunction with the regressive politics of ethnic nationalism and capitalist consumerism, are differentially constitutive of *all of our lives*" (Mohanty 2003:3, emphasis mine), we cannot continue to leave this task to minority and postcolonial feminist scholars and artists who have been doing most of the thinking about these issues so far. Developing a more critical understanding of hybridity would require all scholars to vigorously address the damaging tendency to favor certain aspects of identity in academic examinations of power relations mired in identity politics and limited by disciplinary boundaries, and to more honestly consider the ways in which we are all benefiting in multiple and varied ways from various systems of oppression.

Because constructing gender is "an ongoing activity embedded in everyday interactions" (West and Zimmerman 1987:130), critically engaging with the hybridity/gender articulation in all its multifaceted complexity might help us build the kinds of "micropolitical practices of daily life and daily resistances" that De Lauretis (1987:25) advocates as a means to destabilize hegemonic discourses. Such practices taking place at the local level through subjectivity and self-representations and operating "in the interstices of institutions and in the chinks and cracks of the power-knowledge apparati" (1987:25) emphasize creative tensions between different aspects of individuals' identities and offer the potential for the generation of alternative conceptualizations of gender.

Inserting gender into the hybridity equation at both the local and global levels is also critical to the development of a truly "critical transculturalism" – to borrow Kraidy's term (2005:149) – that refuses to conveniently ignore significant aspects of individuals identities' in the service of economic, political, and/or academic discourses about gender, feminism, class, race, culture, or the nation. A transculturalism which, in other words, more fully addresses *all* of the "oblique powers" (García-Canclini, 1995:258) at work in hybridity.

Chapter Five

Gender and the Hybrid Identity: On Passing Through[1]

Salvador Vidal-Ortiz

Introduction

This chapter is an attempt to develop discussions of "passing through," particularly in terms of transgenderism and transsexuality. My argument here tends less to whether transsexual and transgender people "pass" or "do not pass" (and the related underpinnings of those arguments about passing as becoming normative), but focuses more on what takes place in the "in and through" of the movement between categories. I argue in this chapter that the passing through gender (more specifically, gender borders or lines) is what can illustrate gendered identities and hybridity – sometimes at its fullest. This is not necessarily a new argument, nor one new to sociology – indeed, oftentimes, sociologists explain a social norm by looking at the marginal aspects of the norm, or at the rule breakers of the norm, in order

[1] Portions of this chapter were originally presented at the 2007 American Sociological Association meetings in New York, New York, under the title *Hybridity, "Passing" and Identity Movements: Productive tensions between academics' and their fields of study*. My thanks to Judith Lorber for allowing me to share some of these "ideas in the making" in this panel, to Elisa A. G. Arfini, Karl Bryant, and Elijah Edelman for reading suggestions and conversations in furthering these arguments, and to Keri E. Iyall Smith for inviting me to submit a chapter to this book project, and her encouragement throughout the writing process.

to illustrate it fully.[2] In sex, gender, and sexuality scholarship, for instance, we see the use of intersex, transsexuality, and homosexuality as the outlier cases to explain the social norms of regulating two sexes, an equal number of genders (with an expected hierarchy between male and female), and a similar hierarchy of sexuality, with heterosexuality as the most privileged.[3] What I aim to do in this chapter is to go beyond signaling transsexuality as rule-breaker of normative sex-gender expectations (a view from the outside), in order to theorize the passing-through categories and the meaning-making in that movement (or inside processes). But I am also arguing something else besides the outlier in discussions of gender (or sex, gender, and sexuality). I propose to look at the movement between categories of identities (not the categories themselves) or the passing through them, first, because such movement is heavily under-theorized but nonetheless an important aspect of gender and gender hybridity, but also because the movement itself can show us productive ways of thinking about the categories.

I came about the idea of "passing" as I was thinking and writing about the relationship of race and ethnicity for Puerto Ricans.[4] I had a sense that there was something about the *passing through* of "racial" categories and how, perhaps, Puerto Ricanness was a way to interrogate US ethno-racial categories, so I began to write autoethnographically about complex everyday experience and interaction with others, and frustrations with theoretical frameworks that I felt were void of complexity.[5] As with that previous work, my use of the term "passing" here is not about historical uses of it, as in *passing for*

---

[2] For writings documenting how this has happened in the sociological study of gender (especially through interactionism), see Lorber (1994) and Ekins and King (2006).

[3] See, for instance, Butler (1990), Corber and Valoochi (2003), and Fausto-Sterling (2000).

[4] See Vidal-Ortiz (2004). I focused there on the flexible and movable social identifications for Puerto Ricans in the US. The productiveness between being/moving from Puerto Rican, Latino, and people of color in situational turns (that is, how one can be Puerto Rican in certain spaces, Latina/o in others, and an ethno-racial minority, or a person of color, in others) proved for me to be a way of opening up identities to their social contexts.

[5] I see some similarities between the autobiographical work of transsexuals and my own in terms of racialization, and I draw this parallel in the literature review in order to explore this idea (although the comparison is drawn only to a limit, as the reader will notice). The autobiographical is intrinsic to the study of transsexuality and transgender studies (see Vidal-Ortiz 2008), but more research is needed in terms of understanding this knowledge production.

someone or something, but entering/exiting, or using a connector to move from place to place, as in *passing through.* The temporality of the passing through of categories, identities, and social contexts is a slippery (and less tangible) way of thinking about gender, but it may prove to offer a lot of possibilities for analysis.

I am interested in troubling identity-politics frameworks by going *through* them, but also by arguing *something else, something different,* from what is offered in traditional sociological frameworks of identity and movement. The permeability of borders – and our attempts to go through them, and to challenge them – are central to the arguments elaborated upon here. I am aware that only some people have the possibility of literally passing through categories, be it gender, sexuality, or race, but the chapter is not focusing on whether that opportunity arises to some – instead, my focus is on the structure that depends on the categories, and how it allows for movement between and across the categories. I explore if and the extent to which these movements destabilize or reify social structures, as I illustrate throughout.

Because I bring together gender and sexuality in my writing, a caveat is important. Oftentimes in gender theorizing, sexuality is mentioned as a sub-division or a dimension of gender, one that could never stand on its own. This is especially relevant in feminist studies, where the threat of managing sexuality seems (to some) to overshadow the emphasis on gender as a his-torically relevant axis essential to intersectionality.[6] In my own work, gender and sexuality have posed analytical challenges, since it is hard to maintain them as independent, and oftentimes harder not to explain them as mutu-ally constitutive of each other.[7] That has been the case of some lesbian, gay, bisexual, and transgender (LGBT) scholarship,[8] although I think there is more to be said in that regard.

I start this chapter with a literature review, which builds from sexuality and racial discussions on passing (through) and hybridity, moving into a main section discussing my focus on transgenderism and transsexuality through some critical texts that help trouble the notion of passing (and also complicate the relationship between some of the categories of analysis we

---

[6] For more on this, see Andersen (2005) and the symposium in response to that article published in *Gender & Society* in the February 2008 issue.

[7] Vidal-Ortiz (2002); see also Richardson (2007) and Butler (1994).

[8] See Valoochi (2005).

use), ending with a conclusion on some of the potential contributions of the notion of passing through and its relation to gender studies.

On Passing and Passing through Hybrid Spaces

In *Disidentifications: Queers of Color and the Performance of Politics*, José Muñoz discusses the concept of "hybridity," which illustrates how queers of color insert themselves in a space "not of their own" – a space multiply constituted by subjectivities other than the ones intended to occupy it – in this case, queers of color who seem to defy the neat boundaries of race and sexual homogeneity. This takes place in the context of physical spaces that are either primarily identified by (and exclusive to) whiteness (as in the case of gay neighborhoods), or in terms of sexual normativity (as in ethno-racial minority heterosexual spaces). But the excess formed in not being able to (symbolically) fit within either of these physical spaces may constitute a newer, third space – one where the particularities of the experience of queers of color is valued.

I am bringing to our attention hybridity as a tool to better account for spaces where no single narrative or authority can claim to represent a truth, so we can interrogate concepts such as "gender" and the relationship of gender to sexuality. Gender hybridity, using as foundation Muñoz's interpretation of minority subjects *vis à vis* the State, can be both a space articulated through liminality as well as the expulsion of spaces that interpret gender as male or female.[9] Like Muñoz, I aim to talk about these disidentifications as survival strategies that, while they are not always available to the minority subject, they are still potential ruptures to the structural configurations of racial, gender, and sexual hegemonies. I thus explore here the extent to which they break away from structural repositionings of normativity.

The notion of passing through is especially relevant here. Using Muñoz's work, as well as others' (Amhed 1999, see also Bernstein Sycamore 2006, Schlossberg 2001, and Torres 2007), I look at gender in relation to sexuality

---

[9] It can also be about assumptions that reify sex=gender – see Rubin (1984 [1993]). For a discussion on boundaries, transgender activists, and the Michigan Womyn's Music Festival, see Gamson (1997).

and race – like these other authors do – in order to demonstrate the potential new readings of passing and the capacity to pass through in significant ways that either dissolve a space, produce others, and/or signify a productive tension between the original spaces and the newly constituted ones.

Passing challenges notions of what seems evident at first sight; it also challenges understandings of the natural. According to Schlossberg: "the passing subject's ability to transcend or abandon his or her 'authentic' identity calls into question the very notion of authenticity itself" (2001:2). The notion of passing through, which does not necessarily follow questions of visibility, pride/shame,[10] and coherent (and often individualized) life narratives like passing does (Schlossberg 2001:3–4), offers room to discuss the movement of people beyond notions of fixed sex-gender identities, pure racial backgrounds, and normative versus deviant sexualities.[11] Indeed, the passing through captures the mobility across categories of analysis or identification, creating a space of a non-racial pure subject, a set of gender insignia that trouble binary readings of gender, or a "queer" non-gay or lesbian subject.[12]

Passing here is not about being visible or having authority to speak because one is read as raced, outside (American imaginaries of) traditional gender expression, or outside normative sexual parameters – nor is passing about noticing those normative selves whose experience has nothing to tell us, for instance, because their whiteness is not raced. Not all passings are the same, given that there are various meanings to passing.[13] As Schlossberg

---

[10] For examples, refer to Britt and Heise's "From shame to pride in identity politics" (2000).

[11] See Stacey's "Cruising to Familyland" (2004) for an example of normative discourses within gay movements.

[12] See Johnson (2002) and Harper (1998) for some sexuality and race/class examples of this discussion. See West and Zimmerman (1987) for the discussion of gender insignia in particular.

[13] Moreover, some passings fuse gender and sexuality. For instance, a woman who is perceived by others to be "too masculine" and is generally orientated as heterosexual, passes as lesbian to some. A man whose sexual attractions are toward women, but who is perceived to be "feminine" is thus read by most through the lens of gender cues, and his sexuality is assumed as gay. In either instance, rarely their sexuality is read in a different space – bisexuality – nor is bisexuality read as more than "the middle." These dualistic ideas of gender and sexuality tend to fuse in the image of bisexuality; see Schwartz and Rutter (1998) for more on this. A useful theoretical explanation of the relation between gender and sexuality on discussions of bisexuality can be found in Hemmings (2002).

(2001) notes, while the passing of a sexual "minority" subject often requires his or her ability to remain "in the closet;" the passing of raced (ethno-racial minority) subjects is often denounced, as an act of avoiding (and rejecting the perceived need) to pass as white. As hinted at in the introduction, the passings in gender and transgender people in particular, on the other hand, are thought of as a challenge to the capacity for transgender (or, more specifically, transsexual) people to "be their true selves."[14]

While gender regimes, hierarchical notions of gender based on power, and the movement between genders, gender constructs, and even gender roles, are all movements of passing through, this chapter engages gender as a structured (and fixed) way of living, from which transgender and transsexual people migrate to and from.[15] Clearly, some experiences and identities resonate much more with this concept of passing through and of movement: the figure of the transsexual, a female in a male-dominated field, or the notion of the prostitute are all examples that, to varying degrees, move from traditionally expected gendered notions. Some of the people in these examples "pass," while some others "stick" to an imaginary group of people who break social rules.[16] For reasons of space, personal expertise, and interest, I focus solely on transgender and transsexual "moves," although I use the literature that mentions race and sexuality as a way of engaging the published literature on passing (through).

Sarah Ahmed (1999) incorporates gender, sexual, and racial discussions of passing in her article, "'She'll Wake Up One of These Days and Find She's Turned into a Nigger': Passing through Hybridity" (despite what may seem to some as a racial argument in the title of her article). In the following quote, and after explaining the double passing of two black women understood as whites by everyone else (which is linked to the title), Ahmed illustrates the

---

[14] It is difficult not to relate the "true transsexuality" diagnoses early on in the "treatment" of transsexuality and the notion of a true self used at present time. For a "taken for granted" use of the term in the lives of transgender people, see Brown and Rounsley (1996). For a critique that illustrates a struggle between categories (for instance, cross-dresser, transsexual, transvestite), see Mason-Schrock (1996). Questions of insignia perceived as crucial (e.g., voice pitch) as illustrations of the challenges of a gender system for transgender/transsexual people can be found in Kulick (1999).

[15] For the notion of gender migration, refer to King (2003).

[16] For a more developed discussion on the notion of things that "stick" and affect, see Ahmed (2004).

challenges of thinking about identity and hybridity in relation to the ambigu-ous body and the generalized notion of thinking of it as disruptive:

> How do ambiguous bodies get read in a way which further supports the
> enunciative power of those who are telling the difference? In what ways is
> 'passing' implicated in the very discourse around tellable differences? How
> are social identities fixed and secured? To simply focus on strategies or tactics
> of destabilization, transgression, mimicry, rupture, hybridity, breakage,
> travesty, masquerade, iterability, performativity, citationality, camouflage
> (one must note the proliferation of such terms which celebrate and affirm
> the structural possibility of a displacement from social norms), is to forgo
> an analysis of the complex social and psychic mechanisms for dealing with
> such tactics (such as designating them as undesirable outcomes of the loss
> of social and familial security). (Ahmed 1999:89)

Ahmed is here less interested in the conceptualization of the unreadable body (unreadable through specific markers like gender, race, and class) than she is in the almost immediate realignment of the structurally imposed (and domi-nant) regimes that define gender, race, and class, and reinscribe the normative expectations in any of these markers. She is interested not in the origin or arrival/destiny of the movement, but in the movement itself. First, the passing for something is identified, and perhaps it is so as a threat to the regulatory system it attempts to disrupt. Secondly, the passing through does not always result in a transgression (as also stated by Muñoz), oftentimes resulting in the dismissal, or ejection, of the body that creates the "anomaly." That action tends to reinstate the normative view of the structure one inhabits. In the specific account of the story in *Passing*, which Ahmed recounts in the opening of the article, Claire's narrative, as the main character, does not survive. After that erasure and elimination of the character, Ahmed asks: "Who counts as Black [sic]? Who counts as male? Who counts as female? Who counts as a Black [sic] woman?...The dis-organizing of social identities, here, can become a mechanism for the re-organizing of social life through an expansion of the terms of surveillance" (91). One can only be reminded of this expulsion from the narrative of the story in terms of gender and gender identity and think of transgendered accounts such as Brandon Teena's, whose gender identity self-identification remains unclear, but whose murder because of breaking gender norms acted as a re-organizing of social life by attempting to regulate everyone's gender expressions.[17] However, what makes most of us remember such expulsion has more to do with neoliberal positionings of gay and lesbian middle-class extensions of marginality that in some respects co-opt the marginality and disenfranchisement of transgender people – oftentimes queer youth or youth of color, and sometimes transwomen dependent on informal economies like sex work.[18]

Indeed, the "counting" Ahmed refers to in this last passage challenges readings that single out singular race or gender markers. Being read as a white male or white female, and being read as a black male or a black female in the US offers different sexual and sexualized readings – as it does different perceptions of class and power. For example, in the experiences of African-American transsexual males who grew up in an environment that understood them as female, the shift is monumental, as there are so many stereotypes around black male behavior in the US that impact the reading (and transitioning experiences) of transsexual men differently.[19] While individuals may "pass" and achieve certain things, the act of "passing" here from one gender construct to another has huge ramifications that sustain a traditional (racist, sexist, and heteronormative) structure in place – structures that will judge them even as they transition.

In Sloop's *Disciplining Gender* (2004), we see the power of cultural arguments played out in the public that have to do with gender expression and sexual ambiguity. Sloop does a great job addressing some of the re-structurings mentioned previously by Ahmed. Through the use of five cases of well-known figures and situations in US news, politics, and the arts, Sloop

---

[17] Teena was raped, and later killed in Nebraska by two men who did not respect Teena's gender identity and presentation as male. Brandon Teena's identity has been discussed in media, personal accounts of relatives and people close to Teena, and in academics' writings, as a female to male transgender, a butch lesbian, and sometimes a mix of these two. There does not seem to be an account from Brandon Teena that directly speaks to a self-identity. For more on this, refer to Halberstam (2005), Hale (1998), and Wilcox (2003).

[18] For more on this notion of adding one's fears of death onto the bodies of those killed by homophobia or transphobia, refer to the introduction of "Retheorizing Homophobias" and our (Bryant and Vidal-Ortiz 2008) discussion of Halberstam's introduction to her 2005 book. For the marginality of key trans individuals in the LGBT movement, such as Sylvia Rivera, see Gan (2007).

[19] See, for example, "Any four Black men will do" (Owens Patton and Snyder-Yuly 2007).

shows how regulatory and self-sustaining a gender normative system is. Among these cases was the one centered on the 1999 killing of US military private Barry Winchell and his surviving partner, Calpernia Adams, who self-identified as a "pre-operative transsexual" (Sloop 2004:5). The policing of gender (and sexuality) by both general, mainstream coverage that either assumed their heterosexuality or forced their relationship to be read as the relationship of two gay men, was one of the ways in which gender norms remained in place.

In the example of Winchell and Adams, this story was certainly mediated by the mass media's attempt to simplify their relationship (including their sexuality), which depended on questions of Adams's gender. If we were to use Ahmed's readings, paraphrasing, I would say: "for whom does Adams count as a woman?" Drawing on similarities between this case and Brandon Teena's, Sloop evokes the balance between telling their own (transgender) stories and their perception in the popular media realm. Unlike Teena's case, Adams's includes a chance of speaking and getting a sense of the perception and perspective of her, a chance Sloop took in balancing this chapter's data between the personal conversations he had with Calpernia Adams and the coverage of her deceased partner, their relationship, and her own identity. For most, the first two items were unanswered until the last – her sex-gender equation – was "clarified." But the challenges in "resolving" their defiant statuses (defiant to those gender structures that I referred to earlier) did not stop there. While her gender identity was judged and re-evaluated constantly in a media frenzy, pulling the definition of their relationship, and Winchell's sexual orientation (toward a definition of same-sex desire), to be linked to her identity and choice of self-identification, an additional effect was that *because* her partner's sexual orientation was most often described as "gay" in public, this became a pushing factor to identify Adams as gay (and, perhaps more specifically, as a gay man).

Another significant contribution – and one most relevant to the issue of passing – was the lack of evidence in determining Winchell's heterosexuality (discussed by his mother as the presence of past love letters, and the presumed absence of "gay" love letters, as Sloop points out), paired with his lack of announcing his homosexuality, as enough proof that he was, indeed, heterosexual. Sloop's view of Winchell's sexuality (as deployed in media outlets) does not stay in one place:

> While one could read the term 'passing phase' to indicate a phase of passing
> as heterosexual just before the moment of outing oneself, or, more radically,
> as a phase of passing through a number of different identities with no
> assumed telos, here Winchell's silence, like the silence of the love letters,
> indicates a temporary phase that was coming to an end – an end that would
> eventually reestablish Winchell's heterosexuality. (Sloop 2004:135)

The passing through referenced here is about the possibilities of being in various spaces of experience (although not necessarily identification). This passing through is not so much in between (which depends on categories), but in movement. Indeed, Sloop talks about how Adams saw Winchell's sexuality as "in process." These temporal spaces signify movement and change. But the temporality spoken about in this quote also allows us to notice the normative systems that reconstruct the meaning of such temporalities as slippages from the normative. With his death, the presumed heterosexuality, which is so strongly referenced in and through the "evidence" as well as what is not "there," is reinstated. According to this disciplining system, heterosexuality was, all along, his inherent identity.

This regulatory system impacts both members of the relationship. There was a movement in experience less related to self-categorizations (for Winchell but also Adams) that threatened the possibility of sustaining Winchell's perceived heterosexuality. That is, the dislocation of self-identification takes place for both of them, as Winchell's presumed heterosexual life narrative impacts Adams's portrayal of herself – and the two of them. This passing is not about not being anything, not fitting within any category, or refusing identity altogether; this passing references the threat of the shift in sexuality representation. Because both of them experienced life in a hyper-masculine setting (the military) that reproduces many surveillance strategies that at the same time reify a structure of normativity, the "doubts" about Winchell's heterosexuality can be erased. As others have noted (Ahmed 1999, Schlossberg 2001), passing (as an image used by the individual), often leaves untouched the structures that make the hegemonic system to maintain itself in place.

To sum up, passing through is thus not an element that foregrounds a hybrid sense, if passing depends on the ability to defy an entry point or a final location (as in Ahmed's work) but instead requires that mobility be granted on the account of ambiguity, of a mislocated home, or of a diasporic self in exile. In terms of gender and hybridity, gendering systems that account for two (and only two) genders rely on fixed notions of sex, a continuous defense of insignia that represent one (not the other), and a set of sexual regulations to reify itself, as Sloop (2004) showed us.[20] The following section does discuss the relationship between gender and sexuality, and transgender and transsexual, in order to further the notion of passing (through), but not before clarifying and defining some terms used in my analysis.

The Passing Through in Transgender and Transsexual Frameworks

In this section, I engage the readings of transgender and transsexual scholarship in order to discuss hybridity in the context of gender. In trans studies, there is a (negative) history with the concept of passing, but so little discussion about the extent to which passing (through) gendered systems benefits the trans individual, and/or regenerates the gendered system. Because of this, I want to convey a sense of urgency in thinking about the standpoint of the populations we wish to support, study, or give voice to, especially by not imposing a set of categories ("third gender" comes to mind) to those experiences.[21] Thus, I clarify the terms of these categories before delving into the literature that complicates the relationship of the terms.

Transsexuality is a term historically used to refer to transitions (medical, surgical, and psychological) by gender-crossing individuals, as defined by the medical/scientific establishment (and oftentimes, the medical establishment conducted surgical interventions in the service of gender conformity and heteronormativity).[22] Transgender is utilized to refer to an umbrella term of gender-crossing experiences ranging from cross-dressing, drag-queen-/king-ing, transvestism, and gender bending not associated with transitioning strategies (as in the case of the earlier use of transsexuality). While it would seem that surgery serves as an act that divides transgender and transsexual, as I illustrate next, the line between the two is becoming less plausible.

---

[20] For more on that, see West and Zimmerman (1987).

[21] Towle and Morgan (2002).

[22] For more on the relationship between gender congruity in transsexuals and heteronorms in relation to categorizing the transsexual body as "productive," refer to Irving (2008).

As noted elsewhere (Vidal-Ortiz 2002, 2008), discussing transgender experience requires unpacking the various meanings of the term. Some authors (Kessler and McKenna 2000) have discussed at least three ways of interpreting the prefix "trans" so often used in this scholarship. In their use, this prefix may mean "change," "across," and "beyond." In the first of the three uses, "trans" is utilized to refer to "transsexuality." In the second sense, it represents a movement from one gender category to another (still within a two-gender structure), and in the third and last one, Kessler and McKenna argue for a multiplicity of gender options, as in when a person moves *beyond* gender, or *through it*. Kessler and McKenna point out how it is in this third sense of "trans" that a lot of revolutionary possibilities can take place. But in this instance, scholars often place a greater responsibility on transsexual people to disrupt dual gender systems, whereas all should be made responsible to actively pursue the project of undoing gender – not just transsexual and transgender people. This judgment against transsexuality also emerges through the challenges to the idea of transitioning and "passing," which is conceptualized as a transsexual narrative, because it is understood by some as a "buying into" gender-oppressive systems. In the end, with some exceptions, little communication takes place between gender scholars and transgender and transsexual people.

In terms of gender and sexuality, and specifically in terms of transgenderism, I am reminded of the work by Susan Stryker (1994) at the dawn of transgender studies, where she argued that transsexuals were *something more, something else*, than what the sexological, psychiatric, medical, and psychological establishments made them to be during the 20th century.[23] The hybridity of trans as that something more, something else, is a useful concept for sociological scholarship because it might be through this detachment from a solid, simplistic sense of transsexuality that we will begin to see the possibilities for better understanding and addressing gender identity and expression experiences beyond the male and female. Hybridity is here a concept doable outside identity frameworks.

Let us explore the meaning of this "something more," or take a look beyond the boundaries of what medical and psychiatric professionals instituted as

---

[23] For a history of and the development of these various disciplines and areas of study, see Irvine (1990) and Meyerowitz (2002).

transsexuality, in relation to hybridity and gender.[24] It would seem logical to think that hybridity marks the passing of a person: To talk about a trans-gendered male might mean to some to hold a hybrid identity. Also, as is the case in much sociological scholarship, transgender men have voiced their sense of how transsexuality was a passing through from female to male.[25] Both of these instances illustrate a trajectory: in the first scenario, by fusing transgender and male (or female), and in the second, by using it as a conduit for something else. Others might argue that an androgyny and blending of genders is a hybrid identity that merits attention. But, while I would argue that there is no passing through in a blend, because the movement between these two is moot if the end point is to go across them, this could also mean that there is always a passing through – that one is always in an open state of movement and non-definition. Whether androgyny and the blending of genders challenge the structures that reconstitute the bi-gender normative system, or simply pass – and in passing through this strict bi-gendered system, get digested by it – warrants more specific study.

Stealth is another aspect in studies of transsexuality that merits interrogation. While some scholarship has argued (albeit with anecdotal evidence) that large numbers of transmen leave trans communities after transitioning,[26] this assessment leaves uninterrogated the need to surveil the transition of transgender people, or the validity of their transitioning, unless they remain linked to queer communities. This chapter focuses on the uses of transgender and transsexual, less as a (feminist) project of assigning (gender) privilege, and more as an analysis of the ways in which transgender and transsexual meaning-making is different depending on how the people we are referring to/studying are situated. I want to introduce more productive ways of theorizing hybridity and transgender experience: between gender and sexuality, as well as between the categories (of transgender and transsexual) in current meaning-making and in the experiences voiced at present time. The following discussion brings forth recent works that, while focusing on the transgendered

---

[24] For instance, Stone (1991) develops the notion of a post-transsexual identity as a response to feminist critiques.

[25] See for example, the interviews in Rubin's (2003) and Vidal-Ortiz's (2002) research.

[26] Schilt (2006). Anecdotal evidence is indeed valuable, especially at the beginning stages of research inquiries.

and transsexuality, incorporate the movements between gender and sexuality and between transgender and transsexual.

In Valentine's recent work *Imagining Transgender: an ethnography of a category* (2007), we are introduced to an ethnographic site that speaks not just of the "field" and its people as objects of study, but also, about how these members (social service providers, researchers, and trans people to name but a few) act as producers of the common knowledge of this category we now use to refer to transgender people and expression. Based on an ethnography that took place in the 1990s, Valentine makes a claim that the solidification of the "transgender" category was gaining currency at the very same time that his ethnographic work was going on (in multiple sites in New York City), distinguishing between the sexological and psychiatric scholarly work from the early 20th century as it formed something else – beyond pathologization, but also, a rupture from homosexuality even as it continued to use it as a referent.

More specifically, the project Valentine puts forth is about the oppositional (but significantly constitutive) categories of homosexuality and transgender, or of gender and sexuality. To make this point clearer, I show an excerpt from Valentine's introduction that helps see the connections and the juncture he develops in his writing:

> [I]n what ways does transgender not only *explain* non-normative genders but also *produce the effect* of those differences by effacing others? It is this complex social and political process that I refer to as 'imagining transgender.' Related to this process is another category, one which stands as the implicit Other to transgender: homosexuality. One of the oft-told progressivist stories of the late twentieth century is that of the depathologization of homosexuality. This story rests not only on the social validation of homosexual identity but centrally on the assertion that homosexual identity is not rooted in a gendered inversion. That is, if in the contemporary United States 'transgender' describes a deviation from gender norms, then 'homosexuality' indexes same-sex eroticism between *gender-normative* people. (2007:14–15, italics in original)

This quote illustrates the 20th-century history of sexological knowledge production (in Europe and the United States) that linked homosexuality to gender inversion and later femininity – in ways that have not completely been abandoned.[27] Indeed, as this statement reveals, while there are debates about the relationship between homosexuality and transgenderism in the Diagnostic and Statistical Manual of the American Psychiatric Association, from the exclusion of the former from 1973 (a revision of the 1968 2nd edition), and the insertion of the latter in 1980 (3rd edition), there are various debates that claim the pathologization of transgender (as gender identity disorder) is not an automatic response to the elimination of homosexuality as a mental illness.[28]

But the project Valentine presents here is also about demonstrating that gender-conformant gay men and lesbians are produced out of this differentiation between homosexuality and transgender in ways that exclude any linking of the terms or the categories (especially in relation to women and female-bodied people), as it did in the earlier part of the 20th century. A "clear" sense of distinctiveness between these terms emerges in and through their gender and sexuality significations, at least in the gay and lesbian use of these categories. In feminist theorizing, on the other hand, the complex relationship between gender and sexuality continues to be theorized in relation to each other – and not simply in oppositional stands, as in gay and lesbian organizing. As we learn from the documented ethnography, there are informants that represent a break from the rule: a "transgender" person who says that her experience is of being "gay, a woman," another who says, "gay, transgender, whatever," both diffusing the distinction between these categories of explanation.

The reinsertion within a New York City sexual minority space outside a self-labeling of transgender (and sometimes including gay and transgender together) results in an unfortunate exclusion of people from the general resources (especially organizing funds) otherwise available to LGBT organizations. A violent set of exclusions thus emerges out of this distinction, and an unfortunate education of those who transgress transgender (gender)-homosexual (sexuality) definitional boundaries takes place. Valentine cautions the reader to better understand the relationship between gender and sexuality, and

---

[27] For more on this relationship and transgender and transsexual recent history, see Meyerowitz (2002).

[28] See, for instance, Bryant (2006) and Butler (2006). For some of the history of trans medicalization through this diagnosis, refer to Burke (1996).

between transgender and homosexuality, but he also differentiates between gender and sexuality (without quotation marks or brackets) as categories and experiences, and "gender" and "sexuality" as "cultural and theoretical categories" (2007:239). The assumed ontological basis for differentiating these two, in Valentine's view, needs to be reopened for discussion.

What we get from Valentine's work is that there is a passing through of gender and sexuality, and of transgender and homosexuality, that is heavily guarded and separated into "gender identity" and "sexual orientation" categories, but while scientists, social service providers, and researchers debate the separation between these categories, those categories are inherently fused in the lives of many of the trans people in the ethnographic sites he visited. The passing through of being both "gay, a woman," or "gay, transgender" is a conflation of identities indexing categories that, given our training in thinking through gender and sexuality as distinctive analytical lens, seems illogical. The investment social scientists often hold in reinforcing the distinction of these categories is as much of a focus of study in Valentine's work as people's use of the categories as identities.

Whereas Valentine complicates the relationship between gender and sexuality through transgender and homosexuality nomenclatures, Halberstam (2005) does so through the slippery reading – neither as transsexual, nor certainly as lesbian – of a most referenced individual: Brandon Teena. In Halberstam's writing, the space Teena inhabited was a space that troubles biographical linearity and one that forms a sense of a transgender experience outside the boundaries of the transsexual narrative and of lesbian identity. Instead of dismissing transgender embodiment, as other scholars do (either through the "realness" imposed to transsexuality or the superficiality assigned to cross-dressing and gender crossing), Halberstam points to the impact of the category of "transgenderism":

> [W]e should know what kind of work it does, whom it describes, and whom it validates. Transgender proves to be an important term not to people who want to reside outside the categories altogether but to people who want to place themselves in the way of particular forms of recognition. Transgender may indeed be considered a term of relationality; it describes not simply an identity but a relation between people, within a community, or within intimate bonds. (Halberstam 2005:49)

In this explanation, we can see that those who are validated or described by a transgender category nowadays (as an umbrella term but also as a gender-bending expression) might feel entitled to force their portrayal of a non-traditional gendered expression onto others. Indeed, this transgender expression of blowing up gender altogether is an expression that needs validation, as in those "particular forms of recognition." The passing through dualistic notions of gender here provoke a chance to be read as something else – a transgendered person who actively pursues a challenge to that very binary. This form of transgender recognition stands in contrast to the past notion of transsexuality, where a male-to-female individual (the most commonly visible narrative of transsexuality in medical/psychiatric discourses) avoided a label of homosexuality and reinstated a wish to "pass" from "deviance" to a heterosexual life. Transgender, in the broadest umbrella sense, and as a dominant narrative now, offers a space for community formation, as Halberstam shows. One should assume by the implicit contrast from this definition of transgender to that of transsexuality that the community formation here emerges thanks to the avoidance of a transsexual (passing) narrative of reconceptualization.

On the surface, and given the previous comments, it would appear that for Halberstam, transsexual is more stable (as it has currency and "passes") than transgender, the latter offering a level of fluidity that appears to move faster than transsexual. But the author clarifies: "transsexual is not simply the conservative medical term to transgender's transgressive vernacular; instead, both transsexuality and transgenderism shift and change in meaning as well as application *in relation to each other* than in relation to a hegemonic medical discourse" (54, emphasis in original). Halberstam thus complicates any simplistic distinction between transgender and transsexual, especially one that may assume a reading of passing only on the latter. Instead, we can rethink both transgender and transsexual as figures of a "passing through" that do not intend to reiterate traditional gender expressions.

One only need to pay attention to the anecdotes (and slowly, emergent studies) that show how complicated the line between transgender and transsexual is – you may find female impersonators who get breast implants in order to "do realness" yet do not wish to transition nor identify as transsexual. Similarly, it is more common to find transsexual women whose desire for sexual activity with non-transsexual men does not include having a lower genitalia reconstruction (or the removal of their testicles and penis); while some of these scenarios are often voiced in the area of sex work (where being a penetrative female offers much currency), they are not exclusively the realm of sex work transactions. What I hope these examples show is the blurry space between traditionally conceived (i.e., medically formulated) perceptions of transsexuality (to be a true transsexual is becoming a hetero-sexual woman, whose sole desire is to live heteronormatively), and the more complex space of transgenderism, where some use of hormones, surgical reconstruction, or body alteration may accompany a transgendered identifi-cation. These experiences pass through binary ideas of what an untouched body is, or what constitutes "true" transsexuality or "complete" operations. These very specific situations problematize our understanding of the "real" and the "performative," often aligned with (or imposed onto) transsexual and transgender narratives, respectively.

The crossings that take place between the categories Valentine and Halber-stam theorize help us further our thinking on passing – from the stigmatized use of the term – to passing through and mobility within some of these terms, categories, and identities. The spaces created in the movements may or may not disrupt structural understandings of gender, as Sloop theorized; yet, these ruptures allow for new thinking about the possibilities of movement across category lines and the fruitfulness of some of their effects.

Conclusion

This chapter aimed at departing from the more common tradition in social scientific analysis of charging transsexual and transgender people with the responsibility of breaking from gender dualisms, to instead think about movements between categories and experiences and gender identifications. I also hope this contribution helps us rethink trans as more than a rule/norm breaker (in sociological terms), but to really look within the transgendering that takes place in order to have more informed discussions about whether transgender ought to change bi-gender social norms or dualistic notions of gender. The literature reviewed clearly shows that the movements (passing throughs) are as important in illustrating the social structures that organize, hegemonically, gender scripts and permissible gendered behavior. There is more to be done in terms of this thinking about moving across and passing through.

Possible developments in thinking about the relationship of gender and sexuality outside of looking at the margins is not to fuse categories with identities to the point of essentializing them (transsexuality becoming a shorthand in the case of gender identity, and gay, lesbian, and bisexual identities in the case of sexual orientation), but also to begin to understand a mutually constitutive analysis that incorporates topics such as race, nation, and diaspora. How we enact notions of privilege or oppression, and how we often – as academics – impose a definition and the boundaries of a field, really frames what possible communication we can have among ourselves. Rethinking "passing" as a strategy that better explains marginality or systems of thought, and drawing more complex examinations out of people's experiences, will undoubtedly help in thinking about identity movements inside and outside academia.

While I have used humanities, communications, and anthropological literatures to develop this idea (and these literatures certainly deal with passing through in more productive ways), sociological literature can further aspects of what it means to be gendered from a position of trans experiences. This might require, however, a combination of theoretically dense and less empirical work, or an interdisciplinary framework to study the experiences of passing through some of these identification practices.

Some of the contributions of theorizing "passing through" in relation to hybridity include the capacity to notice the potential spaces created for minority subjects, the non-binary gender readings and how they may inhabit certain gendered communities, the set of unassigned gender insignia's limited impact in restructuring societal norms of "appropriate" or "traditional" gender behavior, and what meaning people living within those spaces give to the experience (whether these movements are discussed in terms of identity or some other construct). Indeed, it might be necessary to develop empirical research that is driven by experience (in a longitudinal way) to account for experience meaning-making through a life course.

Complicating analyses of gender and hybridity will require that we are as aware of the impact of social structures as we are of celebrating gender bending and flexibility. Collapsing gender structures into everyday behavior – and exercising behavioral change to produce a non-gender expression – has been a significant start to defy the categories of gender, but it does little to dismantle them as social organizing principles in our lives. The discussion in this chapter took a look at hegemonic views on gender, so as to bridge the very limiting behavioral adaptations, to the (oftentimes) seemingly untouchable social structures that can regenerate and dismiss the de-gendered behavior. Moving across and passing through may not be the most feasible ways of empirically situating change, but they serve as a start to thinking through a different lens of analysis to support social change and a less oppressive gender system to all.

Chapter Six

Bridging the Theoretical Gap: The Diasporized Hybrid in Sociological Theory

Melissa F. Weiner and Bedelia Nicola Richards

In a nation of immigrants, most American ethnic groups have at some point wrestled with how to reconcile having an identity that is rooted simultaneously in their countries of origin and in the United States, particularly when they are also racialized ethnic minorities. This hybrid identity often blends divergent cultures and traditions. And sociologists, intent on explaining these tensions, have focused on the experiences that have shaped these identities for over a century. As a result, the theoretical roots of contemporary hybridity theories, such as the segmented assimilation perspective, can be traced back to "classical" theorists of race, pluralism, and identity such as Robert Park, Horace Kallen, and W. E. B. DuBois. This chapter examines these roots, with the exception of DuBois's theories of double consciousness (found in Chapter 2), to provide a holistic sociological account of theories of hybrid identities. We suggest that despite the changing nature of immigrant experiences today due to globalization, there is still significant continuity between the processes and outcomes of ethnic identity formation among 19th- and 20th-century European immigrants and the more racially and ethnically diverse post-1965 immigrants to the United States.

In the United States, most immigrants have experienced ambivalence or tension between their hopes for being a part of the American citizenry while simultaneously desiring to retain elements of their homeland cultures. This has resulted in "a close connection between the notion of identity and the awareness of belonging to a distinctive group set apart from others in American society" (Gleason 1992:141). The desire to maintain cultural traditions finds immigrants negotiating a world where two identities exist and vary in salience depending on social contexts and structural conditions.

Until the mid-20th century, European immigrants were not considered fully white but instead existed in an "in-between" status in which they were considered to be neither black nor white. The argument that "the pathway to assimilation was smoothed for the descendants of European immigrants by their racial identification is an anachronism, inappropriately imposing contemporary racial perceptions on the past" (Alba and Nee 1997:845). With Old-World cultures linked to unfitness for citizenship, economic mobility was limited. Therefore, a hybrid identity persisted for generations among poor and working-class immigrants. However, this hybrid identity progressively attenuated among Europeans to the point where they identified only "symbolically" with their ethnic origins (Gans 1979). For contemporary immigrants, the United States remains a racial nationalist state where first-class citizenship rights are limited to those considered fully white. Thus, the likelihood of lasting hybrid identities looms large and necessitates a full understanding of similarities and differences between historical and contemporary immigrant groups.

The Place of the Diaspora in the Diasporized Hybrid

Whether referring to groups arriving in the United States 250 years ago or two years ago, a number of similarities arise with regard to the role of the diasporic experience on identities. Traditionally applied to Jews, the rise of transnational migration has produced diasporic experiences among generations of immigrants. This results in a diasporic consciousness such that migranthood and the journey of the diasporic experiences themselves become integral parts of groups' identities (Hall 1996; Safran 1991). Even as this identity celebrates cultures, the histories of migration, and global historical cultures and forces, it simultaneously reflects the uncertainty of actual residence and community, discrimination and exclusion, and social and economic marginalization (Clifford 1994).

Diasporic identities are characterized by a "continuing relationship to the homeland" that may either be physical, when individuals and group members continue to visit the homeland, or based on an imaginary community with the knowledge that they will not, or cannot, return (Safran 1991:84, Anderson 1991). The latter is particularly common among refugees, those fleeing religious, racial, or political persecution, as in the case of Jews fleeing from Russian pogroms or Nazi Germany, Italians fleeing Mussolini, or Tutsi fleeing Rwanda during the genocide. Diasporic groups also recognize they may never be fully accepted by their new nation and maintain memories, myths, customs, and traditions of the original homelands. These qualifications reveal that hundreds of immigrant groups arriving in America throughout its history likely experienced diasporic identities. Viewing the experiences of most American immigrants through a lens of diasporized hybridity allows us a similar lens with which to examine, compare, and understand the experiences of hundreds of immigrant groups arriving in the United States during the last four centuries.

Historical Hybridity: Classical Theories of Incorporation

The earliest sociological theorists of race, sometimes grudgingly, acknowledged the dualistic nature of immigrant identities. Robert Park (1928), although championing a race relations cycle predicated on the assimilation and loss of Old World cultures, recognized that this did not always occur. As "cultural hybrids," migrants lived and shared "the cultural life and traditions of two distinct peoples" (892). They straddled the boundaries of two different cultures, navigating the new American culture while simultaneously adhering to Old-World standards. One is quickly reminded of contemporary immigrants in reading his discussion of Jews, described as "never quite willing to break, even if he were permitted to do so, with his past and his traditions, and not quite accepted, because of racial prejudice, in the new society in which he now sought to find a place" (892). Unable and unwilling to assimilate, these immigrants exist as "marginal men...on the margin of two cultures and two societies, which never completely interpenetrated and fused" (892).

While Park found the multiplicity of identities problematic when permanent or semi-permanent, Horace Kallen championed cultural pluralism and dualistic identities because of their inevitability and ability to accommodate cultural longevity and renewal. Throughout his work, he rejected assimilatory models in favor of a theory that accurately described the realities of contemporary immigrants, which remains relevant today. Because they spent time in two different worlds impacting both aspects of their identity, work and home, people could not choose one identity, an American or a homeland identity, over another. For, "A man is at once...one in an ethnic and social group and the citizen on a nation" (1924:62). To account for this duality, groups asserted their hybridity by declaring themselves Irish-American, Italian-American, and Polish-American. This hyphenation became a fact, permeating all realms of life.

In the face of massive Americanization efforts, immigrant groups resisted, determined to hold on their ethnic traditions, and it worked. For generations, cultural traditions persisted among every ethnic group in the United States. As groups became more Americanized, so too did they assert their rights to maintain their ethnic cultures.

> As they grow more prosperous and 'Americanized,' as they become freed from the stigma of 'foreigner,' they develop group self-respect: the wop changes into a proud Italian, the hunky into an intensely nationalistic Slav...Their cultural abjectness gives way to cultural pride...In sum, the most eagerly American of the immigrant groups are also the most autonomous and self-conscious in spirit and culture. (106, 114)

In America, ethnic success facilitated the perfection of hybrid ethnic identities. Using Jews as an example, Kallen finds that as they acculturated to American traditions and became more American, so too did they "become rather the more a Jew. The cultural unity of his race, history, and background, is only continued by the new life under the new conditions" (113).

Directly challenging a melting pot ideology predicated on the loss of cultures, Kallen posited hybridity as central to American democracy involving "not the elimination of differences, but the perfection and conservation of differences" (1924:61). He foresaw

> a democracy of nationalities, cooperating voluntarily and autonomously through common institutions in the enterprise of self-realization through

the perfection of men according to their kind. The common language of the commonwealth, the language of its great tradition, would be English, but each nationalist would have for its emotional and involuntary life its own peculiar dialect or speech, its own individual and inevitable esthetic and intellectual forms. (1924:124)

This vision, though perhaps too optimistic because Kallen believed these groups would be immune from discrimination, foreshadows the reality of many immigrant groups today.

Even Milton Gordon (1964), who penned a model of assimilation predicated on the loss of homeland cultures, recognized that, within immigrant communities, people developed organizational networks and informal social relationships encouraging "members of the ethnic group to remain within the confines of the group for all of their primary relationships and some of their secondary relationships throughout all the stages of the life-cycle" (35). This allowed for group self-identification by simultaneously refracting "the national cultural patterns of behavior and values through the prism of its own cultural heritage" (38). Combined with class identities, these hybrid identities incorporated both American and ethnic group practices.

However, Gordon believed this identificational multiplicity was transitory as immigrants move toward identificational assimilation, when immigrants identify as "American" without any hyphenated identity. Heavily critiqued by other sociologists, this phenomena presumes a disinterest in cultural retention and requires "the extinction of any form of ethnic identity in favor of an exclusively national, American identity" (Alba and Nee 1997:831). Immigrants must expunge all familial and extra-American origins and traditions from the collective memory, which "flies in the face of the data demonstrating that the overwhelming majority of Americans still acknowledge some non-American ethnic ancestry" (Alba and Nee 1997:831, Alba 1990).

Revisiting Historical Hybridity: New Immigration Historians

Greater scrutiny of older ethnographical sociological studies of urban community find clear evidence of the maintenance of multiple ethnic and immigrant cultures while simultaneously assimilating to some degree into larger American culture (Bodnar 1987, Handlin 1941, Thomas and Znaniecki 1918). These immigrants lived in a world governed by a "culture of everyday life" shaped simultaneously by their folk cultures and their "present realities" in America (Bodnar 1987:209). As a result, their identities, rooted in neither new nor old countries, coalesced, forever shifting with new experiences in their new homeland.

Recent work examining white immigrant groups has focused on tensions they experience upon arriving in the United States, necessitating the negotiation of racial and ethnic boundaries that often placed them as "in-between" peoples who were "not-yet-white" (Barrett and Roediger 1997). Indeed, they existed in limbo with hybrid identities. This literature emphasizes the constructed nature and selective persistence of culture and identity among immigrants who became white in the 20th century (Vecoli 1964, 1990). These hybrid cultures not only existed but were integral to immigrants' ability to adjust and succeed in the United States. Confirming Kallen's findings nearly 50 years later, "as demands for loyalty and conformity to 'American' norms increased, immigrant groups responded by asserting and demonstrating the compatibility of their ethnocultures with national ideals" (Conzen et al. 1992:13).

Revisiting identity formation experiences of European immigrants, scholars find hybrid, or ethnic, identities constructed, negotiated, and adapted upon arrival to and throughout their time in America (Sollors 1989). This model, like contemporary discussions of hybridity, attributes agency to individual actors and groups in defining their own identities, cultures, and solidarities. This process entailed the fusion of "ancestral loyalties (religious, linguistic, and cultural) with American circumstances, political ideals, and participation in American political institutions" (Fuchs 1990:20). Therefore, ethnicity, like hybridity, is "a process of construction or invention with which one incorporates, adapts, and amplifies preexisting communal solidarities, cultural attributes, and historical memories…grounded in real life context and social experience" (Conzen et al. 1992:4).

This ethnic culture, repeatedly modified as groups in residence in the US expanded and acculturated to American customs, served a number of purposes. It has the power to "provide the basis for solidarity among the potential members of the group; mobilize the group to defend its cultural values and to advance its claims to power and status, and resources; and, at the same time, defuse the hostility of the mainstream ethnoculture by depicting the compatibility of the sidestream ethnoculture with American principles and ideals" (Conzen et al. 1992:5–6). Perhaps most importantly, ethnic cultures provide new immigrants access to ethnic niches and networks, which allow for citizenship-based access to social, political, and economic resources (Gans 1962, Waldinger 1996). Simultaneously, proximity to other ethnic groups also increased immigrants' likelihood to maintain their cultural identities, thereby mutually reinforcing the benefits of hybridity. Ethnic groups living in rural areas were more likely to maintain their cultures and not face assimilative pressures (Conzen et al. 1992) than those living in larger multiethnic cities.

Like today's immigrant groups, nearly all immigrant groups arriving pre-1965 – the Dutch, Germans, Irish, Italians, Jews, Czechs, French, or Poles – engaged in some form of voluntary pluralism, separatism, and attempts to maintain their own identity for at least some period of time, often a century or greater, in the form of hyphenated or hybrid identities (Bodnar 1987, Fuchs 1990, Vecoli 1990). Members of groups experiencing these conditions have been described as "multicultural" individuals (Adler 1974, Alexander 2001). They resemble marginal men with "no clear boundaries between him and himself and the varieties of cultural contexts he may find himself in," such that he is "very much a formative being, resilient, changing, and evolutionary" (Adler 1974:369–71).

Many link white ethnicity to class and urbanism, arguing that as immigrants become upwardly mobile and suburbanize, they assimilate into the dominant society and lose all but their most symbolic forms of ethnicity (Gans 1979, Steinberg 1989). Like contemporary immigrants with hybrid identities, European ethnics experienced conflict because becoming American necessitated the dissolution of strong family and community ties to promote economic success (Gans 1962, Whyte 1993). However, a majority of ethnics, even in the third generation, identify with their ancestor's homeland (Alba 1990, Greeley 1974, Tricarico 1984). It is not trivial that people choose, consistently, to retain their cultural backgrounds and become hyphenated Americans.

The above research highlights the extent to which white ethnicity was important to the communities that enacted these cultures from their native lands as ways to both assert their difference from native whites and utilize these cultures in their transition from one country to another. Throughout American history, immigrants have experienced and adopted "a double identity that included 'American' self-definition" (Kazal 1995:462) alongside (real or imagined) customs, values, and traditions of an ancestral homeland.

The Diasporic Hybrid in Contemporary Immigration Theory

Lacking a transnational perspective until recently, the immigration literature has traditionally been more concerned with how immigrant identities are shaped in response to social and structural factors within the United States. Yet the magnitude of post-1965 immigration to the United States has yielded an even greater geographical concentration of immigrants in certain metropolitan areas in the United States, such as in New York City, Los Angeles, and Miami, creating ideal conditions for the formation of diasporic hybrid identities. The influx of these racially and ethnically diverse populations in the post-1965 immigration era has challenged sociologists to develop new concepts and frameworks for describing ethnic identity formation processes and outcomes. The segmented assimilation perspective was derived to capture these new ways of becoming and being ethnic Americans.

The segmented assimilation perspective posits that the way in which new immigrants are incorporated into American society will affect whether the second generation will experience ethnic identity formation as a "linear," "selective," or a "reactive" process (Rumbaut 1997, Portes and Rumbaut 2001). In particular, ethnic identity formation varies depending on where immigrant groups settle, whether there is an existing ethnic community, and whether they are accepted or discriminated against by the native-born majority group (Portes and Zhou 1993). These contextual factors shape "divergent modes of incorporation [that are] accompanied by changes in the character and salience of ethnicity" and ethnic self-identification (Rumbaut 1997:948).

As discussed above, the linear path has traditionally been associated with early 20th-century European immigrants for whom ethnic identity grew progressively weaker over time (Gans 1979). Children of immigrants today who are racially classified as white follow a similar path of cultural assimilation into mainstream white America. However, this option is not available to Asians, Hispanics, Africans, and Afro-Caribbeans, who are vulnerable to racial discrimination as ethnic minority groups in the United States. Some of these ethnic groups "selectively" assimilate into American society, while continuing to identify primarily with their ethnic origins into the second generation. Among second generation youth, this selective assimilation process is consistent with the formation of a diasporic hybrid identity. Recall that the diasporic hybrid identity recognizes that two or more cultures can become united within a single individual. Further because "a member's adherence to a diasporic community is demonstrated by an acceptance of an inescapable link with their past migration history and a sense of co-ethnicity with others of a similar background," the diasporic hybrid identity transcends space and time (Brettell 2003). So, it allows for an identity that can emerge, reside, and survive outside of the immigrant homeland. Today, ethnic enclaves nourish and sustain a diasporic consciousness among second-generation youth and serve as spaces where immigrant and American cultures morph into hybrid ethnic identities.

In the United States, reactive identities tend to boomerang depending on a number of social, economic, and political factors. They are particularly responsive to direct experiences with racial discrimination and to the hostility and marginalization that ethnic minority groups often face within American society. As a result of these experiences, some groups are likely to make a conscious effort to maintain a strong attachment to their ethnic origins and solidarity with co-ethnics as a way of defending themselves from the threat of the larger society. This reactive ethnic identity formation process is associated most with inner-city black and Hispanic youth. For example, protests against proposition 187 to deny illegal immigrants healthcare, education, and other social services in California influenced a rise in group consciousness among Hispanic youth during the mid-1990s (Portes and Zhou 1993). However, because these identities are perceived as situational responses to social events inside the United States, immigration scholars tend to treat them as more American, and therefore less authentically ethnic compared to those who selectively assimilate into American culture.

Criticism, Gaps, and Future Directions

Contemporary studies of ethnic identity formation among second-generation children of immigrants use ethnic labels to track their cultural assimilation into different segments of American society. For instance, in their study of second generation immigrant children in Florida and California, Portes and Rumbaut's (2001) survey uncovered four ethnic labels used by second-generation youth. They determined that children of immigrants who identify based on the national origins of parents have the strongest attachment to their ethnic origins, followed by those who use hyphenated ethnic labels. Next on this continuum are those who use unhyphenated American national origin labels or pan-ethnic minority labels such as black, Hispanic, or Asian. The last two pan-ethnic labels are assumed to signify estrangement from the immigrant experience and awareness of their status as marginalized minority group members. In both classic and contemporary immigration literatures, the hyphenated ethnic label is used to identify individuals whose identities represent a fusion of American and immigrant cultural influences.

Immigration scholars also use hyphenated ethnic labels to signify movement away from an immigrant ethnic identity, and so they perceive the blending of two cultures as a transitory stage towards Americanization, not the creation of something new. Here, the distinction between cultural assimilation and cultural hybridization is critical. According to Oyserman, Sakamoto, and Lauffer, cultural assimilation, a primary focus of study for immigration scholars in sociology, is distinct from cultural hybridization:

> Hybridization involves the melding of cultural lenses or frames such that values and goals that were focused on one context are transposed to a new context. Hybridization has the potential of allowing individuals to express cultural values, even when the original contexts no longer exist, and also may create a bond or connection between individuals and their new contexts by allowing a socially approved forum to express their identities. (1998:1606)

Individuals who selectively assimilate into American society might certainly fit this definition of hybridity. However, sociologists are more focused on the fact that such an individual will eventually become "fully" assimilated into American culture. As a result, sociologists have theorized about the stages that take immigrants from being ethnic to being Americans but have paid less attention to how immigrant and American cultures interact to form new identities.

The creation of new identities has a longer history in other related disciplines, where cultural formation is a primary or significant focus of inquiry (Itzigsohn 2000). For example, borrowing from Caribbean studies, anthropologist Nancy Foner (1997) conceptualizes the formation of new (hybrid) identities among Jamaican immigrants as a "creolization" process such that "Jamaican immigrants do not become exactly like Americans, black or white. Nor are they any longer just like Jamaicans in the home society. [Instead,] new meanings, ideologies, and patterns of behavior develop among them in response to conditions and circumstances they encounter here [in the United States]" (967). We agree with Dewind and Kasinitz, who suggest in the concluding section of the special volume in which this article appears, that creolization might be a more useful alternative to the segmented assimilation perspective in accounting for "the complexities of interaction between immigrant and American cultures and behaviors (1997:1103).

The research on ethnic identity formation among second-generation black immigrant youth is one example of how the immigration literature could benefit from a more textured understanding of hybridity in analyses of ethnic identity formation. In her seminal work on West Indian immigrants and their children, Waters (2001) divides her sample into three categories: the immigrant identified, the ethnic identified, and the American identified. She suggests that her middle-class sample were more likely to identify "ethnically" based on the nationality of their parents, but that working-class youth were more likely to identify "racially" with African-Americans.

The categorization of West Indian youth into such discrete categories has been challenged by the research of other scholars whose work focuses on the identities of second-generation West Indian youth. While these scholars address this complexity in different ways, they tend to describe the identities of West Indian youth as "bicultural" as a way of indicating that they are equally competent in the ethnic world of their families and the American world of their peers (Zepir 2001, Butterfield 2001). Most recently, Butterfield has admonished scholars for treating the identities of West Indian youth as a dichotomous choice between two categories. Specifically, she contends that scholars "must stop framing the question as a matter of second-generation West Indians choosing between racial and ethnic identities... [because] that formulation mistakenly implies that the choice is dichotomous – [In fact, she suggests that] choosing to emphasize one identity does not negate the other" (2004:306).

Although the social categories used by immigration scholars are limited in capturing some aspects of ethnic identity formation among children of immigrants, recently sociologists have begun to engage with critical feminist scholarship, particularly Chicana studies, that describe newer versions of Park's marginal identity. Anzaldúa's (1987) "border" or "threshold" identities are constructed of *mestizaje* consciousnesses in which multiple strands of consciousness and identity are negotiated and practiced. The

> mestizaje consciousness is a consciousness of the borderlands, a conscious-
> ness born of the historical collusion of Anglo and Mexican cultures and

frames of reference. It is a plural consciousness in that it requires understanding multiple, often opposing ideas and knowledges and negotiating these knowledges (Mohanty 1991:34–35).

This consciousness is a "fluid, transformational thinking process that breaks down the rigid boundaries between apparently separate categories of meaning" (Keating 1996:7) but at the same time "is plagued by psychic restlessness" from internal strife, insecurity, and indecisiveness (Anzaldúa 1987:78). This re-invigoration of Park's concept of a marginal identity, along with the criticisms of immigration scholars above, all point to new possibilities for how hybridity might be further developed within contemporary immigration theory.

It isn't that sociologists do not recognize that ethnic identity is a complex and multi-dimensional concept. In fact, in addition to ethnic labels, Portes and Rumbaut's (2001) study of second-generation racial and ethnic identities also focuses on how salient these identities are to children of immigrants and the extent to which these identities change over time and across varied social contexts. But there is good reason why sociologists continue to use hyphenated ethnic labels to convey a hybrid ethnic identity and have focused less explicit attention to how new identities are formed. From its point of origin, classic studies on immigrant adaptation used ethnic labels to measure and predict social and economic integration into American society, and this practice has continued to the present day. For instance, ethnic labels are now consistently associated with variation in academic outcomes among children of immigrants, and this helps sociologists to predict how well these young people will do in the labor market. So while a focus on "cultural hybridization" or "creolization" would be useful to sociological discourses on ethnic identity formation, a focus on consciousness limits their usefulness in predicting the academic and economic outcomes that are at the core of classic and contemporary literatures on immigrant adaptation.

Diasporic Links between Historical and Contemporary Immigrants

Central to these accounts of identity construction among new and earlier immigrants is the role of the diaspora. This role may be minimal, as in the case with the descendants of European immigrants who selectively incorporated elements of their ancestral homeland into their identity without it critically impacting their daily life. In the case of refugees, the experience of having been displaced makes it all the more important for them to want to remain connected to their homelands by incorporating cultural practices into their daily lives while living elsewhere. Over time it is likely that this diasporic consciousness will increase or decrease in salience depending on the situation or as a result of larger social, political, or historical forces.

The diasporized hybrid identity makes explicit the role of border crossings and the potential or prohibition of return due to larger global processes and conflicts. Similarly, the reason for leaving the homeland, whether for political, economic, or familial reasons, or a combination of all three that often result from such events as famine, war, or industrialization, are key to this identity. Therefore, the diasporized hybrid must take into account not only the old and new cultures in which the group previously and currently resides but the entire transnational experience of movement and the social, political, and economic reasons behind this migration. The diasporic experience, then, represents a bridge between multiple locations that will always exist, even if it is never again crossed. Though Jewish identities are deeply tied to multiple diasporic experiences, many American Jews will never visit Israel, and even fewer will return to live there. Nor will many Jews from other nations, unless they experience persecution, as in the case of Russian Jews who fled to Israel during the 1970s and 80s. On the other hand, a variety of contemporary immigrant groups to the United States, such as those from South American and Asian nations, retain sustained ties to people, cultures, and villages from which they emigrated with frequent return trips home.

However, the diasporized hybrid identity does not have to center on a particular shared homeland or host location. Many immigrants to the United States, regardless of where they initiated, identified with their home villages and not with a nation state, as in the case of Italians identifying as Sicilian, Jews identifying from Bialystok, or Mexicans identifying with Juarez (Moya 2005, Soyer 1997, Vecoli 1964). Instead, this protonational aspect of the hybrid identity was created during and after relocation as a result of local, national, and global developments, in conjunction with the United States' tendency to categorize immigrants by nation, rather than the village from which they came. Only after living in their new nation did they become Italian-, Jewish-, and Mexican-Americans. Instead, a shared history of displacement results in potentially global imagined communities. For example, Paul Gilroy's *Black Atlantic* features a diasporized hybrid identity linking all British, American, and Caribbean Africans dispersed by the slave trade to propose similarities based on the diasporic experience itself but transcending specific national boundaries. The simultaneous discomfort with the former homeland as a result of displacement and deep attachment, usually in conjunction with a longing for return, results in a complicated interplay of consciousnesses that are then fused with developing norms and cultures rooted in the cultures and customs of the host nation and local community. For example, Somalian refugees in Minnesota (Darboe 2003) remain attached to their former homelands even as they have been exiled for political reasons (sometimes under threat of death). They do this, in part, to maintain cultural traditions, but also to signal to local residents that they are not American blacks. This collective memory of cultural trauma (Alexander 2003) in their former homeland, in conjunction with experiences of potential discrimination in America, therefore feature prominently in the construction of diasporized hybrid identities.

Immigrant groups who maintain diasporized hybrid identities can never be fully identificationally assimilated with their new national communities because of cultural allegiances to other nations and cultures. Identities and cultures relating to the former homeland, as well as the experiences that precipitated the transnational movement, persist perennially and across generations. The salience of this persistence is largely dependent upon the reception from (i.e., whether groups are welcomed and readily incorporated or subject to racism, discrimination, and isolation) and similarities to cultures in the host country. As a result, decisions made and actions undertaken with regard to citizenship are never holistically rooted in their current situation or place of residence. Rather, they are reflective of diasporic experiences, consciousness, and cultures.

These experiences, whether personal or in the repositories of a group's collective memory and consciousnesses, result in different worldviews and lived experiences than those of the members of the dominant group in the new host nation. For example, while many Jews have achieved tremendous social and economic assimilation, the persistence of a diasporized hybrid identity finds adherents always viewing the world through the lens of an outsider, real or imagined, and is critically influenced by the particular residential location and concentration of group members.

The diasporic aspect of the diasporized hybrid identity is therefore a central feature of both historical and contemporary immigrants. The diasporic hybrid identity is formed in part, but is certainly not limited to the actual experiences of planning the migration, the reason for leaving the country of origin, the journey itself, and finally, the context of reception in the host society. Taking into account the variety of ways in which these different aspects affect contemporary and historical immigrants' experiences and identities will allow researchers to more accurately compare and contextualize similarities and differences between groups arriving from and departing to a wide variety of locations, which will become increasingly important as transnational migration proceeds in an increasingly global and transitory world.

Conclusion

From the perspective of American society today, there are significant differences between the experiences of 19th- and 20th-century European immigrants and today's Asian, Hispanic, and African descended ethnic groups. It is difficult, for example, to foresee a time when black immigrants will be fully accepted within the mainstream of American society as were the Irish, Italians, and Jews. For African-Americans have had a long history of knocking at the door of opportunity, and have yet to gain America's full embrace. Historically, the color line has been pushed, prodded, and pummeled against by a number of ethnic minority groups, people of African descent in particular, but never severely damaged nor destroyed. Nonetheless, the "in between" status of European immigrants is often ignored when comparing their experiences of adapting to American society in comparison to today's racial and ethnic minority groups. Accordingly, there is a propensity to study these groups in isolation, using different theoretical perspectives. As a result, the historical continuities in their experiences become invisible or seem irrelevant.

Theoretical discussions of hybrid ethnic identities represent an area of convergence between the European experience of adapting to American society and that of more racially and ethnically diverse population streams in the post-1965 immigration era. First, discrimination and social exclusion fostered and maintained hybrid ethnic identities among European immigrants, similar to the reactive ethnic identities produced among racial and ethnic minorities of today. Similarly, separation from the mainstream, whether it occurred in isolated rural communities, segregated urban ghettos, or today's ethnic enclaves, fuels the development of hybrid identities. In the communities that are formed, sometimes voluntarily and other times not, the sustained day-to-day interactions that take place primarily with co-ethnics reinforce a common culture and identity. Ethnic groups who are marginalized from the mainstream of American culture are more likely to develop and maintain hybrid ethnic identities because this kind of exclusion reinforces the fact that they are different from majority group members. Due to the hostility that they face, these groups are likely to actively differentiate themselves from majority group members. Experiences with discrimination may also heighten a pre-existing attachment to an immigrant group's country of origin, strengthening and promoting a diasporic consciousness among first- and later-generation children of immigrants. Clearly, hybridity has deep roots in the sociological literature due to its utility for understanding the similarities in how different racial and ethnic minorities groups have identified with their ethnic origins over time. Yet it has been underutilized within the contemporary immigration literature. In the future, scholars might consider further incorporating existing concepts and knowledge from within other subfields in sociology (such as the literature on feminism) or from other disciplinary perspectives such as anthropology or cultural studies.

Chapter Seven

Geoculture and Popular Culture: Carnivals, Diasporas, and Hybridities in the Americas

Keith Nurse

Introduction

Almost every country and major city in the Americas (i.e., the Greater Caribbean, South and Central America, and the Southern United States [e.g., New Orleans]), has a carnival festival, and they have grown in stature and importance as socioeconomic and politico-cultural phenomena. The carnivals of the Americas that are focused on in this paper are those forged in the colonial era and that are associated with plantation society. Particular emphasis is given to the "big three" carnivals: Rio Carnival in Brazil, New Orleans' Mardi Gras, and Trinidad Carnival. These carnivals are transnational and transcultural formations, the consequence of the parallel processes of globalization and diasporization (Nurse 1999).

The region's historical development has been shaped by the virtual extermination of the indigenous population, the domination of a transplanted European elite, the enslavement of Africans, the indentureship of Asians, and the integration of other groups from the "Old World." The attendant processes of colonization and diasporization created in their wake a new society and a modern culture, one grounded in cultural hybridization and all informed by racial, gender, ethnic, and status-based oppression (Mintz 1993). From this perspective, international migration is one of the defining features of the history of the Americas.

For most of its history, the Americas have been a point of arrival and a net importer of labor. It is the first area of the non-European world to be fully incorporated into the service of global capitalist development through export-oriented production systems and import-dependent consumption structures (James 1962). In this vein, the Americas have the most extraverted societies with the highest level of inequality among regions in the world (Quijano and Wallerstein 1992).

In the context of these structural rigidities, the region has developed a capacity to engage *modernity* and *globalization* creatively and politically by drawing upon folk, religious, and popular cultures as a source of cultural identity while participating in the dominant Europeanized culture. Therefore, in American culture, one can say that there are no pure forms and that everything is hybridized or the result of the confluence of several cultural traditions. The dynamics of this experience on the Americas has been described as one of *double consciousness* (Gilroy 1993).

The aim of this paper is to theorize about the linkage between geoculture and popular culture with reference to carnival festivals in the Americas. The popular culture and carnivals of the Americas are diasporic and hybrid sites for the ritual negotiation and reinvention of cultural identity and practice between and among various social groups in the Americas. Geocultures, on the other hand, represent official culture. It is the ideational underside of the world system, that part of global culture that is embedded in "custom," rendered invisible, and, thus, facilitates the reproduction of the hegemonic world order by evading scrutiny (Wallerstein 1991:11).

The paper argues that popular culture gives insight into the configuration of global social forces and allows for the unmasking and reimagination of geocultural and hegemonic constructions embodied in notions of empire, nation, class, race, gender, sexuality, ethnicity, and even development. As such, the paper starts from the premise that popular culture, carnival, and festivals are not just an aesthetic and commercial space where psychic and bodily pleasures are enacted, represented, and marketed. It is an arena where social values and meaning are put on public display, negotiated, and contested.

Geoculture and Popular Culture

> Culture has always been a weapon of the powerful...But culture has always cut both ways. If the powerful can legitimate their expropriations by transposing them into 'custom,' the weak can appeal to the legitimacy of these same 'customs' to resist new and different expropriations. This is an unequal battle to be sure, but not one that has had no effect...There have long been relatively stable popular cultures which have asserted their values and their forms against elite cultures...And the very stability of popular cultures has been their weakness as well as their strength. They have more often led to social anesthesia than to social revolution. (Wallerstein 1991a:193)

Geocultures of the modern capitalist world-system are the cultural framework that facilitates the reproduction of the hegemonic world order. It operates as the ideational underside rather than the institutional superstructure of the world-system. It is "the part that is more hidden from view and therefore more difficult to assess, but the part without which the rest would not be nourished" (Wallerstein 1991a:11). The power of a geoculture comes from its invisibility and naturalization. Wallerstein (1991a:167) argues that the modern world-system is able to reproduce the social configuration of power and world order not through coercion but by the ways in which the antinomies and contradictions of integration and resistance, assimilation and difference, inclusion and exclusion are balanced over time and space, from one historical conjuncture to another, in a continuous ideological zigzag. This is evident in the ideological tension between the doctrine of universalism, which asserts equality and meritocracy (e.g., all humans are equal; all nations are equal), and the anti-universalistic doctrine of racism-sexism, which institutionalizes oppression and discrimination based on ethnicity and gender (e.g., some humans and nations are more equal). Thus the zigzag pattern results because "there are always efforts to push one side or the other of this equation 'too far'" (Wallerstein 1991b:35).

There are several implications that emerge from Wallerstein's thesis. The first is that ideologies such as racism and sexism are not standalone ideologies in that they are reinforced by other anti-universalist ideologies such as eurocentrism, nationalism, and imperialism, while being juxtaposed with universalistic ideologies like liberalism, modernism, developmentalism, and scientism. Racism and sexism are intimately linked because they are the main means by which oppression is justified and legitimated. There is a high correlation between a group's position in the geocultural divide and its status and income in the world system (Wallerstein 1991a:175).

What does all this have to do with popular culture? The argument is that while geoculture is ideational underside of the world-system, popular culture is the most observable and accessible feature of global culture. It is the space within which identities are visibly constructed and represented. It is also the space in which the geocultures are contested, or at least engaged. Popular culture, in effect, employs an "aesthetic of resistance" that confronts and subverts hegemonic modes of representation, and thus acts as a counter-hegemonic tradition to the geocultural constructions embodied in notions of empire, nation, class, race, gender, sexuality, and ethnicity (Shohat and Stam 1994, Storey 1996). The popular cultures of the Americas, as "New World," postcolonial cultures, are an expression of what Stuart Hall calls the "redemptive move" associated with most diasporic cultures that are "born of traveling, rupture, appropriation, loss, exile" (1997:27).

This paper argues that popular culture in the Americas was born of opposition, rebellion, protest, and resistance to the colonial and neo-colonial power structure. In this sense, popular culture is not just about loss; it is also about redemption, resignification, and indigenization. However, in the contemporary context it operates in a contradictory and contested space of commercialization, which, we argue, does not lend itself to simple binary oppositions of resistance versus incorporation (Hall 1992). From this standpoint, this paper calls for an approach that embodies an understanding of popular culture as complex, ambivalent, and contested (Hesmondhalgh 2002).

Elsewhere I have argued, for example, that Caribbean popular culture is a counter-culture or counter-narrative that challenges hegemonic structures and ideologies, deploying aesthetic forms to contest inequality, social injustice, and cultural deprivation, thereby providing meaning, hope, and affirmation to diasporic communities. But, at the same time, it becomes readily commodified through widespread consumption and industrialized production structures and technologies. Caribbean popular culture is also seemingly contradictory in the political realm. On one hand, there is limited governmental support and philanthropic or corporate sponsorship of the arts, but on the other hand the arts are often used to mobilize domestic populations at election times. So although the art forms give expression to social protest among the marginalized and dispossessed, they are also often co-opted in advancing the interests of powerful and hegemonic groups (see Ho and Nurse 2005).

Carnival, Popular Culture, and Geoculture

> Carnival is not a spectacle seen by the people; they live in it, and everyone participates because its very idea embraces all the people. (Bakhtin 1984:7)

Carnival comes from the Latin word *carnivale*, meaning "farewell to the flesh," essentially referring to a period of celebration of the body, of physical abandon, where licentiousness, hedonism, and sexual excess are expressed in music, dancing, masquerading, and feasting. In the Euro-Christian cultural framework, the culmination of carnival activities on "Shrove Tuesday" is the time when sins are shriven, or confessed. Carnival, therefore, evolved to be the "last fling" before the Lenten period in the Christian calendar, hence the reason it is called *Mardi Gras* in France and *Fastnacht* in Germany.

Almost all cultures have something like a carnival event in their ritual calendar. For instance, you can find the carnivalesque spirit in most market fairs, harvest celebrations, and spring fertility rights. This is evident in pagan European festivities as much as in festivals in other regions such as Africa, Asia, and the Americas (Scott 1990).

Mikhail Bakhtin, the Russian theorist, argues that carnival "is always essentially related to time, either to the recurrence of an event in the natural (cosmic) cycle, or to biological or historic timeliness" (1984:9). He also sees it as "the people's second life," a utopian realm of community, freedom, equality, and abundance. He views it as a special type of communication that is impossible in everyday life in that it allows for "the temporary suspension, both ideal and real, of hierarchical rank" – a time when *the world is turned upside down* (Bakhtin 1984:8–10).

Carnival's logic is one of ambivalence to the structures and strictures of life, and particularly to official cultures or geocultures. It circumvents dominant modes of representation and objectification and confronts the limitations of binary oppositions. Thus, the people involved in it are both actors and spectators simultaneously. The people involved in it are both subjects and objects of laughter. Mimicry, parody, satire, role reversals, and symbolic social inversion are the aesthetic methods used to confront various modes of oppression (Bakhtin 1984).

There is much debate about whether carnival is a liberating social ritual as articulated by Bakhtin. Critics like Terry Eagleton argue that carnivals are a "licensed affair" institutionalized by elites as a safety-valve or "permissible rupture of hegemony" for social release and political control (quoted in Stallybras and White 1986:13). Indeed, one can argue that there have always been attempts by dominant or hegemonic groups to tame and sanitize carnivals, or to eliminate them altogether. The modern history of European carnivals is instructive in this regard.

The European carnival form has become less rebellious and politically vibrant in the last 200 years. In Britain, by the mid-1850s the carnivalesque fairs were considered "out of date and too rowdy for the respectable mid-Victorians" (Berland 1992:41). Shohat and Stam argue, "European real-life carnivals have generally degenerated into the ossified repetition of perennial rituals" (1994:302). A long-term view suggests that the decline of European carnival relates to systemic social change rather than the efforts of powerful social groups. Samuel Kinser argues, for instance, that the decline of carnival can be attributed to:

> The combined forces of industrialization, bourgeois standards of orderly respectable behavior, and diminishing Christian traditionalism reduced people's interest in and understanding of the occasion. (1990:7)

It can thus be argued that carnivalesque rituals and arts are neither about outright rebellion or passive acceptance. Instead, it can be argued that carnival embodies a "ritual of intensification" in which the forces that govern ordinary life are expressed with a particular salience, clarity, and eloquence" (Burton 1997:157). What this suggests is that while "oppressed people might have difficulty in imagining the precise contours of an alternative society, they have no trouble in imagining a reversal of the existing distribution of status and rewards" (Shohat and Stam 1994:304). In summary, the counter-argument to the safety-valve thesis argues that:

> It is surely not accurate to proceed as if carnival were set up exclusively by dominant groups to allow subordinate groups to play at rebellion lest they resort to the real thing. The existence and the evolving form of carnival have been the outcome of social conflict, not the unilateral creation of elites. (1990:178)

While the jury is still out on how revolutionary carnivals are, it may be more useful to see carnival not as a victory for one social group over another but as a ritualized space where these conflicts are contested. From this perspective, carnival is a reflection of the configuration of social forces and an arena for the public display and negotiation of the varied social tensions and struggles of the society. One analyst suggests that carnival is about the aestheticizing of politics and "is thus politics masquerading behind cultural forms" (Cohen 1993:132). Kinser similarly argues that:

> Carnival deals with the barriers omnipresent in daily life not by tearing them down or turning them topsy-turvy but by stepping over them and back again in an exemplary although impractical enlargement of the everyday. Daily life is enlarged theatrically; it is also enlarged in a particularly bodily way. (1990:xvii)

Diaspora, Hybridities, and the Carnivals of the Americas

> Today, if one listens to the sounds, the images, the symbols, and the utopia of the Americas, one must acknowledge the maturation of an autonomous social pattern, the presence of a process of reinvention of culture in the Americas. (Quijano and Wallerstein 1992:556)

In contrast to the European carnivals, the carnivals of the Americas have been growing and have evolved to be dynamic and politically engaging. Throughout the Americas – from Rio's carnival in Brazil to New Orleans' Mardi Gras – carnivals are a reflection of the social order and the attendant social conflict as well as the submerged aspirations and tensions of the respective societies. In Brazil "the carnival is informed by cultural memories of the African ancestral past, a pagan influence that subverts the official Catholic institution" (Lawlor 1993:2). Throughout the Caribbean, the carnivals in the post-independence period have been expressions of island identity, regional harmony, and black identity (Manning 1978).

Carnivals of the Americas are popular festivals that allow for the negotiation of cultural identity. Several of these carnivals occur either as pre-lenten festivals, thereby following the Christian calendar, or at times of emancipation and/or national celebrations. For example, carnival in Cuba has been celebrated in the month of July since 1959 to commemorate the 1953 failed overthrow attempt, which at the time was strategically scheduled to coincide with the July carnival in Santiago de Cuba. In Trinidad and Tobago, the carnival was brought into line with the Christian calendar at the turn of the 20th century. Prior to this, in the post-emancipation period, the carnival was celebrated in August to commemorate the end of slavery.

The Trinidad Carnival, along with the Rio Carnival and the Mardi Gras in New Orleans, are probably the best known and most publicized. Throughout the Caribbean – from the carnival of Santiago de Cuba (Brea and Millet 1995) to the Barranquilla carnival in Colombia (Martinez and Aldana 1994) and all the carnivals in-between – the carnival is informed by an ancestral past, which recalls the indigenous Indian, African, Asian, and European heritage of the peoples that populate the region. Almost all the cultures that came to the Americas have something like a carnival festival. In the same carnival, one can view diasporal and hybridized expressions such as the re-enactment of Egyptian mystery plays, elements from the Greek Dionysian and Roman Saturnalia festivals, and portrayals of authentic Native American traditions.

Another remarkable feature of the carnivals of the Americas is the extent to which there are parallels between the various festivals beyond what intraregional migration and travel would suggest. For the time period there would have been little, if any, direct or sustained contact between the locations. The suggestion is that the festivals are "separate but parallel developments with some cross-fertilization, based on West African models" (Mitchell 1999:115). Mitchell, in his study of New Orleans, observes that several of the masquerade costumes found in New Orleans are also found in other carnivals:

> The tradition of black people masking Indian is widespread in Caribbean Carnival. There are such 'Indians' in Trinidad, Bahia, and Cuba. Christmas maskers in Jamaica, St. Kitts, and the Dominican Republic include Wild Indians. Gombey dancers in Bermuda also dress as Indians... With the Mardi Gras Indians, the working-class black people of New Orleans too 'invented a tradition.' (Mitchell 1999:115)

Carnivals of the Americas also speak to the new and ever-changing identities forged by colonialism and globalization. In its expression, the carnival symbolizes syncretism as well as competition between the varied cultural traditions. One of the enduring features of carnivals in the region is the perennial debate about what is respectable and what is vulgar, often defined in terms of race, ethnicity, and gender. What is often constructed in the discourse is an insider versus outsider debate.

In this respect, the carnivals of the Americas are arenas for the contestation of European cultural hegemony and the assertion of the cultural rights of the formerly enslaved Africans, indentured Asians, and colonized indigenous peoples. In these carnivals, the dualistic nature of the festival is ever-present. In many respects it can be argued that there are really two or more carnivals bound together. An example of this is the carnivals in Puerto Rico. The carnival of Ponce, a southern coast city, is a pre-lenten festival that draws on European traditions and involves the creation of devilish masks made of papier-maché that are painted in a variety of bright colors. The other Puerto Rican carnival is in the north coast town of Loiza. The Loiza St. James festivities have carnival masks made of coconut husks and draw on African Yoruba culture that was banned and then altered to at least outwardly reflect Christian practices.

The sharpest cleavage among carnivals in the Americas is evident in the New Orleans Mardi Gras. For instance, if you were to watch the Mardi Gras parade on TV (on any one of the top American networks), what is advertised and covered as the carnival is the white-run carnival. The black carnival, which takes place on narrower streets or in black areas, is never commented on. This observation leads Kinser to argue that:

> ...playful as it is, richly inventive as it has been, Carnival at New Orleans and Mobile conserves the black-white barriers which can be observed nearly everywhere in American society and which developed with force in slave society of this southern area's first century and half of existence...The rituals all make reference, consciously or unconsciously, to race relations. (1990:xix–xx)

The *problématique* of race can be said to be the defining issue in the carnivals of the Americas. This is the basis upon which the case for stopping the carnival has been made. For example, the colonial authorities in Cuba in 1675 prohibited the carnival "under the pretext that masked and disguised revelers ridiculed the governmental and episcopal hierarchies" (Martinez and Aldana 1994:187). The Bahian carnival in Brazil saw the rise of black carnival clubs after the abolition of slavery in 1888. However, "within a decade, these organizations were banned from the Bahian Carnival by elite white authorities who feared the Africanization of local culture" (Dunn 2001:3). Resistance to class and racial inequality, a dominant theme, is often expressed in songs of protest, as exemplified by calypsos in Trinidad Carnival, mereng in the Haitian

Carnival, or the cumbia songs in the Barranquilla Carnival of Colombia. No wonder there have been so many attempts to censure or ban these songs and even stop the carnivals.

In Trinidad, several attempts were made to abolish the carnival between 1878 and 1881. The police applied strong controls on the carnival. Things finally came to a head in 1881, resulting in what is known as the Canboulay riots. In the wake of the riots, an accommodation was brokered between the colonial authorities and the revelers. Subsequent years saw the carnival become more orderly and sanitized. Masquerading at night, the carrying of lighted torches, stickfighting, drumming, dancing, and congregations of people numbering ten or more became prohibited under the 1884 Peace Preservation Ordinance. By the 1890s, the carnival was brought under more effective control by the police, the colored middle-class began to participate in the festival, carnival competitions were sponsored by the merchant class as the commercial benefits of the carnival became evident (Rohlehr 1990).

Many of the changes that occurred in the Trinidad Carnival in the late 19th century (e.g., incorporation into the mainstream, commercialization and professionalization of the arts, festival tourism) also happened in several of the other carnivals in the Americas. The festival took on its modern-day form, which in many ways, is still evident today.

In spite of all the attempts to quash the carnivals, they have survived and thrived. An important element of this is the ways in which the festivals have been incorporated into the economy. Many of the carnivals in the Americas, especially the "big three," enjoy massive economic returns, particularly from festival tourism. New Orleans has long adopted a tourism strategy in relation to the festival. Tourism had become an important element of the festival as early as the 1870s (Mitchell 1995:83). By 1977, Mardi Gras was contributing $50 million, or ten percent of annual visitor expenditures (Kinser 1990:9).

In Trinidad, since the 1990s carnival has become big business, especially in terms of festival tourism and entertainment industry in each of the three key art forms: mas, pan, and calypso. The Trinidad carnival has grown to be the premier festival in the region, attracting 40,000 visitors and generating foreign exchange earnings of over US$20 million. The carnival arts have emerged to be the lynchpin of the entertainment industry sector, which is in the top ten foreign exchange earners in the economy (Nurse 2002).

In the Rio Carnival, similar trends are observed. Visitor estimates range as high as 100,000, and visitor spending is in the tens of millions. The impact of this wave of commercialization is not without its critics. One observer argues that "Rio Carnival is all about money, publicity, and silicone" for breast implants (Holtwijk 2001). The analyst goes on to note some other problematic changes in the Rio Carnival:

> By the 1960s, Carnival, which is actually a competition, had become more professional. The costumes were more luxurious and stars, including white stars, had begun to appear on the floats...Since the 1980s, Carnival has rapidly 'whitened up.' Poor people can no longer afford the costumes. Either it's the middle class who buys the costumes, and often by means of the Internet, or it's the tourists who head straight to the parade from the airport. (Holtwijk 2001:76)

However, these trends present new challenges and generate new areas of contestation. The carnivals of the Americas, to different degrees, have acted as a ritual site for socio-cultural contestations and aesthetic resistance, between a hegemonic European group and subordinate indigenous, creole, mestizo, and African peoples. They generally embody rituals of social protest that critique and parody the process of enforced hybridization and transculturation embedded in colonial and neo-colonial society. Many of the carnival celebrations involve transgressive activities that are aimed at redefining or accommodating the resultant heterogeneous cultural and racial identities and contested cultural spaces that are an outcome of globalization and diasporization processes.

Conclusion

> The planners of cultural resistance, in planning the assertion of some particular culture, are in effect (re)legitimating the concept of universal values...The contradictions of planned resistance are inescapable. (Wallerstein 1991a:195)

Historically, the carnivalesque spirit of festivity, laughter, and irreverence feeds off the enduring celebration of birth, death, and renewal and the eternal search for freedom from the strictures of official culture (Bakhtin 1984). From this perspective, carnivals of the Americas confront and unmask socio-hierarchical inequalities and hegemonic discourses as well as reinforce historical and geocultural tendencies. Aesthetic and symbolic rituals operate as the basis for critiquing the unequal distribution of power and resources and a mode of resistance to colonialist and neo-colonialist cultural representations and signifying practices, while at the same time fulfilling the commercial and political goals of the hegemonic culture.

The cases of Brazil, New Orleans, and Trinidad illustrate that carnival is a contested space born out of the struggle between marginalized peoples and a hegemonic European culture. The carnival thus shows elements of both resistance and integration, liberation and accommodation, social catharsis and social control. What the cases do show is that the carnival arts do confront and contest the conventions, strictures, moral codes, and hierarchies of the day, if only temporarily and symbolically.

The value of the carnivals to the cultural political economy of the Americas is not an uncontested space. Concerns about commercialization and ethnic exclusion are ever present in the discourse. The question that emerges, however, is what is the transformational potential of the carnivals in terms of deepening cultural confidence, building cultural identity, and facilitating the use of indigenous resources and capabilities? Nettleford echoes these concerns:

> But to the ordinary people, festival arts are more than minstrelsy; they affirm the use of the mask, literally and metaphorically, in coming to terms or coping with an environment that has yet to work in their interest, a society that is yet to be mastered and controlled by them, despite the coming of Independence. (1988:194)

The above analysis illustrates how far and deep geocultures run. It shows that the legacies of geocultures are multi-dimensional and pervasive. It also illustrates that there are ebbs and flows, periods when there are crisis tendencies as opposed to times of relaxation. The counter flow of popular cultures and carnivals suggest a cyclical pattern and can be explained as part of the ideological tensions of historical capitalism.

Chapter Eight

The Internal Colony Hybrid: Reformulating Structure, Culture, and Agency

Roderick Bush

> After the Egyptian and Indian, the Greek and Roman, the Teuton and Mongolian, the Negro is a sort of seventh son, born with a veil, and gifted with second-sight in this American world...It is a peculiar sensation, this double-consciousness, this sense of always looking at one's self through the eyes of others, of measuring one's soul by the tape of a world that looks on in amused contempt and pity. One ever feels his twoness – an American, a Negro; two souls, two thoughts, two unreconciled strivings; two warring ideals in one dark body, whose dogged strength alone keeps it from being torn asunder.
>
> (DuBois 1961:16–17)

Colonialism is generally considered to be the extension of a nation's sovereignty over territory beyond its borders. In the modern world, the model of colonialism is the extension of European dominion over much of the world's territory in the Americas, Africa, Asia, and the Pacific Islands. In some cases enslaved people were moved to another territory, or states actually expanded their territory to encompass territory formerly controlled by other populations, thereby forming what some have referred to as internal colonies. Many indigenous populations fit this category, as do formerly enslaved Africans in territories dominated by descendents of settler colonists from Europe. Colonialism has tended to be conceived in geographical and geopolitical terms. What I intend to do here is to view the concept of internal colony more in structural terms and assess the impact of such structural relations on the development of hybrid cultures among the internally colonized populations and, consequently, on how these populations come to view themselves as change agents within the landscape of these societies. Such people almost always develop what DuBois refers to as a double consciousness, which gives them a special insight about the dominant culture not easily accessed by those who view their own societies only from the perspective of the dominant culture. The hybrid culture then becomes a source of agency that is important in the ability to impact change within these societies.

During the 1960s, the concept of internal colonialism obtained substantial utility in explaining significant populations within some nation-states who were born within the territorial boundaries of those states, and thus legally integrated into the state and economy, but who remained structurally, culturally, socioeconomically, legally, and socially marginal. These so-called "second-class citizens" were not only disproportionately concentrated at the bottom of the economic ladder, with scant political power, they were also scorned in the public imagination.

African-Americans are only one example of a group that has been identified by some as an internal colony. Mexican-Americans, Puerto Ricans, and Native Americans are also commonly considered internally colonized populations within the United States. In Canada there are, of course, the Quebecois and the First Nations, in France the Ocitans, in Spain the Basque, and indigenous populations throughout Latin America.

All of these populations, which seemed outside of the socio-economic mainstream of the so-called advanced industrial nation-states, were often said to constitute a subculture of the mainstream culture or to be afflicted with a culture of poverty. While the marginality of these populations were almost always the focus of observers in the social sciences, there were always some in the humanities who recognized that the efforts of such populations to seek justice and equality constituted a fundamental challenge to the democratic and egalitarian pretensions or aspirations of these societies. It was often recognized that the hybrid culture of these outsider groups gave them an insight into these societies (what DuBois referred to as the gift of second sight) that was much more critical and perceptive than that of the more accepted groups, but that their very hybridity gave them a connection to the larger society and enabled them to communicate their insights across the cultural barriers they faced. From the perspective of the longue duree of historical capitalism, the most notable movements that arose to challenge the social inequalities of local, national, and global power structures during the 19th and 20th centuries were the workers' movements of the industrialized countries and the national liberation movements of the colonized, semi-colonized, and dependent zones of the world-system. While the First World War occasioned much talk about the crisis of European civilization or of white world supremacy, radicals argued that monopoly capitalism was the imperialist stage of capitalism, that capitalism was now a world system, and that it was moribund capitalism. The social movements of this period subsequently began to increasingly argue that revolution was the only solution, but they were in practice offered assimilation and inclusion by the dominant strata of the world-system. Although there had long been fierce debates between the national movements and the social movements, some came increasingly to equate the social question with the colonial (or national) question, arguing in effect that there was not a fundamental difference between the metropole-colony relationship and the capital-labor relationship. During the 1960s this position was reaffirmed, but with heightened emphasis on what Patricia Hill Collins refers to as the "outsider-within," represented in part by internally colonized populations, or what opponents of pan-European racism often refer to as the "third world within" (Blauner 1972, Collins 1991, Wallerstein 1979). The democratic aspirations of these groups were often more far-reaching and potentially transformative than those of the lower strata of the dominant ethno-racial population because they were unlikely candidates for assimilation and required a more fundamental transformation of the existing social system. The low social status of these populations, however, meant that they were disproportionately concentrated among the sub-proletarian strata, or what has come to be called the "underclass" in the core zones of the world-system. The social isolation of these populations have therefore made them particularly susceptible to public scorn among other social strata and thereby blamed as being responsible for much of the nation's ills and their own low social position.

But as the proportion of the "third world within" continues to increase in the population of the core states (most pronounced within the United States), political efficacy for the lower and lower-middle class strata will require that they face the challenge of creating an effective rainbow coalition to contend with the ideological weight of pan-European racism, which will confine them to a subordinate role in the polity, economy, and society. The defenders of the status quo have recognized this issue since at least the early part of the 20th century, when the New Negro radicals animated a variety of organizations and movements, from the Messenger Group to the African Blood Brotherhood, to the Garvey movement, to the Communist Party. To the distress of the defenders of the status quo, such movements always tended leftwards. American elites have been attentive to the threat to their hegemony coming from this quarter since the proletarian insurgencies of the World War I – era during the reign of the New Negro. Woodrow Wilson's program for the self-determination of nations was a response to the threat of Bolshevik anticolonialism, which he thought was most likely to be introduced in the United States by blacks. Long before COINTELPRO, American security forces were employed to eliminate, discredit, and harass black leaders of whom they did not approve. The list includes many, and perhaps most, of the most respected leaders and intellectuals within the African-American community: Marcus Garvey, A. Philip Randolph, Chandler Owen, William Monroe Trotter, Hubert Harrison, Cyril Briggs, Claude McKay, Wilfred Domingo, Harry Haywood, William Patterson, George Padmore, W. E. B. DuBois, Paul Robeson, Elijah Muhammad, Langston Hughes, and C. L. R. James (Kornweibel 1998, 2002). During the 1960s, of course, we add to this list some of the main targets of COINTELPRO: Martin Luther King, Jr., Malcolm X, Adam Clayton Powell, Jr., James Baldwin, Medgar Evers, Bayard Rustin, Stokely Carmichael, Huey Newton, Bobby Seale, Fred Hampton, and Bunchy Carter (O'Reilly 1989, 1994; Churchill and Vander Wall 1988). Even the centrist leader Jesse Jackson was too much of a threat for the liberal establishment (Bush 1984, 1999). Perhaps in Barack Obama some among the centrist liberal establishment and among the white public feel they have found an acceptable candidate whose low racial profile symbolizes reconciliation between the races in the direction of a color-blind society called for by neo-conservative intellectuals in the camp of President Ronald Reagan, and since diffused to other sections of the populations. This is a crucial issue of legitimization and hegemony in the United States.

I follow the lead of Peruvian sociologist Anibal Quijano, who argues that the coloniality of power (which is heir to the colonial situation) accounts for the formulation of a worldwide system of social classification based on the idea of race. This idea, he argues, accounts not only for the patterns of social classification, but also for its dominant cultural logics, forms of knowledge, and modes of (inter)subjectivity and identification. The Eurocentric racial discourse thus established is the cornerstone of Western hegemony under the leadership of the United States and a central organizing feature of the modern constellations of power. But although coloniality is the substance of the domination of the pan-European world over the non-European world, its strategies of legitimization require that it appear as a universalistic, neutral, objective enterprise unlike the essentialist (often equated with fundamentalist) perspectives of the less-developed zones of the world-system. I also follow Kelvin Santiago-Valles, whose definition of the colonized is not dependent on the territorial formulation, but on being subjected to "degraded forms of social embodiment" and other substandard conditions of life associated mostly with those groups who are identified with racially depreciated labor (Santiago-Valles 2003:103).

The internal minorities or the internally colonized who will grow as a proportion of the population throughout the core states of the world-system are key to any system of political alliances needed to determine the whether we maintain the power relations embedded in the hegemony of the pan-European world under the leadership of the United States. As we approach the twilight of the American Century, realists within the ruling establishment might favor a strategy that takes advantage of the "multicultural" hue of our population and the positioning of a pro-imperialist leader of African descent who might allow the US to somewhat maintain its position of influence within the world-system.

Origins of the Internal Colonialism Concept

George Balandier's "The Colonial Situation: A Theoretical Approach," written originally in 1951, cites Jean Guitton, who equated the "colonial question" with the "social question." Guitton is said to have argued that "they are not fundamentally different because the *metropole-colony* relationship is in no sense different from the *capital-labor* relationship, or the relationship Hegel has termed *master-servant*" (Balandier 1951:40). Balandier adds support from Paul

Reuter, who points out that "in both cases we are dealing with a population who produces all the wealth, but does not share in its political or economic advantages and constitutes an oppressed class" (Balandier 1951:40).

This has, of course, been the basis of the political coalition between the workers' movement in the core states and the national liberation movements in the periphery of the world-system. But Balandier highlights Stalin's studies on the colonial question, which held that "Leninism...destroyed the wall separating [w]hites from [b]lacks, Europeans from Asiatics, the 'civilized' from the 'non-civilized' slaves of imperialism." Furthermore, he argued that "the October Revolution *inaugurated* a new era, the era of *colonial revolutions in the oppressed countries* of the world, in *alliance* with the proletariat and *under the direction* of the proletariat" (Balandier 1951:40, emphasis in original). Alvin Gouldner has a slightly different take on this position as a critique of Stalin's practice within the Soviet Union, which involved a strategy of primitive socialist accumulation on behalf of an urban elite that imposed unfavorable rates of exchange upon a rural society they did not consider to be a part of the same moral community. Gouldner held that the peasants in the countryside were the Soviet Union's versions of Indians, and the Soviet countryside itself was viewed as a continental reservation (Hind 1984:545–546).

While some may view Gouldner's claims with some skepticism, the relationship between the workers' movement and colonized strata have long been problematic. During the period of the Great Migration in the United States, African-Americans' political agency emerged in the form of the New Negro movement. The New Negro radicals closely identified themselves with world anticapitalist and anti-imperialist forces and debated whether race was a component of capitalist stratification (race first) or whether race was clothing for class stratification (class first). During the 1930s and '40s, these social strata made the issue of racial justice central to the overall fight for social justice, though the "race first" radicalism of the New Negro (now represented by DuBois) was sidelined in the interest of a united front against fascism.

The Communist International, which was founded in the wake of the Bolshevik Revolution, rejected the "class first" ideology of traditional socialism and was constituted by an alliance between the workers' movements and the anticolonial movements. This was an unstable alliance, however, since there was general agreement on the issue of "proletarian leadership," which meant the leadership of the civilized over the non-civilized and the Europeans over the non-Europeans.

Some have argued that indeed beneath the political and economic causes still dividing the white race and the colored people, there is almost always a racial motive. Though Balandier seems to accept the presumed naturalness of racial differences, he does show that the inferior status of the Negro and a justification for racial prejudice cannot be made to appear as natural because "cultural differences are virtually imperceptible and a common identity of rights have been affirmed" (Balandier 1951:54). For Balandier, this only shows that it is not possible to separate the study of cultural contacts from that of racial contacts.

In the 1960s in the United States there arose, primarily in response to the militancy of the urban black masses and secondarily because of the black power movement, a burgeoning, if unevenly sophisticated, literature that defined the nature of the African population within US borders as a colonial situation. By the 1980s, one rarely found authors who supported such a view. Both Robert Allen[1] and Robert Blauner, who had been among the most influential scholars espousing that thesis, had recanted and adopted more pragmatic positions. By the time the tumultuous sixties subsided, white America's willingness to entertain the grievances of the black population had dramatically declined. How did we get to that point?

The Heyday of the Internal Colonialism Concept

Using internal colonialism to conceptualize the situation of black people within the United States stems from the notion – which goes back to the late 18th-century formation of the Free African Society and the African Methodist Episcopal Church – that African-Americans constituted a nation within a nation. These ideas were crystallized in the National Negro Convention Movement from 1830–1861. Henry Highland Garnett (1815–1882), Martin Delaney (1812–1885), Alexander Crummell (1819–1898), and W. E. B. DuBois (1868–1963) were some of the more prominent exponents of that formulation.

Though black nationalism had been a constant feature of the landscape of the Black Freedom struggle throughout the 19th century, it would be dramatically ratcheted up at the opening of the 20th century at the Pan-African Conference, where DuBois announced that the problem of the 20th century

---

[1] Robert Allen (2005) has been moved recently to reassert the issue of internal (neo)colonialism, to some extent along the lines that I do here.

would be the problem of the color line. Though this was, indeed, an ominous announcement, the relations at this time only allowed for a liberal anticolonial position. A few years later, DuBois joined with a group of black radicals who formed the Niagara Movement, some of whom would later form an alliance with white socialists and reform liberals in the NAACP. But the urbanization and concentration of blacks during the first Great Migration created the social conditions that, along with the First World War, gave rise to a new social force: the New Negro.

The New Negro radicals who came to the fore during and after the first Great Migration soon came to view themselves politically as part of world anticolonial and anticapitalist forces. They identified themselves with and arguably belonged to a Pan-African social strata in world society. Though they came to prominence in a pre-existing political community dominated by the towering figure of DuBois, he was nevertheless viewed by the young radicals as part of the "Old Crowd Negroes" (due, in part, to his "Close Ranks" editorial in *The Crisis*).

It was New Negro radicals such as Hubert Harrison, Marcus Garvey, Cyril Briggs, A. Philip Randolph, and Claude McKay who established the radical tradition that would dominate the African-American intelligentsia throughout most of the 20th century. During the early 20th century, they debated whether racial stratification was the foundation of American and capitalist stratification (race first) or whether racial stratification was simply an expression of class stratification (class first). Some of the "race first" radicals took their position to the newly formed Communist International (consisting of revolutionary organizations disproportionately located in the semi-colonial [Russia, China, Mexico], colonial, and dependent zones of the world economy), who then endorsed the idea that the Negro within the United States constituted a nation within a nation (but limited this definition to the Black Belt South). Some of these New Negro radicals then joined the Communist Party of the United States (CPUSA), who were obliged to accept the position of the international body (also known as the Third International). During the 1930s and '40s these social strata made the issue of racial justice central to the overall fight for social justice, though the "race first" radicalism of the New Negro (now represented by DuBois) was sidelined in the interest of a united front against fascism, which, among African-Americans, took the form of an informal grouping that has since come to be called the Black Popular Front. But the quest for US economic, military, and political preeminence in the postwar world system ran counter to the egalitarian and cooperative sentiment of the 1930s and '40s, establishing in its stead an imperial project dubbed "the American century," which demanded an unprecedented ideological conformity that narrowed the scope of theorizing about race and racial discrimination to the attitudes and practices of individuals, except within the Jim Crow South.

However, the postwar rise of opposition to imperialism in Africa, Asia, and Latin America created an echo among the internal minorities in the US and brought the radicals of the Black Popular Front to an engagement with the social forces involved in the all-out rebellion against the Jim Crow system. And though the militants of this movement spoke largely in terms of the Southern Movement, they were themselves quite cosmopolitan in origin and understood the deep strains of structural and ideological racism as well as plain old prejudice and discrimination outside of the South. Many had worked on the issue of civil rights in New York City during the 1940s.

While the Southern Movement was equated with the struggle against Jim Crow and followed the formal line of the CPUSA about the Negro nation within a nation, in fact it was closer to the internal colonialism concept than most admit, as is indicated in some of the commentary that follows.

The debates of the 1960s and early 1970s arose as means to articulate the political motion of the black population in a period of intense mobilization. Such theories were also propounded in the first quarter of the 20th century, the period of the initial mass migration of black people to the urban areas of the Northeastern, Midwestern, and Western United States. The Garvey Movement, the largest social movement of the black population in the United States, undoubtedly influenced the formulations of a nation within a nation by the African Blood Brotherhood, and eventually by the CPUSA. While the CPUSA ceded to the Communist International's insistence that they give priority to what was called the Negro National Question (because the US-based African Blood Brotherhood took its own position directly to the Communist International), the implementation of the line tended to be uneven and confused, as the CP cadre tended to use the theory as a means to both recruit cadres of the Garvey movement and to theoretically justify their elevation of the importance of the struggles of the black population within the US. Eventually they abandoned the theory, arguing that conditions had changed, blacks had migrated away from the historical black nation in the

Black Belt South, and furthermore that the main thrust of the black population was for equality and justice within the United States.

Although the CPUSA was an important organization in the general working class struggles of the 1930s and '40s and in the struggle for racial justice, at the highest levels of the organization, their notions about the black struggle within the United States tended to be very mechanical. Though the infusion of militants from the African Blood Brotherhood pushed them to the forefront of the struggle for racial justice, their understanding of the inter-subjectivity of African-Americans was not really superficial, as I have argued elsewhere, but more tone deaf, for the obvious reason that they held the "race first" radicals of the New Negro movement at arm's length. Harold Cruse places his finger on this phenomenon:

> American Marxism has neither understood the nature of Negro nationalism, nor dealt with its roots in American society. When the communists first promulgated the Negro question as a 'national question' in 1928, they wanted a national question without nationalism. They posed the question mechanically because they did not understand it. They relegated the national aspect of the Negro question to the 'black belt' of the South, despite the fact that Garvey's 'national movement' had been organized in 1916 in a northern urban center where the Negro was, according to the communists, a 'national minority,' but not a 'nation,' as he was in the Southern states. Of course the national character of the Negro has little to do with what part of the country he lives in. Wherever he lives, he is restricted. His national boundaries are the color of his skin, his racial characteristics, and the social conditions of his substructural world. (Cruse 1968:78)

Cruse's corrective to the orthodox Marxist mechanistic notions was part of the sweeping reevaluation of a global new left, of which the black power movement was a part. Frantz Fanon's *Wretched of the Earth* was the key political document. From the ideas elaborated in his work came the main impetus for the revival and correction of an "internal colonialism" perspective within the black power movement.

But these theories about internal colonialism within this new Left did not spring fully formed in the minds of the young militants. Harold Cruse, Stokely Carmichael, Jack O'Dell, and Malcolm X all had ties to the old Left, or had been members of the old Left. The positions that came to be articulated in the

1960s and '70s (below) derive mostly from the influence of DuBois, Robeson, and Briggs, who continued to hold the "race first" position throughout the 1930s and '40s.

In *Black Power: the Politics of Liberation in America*, Carmichael and Hamilton (1967) had argued that the black condition in the United States is essentially a colonial condition, not perfectly analogous to classic colonialism in the sense that there is not a separation of territory and no exploitation of raw materials. Such a distinction, however, was viewed as merely a technicality, since politically, economically, and socially the black community is controlled by predominantly white institutions, although they also make use of indirect rule. For Carmichael and Hamilton, the key role for black people in the United States is as a source for cheap and unskilled labor. The captive black communities also provide a market for cheap and shoddy goods for merchants, creditors, real estate interests, etc.

It should be noted that the emphasis of the Carmichael and Hamilton book was on what they called the "colonial analogy." Robert Allen would later try to take the discussion of internal colonialism beyond the level of an analogy by arguing that "Black America is an oppressed nation, a semi-colony of the United States" (1970:1), and that the implication for social change is that the black freedom struggle should take the form of a national liberation movement. He argued further, however, that there is a tension between a revolutionary thrust and a reformist thrust within the movement, despite the fact that most spokespersons used the "language" of revolution. Unlike Carmichael and Hamilton, Allen sought to avoid the "lack of perfect fit" by looking to Jack O'Dell's clarification on the issue of territoriality. O'Dell had argued:

> In defining the colonial problem it is the role of the institutional mechanisms of colonial domination which are decisive. Territory is merely the stage upon which these historically developed mechanisms of super-exploitation are organized into a system of oppression. (O'Dell 1967:8)

And, thus, for Allen, colonialism was the "direct and overall subordination of one people, nation, or country to another with state power in the hands of the dominating power" (Allen 1970:8).

Allen and others have argued that in the United States the urban rebellions of the 1960s gave rise to a more neo-colonial form of control, which utilizes indirect rule. In this scheme, black power became black capitalism, and a black middle class, militant rhetoric and all, would be allowed to get a larger piece of the pie for itself.

But there was still unease about the concept, so those involved in using the concept as a guide to social struggle turned increasingly to Robert Blauner's theory of internal colonialism; his systematization of the concept made the concept more elegant than it had been in the writings of those who were closer to the movement. He contended that the conditions of black people do not really fit the traditional criteria of colonialism, which refers to the establishment of domination over a "geographically external political unit, most often inhabited by people of a different race and culture" (Blauner 1972:83).

What is common to classical colonialism, and what Blauner calls "internal colonialism," is that since they developed out of similar technological, cultural, and power relations, a common *process* of social oppression characterized the racial patterns in the two contexts (Blauner 1972:84). The components of Blauner's internal colonization process were said to be: (1) the mode of entry into the dominant society – forced versus voluntary; (2) a process of destruction of the indigenous values, orientations, and ways of life; (3) a special relationship to the governing or legal order in which the colonized view themselves as being managed and manipulated by outsiders; (4) the racist characterization of a group as inferior because of biological characteristics, in a process of social domination by which the group is exploited, controlled, and oppressed socially and psychically by a super-ordinate group; and (5) a separation in labor status between the colonized workers and the immigrant minorities.

Much of our public attention to the concept of internal colonialism as it was elaborated during the 1960s focuses on the intellectuals mentioned above, but an influential articulation of internal colonialism was published in *Studies on the Left* in 1962 by Harold Cruse (reprinted in his *Rebellion or Revolution*). The article, "Revolutionary Nationalism and the Afro-American," framed his analysis in a longer intellectual history than most of the more popular exponents of the theory. He situated the black domestic colony in the colonial empire established by pan-European capitalism. But the United States did not establish a colonial empire in Africa, it brought the colonial subjects home and installed them within the southern states. From that time, the Negro has existed in a condition of domestic colonialism everywhere within the United

States. Cruse is critical of the Black Belt nation theory promulgated by the communists in 1928. Cruse views the colonial revolution against capitalism as the leading edge of the revolutionary struggle, rather than the western workers' movement. Members of the early 1960s black radicals, such as the Revolutionary Action movement, studied the article and circulated it among a wide circle of black radicals during that period. While most of the exponents of the theory thus far have been concerned with movements for social change, including Kwame Nkrumah (1970:87), there were also economists whose views we should examine. Some of these views use the "colonial analogy," and some use a more rigorous formulation.

William Tabb argued that there are two key relationships that must exist before the colonial analogy can be accepted: (1) economic control and exploitation, and (2) political dependence and subjugation. The maintenance of such relationships requires separation and inferior status (Tabb 1970:23). Tabb agreed with black radicals who argued that the issue of spatial separation of the colony from the colonial power was secondary to the actuality of the control of the ghetto from the outside.

Following Tabb, Bennett Harrison (1974) viewed the internal colony as a social entity similar to a "'less developed country' with a severe 'balance of payments' deficit and with 'foreign' control of the most important local, political, and economic institutions" (Harrison 1974:4). Interestingly, some analysts reject the internal colonialism model while accepting the striking similarities between the structural dualism pervading so many less developed countries and the segmentation of the American economy into a growing "core" and ghetto "periphery" (Harrison 1974:6).

Barry Bluestone had earlier expressed a more nuanced view of the ghetto economy. He thought that striving toward an inner-city economy would be the organizing base for strengthening the black community as a force to gain concessions from the government and from the corporate establishment, similar to DuBois's arguments in the 1930s.

Ron Bailey's analysis is distinguished by his combined emphasis on social movements and political economy. Bailey stresses the racial dimension in internal colonialism, defining it as "the forceful conquest of people of color by Europeans for purposes of economic exploitation" (1973). Bailey holds that "race has always been a significant and relatively independent force in shaping material reality in capitalist society" (1973:162). He is critical of conventional Marxist analysis, which has not accorded to race its proper significance, because he sees "internal colonialism as the domestic face of world imperialism and the racist conquest and exploitation of people of color by Europeans" (Bailey 1973:162).

Bailey traces the black colony to the enslavement of Africans in the Americas as part of a global capitalist world-system. Bailey establishes that the black internal colony is a reservoir of superexploited labor, relegated to the lowest paid and least desirable jobs, alongside a large pool of unemployed workers that facilitates the exploitation of non-colonized workers. It is a zone of dependent development locked in the logic of spiraling impoverishment, and an expendable buffer zone to cushion the antagonism-producing operations of the American capitalist economy.

Bailey argued that relations of monopoly and dependency were at the heart of the economic domination of the black internal colony. The black internal colony is a zone of white control both internally and externally. Whites control and monopolize the mechanisms of production, exchange, and distribution, in addition to mechanisms of economic diversification (such as banks, credit, and technology). This dependent position of the black colony is a by-product of capitalist growth *outside* of the black internal colony. The enclave structure of the black community generates employment *outside* the black community while black labor goes unemployed (Bailey 1973:175).

For Bailey, dependency theory offered a set of organizing ideas that clarified how the black internal colony is a consequence of a set of historical forces and structures that consign it to underdevelopment and dependence (Bailey 1973:176).

Bailey concludes that the essential role of the black internal colony is to ensure the smooth functioning of the relations of production and exploitation and the system of domination and dependence, but that there must also be a system that guarantees the continuing existence of this entire edifice, which is the pacification of the black bourgeoisie, the strategy of tokenism.

In the same volume, Bailey and Flores caution against a rote invocation of the phrase colonialism based on assumptions about classical colonialism. They argue that discussion about internal colonialism too often included an undue emphasis on certain features of classical colonialism, especially the issues of an overseas army, and the domination of an overseas territory far from the conquering country. To illustrate their point, they cite Jack O'Dell's classic article on the issue in *Freedomways* in 1966–67.

This allows them to notice that despite the affluence and power of the United States, "racial minorities remain unconquered by policies of forced assimilation, acculturation, and cultural extermination" (Bailey and Flores 1973:158). Bailey and Flores point out that the colonized minorities within US borders are distinct from their people of origin, but are also distinct from the white society within the United States, where they are rejected by the society that they built. But Bailey and Flores are not intimidated by such unwantedness; they view this strata's counter-hegemonic critique of US racist oppression as a badge of honor rather than shame.

Indeed, the "national liberation struggles of racial minorities within the US are important negations of US capitalist domination inside its borders and converge with and strengthen the national liberation struggles of other third world peoples" (Bailey and Flores 1973:158). Bailey and Flores writing in the early 1970s are most assuredly an indication of the confidence of a rising class of radical intellectuals from the internally colonized minorities within US borders and their allies among a radicalized young intelligentsia among whites themselves.

The 1960s had brought the US back to a time when many equated the "colonial question" with the "social question." This had been the basis of past coalitions, but there had also been controversy over which of the two were primary. The old Left consistently argued for the leading role of the working class (class first), a position that was defeated during the heyday of the internal colonialism concept.

Decline of Internal Colonialism Concept

The fierce repression of revolutionary nationalists associated with the Black Panther Party, the Revolutionary Action movement, and the Republic of New Africa led to a reassessment of the revolutionary strategy that had come to be accepted by these groups. The demise of those organizations resulted in an increasing acceptance of the "universal" ideas of Marxism. The Black Left, the Chicano Left, and the Puerto Rican Left moved to more multinational forms of organization and to an embrace of Third Internationalist forms of Marxism. As I argue above, Third Internationalist Marxism, drawing disproportionately from social movements outside of the core zones of the world economy, constituted a compromise, though unstable, between "class first" and "race first."

Within the academy there arose increasing critiques of the internal colonialism perspective. But these critiques were never merely theoretical – they reflected changing estimates of the relations of force on the ground. One influential rebuttal of the internal colonialism model is that of Michael Burawoy (1974). Burawoy criticizes Cruse's stress on the exclusion of the Negro from US society, as a group set aside and systematically exploited for the benefit of the mother country. Burawoy argues that the Negro is an essential part of advanced capitalist societies such as the United States. Burawoy, on the other hand, defines a colony as of marginal value to the metropolis. And he relies firmly on the classical definition of a colony as a separate territory.

In the meantime, a decisive shift in rapports de force cut the ground out from under the positive notion of internal colonialism as the basis of mobilization by agents of social change. First there was a sense that the radicalization of the working class struggle called most of all for the unity of the great multinational US working class in the language of that time, and the Black Left called for black leadership of this working class movement, which all led to a movement away from nationalist forms of theoretical formulations. The Watergate crisis resulted in the resignation of President Nixon, and Crozier, Huntington, and Watnuki published a book entitled *The Crisis of Democracy* for the Trilateral Commission.

The authors argued that the 1960s had been a period of democratic upsurge:

> The 1960s witnessed a dramatic renewal of the democratic spirit in America. The predominant trends of that decade involved the challenging of the authority of established political, social, and economic institutions, increased popular participation in and control over those institutions, a reaction against the concentration of power in the executive branch of the federal government and in favor of the reassertion of the power of Congress and of state and local government, renewed commitment to the idea of equality on the part of intellectuals and other elites, the emergence of the 'public interest' lobbying groups, increased concern for the rights of and provisions of opportunities for minorities and women to participate in the polity and economy, and a pervasive criticism of those who possessed or were even thought to possess excessive power or wealth... It was a decade of democratic surge and of the reassertion of democratic egalitarianism. (Crozier, Huntington, Watnuki 1975:59–60)

In addition to increased political participation, the authors argued that there was "a marked upswing in other forms of citizen participation, in the form of marches, demonstrations, protest movements, and 'cause' organizations" (Crozier, Huntington, Watnuki 1975:61). There were "markedly higher levels of self-consciousness on the part of blacks, Indians, Chicanos, white ethnic groups, students, and women," all seeking "their appropriate share of the action and of the rewards" (Crozier, Huntington, Watnuki 1975:61).

> Previously passive or unorganized groups in the population now embarked on concerted efforts to establish their claims to opportunities, positions, rewards, and privileges, which they had not considered themselves entitled to before. (Crozier, Huntington, Watnuki 1975:61–62)

Thus, some of the problems of governance in the United States were said to stem "from an excess of democracy." But, the authors argued, "needed instead is a greater degree of moderation in democracy" (Crozier, Huntington, Watnuki 1975:113). The authors argued that such "moderation" comes in two forms: reassertion of undemocratic authority and cultivation of political apathy. Too much democracy was said to be an inefficient method of governance. All democracy "usually requires some measure of apathy and noninvolvement on the part of some individuals and groups. In the past, every democratic society has had a marginal population, of greater or lesser size, which has not actively participated in politics" (Crozier, Huntington, Watnuki 1975:114). The authors conclude that greater inclusion of such marginal groups in the democratic societies requires more self-restraint on the part of all groups.

In 1965, the civil rights activist and strategist Bayard Rustin had called for a movement from protest to politics. The deepening of the civil rights goals of social equality for people of color would require a form of coalition politics similar to the 1930s New Deal. By the 1970s, writes Norm Kelley, some of these leaders became, in effect, a national black political directorate, with power centered in the Congressional Black Caucus. Meanwhile, black America retired itself from the kind of political action that disrupted business as usual. Political energy was channeled into voting, the only legitimate form of redress of grievance as seen by dominant political elites. This process enabled black mobilizations to place more black elected officials at the table, but the requisites of maintaining political power limited their options, and it led to the effective demobilization of one of the more democratic publics within the United States.

The internal colonialism concept had always operated within a radical milieu. With the institutionalization of black politics within a liberal polity, and the necessity to operate within that polity during the mid-1970s, the forces on the Left began to question themselves. The Black Liberation Movement, the Puerto Rican Liberation Movement, the Chicano Liberation Movement, and the Native American Movement were all said to have gone too far. There was now a sense among some that the militants of the 1960s and early 1970s had brought much of the drama of state repression on themselves. Their adventurism and their elevation of identity politics to a principle had brought us to the twilight of our common dreams (Gitlin 1995).

Toward the end of the 1970s, William Julius Wilson sought to intervene to stem the hemorrhaging of liberal social policy that had occurred in that decade. He argued that race had actually declined in significance since the victory of the civil rights movement over Jim Crow and called for universal programs rather than race-specific programs. Wilson held that the main problem of the urban underclass in the inner cities of the United States (the black underclass or the truly disadvantaged) was not racism but impersonal economic forces that dramatically undercut their life chances and created a situation of social isolation and highly concentrated poverty. This came to be a new consensus not only on the Left, but in the Center and on the Right as well.

From the Left, Jesse Jackson encouraged the activists who called upon him to address the racism of the Howard Beach thugs who chased Howard Griffith to his death, and he warned that they should beware of the racial battleground and seek the economic common ground because there are more black people in Howard Beach than in the boardrooms of CBS, the New York Times, etc. On the Right, Ronald Reagan enjoined us to remember Martin Luther King Jr.'s call for a color-blind society. From the Center, Bill Clinton said that if King was alive today, he would not be involved in the fight for social equality and justice but in the fight against black on black crime. The internal colonialism framework had been a recognition of the significance of African-Americans as a constitutive part of American society, despite their marginalization. The history of African-Americans not only lent a semi-autonomous logic to their struggle, but it had profound implications for American society as a whole, and for its position in the wider world. During the 1970s, there was movement toward an elite consensus reflected in the deliberations of the trilateral commission that the democratic renewal sparked by the civil rights movement was too much of a threat to social order. In the meantime, the institutionalization of black politics, which is discussed above, placed those who articulated the internal colonialism perspective in a position where such discourse was simply not acceptable. One by one, those who had argued for the concept of internal colonialism recanted.

Why the Need for a Reassessment of Internal Colonialism?

Despite the tactical sophistication of William Julius Wilson's response to the era of conservative hegemony within social policy during the Reagan-Bush administrations, there were some who were not willing to concede that the efforts of conservatives were well intended, or that the liberal/social democratic strategy of Wilson was appropriate for the difficulties faced by the truly disadvantaged.

During the 1990s, the seasoned scholar and former Congress of African People militant Komozi Woodard wrote *A Nation Within a Nation: Amiri Baraka and Black Power Politics*, in which he called attention to Arnold Hirsch's *Making of the Second Ghetto*. Hirsch details how Chicago neighborhood associations, urban institutions such as the University of Chicago and Illinois Institute of Technology, and government agencies such as the Chicago Housing Authority all agreed on the need to restrict black access to housing stock outside of the ghetto areas allotted to them. At the same time Chicago's Serbs, Croats, Poles, Italians, and Irish overcame intergroup suspicion and came together around their common interests as whites to stem black influx into highly desirable city neighborhoods (Hirsch 2000).

The Los Angeles Sentinel penned an editorial entitled "Ghettoes, American Style" at the end of 1938 that warned that "those who have been protesting Hitler's despicable plan to herd German Jews into ghettoes will be surprised to learn that their own government has been busily planning ghettoes for American Negroes through the Federal Housing Authority [sic]" (Hirsch 2000:158). Twenty years later, the US Commission on Civil Rights would reach a similar conclusion about how the efforts of the Federal Housing Administration, the Housing and Home Finance Agency, the Public Housing Administration, and the Urban Renewal Administration all contributed to the residential isolation of African-Americans.

In some recent work, Michael B. Katz sought to explore the relative quiescence in US cities, since many of the conditions thought to have caused unrest during the 1960s and 1970s persist, and in some cases have worsened (Katz 2007, 2008).

Katz argues that black political control of central cities has not sufficiently altered the lives of most inner-city residents. "African-Americans inherited city governments at the very moment when de-industrialization, cuts in federal aid, and white flight were decimating tax bases and job opportunities while fueling homelessness, street crime, and poverty" (Katz 2008:191). While rural to urban migration in the United States brought political power to black politicians, in the ensuing reorganization of urban space, class-based contestations operating to the disadvantage of the lower strata have consistently maintained distance between the urban racialized lower strata and the higher social strata. For Katz, the upshot of this transformation of urban space means that the new ecology of urban power dampens the potential for civil violence by organizing race and class segregation alongside the devolution of control over urban space to previously marginalized groups. On the whole then, white abandonment, selective incorporation, and mimetic reform resulted in indirect rule, which Katz concedes in a footnote was developed as a part of the theory of internal colonialism advanced by black writers such as Stokely Carmichael (Kwame Ture) and Charles Hamilton in the late 1960s (Katz 2008:206). But the strategies suggested by these radicals were viewed as a minimum program for increasing the political power of the internal colony, from which more comprehensive struggles would ensue. Katz recognizes this briefly in one of the essays when he talks about a global crisis of legitimacy spawned by revulsion against Cold War politics, the Vietnam War, and the growth of impersonal and bureaucratic domestic institutions.

The increased political power in the cities did not fundamentally change the place of the black ghetto or the internal neocolony in the ecology of power because of the limitations of local government, which is constrained by the authority of the state and federal government. The newly elected black city leadership were also often caught between the constituencies that elected them and corporations that limited their authority by threatening to move and take much-needed jobs with them if the city did not grant them certain concessions.

The Continuing Relevance of Internal Colonialism Theory

Members of the Association of Black Sociologists have periodically sought to promote a dialogue on internal colonialism. Representative of efforts to revive the issue of internal colonialism is Charles Pinderhughes's paper on the continuing relevance of internal colonialism theory. Pinderhughes ranges far and wide over the landscape of the internal colonialism debate, effectively debunking some of what I have noted as faulty propositions in this chapter, but he also includes some remnants of a too-singular focus on juridico-political territories that I feel has been a hindrance to effective theorizing.

Throughout the paper, Pinderhughes uses the designation African-America rather than African-Americans. Yet he argues that African-Americans, or the internal colony(ies), do not constitute a nation. Then what does the designation African-America refer to? If we are to avoid the dead weight of the past in taking a new look at the concept, why the fealty to the definition of a nation established by Stalin in 1912, and used by some in the Communist International to maintain the leadership of the working class within the international revolutionary movement? It seems to me that this can only mean maintaining the leadership of the white working class.

Overall, Pinderhughes's critique is easily the broadest and most penetrating analysis of internal colonialism since Bailey's article of the early 1970s, but I would like to raise a few questions that the document raised for me.

Rather than rely on dry formulaic analysis, Pinderhughes views internal colonialism as a manifestation of popular discursive formulations such as the ghetto and the inner city to reference internal colonies on American soil. He points out how we speak easily of a colony of Italians, of Dutch, of artists, etc., but when one speaks of a colony of African-Americans, it evokes considerable disagreement. Though he says "to some," the extent of opposition seems much more considerable.

Pinderhughes describes the internal colonies as identifiable areas of concentrated exploitation and focused oppression (Pinderhughes 2007:4), which always seemed to be the subtext of William Julius Wilson's work in *The Truly Disadvantaged*. But he is quick to point out that internal colonialism is not a systematic commentary on all forms of race relations in the United States or elsewhere.

While Pinderhughes gives some respect to Stalin's definition of a nation, he relies primarily on Harry Haywood to outline (very briefly) the efforts of the CPUSA to organize blacks (Pinderhughes 2007:6). To the extent that the CPUSA engaged in effective practice, Pinderhughes hints that this was related to its correct analysis of African-America as an internal colonial situation in the form of an oppressed nation. This seems to compress too much in a very brief commentary. Pinderhughes allows pride of position to the white cadre who came to political consciousness in the "class first" outlook that dominated the radical section of the pan-European Left from day one. But what of the black internationalists like Cyril Briggs and Richard Moore of the African Blood Brotherhood, who came to the CPUSA via the Communist International? It is not clear from this treatment what Pinderhughes makes of the intergenerational Left associated with *Freedomways* magazine in the 1960s, which clearly was associated with the CPUSA. Claude Lightfoot and other members of the CPUSA worked with the Nation of Islam during the 1960s. While DuBois joined the CPUSA in 1961 just before moving to Ghana, he had clearly worked with them since the late 1940s. Pinderhughes seems to adopt a Crusean attitude toward the CPUSA that underestimates the tension within the organization over the "class first" approach.

While Pinderhughes pays some attention to Cruse's elaboration of the domestic colonialism position in *Rebellion or Revolution*, which was published in 1968, he does not associate this position with Cruse's trip to Cuba and the publication of "Revolutionary Nationalism and the Afro-American" in *New Left Notes* shortly after his return in 1962. What is the source of Cruse's position on revolutionary nationalism? Does it have anything to do with his involvement with the CPUSA in the 1940s, the heyday of the Black Popular Front?

Overall, Pinderhughes confronts the critics of the internal colonialism thesis on what most feel is their strongest point, that the implications of the theory for praxis are bleak. Here he takes on both Blauner and Burawoy most effectively. He focuses on Blauner's remarks:

> During the mid-1970s I stopped using the colonial analogy. At the time, I was still enough of a Marxist to believe that a good theory must point the way to a political practice that resolves the contradiction the theory helps us understand. There was a practical solution to overseas colonialism; the colonizers could be sent back to Europe. And for the most part they were. But I could find no parallel solution for America's domestic colonialism.

Such a disconnect between theory and practice suggested to me an inherent flaw in the conceptual scheme itself. (Blauner 2001:189)

Here Pinderhughes pins Blauner to the wall. If short-term or middle-run praxis proves the validity of a theoretical formulation, why have some theoretical formulations persisted long after the futures that they heralded have not been validated? Since we are concerned mostly with Marxist-inflected intellectuals, how about Marxism itself? How much more time is needed? After all, *The Manifesto of the Communist Party* was written in 1848. Blauner thinks that the movements for decolonization in the overseas colonies constituted obviously "practical solutions." They sent the colonizers back to Europe. But one might reply to this facile statement that it is all too obvious today that decolonization did not solve the more deeply entrenched coloniality of power that was the deeper concern of colonized people in the overseas colonies. Movements and intellectuals today are focusing on what a more thorough-going decolonization might consist of (modernity/coloniality, decoloniality group and movement).

Pinderhughes, like many of us, having been immersed in the debates of the Black Liberation movement, introduces the national question into his analysis of the concept of internal colonialism as it affects African-America. He argues that an internal colony that is an oppressed nation can opt for separation since that is achievable for a nation. An oppressed nationality, on the other hand, does not have the option of self-determination; the redress that they seek must be within the political sphere of the oppressor nation, resulting ultimately in socially transformative change within the oppressor nation. This is an extremely important point, but it is a struggle that is quite a bit more difficult than sending colonizers back to their homes. Blauner might do well to consider the implications of this. But Pinderhughes might also think of the example of the impact of the liberation of the Portugal's African colonies on Portugal itself.

In my view, much of the opposition to the concept of internal colonialism exists in countries with social groups who have a high potential of defining themselves as an internal colony. The intellectual objection to the concept of an internal colony, or more precisely of seeing certain social groups as an internal colony, is a political objection. This is not an objection to attempting to see the real-world consequences of theoretical formulations but to allowing short-term or middle-run calculations to dominate our understanding of the world, and thereby of our conception of the larger possibilities for social change.

To my mind, Pinderhughes seems on the whole correct when he insists that the definition of the entire domestic diaspora inside of the US as a single colony is not functional. If one does not have a single geographic location, then how does one carry out democratic reforms and administrative transformation? Pinderhughes's response to this conundrum is to view each individual location as its own internal colony (Pinderhughes 2007:23). But if one hews to the geographic rather than the socio-structural logic of coloniality, it lends to the domination of strategy over analysis, which seems to be a reversal of the order of successful praxis. First, we are all a part of the social world, we are not gods standing outside of the social situation. We seek to understand our situation in order to change it. If our analysis does not provide immediate or middle-run results, do we simply assume that our analysis is wrong or do we need a more sophisticated analysis of the larger social system and of the plurality of social times? Otherwise, we should simply accept Blauner's position.

If colonialism can only be an issue for overseas territories being subjected to the domination of an external political entity, do we miss the historically constituted structural relationship that has been defined as a colonial situation, involving the conquest of one people by the political institutions of a foreign power? This seems to clearly apply to African slaves who were stolen from Africa and enslaved in the Americas, and who were never assimilated into most of the societies that came to exist in the Americas. In the United States, this seems also to apply to Mexicans colonized on stolen land, Amerindians whose lands were confiscated and the people removed or eliminated, and to Puerto Ricans.

Are any of these internal colonies still nations? Clearly one might say that the American Southwest is a territory on which the residents might constitute a nation. This is not true of the other internally colonized groups, but this is not a dilemma, as has so often been posed. Pinderhughes almost allows these definitional difficulties to overwhelm his analysis when it is a tension that makes a strategy more difficult, but once figured out and understood within appropriate social times it can be more transformative, which is much more the object of struggle than self-determination conceived in nation-building or state-building strategies. Pinderhughes himself argues similarly in his proposition that internal colonialism points to "the necessity of a systemic and systematic solution to the oppression and exploitation of its population, not just a reliance on democratic incrementalism" (Pinderhughes 2007:25).

Pinderhughes distrusts what he refers to as "democratic incrementalism" because it cedes disproportionate authority to the prejudices and misconceptions of the non-colonized white population. But one should resist the danger of seeing this as a closed box, when the binding of the internally colonized within the belly of the beast has implications for rapports de forces both within the US and within the larger world-system. This is an issue of great significance that Pinderhughes seems to dismiss with a preponderant emphasis on a state-centric approach, which he opposes to the world-systems approach of the modernity/coloniality, decoloniality group as presented in the work of Ramon Grosfoguel (2003).

While Pinderhughes's contention that the coloniality of power is a redefinition of neo-colonialism in the sense that it is used to describe (frequently nonadministrative) structural survivals of past colonialism is accurate, he does not completely explore the full implications of the difference between the concepts except to disparage efforts that do not focus sufficiently on the state (shades of the conflict between revolutionary nationalism and cultural nationalism). But the implications of Pinderhughes's position here may be precisely the fetishization of state power that Grosfoguel criticizes. To the extent that Grosfoguel uses the term internal colonialism, Pinderhughes is critical of what he sees as the "world-systems" flavor of his analysis, which he thinks is dismissive of initiatives for radical political and social transformations at the nation-state level (Pinderhughes 2007:32). Pinderhughes is clearly more grounded in the struggle of internally colonized populations within the United States and in his involvement in US-based black radical movements.

Pinderhughes, of course, is not unaware of the symbolic and real changes in the conditions of African-America over the last 40–50 years, but he is clear-eyed about the overall balance of an expanded professional managerial strata who are intertwined in various ways with the black internal colony, the base of a transition to what Robert Allen has recently referred to as internal neo-colonialism. But the base of the internally colonized African-America is made up largely of residents of what Loic Wacquant refers to as the hyperghetto. Pinderhughes counterposes the hyperghetto with the rising role of the special blacks (Condoleezza Rice, Barack Obama, Bill Cosby, and Halle Berry) and token blacks. This evolution of African-America feeds the illusion that the only remaining barrier to racial equality is personal prejudice and personal failings (Pinderhughes 2007:40).

On the whole, I view Pinderhughes's "The Continuing Relevance of Internal Colonialism Theory to Africa-America" the best analysis of this issue since Ronald Bailey's articles of the early 1970s. But I am puzzled by his criticism of the internationalism of world-systems analysis, even if Ramon Grosfoguel cannot properly be viewed as a representative of the world-systems perspective. It seemed to me that Huey Newton had made the best application of world-systems analysis in his concept of revolutionary intercommunalism and the movement of Newton and the BPP from revolutionary nationalism to revolutionary intercommunalism.

According to Kelvin Santiago-Valles, races are built around unevenly structured populations or nationalities rather than necessarily being organized on the basis of juridico-political territories. For Santiago-Valles, this form of social order means that "race, modernity, and capitalism, as well as chattel slavery and its legacy, are historically and conceptually bound together as coloniality. This includes both formal colonialism and neo-colonialism as well as the Occidentalist culture of both" (Santiago-Valles 2003:218). This is the ensemble of structures that has undergirded the modern/colonial/capitalist world-system.

Lerone Bennett Jr., who many consider to be the dean of African-American history, tells us that "the history of black America is an act in the larger drama of the worldwide colonization of peoples of color by Europeans and the progeny of Europeans" (Bennett 1993:208). According to Bennett, this colonial system perpetuates the political, economic, and cultural exploitation of non-Europeans. Despite the specificity of the black experience in the United States, it is clearly a variation on a universal European theme: the exploitation of the labor power and resources of the colonized. As elsewhere, the system changed its skin at various junctures in order to protect its essential content.

Bennett dutifully notes the customary conceptualization of colonialism as an external-internal relationship between a metropolitan government and transplanted or indigenous people beyond its borders. But this is not the only situation that might be deemed a colonial one. When an alien group subjugates and exploits an indigenous or transplanted people within the borders of a single country, it might be deemed an instance of internal colonialism. Bennett holds that "the decisive factor in colonialism is not geography but the sociopolitical relationship between a colonial center and the indigenous or transplanted people forcibly brought within the orbit of the colonizer's influence" (Bennett 1993:209). Interestingly, Bennett uses the imagery of a developing center and an underdeveloped circumference within the borders of the same country to describe the internal colonial situation. Although the myopic focus on geography and changing forms of dominance might obscure the nature of a colonial situation, Bennett tells us, and as I argue throughout this chapter, that colonialism is "an organic structural relationship between a dynamic, developing, dominating center and a stagnant, underdeveloped, dominated circumference" (Bennett 1993:216). For Bennett, the center-circumference relationship is pivotal, as has been articulated in dependency theory and world-systems analysis. He then states in classic dependency language: "The underdevelopment of the circumference is a function of the development of the center."[2] The dynamic center expands at the expense of the stagnation and underdevelopment of the colonized periphery.

Although Bennett holds that colonial situations are always characterized by political control, economic exploitation, cultural repression, racism, and force, he underlines the primary role of force in forging and maintaining the colonial relationship. He illustrates with a conversation between a prominent white citizen and Booker T. Washington's successor at Tuskegee Institute in 1923: "You understand, the prominent white citizen said in 1923, that we have the legislature, we make the laws, we have the judges, the sheriffs, and the jails. We have the hardware store and the arms" (Bennett 1993:211).

But despite the role of force in the establishment, institutionalization, and maintenance of the colonial situation, force alone is not sufficient. Force must be used to penetrate into the "secret zones of the minds and bodies of the victims" (Bennett 1993:211). Here enters the role of denial of education or miseducation, white supremacy or racism, and the divine right of white folk to steal, as DuBois had earlier noted.

---

[2] This recalls a cartoon of a well-to-do white couple who look to be in their late 50s or early 60s riding an elevated commuter train through some American ghetto. The husband is saying to the wife, "The solution to the problem of the ghetto? My dear, the ghetto is a solution."

Bennett shows that, initially, the colonial situation in the US was established by laws and conscious acts of institutional subordination during the slave regime. But over time, the colonial regime evolved into an autonomous entity propelled by its own social dynamics. Clearly the slave regime established the colonial situation, but the practice of both elite whites following their class and political interests and subaltern whites following their status and material advantage interests subsequently engaged in social, political, and economic practices by which this system became the established regime, which periodically changed its skin but maintained the fundamentals of the social relationship described above.

After Reconstruction, the colonial elite sought to establish indirect rule via the promotion of an accommodationist or comprador leadership strata within black America. Booker T. Washington and his successor at Tuskegee Institute, Robert Moton, were exemplars of this strata. They were strenuously opposed by more radical leaders such as W. E. B. DuBois, Ida B. Wells, and William Monroe Trotter, but the rapports de force tended to push all leaders in the direction of accommodation. An example, of course, is DuBois' infamous "Close Ranks" editorial in *The Crisis*, advocating black participation in the US Armed Forces during World War I.

While the social structure of black America itself underwent some changes over the first part of the 20th century, neither the Supreme Court decision of 1954 nor the reforms of the 1950s and '60s went to the heart of the colonial relationship. Bennett argues that, by that time, the colonial idea was so deeply embedded in institutional practices not directly related to race (and, I would add, embedded also within the superegos of the American public of all races) that the "abolition of legal segregation and discrimination had little immediate impact on the functioning of the system" (Bennett 1993:220).

Structural Oppression and Violence

While some opposition to the concept of internal colonialism is based on the desirability of peaceful integration of African-Americans into the US economy, internal colonialism or domestic colonialism is precisely based on such integration. However, this integration has not been peaceful, but has been based on structural oppression and violence. Kamara and Van Der Meer (2007) cite Painter's contention that enslaved Africans provided the foundation of the

American economy as a basic commodity in the New England–West Indian trade, as workers producing agricultural goods for the world market, and as property (Pinter 2007). They were not considered persons, but personal property, and were thus the objects of structural violence. While the carefully delineated color categorization clarified the divide between the enslaved Africans and those descendants of Western Europe, it also underlined a sense of social purity among the descendants of Europe who coalesced into "whites," which was posed against the "negative, evil connotation of blackness" (Kamara and Van Der Meer 2007:384).

Thus, people of African descent came to occupy a variety of legal statuses within the United States, but their social identity has not been disentangled from the "in but not of" social psychology of the dominated blacks and dominant whites. From the beginning, the enslaved Africans were unacknowledged witnesses to a discussion about freedom and liberty for all among whites. How else were they to understand the master's conversation about freedom and liberty in their presence except to conclude that they did not exist as human beings in the eyes and hearts of the master and in those members of the master race who took part in this conversation without recognizing the presence of enslaved Africans on US soil? Perhaps there is no need to point out that the very privilege of the master and the master race are "inextricably tied to the existence" of enslaved Africans (Kamara and Van Der Meer 2007:384). The social relationship of the master and the enslaved, and the free people and the enslaved African, established a status hierarchy with material and psychic benefits that was lodged deeply into the interstices of the American commonsense and was of the very fabric of the American social structure. It was maintained by a system of structural oppression and violence that seemed to contradict the vision of the United States as a land of opportunity, with liberty and justice for all. This social violence, from lynching to intimidation to cross and church burning, to genocidal imprisonment rates, to denial of the franchise, to inadequate housing, education, and jobs, to poorer healthcare, has reinforced the internalized sense of superiority of whites and the internalized feelings of failure among large segments of the African-American population (Kamara and Van Der Meer 2007:385).

It is important to appreciate the social dynamics here. Black folk are not merely inferior and lacking in values, they are immoral or amoral. For Kamara and Van Der Meer, Frantz Fanon's description of the colonizers and

the colonized in *The Wretched of the Earth* captures this social dynamic in a
depressingly elegant manner:

> It is not enough for the settler to delimit physically, that is to say with the
> help of the army and the police force, the place of the native. As if to show
> the totalitarian character of colonial exploitation the settler paints the native
> as a sort of quintessence of evil. Native society is not simply described as
> a society lacking in values. It is not enough for the colonist to affirm that
> those values have disappeared from, or still better never existed in, the
> colonial world. The native is declared insensible to ethnics; he represents
> not only the absence of values, but also the negation of values. He is, let us
> dare to admit, the enemy of values, and in the sense he is the absolute evil.
> He is the corrosive element. Destroying all that comes near him, he is the
> deforming element, disfiguring all that has to do with beauty or morality;
> he is the depository of maleficent powers, the unconscious and irretrievable
> instrument of blind forces. (Fanon 1963:35)

Despite the clear hostility of much of the white public to African-Americans
who also seek to instill these ideas in other sectors of the American public, the
admission of a large sector of the African-American professional-managerial
strata into the mainstream of American society has been used as a justification
for the demonization of the lower strata of the African-American population.
Many of the black professional-managerial strata serve as a comprador elite
within the black community that participates in the subjugation or helps to
justify the subjugation of the lower strata of the community.

Kamara and Van Der Meer cite Martin Luther King Jr., who is moving
closer to DuBois and Malcolm X and the younger Black Power militants in
his last book, *Where Do We Go From Here: Chaos or Community*. In calling for
a new program of action in the aftermath of the passage of the Civil Rights
Act of 1964 and the Voting Rights of 1965, King argues, "We have left the
realm of constitutional rights and we are entering the area of human rights"
(King 1967:130). Then he directly addresses the black middle class:

> It is especially important for the Negro middle class to join this action
> program. To say that all too many members of the Negro middle class have
> been detached spectators rather than involved participants in th[is] great
> drama of social change... is not to overlook the unswerving dedication and
> unselfishness of some. But many middle-class Negroes have forgotten their

roots and are more concerned about 'conspicuous consumption' than about the cause of justice. Instead, they seek to sit in some serene and passionless realm of isolation, untouched and unmoved by the agonies and struggles of their underprivileged brothers. This kind of selfish detachment has caused the masses of Negroes to feel alienated not only from white society but also from the Negro middle class. They feel that the average middle-class Negro has no concern for their plight. (King 1967:131–132)

Like his revolutionary call that we unite with the barefoot people of the world at Riverside Church on April 4, 1967, his speech honoring DuBois at Carnegie Hall on February 23, 1968 on the 100th anniversary of DuBois' birth, and his movement toward an alliance with Malcolm X during the last month of Malcolm's life demonstrates his stance with the revolutionary people of the world and affirms the centrality of anticolonial struggle for the African-American liberation movement, which must be joined by all people of good will.

Less than six weeks later, King had been shot dead by an assassin (or assassins) in Memphis, Tennessee, where he had traveled to support a strike by black sanitation workers. This unleashed a fury of indignation within black communities all over the country. While the collective violence of this period was unprecedented, the real story here was an ongoing counter-insurgency that was removing anticolonial black leaders from the scene. While I detail some of this activity above, it is important that we understand how this kind of violence is part of the institutional structure of the United States.

Martinot argues that behind the constitutional state lies a contra-state, a self-defined para-political state, cohered around the principle of white entitlement. He calls it a byelocolonial state (*byelo* is Greek for "white"). This state is both white and colonialist toward those it insists upon excluding. This state acts consensually within a white supremacist cultural framework. Its violence and judgments are said to trump the legalisms of the Constitutional state, though it calls upon the constitutional state when its actions require more than self-legitimization.

Police action against black people that violates legality, such as profiling, arbitrary arrests, and torture, represent the para-political violence of the byelocolonial state, even though the police are officials of the constitutional state. Martinot illustrates the interface between the two structures by explaining that the role of the police is to fine a suspect when a crime is committed. But profiling involves finding a suspect and then finding a crime for that suspect to be charged with (Martinot 2007:374).

According to Martinot, racialization defines "an allo-social form of dehumanized life devoid of birthright" (Martinot 2007:375). White supremacy is said to be an inherent derivative of this project, of which enslavement was one vehicle for enforcement. When whites define other people as non-white in order to define themselves against that otherness, the other is deemed devoid of humanity and thus divested of human recognition (Martinot 2007:376).

For Martinot, the dual state that he has analyzed reflects the existence of a dual class structure: a white class structure organized in what he refers to as the typical capitalist manner, and a racialized class system organized along a byelocolonial division between white society as a whole and the many classes and groups of racialized people dominated both within American society and within its global reach (Martinot 2007:378). What this means for efforts at social change or social transformation is that the transformation of class relations will not be sufficient to alleviate the exploitation of the byelocolonial state, which will simply reconstitute the constitutional state that it needs.

Social movements may be steps toward the allo-cultural, but they will not survive as such if they are not able to become marked as simply another "special interest" within the constitutional state, which was the fate of the New Deal coalition, the labor movement, and the civil rights movement in the post-civil rights era. The transformation of cultural structures such as the byelocolonial state cannot be achieved through rebellion against or class struggle against the constitutional state. A theory of the transformation of cultural structures has to be developed. Such a theory would require an understanding of the relationship between the Intermediary Control Strata (ICS), who play the role of policing the racialized strata; the byelocolonial state; and white racialized identity on the one hand, and the constitutional state, its class structure, and is structures of racialization on the other.

The World Context of Internal Colonialism

Mignolo argues that Creole consciousness formed in relation to Europe was a geo-political consciousness, but that Creole consciousness forged internally was racial, against Amerindian and Afro-American populations. This transformation of reproduction of the colonial difference has been termed "internal colonialism" (Mignolo 1998:34).

Mignolo argues that Latin America is not a subcontinent naturally named by God, it is an invention of the Creole elite of European descent in the 19th century with French imperial designs. Ethnicity in Latin America is thus a "site of struggle, the site of the coloniality of power, of knowledge, of being" (Mignolo 2007:43). But rapports de force are rapidly shifting following the increased assertiveness of Indians and people of African descent who are "shifting the geography of knowledge and taking epistemology in their own hands" (Mignolo 2007:44). Mignolo distinguishes this process from what we now refer to (often dismissively) as identity politics with what he calls identity in politics, which he feels is necessary "because the control of identity politics lies precisely in the construction of an identity that doesn't look as such but as the natural appearance of the world," which one finds in white, heterosexual men. These hegemonic identity politics denounce opposing identities as fundamentalist and essentialist. One must speak from the identities that have been allocated in order to de-naturalize the imperial and racial construction of identity in the modern world-system. Such constructions have not expelled certain people from the system but have marked them as exteriorities, as stigmatized beings by their superiors for purposes of maintaining the interior space that they inhabit.

Mignolo sees the emergence of a de-colonial way of thinking in various parts of the world, which he describes as confronting the hegemonic designs of Western thought from the borderlands, which is a position from which one can avoid Western and non-Western fundamentalisms.

But this struggle requires an internal organization of these internally colonized populations as a matter of survival, and an external organization to fight against imperial/colonial infiltration/destruction of their residential areas, economic and social organizations, culture, etc.

For Mignolo, the consequence of 300 years of direct colonial rule and 200 years of internal colonialism has been the growing force of nations within nations, where in Latin America metizaje became the ideology of national homogeneity, while an Anglo-Protestant culture core into which others would assimilate characterized the United States. But de-colonial thinking is the road to pluri-versality as a universal project. This is posed in opposition to an abstract universalism, whether of the liberal or the radical (Marxist) variety. For Mignolo, the defense of human sameness above human differences is always a claim made from what he refers to as the "privileged position of identity politics in power" (Mignolo 2007:55).

Mignolo argues that epistemic fractures are taking place around the world, not just among indigenous communities in the Americas, New Zealand, and Australia, but also among Afro-Andean, Afro-Caribbean, and Islamic intellectuals and activists. Contrary to what might be assumed, this process has led to a retreat of nationalism, conceived as the identification of the state with one ethnicity and, therefore, to the fetishization of power. If the state is identified with one ethnicity, then there is no difference between the power of the people and the power in the hands of people of that ethnicity who represent the state. And the model of this form of organization is the Western bourgeois state based upon the political theory from Plato and Aristotle to Machiavelli, Hobbes, and Locke. The de-colonial option came to the fore when indigenous people around the world began to claim their own cosmology in the organization of the economic and the social, of education and subjectivity, and when Afro-descendant groups in South America and the Caribbean followed the same path. It will gain significant momentum when Islamic and Arabic intellectuals and activists also follow that path.

The de-colonial option is being exercised more and more today because the logic of coloniality (capitalism, state formation, university education, media, and information as commodity, etc.) is indeed flattening the world, as has been enthusiastically charted by Thomas Friedman (2005). The de-colonial option moves away from Western civilization's expendability of human lives and civilization of death (massive slave trade, famines, wars, genocides, and the elimination of difference at all cost, such as in Iraq and Lebanon).

The American model of multiculturalism conceded "culture" while maintaining "epistemology." Andean intellectuals introduced the term "interculturality" as a means of claiming epistemic rights (Mignolo 2007:62). For Mignolo, the struggle for epistemic rights is fundamental to any strategy for transformative social change because this struggle is what will determine the "principles upon which the economy, politics, and education will be organized, ruled, and enacted" (Mignolo 2007:65). These principles will allow many worlds to co-exist and not be ruled out in the name of simplicity and the reproduction of binary opposition. This approach allows for the rise of a communal system (different from the capitalist and socialist systems) in which power is not located in the state or in the individual (or corporate) proprietor but in the community.

It is within this context that the internally colonized will be able to come into the light and be fully acknowledged. This will be unavoidable for the same reason that the internally colonized have been shunted into the shadows since the 1970s: they had been the principle challenge to white supremacy in the US, had mobilized large sections of the American population against the imperial role of their government in the world arena, and had argued for an increase in the democratic and egalitarian character of American society. All of the efforts at silencing these forces via a neo-liberal closing down of the welfare state, ending the discussion about racial justice via the argument for a color-blind society, and blaming the poor for their own poverty via a discourse about the underclass and a culture of poverty. The withdrawal of the state from inner-city sites of concentrated poverty, or what I would call internally colonized populations, led to replacement by a carceral state. The professional-managerial strata from these populations are incorporated into the class structure of the larger system through affirmative action and pro-grams of diversity, a program of limited integration or assimilation of these strata into the larger society. But there remains a significant section of the intelligentsia that is scornful of this option, and who will likely in time come together with the oppositional culture of the youth and the older organic intellectuals of these communities to espouse and develop a de-colonial option. Since these communities are located in what used to be called "the belly of the beast" in the 1960s, these movements will ally with and draw sustenance from similar movements in the Caribbean, Africa, Latin America, Asia, the Pacific Islands, and Central Europe, and constitute a fundamental challenge to the system of white world supremacy, which was a constitutive feature of the founding of the Americas and the establishment of the capital-ist world economy. While the capitalist world economy itself is entering into a structural crisis, the inability of the workers' movements and the national liberation movements to transform capitalism in the past will be augmented this time by populations who will not accept the gift of assimilation but who will seek to overcome not only capitalism but its coloniality of power, of knowledge, and of being.

The old order is now in a period of transition, and the delinking of these internal colonies from the centers of power will constitute a significant and strategic rebuilding of old structures of power, knowledge, and being. It will foster a situation in which we are not likely to have a new system with global designs, but a system with a true plurality of centers, not of a universal society, but a pluri-versal one, where there is a genuine right of difference.

Samuel Huntington's Hispanic challenge is really a multifaceted challenge to the coloniality of power of the pan-European world, and especially to its declining hegemony, the United States of America. But this will be a liberation from the defensive, oppressive police of the world-system and a release of the concentrated power that will allow the rest of the world to dream their own freedom dreams, and to realistically take steps toward their realization.

Part II. Empirical Studies on Hybrid Identities

Chapter Nine

An Introduction to Empirical Examinations of Hybridity

Patricia Leavy

Hybridity research centers on the relationship between identity and context. Empirical studies of hybrid identities center on the dialectical and mutually productive relationship between a multiplicity of hybridized identities in a shifting, globalizing context. How do different groups, confronted with specific and diverse cultural forces, economic forces, and institutional settings, negotiate identity and cultural space within this context? In what ways are the cultural spaces created by the fissures between, and fusing of, divergent cultural elements in fact *productive spaces* in which identities are constructed and contested?

Empirical scholarship on hybrid identities draws on hybrid, postcolonial, critical race, and feminist theories in order to interrogate the complex processes of identity construction and meaning-making prevalent in the globalizing world. Using data derived largely on the micro level, scholars are conducting research that links "the particular" and "the universal" in multidirectional ways, as suggested by Iyall Smith in the introduction to this volume.

When thinking about this emerging body of research on identity, it is important to have a working understanding of "group identity." Most simply, group identity is dependent on an imagined community bound by the perception of shared heritage, history, or struggle (Leavy 2007). In his collective memory research on national identity, John Gillis (1994) suggests a national memory is shared by a group of people that are only attached by an assumed common identity resulting from the perception of shared history. In this regard, it is not surprising that interdisciplinary studies in collective memory are increasing exponentially, as, simultaneously, research on diasporized hybrid identities is increasing. Collective memory most generally refers to a set of shared, although contested, cultural narrative about the past. Collective memories are dependent on assumed group identities and have implications for how the past impacts the present in political, social, and cultural contexts. In this regard, the expansion of diasporized hybrid identities raises questions about how groups geographically divorced from their homeland self-identify, and thereby engage in rituals of collective remembering (and forgetting) that are pertinent to identity construction and identity politics.

Empirical investigations of hybridity explore the development of complex, relational, and shifting identities. Cultural studies scholar Stuart Hall (1992) refers to identities as "positionings" that are both dynamic and contextual. Grounded in critical theoretical perspectives, studies in hybridity challenge essentialist notions of identity (Terkessidis 2000). As such, hybridity scholarship has the potential to radically alter how identity politics are conceived both within and beyond the academy, particularly as the move towards public sociologies continues. The social justice underpinning of sociology, coupled with efforts toward making sociology useful to the public, creates a space for empirical investigations of hybridity to impact how disenfranchised groups conceptualize group identity for political, social, and economic purposes.

Advances in embodiment theory also underpin many explorations of the lived experiences of hybridity. At the forefront of this scholarship, Elizabeth Grosz (1995) distinguishes "inscriptive" and "the lived body" approaches to embodiment research. The inscribed body serves as a site where social meanings are created and resisted. Influenced by the work of Michel Foucault (1976) and Susan Bordo (1989), Grosz writes, "The body is not outside of history, for it is produced through and in history" (1995:148). The inscriptions may be "subtle" or "violent" but are ultimately cumulative in effect (141).

The way we sex or gender or race the body is deeply implicated in existing relations of power (141–142). It is in theories of "the lived body" that a clear link between embodiment research and phenomenology is evidenced. In embodiment scholarship, "the lived body" refers to people's experiential knowledge. Grosz is influenced by Merleau-Ponty (1962), who posits we must look at the "necessary interconnectedness" of the mind and body (Grosz 1995:86). He argued that experience exists between the mind and body (Merleau-Ponty 1962). Therefore, the body is not viewed as an object but rather as the "condition and context" through which social actors have relations to objects and through which they give and receive information (Grosz 1995:86). Put simply, the body is a tool through which meaning is created. Tami Spry (2006) suggests that in order to access experiential knowledge, researchers must find ways to access "enfleshed knowledge." This holistic view of experience as bodily, and of the mind and body as interconnected, has influenced empirical research on hybridity and identity development.

The relationship between theories of embodiment and explorations of hybrid identities can be viewed via an example. By way of illustration I turn to the issue of "the veil" first explored in the introduction to this volume. Building on anthropological research that focuses on the role of dress with respect to identity formation, Claire Dwyer (1999) conducted in-depth group interview research with forty-nine young British women regarding their gender and ethnic identity construction. Dwyer's research posits that dress becomes an over-determined signifier for Muslim women, with "the veil" becoming a primary discourse for the development of female Muslim identity. Dwyer's research explores how embodied differences are negotiated "in the construction and contestation of group identities and group boundaries" (1999:5). By drawing on notions of identity grounded in hybridity, Dwyer explores how her participants could construct alternative hybrid femininities as they move through different spaces.

In this context, research on the veil highlights the role the symbolic realm plays in identity development in a global context. As socially constructed imagery crosses formerly distinct cultural borders, further impacted by technological advances that allow for the immediate dissemination of images and texts, the role of mass-mediated imagery in identity struggles is simultaneously diluted and reified. In other words, in the contemporary landscape, in what ways do mass-mediated stereotyped images impact group identity?

How, for example, do images that exoticize "the Other" on the basis of the interconnections between gender, race, and ethnicity play out in an environment with shifting cultural borders?

Again, for continuity we can return to empirical studies of the veil. Mark Tekessidis (2000) examines how the veil has been used as a symbol of undesirable difference in Germany, despite cultural rhetoric about fostering a "hybrid community" (2000:224). Tekessidis, therefore, refers to the veil as an "anti-image of hybridity" (2000:224). In support of his argument, Tekessidis cites the 1998 decision by a school board in Baden-Wurttemberg that would not employ Fereshta Ludin, an Afghan-German teacher, because she wore a veil. The Secretary for Cultural Affairs referred to the veil as a "symbol of cultural demarcation," which was (ironically) deemed incongruent with "the principle of tolerance advocated by the Federal Republic of Germany" (Tekessidis 2000:226). Additionally, Tekessidis examined media images of women wearing veils (note how agency changes when using the term "veiled women" instead). The data consisted, in part, of photographs of model Yasmeen Ghaur (of Pakistani and German descent). The editors of the German version of GQ used Ghaur's veiled image to "contrast secularized openness with religious closure. But freedom and openness were reduced to the exotic strip. The strip guaranteed the inclusion of the exoticised female body in the machine of difference consumption, whereas the veil represented a barrier to this inclusion" (Tekessidis 2000:227).

In other words, according to Tekessidis, the veil prevents the dominant group from consuming "the Other," in bell hooks' terms (1990). Moreover, freedom for women is equated with embodying Western heterosexual male definitions of sexuality, artificially placed in opposition to religiosity. The trivialization and sexualization of women's freedom can be seen in other contexts as well. For example, Jeanne Kilbourne's (2000) work highlights the role of Western advertising in the trivialization of female freedom and power in the United States by equating liberation with the ability to purchase beauty products. In this light, empirical scholarship on Muslim-feminine identity contributes to our understanding of the complex and shifting relations of dominance and subordination that are in play as group identities are contested across spaces.

Organization of Part Two

It is important to note that the categories employed in this book (borderland identities, double consciousness, and so forth) are useful for organizational and conceptual purposes; however, these are overlapping, non-discrete categories. The slippage between many of these terms in hybrid theory, and the cross-pollination of identity processes, becomes much more evident when turning from theory to empirical scholarship. For example, in some instances distinctions between living with double consciousness or living with a diasporized hybrid identity are virtually obsolete. In this vein, section two offers a range of exemplars in the field of hybridity research, categorized by where they most fit with relation to existing theoretical scholarship.

The critical sociological perspective of the authors in part two culminates in a unique body of empirical scholarship that explores the complex relationships between the micro and macro levels of analysis. The contributors in this volume approach their research projects through a wide range of epistemological, theoretical, and cross-national perspectives while maintaining a commitment to investigating hybrid identities through a particular disciplinary lens. C. Wright Mills (1959) proposed that the promise of sociology manifests in the "sociological imagination," which calls on sociologists to examine the relationship between history and biography. The contributors in part two, each in their own way, have taken this as their challenge.

Borderland Hybrid Identities

In the globalizing world, borders are shifting, and individuals and groups respond to these shuffling borders via (re)negotiating collective identities. In this vein, shifting borders can both reify and alter group identities. The material and discursive borders of nation-states exist so that a sense of national identity can be forged by demarcating nationalistic borders and thereby separating the assumed identities of those within the borders from those outside of the borders. As hybrid theoretical scholarship posits, the concept of national identity itself is based on an idea of an "imagined community" (Anderson 1991, Bhabba 1990).

Some of the most profound borderlands work has developed out of Chicano identity studies. Gloria Anzaldúa's groundbreaking scholarship on the

Mexico-US border, detailed in *Borderlands/La Frontera*, pushes our understanding of borders way beyond geographic space, as she posits the border is a "vague and undetermined place created by the emotional residue of an unnatural boundary" (1987:3). Anzaldúa notes that within this context, "plural personalities" emerge, thus producing more heterogeneity:

> [She] learns to be an Indian in Mexican literature, to be Mexican from an Anglo point of view. She learns to juggle cultures. She has a plural personality, she operates in a pluralistic mode...she turns the ambivalence into something else. (1987:79)

Juan E. de Castro suggests this "borderland paradigm" transcends particular multicultural identities and implies those who walk the borders are able to "live in more than one culture at a time" (2001:117). Castro contrasts this perspective with earlier work by Richard Rodriguez (1982), in which he naturalized a dichotomy between Mexican identity and mainstream US identity (Castro 2001:103).

In the opening empirical chapter Trinidad Gonzales explores borderland identities as a particular enactment of hybridity. Gonzales provides an empirical case study of how the Mexico/United States transnational border impacted ethnic Mexican identity from 1900–1930. Gonzales explores the effect of the border, and the shift from an "open" border (one that can be crossed without a clear sense of national space) to a "closed" border (with a clear sense of crossing national spaces, and corresponding surveillance and policing procedures for doing so), as a means of accessing a more nuanced understanding of hybridity.

Double Consciousness

As noted in the introduction to this volume, "double consciousness" refers to a form of hybridity in which individuals occupy space within two cultural groups (DuBois 1996, 1903). Individuals who have developed a double consciousness must negotiate between these two group identities. Empirical examinations of this form of hybridity focus on individuals or groups who may experience "two-ness" (DuBois 1996, 1903) as they try to merge and negotiate competing identities. At times, this hybrid identity is conceptualized as experiencing a duality as a complex dialectic occurs between insider and outsider identities.

The majority of sociological research on double consciousness has centered on the African-American experience, and it is in this tradition that Sharlene Hesse-Biber and Emily Barko present their empirical study of African-American women attending predominantly white colleges. Hesse-Biber and Barko consider their research population first as a group that experiences "double jeopardy" with respect to their gender and racial status. Within this context, Hesse-Biber and Barko engaged in a multi-method qualitative interview study in order to explore the multiple racial identity negotiations this population engages in, and the various hybrid identity typologies that emerge as a result.

Tess Moeke-Maxwell's chapter on bi/multi racial Maori women's inclusion within New Zealand Mental Health Services has developed out of a confluence of personal and professional circumstances. In this vein, Moeke-Maxwell's chapter offers a highly personal account of the lived experience of double consciousness while simultaneously examining broader issues of raced and gendered corporeality within a particular institutional setting. Moeke-Maxwell self-identifies as a fair-skinned Maori (indigenous) and Pakeha (European/ New Zealander) lesbian. Within the society in which she grew up, Maori and Pakeha identities were constructed as dichotomous. Moreover, related experiences with alienation led her to seek mental health services, a context in which her Maori/Pakeha identities were again starkly polarized. These experiences, and later work as a mental health clinician, underscore Moeke-Maxwell's chapter, which argues for the development and use of a Maori hybridity concept. The author makes a persuasive case for encouraging a holistic model of "ethnic pluralism" that can be integrated into the assessment and intervention frameworks of the mental health system.

Women Occupying the Hybrid Space

As studies of hybridity initially emerged out of racial and ethnic identity scholarship, linkages between hybrid theory and hybrid gendered identities have not been robust. However, as hybrid theory has been gaining prominence in sociology, and studies in gender and sexual identity are on the rise, research on gender and the hybrid space are likely to increase. Moreover, in a post-September 11th context, increased attention has been paid to Muslim-American women's negotiation of competing femininities, which also contributes to our understanding of how women occupy the hybrid space.

It is likely that in the tradition of earlier feminist scholarship (Jaggar 1989, Sprague and Zimmerman 1993), this research too will challenge the dichotomous notions of gender, sex, and sexuality that limit acceptable notions of personhood within varying contexts. In this regard, feminist explorations of the hybrid space are also likely to challenge the myopic imagery that helps to culturally define femininity and masculinity.

Helen Kim's empirical study of women occupying the hybrid space builds on two decades of critical feminist scholarship that examines the interlocking nature of race, class, and gender as means of understanding how gender is enacted within "vectors of privilege and oppression" (Hill Collins 1991). Earlier feminist standpoint theory or standpoint epistemology, building on Karl Marx's ideal of class consciousness, posited that men and women occupy different positions (or standpoints) within the social order (a hierarchy), resulting in different earned perspectives (Hartsock 2004, Smith 1987). Later, black feminist thought or critical multicultural feminism posited that gender identities are negotiated at the interconnections of multiple status characteristics. It is within this context that Kim presents her empirical research on second generation Korean-American women attending a prestigious Midwest public university. Kim investigates how these women "do gender." In particular, Kim explores how these women negotiate competing femininities, including racialized femininities, as they simultaneously negotiate their gender and ethnic identities.

The Diasporized Hybrid

As discussed in the introduction to this volume, diasporized populations are tied to their homeland via a sense of shared national identity; however, they live beyond the physical borders of their homeland. As world borders continue to shift, becoming both more and less important, and hybrid theory allows for increasingly inclusive definitions of diasporas, empirical scholarship is investigating a wide range of diasporized hybrid identities. These studies address the diverse ways that diasporas adopt hybrid identities and/or maintain identities that are strongly connected to their homeland.

Bedelia Richards's work on the diasporized hybrid in Brooklyn, New York, considers the identity negotiations of West Indian Immigrants in Brooklyn. Richards posits that Brooklyn is a unique environment that is itself "a fusion of West Indian and American cultural influences" as a result of a history of Caribbean nationals seeking economic opportunities in New York. Through a qualitative research project, primarily reliant on in-depth interviews, Richards provides an examination of ethnic identification and cultural orientation among second-generation West Indian high school students in Brooklyn. Through this case study, Richards contributes to our understanding of the particular identity negotiations of this group within a unique city while also noting patterns that link this group's experiences to larger patterns with respect to diaspora hybrid identities.

Helene Lee's work focuses on how migration and labor histories have influenced the development of hybrid identities within the Korean diaspora. Lee's work explores two immigrant communities: Korean-Chinese and Korean-American, examining how these two groups create definitions of "Koreanness" by producing identities linked to their homeland. Rather than replicating research that studies hybridity in a unidirectional manner, Lee, paralleling the dialectical nature of globalizing processes, also considers migration patterns back to the homeland, South Korea. As such, her research raises important questions about how definitions of "authentic" Koreanness come to be, and what this means with respect to identity construction and negotiation. Lee uses empirical data collected from sixteen months of ethnographic research conducted in Seoul, South Korea, and semi-structured interviews with more than sixty research participants in order to explore the lived challenges of diasporized people who adopt a hybrid identity.

Third Space

Through the globalizing process, as multidirectional cultural pathways cross and intermingle, new spaces emerge, new hybrids. The "third space" emerges when two cultural forms interact to create a new form that is not reducible to the sum of its parts (Bhabha 1993). Empirical studies of the third space are shedding light on the complex cultural exchanges occurring and how varied groups occupy the third space. Many examinations of the third space consider the development of new cultural forms, such as hybrid forms of popular culture. For example, consider the urban musical genre called "British bhangra" that has emerged as a popular style of music regularly played on the radio and in dance clubs in Britain. This music combines elements of folk music from the Punjab people, located along the diverse and expansive borders of Pakistan and India, with black music genres and British pop music (Dudrah 2002:363). Specifically, British bhangra combines Punjabi lyrics, Indian drum beats, the dhol, black musical genres, and British pop sounds (Dudrah 2002:363). Both the emergence of this hybrid genre of music, as well as its acceptance into mainstream British music (and society), speak to larger issues pertaining to the arts, processes of cultural globalization, and identity negotiations among British South Asian audiences (Leavy 2008).

David Brunsma and Daniel Delgado's work contemplates whether or not, and in what ways, multiracial people exist in a third space. Springboarding off of previous research on racial identity and multiracial people, Brunsma and Delgado's chapter moves this conversation forward by drawing on hybrid theories of the third space and negotiating multiracial identity as a hybrid identity. Situating their scholarship in critical race theory, Brunsma and Delgado consider how multiracial people navigate space as their identities develop within vectors of privilege and oppression based on the intersections of race, class, gender, and sexuality. Moreover, Brunsma and Delgado consider the advantages and disadvantages of conceptualizing this process as a third space experience. Using data from a study of black-white multiracial people, Brunsma and Delgado explore the lived experience of occupying the third space while also theorizing about the usefulness of such conceptualizations.

Alex Frame and Paul Meredith uniquely contribute to the current body of knowledge on hybridity by taking their analysis into an institutional realm: the law. Frame and Meredith address "legal hybridity" as a third space hybrid form in which an interactive and productive space produces new opportunities that challenge and transcend present boundaries. By examining legal hybridity in relation to the Maori peoples of Autearoa/New Zealand, Frame and Meredith unravel the process of hybridization in which two customary systems engage in a complex interaction through which new forms become possible.

The Future of Empirical Hybrid Identities Research

As globalizing processes continue to rapidly transform issues of place, space, and identity, increases in hybridity scholarship, both theory and practice, will abound. The nature of this collection provides insights into what areas may be explored in future research. By and large, the scholars in part two have drawn on theories of hybridity and designed research projects employing conventional methods such as interviews, ethnography, and historical comparative methods. As our understanding of hybrid identities increases, research questions will be refined. Traditional qualitative methods may not suit every research project. I therefore suggest that methodological innovation is a primary area for future hybridity research, as already indicated by current methods literature.

Typically, theoretical advances promote methodological innovation. Hesse-Biber and Leavy (2006) identify a "methods lag" that can occur as theoretical scholarship opens up new research questions but traditional methodological tools are not able to "get at," reveal, or illuminate those aspects of social reality. When this occurs, new or "emergent" research methods may develop (Hesse-Biber and Leavy 2006). Currently, methodologists are building tools for accessing knowledge about the experience of hybridity as evidenced by the emerging field of indigenous and critical research practices (see Denzin, Lincoln, and Smith 2008). Coupling theoretical and methodological innovations will continue to expand the current body of knowledge on hybrid identities.

Chapter Ten

Conquest, Colonization, and Borderland Identities: The World of Ethnic Mexicans in the Lower Rio Grande Valley, 1900–1930

Trinidad Gonzales

This case study is of a border born from United States conquest and colonization that affected ethnic Mexican identity in the Lower Rio Grande Valley from 1900 to 1930. For simplicity, I use "ethnic Mexican" as a means to describe people of Mexican and México Texano cultural descent (Gutiérrez 1995:218, endnote 3). The Lower Rio Grande Valley is presently composed of Starr, Hidalgo, Cameron, and Willacy counties in the southern tip of Texas along the United States/Mexico border. The intent of this study is to examine how the United States/Mexico border affected ethnic Mexican group identity during a specific period. Group identities are how people unify themselves in relation to other groups of people. Three group identities existed from 1900 to 1930. They included the México Texano, Mexicano, and México Americano. The first two existed in 1900, while the last emerged by the 1920s. Identities by their nature are hybrid, but for analytical purposes this study traces the history of the border's effect on the existent México Texano and Mexicano identities (not their hybrid nature), and the emergence of the México Americano (hybrid) identity. By analyzing the border's affect on group identities over time, hybridity as a process is examined.

The change from an open border to a closed border led to the emergence of the México Americano identity by the 1920s – an identity that differed from the México Texano and Mexicano identities. The terms "open" and "closed" are not utilized in the literal sense. Instead, "open" denotes a border easily crossed without a clear sense of national spaces, and "closed" denotes a border policed and difficult to cross with a clear sense of national spaces. It is the contention of this case study that the México Texano and Mexicano group identities that existed in 1900 continued and changed by the 1920s, with some members of the former engaging in a reconstruction forming a new identity, México Americano, and the latter maintaining its identity. The change from an open border to a closed border occurred as a result of structural forces and human agency. It is important to note that this is not a structural history of a border affecting passive persons, but a historical analysis of structural forces and human agency as intertwined processes.

Theory and Concepts

A relational paradigm of identity centers my conception of group identity. How members of a group viewed themselves and their relations to another group as a means of centering their location within the world provides the best avenue for interrogating the meaning-making phenomena behind the labels groups of people used to identify themselves (Maines 2000, Lamont 2000). My methodology focuses on tracing the use of the labels México Texano, Mexicano, and México Americano as they appeared in printed documents. These texts include Spanish language newspapers, books, political speeches, letters, music lyrics, names of *mutualistas* (community-based mutual aid societies), and the English language version of these labels in contemporary scholarly works from 1900 to 1930. The use of these labels by various authors dispersed over space and time indicate their discursive power as identifiers. In essence, I accept that these labels truly reflected the ethnic Mexican community's internal sense of group identities.

An international border between two nation-states is a material and discursive phenomenon with a transnational history. Particular activities occur at border locations that do not happen at the center of a nation-state, such as cross-border commerce and immigration. Nationalism and citizenship as discourses also harden in border locations. An international border is a location that two nation-states utilize to mark their physical boundaries in order to distinguish their respective citizens from each other. How an international border originated and changed over time represents its history. Within this case study, the United States/Mexico border originated from the War of Aggression of 1846. The border changed over time as a result of colonization, nationalism, and citizenship. From 1848 to 1915 the border was relatively open. By 1915, the United States government began to police the border in an effort to close it. During the 1920s, the border was further closed as nationalism and citizenship gained importance at a macro and micro level. The change from an open to a closed border directly affected identities.

A meso-level analysis filtered through a historical narrative description is utilized to examine structural forces and agency over space and time (Jacobs and Spillman 2005:3, Sewell 2005). This case study examines the relationship between the macro phenomenon of a border and the micro phenomenon of group identity. I utilize the concepts of "construction" and "reconstruction" to describe group identity as a socio-historical process that describes continuity and change. Implicit for understanding group identity is "place construction," which describes how people construct space into a meaningful cultural and national place. Physical places, buildings, and other structures do not have agency but do affect how people conduct themselves and construct their identity, in particular when place construction becomes intertwined with processes of border formation, nationalism, and citizenship (Gupta and Ferguson 1997:4). For this case study I focus on place construction as it affected and was affected by the processes of border formation, nationalism, and citizenship in the Lower Rio Grande Valley during the early part of the twentieth century.

Hybridity is a process of intertwined macro and micro phenomena (Canclini 2003). The key argument for this case study is that the United States/Mexico border's closing led to the emergence of a new identity, México Americano. Thus, the macro-level phenomena of a policed border, nationalism, and citizenship, and the micro-level phenomena of group identity construction and reconstruction represents hybridity – if viewed as a process that encompasses these phenomena as a whole. Hybridity both stabilizes and destabilizes group identities, that is, construction and reconstruction. For the Lower Rio Grande Valley, by the late 1920s this process led to the existence of three group identities when only two existed during the early 1900s.

I use the concepts of nationalism and transnational within this chapter. Nationalism is an incomplete discourse where disparate people unify themselves in an imagined community (Anderson 1991). Conquest, colonization, and immigration represent transnational phenomena. Conquest and colonization occur when a national border crosses and/or divides a community. Immigration occurs when a person moves between two nation-states. The origins and development of the United States/Mexico border area is examined through a transnational lens that traces the history of a conquered community as a policed border, nationalism, and citizenship that acted as structural forces that affected ethnic Mexican identities.

Group Identities

The México Texano identity relates to ethnic Mexicans who developed a colonized transnational identity after 1848 within the United States. By colonized transnational identity I mean an identity construction where the conquered viewed themselves and the land they lived on as continuing to belong to the defeated nation, but adapted to an unsettled socioeconomic and political world created by conquest and colonization. México Texanos used both United States and Mexican institutions for dealing with political and economic problems after 1848. Most importantly, México Texanos worked along side Mexicanos during the early part of the 20th century to seek out solutions to problems all ethnic Mexicans faced in relation to racism and segregation. México Texanos maintained a strong sense of Mexican nationalism and were at best ambivalent United States citizens.

A Mexicano identity relates to people who developed an immigrant transnational identity as temporary residents of the United States and as non-United States citizens. By immigrant transnational identity I mean an identity where immigrants continued to view themselves as belonging to the nation they left, but adapted to an unsettled socioeconomic and political world created by their movement into a new national space. Mexicanos sought solutions to their political and economic problems within the United States by predominantly appealing to the Mexican government and to upper-class México Texanos. Both the Mexican government and upper-class México Texanos provided support to Mexicanos by maintaining shared ethnic Mexican socioeconomic and political networks that helped during times of crisis.

The México Americano identity relates to ethnic Mexicans who once exhibited a México Texano identity but re-constructed their identity to the former with an emphasis on United States nationalism and citizenship. Hence, a México Americano identity is the reconstruction of a México Texano identity that represented a change from a colonized transnational identity to a national identity. By national identity I mean an identity construction (in this case a reconstruction) where descendants of the conquered came to fully accept the conquering nation and the conquerors as their homeland and fellow citizens. Those with a México Americano identity distanced themselves from Mexicanos. México Americanos solely utilized United States institutions for their political and economic problems. While México Americanos distinguished themselves from México Texanos and Mexicanos based on an emphasis of United States citizenship and a desire for greater English proficiency, they did not abandon their cultural roots or Spanish language. It was through the voting booth, bilingual press, and lawsuits that México Americanos advocated for civil rights. México Americanos re-constructed an identity that eliminated the transnational quality that both México Texanos and Mexicanos shared.

Case Study

The Spanish settled the area known as the Lower Rio Grande Valley during the 1740s by establishing communities on both sides of the Río Bravo/Rio Grande. The settlements came under Mexican control in 1821, and the Republic of Texas claimed the area in 1836. The United States continued Texas' claims after it became a state in 1845. It was here that the United States first sent troops to enforce the Río Bravo/Río Grande as the boundary between both countries, and it was here that the first battles occurred in what became known as the Mexican War, or War of Aggression, of 1846. Despite the military victory by the United States, defeated Mexicanos living in what became known as the Lower Rio Grande Valley continued to live on both sides of the river, crossing back and forth as they pleased. As ethnic whites entered the area during the late nineteenth century, inter-ethnic relations exhibited a harmonious character that was punctuated by bursts of violence (Montejano 1987, González 1930b:102). Newcomers arrived in earnest with the railroad in 1904 and shifted the area's economy from ranching/merchant activities to commercial agricultural enterprises by the 1920s. Ethnic whites who arrived during the 20th century are labeled newcomers, while ethnic whites who arrived during the 19th century are labeled old-timers. Newcomers tended to isolate themselves, while old-timers integrated with ethnic Mexicans. Ethnic Mexicans by the 1910s lived in a harsher environment because of the economic shift and arrival of newcomers (Montejano 1987).

Ethnic Mexicans continued to construct the Lower Rio Grande Valley as a Mexican place during the first decade of the 20th century. Jovita González, a contemporary México Americana scholar from the area, wrote, "The Texas-Mexicans had lived so long in their communities that these were home to them – and home meant Mexico. They lived happily ignorant that they were foreigners in a foreign land" (González 1930a:467). The attitude González described existed because ethnic Mexicans at the beginning of the 1900s continued to influence important structures such as border crossings, economic activity, and educational activities. A result of ethnic Mexican continued power was the presence of Mexican nationalism on United States territory, and an open border.

In 1901 Henry Terrell, a United States attorney, recounted his visit to the area by stating that, "everything in this country is bought and paid for in Mexican money. In fact, it is difficult to believe that you are in the United States at all. Language, customs, people, and money are all Mexican" (*Brownsville Herald*, April 4, 1901). He also foreshadowed the changes the railroad would bring. "While a railroad to this end of the United States would be a great thing for commercial reasons and would soon become profitable, it would forever change one of the most lovely towns (Brownsville) of yesterday, into a town of today" (*ibid.*). The railroad arrived in 1904 and began the process that Terrell predicted.

One of the key structural factors that maintained the strength of a Mexican place and ethnic Mexican identities was the use of ferries to cross the Río Bravo/Rio Grande regularly. There existed 40 to 50 ferries operating from Brownsville to Roma (Department of Labor 1993, Reel 1, frames 0855–0856; Reel 5, frames 0175–0176; Reel 6, frames 0011–0015). The local immigration inspector in charge of Brownsville complained in a letter to his superior that the ferries operated unregulated and posed problems for controlling the flow of people crossing the river but noted shutting down the boats would create "a revolution in affairs in South Texas" (*ibid.* Reel 1, frames 0855–0856). The inspector stated, "To interfere with these boats will mean the interruption of a practice that has continued for generations, and necessarily with the comfort and convenience of the people living adjacent to the river" (*ibid.*). The everyday ease with which people crossed the border from 1900 to 1914 helps explain why a Mexican place construction and nationalism persisted. The persistence of this phenomenon resulted from an open border that facilitated the existence of the México Texano and Mexicano identities.

The importance of education for ethnic Mexicans, in particular the ability to read and write, dated to 1796 with the first efforts at providing public education (Kearney, et al. 1989:2). *Rancheros* and other ethnic Mexicans continued such educational efforts by seeking Mexican-trained educators to teach their children during the late 19th and early 20th centuries. For instance, Jovita González's father, a teacher from Saltillo, Coahuila, was hired because he had "the culture and training of Mexico" (E. E. Mireles and Jovita G. Mireles Papers, Autobiography: 4). The three educational institutions ethnic Mexicans controlled included religious schools, ranch schools, and the private Mexican schools (San Miguel Jr. 2001:8–13). Besides teaching students reading and writing, these institutions instilled pride in being Mexican by emphasizing Mexican history and nationalism. For instance, in 1887 Ellen Smith's family migrated from Rockport, Texas, and settled in Santa Maria, Hidalgo County, where she attended the Esterito School under the instruction of Don Juan Izquierdo. The schoolroom displayed a Mexican flag and the instruction included lessons about Mexican heroes. By 1898 the city of Matamoros, a border city across from Brownsville, founded a teachers college that emphasized a capitalist, positivist, Mexican nationalist curriculum as the official instruction for teachers from the area (Kearney, et al. 1989:7). Many of these teachers crossed the river to teach ethnic Mexican children on the United States side of the border. Names for schools reflect a group's socioeconomic and political position within a local community. So it is not surprising that local school names included Escuela Mexicana, Escuela Cinco de Mayo, and Colegio Fronterizo.

Ethnic Mexican literacy at the beginning of the 20th century reflected their educational efforts. In 1900 the literacy rate for the total population of the Lower Rio Grande Valley was 61 percent, and it rose to 72 percent in 1910, according to the United States Census Bureau (Gonzales 2008). These rates do not determine the ethnic breakdown for persons who were literate. However, the ethnic Mexican demographic majority, the community's commitment to education, and wide circulation of Spanish language newspapers strengthens the view of ethnic Mexican literacy. This evidence helps belie the myth of ethnic Mexicans as simply an oral community. México Texanos and Mexicanos maintained their worldview by controlling these educational institutions, particularly through a textual understanding of that world. As Anderson pointed out, print culture is an important factor for maintaining nationalism and identity (1991).

While ethnic Mexicans continued to influence these structures during the 1900s, United States colonization began in earnest by the 1910s with *barrioization*, the increasing expansion of public schools as the dominant educational institution for the area, and the restriction of ferries for crossing the Río Bravo/Rio Grande. *Barrioization* is the process by which ethnic Mexicans were segregated into separate neighborhoods as a method for socioeconomic and political control. Segregation occurred in the newcomer cities of Raymondville, Lyford, Sebastian, Harlingen, San Benito, La Feria, Mercedes, Weslaco, Donna, Alamo, San Juan, Pharr, McAllen, and Mission. These communities developed from train depots that began in 1904 and were controlled by newcomers who tended to view ethnic Mexicans as inferior. David Montejano states that these communities were "transplanted societies from the Midwest and the North," which brought racial segregation into the area (104). The cities operated as ethnic-white enclaves that disrupted the construction of a Mexican place and represented centers of United States colonization.

Public schools were institutions utilized for dismantling the construction of a Mexican place. During a United States holiday in 1914, a public school principal raised the United States flag, but "some of her Mexican patrons protested to the school board and she was advised to desist (from raising the United States flag) because it would be offensive to the Mexicans" (Department of Labor 1993, Reel 5, frames 0536–0539). Ethnic white parents protested against the school board's actions, and the United States flag was flown as a symbol of sovereignty. The effort to enforce United States symbolic sovereignty within the school system did not always emanate from newcomers, but from México Texanos as well. José Tomás Canales, elected Cameron County superintendent of public schools in 1912, instituted an English-only policy for schools. He probably instituted this policy to prevent school segregation between ethnic white and ethnic Mexican children based on language differences (Ribb 2001). It became a common practice in Texas to segregate ethnic Mexican children to inferior schools based on their weak English skills. Canales's reaction represented an effort to ensure ethnic Mexican children received a quality education. The threat of segregation reflected the macro-phenomenon of United States colonization that prompted his policy decision. This structural change did more than just train ethnic Mexican children to speak English, it also created a process to instill United States nationalism into the worldview of ethnic Mexican children. Reflecting on this event, Canales stated:

> I can safely say that from 1912 on, our common schools in Cameron County began to render a very valuable service, not only by training future generations, but in transforming the Latin American children from regarding themselves as 'Mexican' by becoming loyal citizens of the United States of America. (Canales 1945:18–19)

Taken together, both events help illuminate how United States colonization incorporated nationalism as a discourse to help dislodge the ethnic Mexican view of the Lower Rio Grande Valley as a Mexican place. The newcomers wanted a clear claim to the area as American and utilized nationalism as a discursive weapon to achieve that aim through the displaying of the United States flag and English-only polices for public schools. As a whole, this process represented colonization at a discursive level that, once linked to a material closing of the border, would affect in particular the México Texano identity.

By 1907 the Brownsville immigration inspector created guidelines to limit the flow of people who used ferries along the Río Bravo/Rio Grande. He notified boatmen that the only legal ports of entry were Brownsville, Santa Maria, Hidalgo, and Rio Grande City. Only registered Mexicans living along the river could cross back and forth on county licensed ferries. The new guidelines stated that no "diseased" or "contract" labor Mexicans should be allowed to cross the river other than at legal ports of entry. Boatmen in violation of these orders would be fined up to $1,000 and/or sentenced to two years in prison (Department of Labor 1993, Reel 1, frame 0867). These efforts failed to materialize, and the border continued to operate as it did during the late 19th century. However, the dismantling of the ferry system did begin during 1915 as a result of the México Texano Revolt.

While the process of newcomer colonization began by the 1910s, it did not close the border. Thus, the structural shift from an open to closed border originated during this period. Before the border could truly close, both material and discursive shifts were necessary. Even though the United States's symbolic presence increased during this period through the use of flags and English-only policies for public schools, it would take more to close the border. Not until two other structural changes occurred did the border close. First, the United States began to police the border in order to end the free flow of people crossing the river. Second, United States and Mexican nationalism linked itself to citizenship concerning voting and civil-rights policies during the 1920s. The first change represented a material closing of the border, and the second change represented a discursive closing of the border. These changes occurred from the 1910s to the 1920s and represent the closing of the border that left a lasting affect on ethnic Mexican identity construction.

In response to *barrioization*, school segregation and violence against ethnic Mexicans, both Mexicanos and México Texanos met at the 1911 *Primer Congreso Mexicanista* in Laredo to discuss solutions to their community's plight. The congress represented a peaceful response to the increased hostility that ethnic Mexicans faced during the last phases of colonization. Delegates from different parts of Texas, including the Lower Rio Grande Valley, converged on Laredo to reaffirm their Mexican nationalism, cultural pride, and unity (Orozco 1992:170–171, *Primer Congreso* 1912:3–5). Of the 36 official delegates, eight were from the Lower Rio Grande Valley (22 percent of the official delegates). The delegation from the Lower Rio Grande Valley represented a mix of individuals that were either United States or Mexican citizens. Their ethnicity and Mexican nationalism operated as a unifying element in this first statewide meeting concerning issues of discrimination.

It is important to note that the speakers' understanding of rights in 1911 continued a 19th-century notion of natural rights. The difference between current notions of civil rights and natural rights is that the former is a concept of rights granted only to citizens, and the latter is a concept of rights granted to persons in general. As nationalism and citizenship strengthened during the 1920s, the concept of civil rights replaced that of natural rights. For México Texanos and Mexicanos, the concept of natural rights was expressed through Mexican liberalism, and they objected to discrimination against ethnic Mexicans as violations of their natural rights "to life, liberty, and the pursuit of property." Thus, the congress represented a transnational phenomenon because ethnicity – not citizenship – unified México Texanos and Mexicanos. Instead, descendants of defeated México Texanos and Mexicanos expressed unity through Mexican nationalism and an understanding of natural rights. A result of the congress was the creation of the *Gran Liga Mexicanista*. Both México Texanos and Mexicanos were allowed to join this *mutualista* (mutual aid society). The primary purpose of the league was to provide protection for ethnic Mexicans against discrimination and violence. However, the league failed to materialize into a viable organization because ethnic Mexicans continued to appeal to the Mexican government, elites, and local *mutualistas* for protection.

The continued loss of socioeconomic and political power after the congress by ethnic Mexicans explains the México Texano Revolt of 1915. The revolt, popularly known as the Plan de San Diego, represented a violent response to the last phase of United States colonization that sought to return South Texas to Mexico (Sandos 1992). In their manifesto, the leaders of the revolt referred to issues of discrimination and violence against ethnic Mexicans. They stated: "How does one remain indifferent and accepting of such civil abuses? How does one allow discriminatory offenses against our people? Or has our deep humanity and patriotism dissipated? No! It slumbers but it is easily wakened" (my translation; Sandos 1992:95). México Texanos and Mexicanos fought against the United States military and other forces. Because the revolt was a local insurgency against the United States, commanders constantly complained about their inability to distinguish ethnic Mexicans as either friend or foe.

Space does not allow for an extended examination of the insurgency, but there were over seventy engagements in total that ended with the revolt's failure (Rocha 1981:279). The largest and longest firefight lasted over two hours as United States soldiers chased eighty insurgents across the Río Bravo/Rio Grande into Mexico from the United States. Mexican forces provided covering fire for the insurgents as they crossed the river. The engagement resulted in 3,000 rounds fired (Department of State 1971:812.00/16302). As the result of cross-border raiding, the United States military dismantled the ferry system along the river and limited border crossing to official ports of entry.

In response to the revolt, it is estimated that Texas Rangers and newcomer paramilitary groups killed 300 to 3,000 ethnic Mexicans during what became known as the *matanza* (massacre) of 1915. One historian points out that ethnic Mexicans killed represent a higher rate of deaths than Argentina's Dirty War of 1976–1983 in a shorter amount of time (Ribb 2001: note 1, 2). The killing of ethnic Mexicans became such a normal practice that E. P. Reynolds, immigration inspector in charge at Brownsville, failed to begin deportation proceedings for Pablo Diablo, a Mexican citizen, after Texas Rangers captured him in Pharr. He stated, "[Diablo] will probably be kept in jail for some time, if he is not lynched." In the same report, Reynolds stated 31 ethnic Mexicans were killed in a 24-hour period (Department of Labor 1993, Reel 5, frames 0202–0204). Cosme Casares Munoz recalled this incident in an oral interview (1987). Texas Rangers lynched 15 ethnic Mexicans on one side of Alamo, a newcomer city, and another 15 on the other side of the city, he stated. One was taken into custody.

Newcomers created black lists that targeted ethnic Mexicans for death. Their contribution to Texas Ranger and other law enforcement extra-legal killings facilitated the process of ethnic cleansing, according to R. B. Creager, who testified in front of a special Texas investigative committee looking into Texas Ranger activities (State of Texas 1919:355). As a result of the *matanza*, many ethnic Mexicans fled to the Mexican side of the river for safety. The use of violence to discipline ethnic Mexicans regardless of their culpability in the revolt marked the border on the north side as belonging to the United States. The ethnic Mexican view that the Lower Rio Grande Valley was a Mexican place under United States jurisdiction began to shift after this point to the view that the area was an American place with a Mexican past. México Texanos began to see themselves as foreigners on foreign land, and this growing awareness strengthened during the 1920s. Thus, the revolt reveals the microphenomenon of human agency in relation to the macrophenomenon of United States colonization, which was exhibited through the policing of the border and the *matanza*. The outcome of this clash led to a strengthened United States colonization and a permanent retreat from the use of political violence by ethnic Mexicans.

World War I marked an important turning point for México Texano identity construction. The small number of México Texanos who served became the vanguard for adopting United States nationalism as part of their identity. However, most México Texanos continued to be ambivalent about being United States citizens, especially in light of the *matanza*. As a result, many México Texanos failed to register for the draft. José de la Luz Sáenz, a World War I veteran, stated that two types of México Texanos avoided the draft. The first group did so because public school officials never inculcated México Texanos with Americanism. Instead, officials treated México Texanos as foreigners. The second group evaded the draft because of discrimination the community suffered. To make matters worse, German propagandists took advantage of this tension by encouraging México Texanos not to serve a country that discriminated against them (de la Luz Sáenz 1933:13). The *matanza*, failed Americanization, and discrimination explain México Texano evasion of the draft. Despite these factors, a small group of México Texanos served in World War I. The veterans came to use their service for understanding not only their relationship to the United States, but to other ethnic Mexicans. These México Texanos became the first group that engaged in a reconstruction of their identity to México Americano during the early 1920s.

Policing of the border, nationalism, citizenship, and restrictions on voting rights further closed the border materially and discursively. Beginning in 1915, the border was policed in earnest. After the United States military left the Lower Rio Grande Valley, mounted inspectors continued to patrol the border. The border patrol replaced the mounted inspectors in 1924, creating a more effective military force, but one still not large enough to prevent all crossings. By 1917, the United States Congress passed the first set of restrictive immigration laws for Mexican immigrants. Mexicanos crossing into the United States needed to pay a head tax of $8 and pass a literacy test. Both the policing of the border and new immigration restrictions led to a material closing of the border that once was freely crossed on a daily basis. During the 1920s, United States and Mexican nationalistic expressions increased, and voting rights in the United States were restricted to citizens. These changes divided the ethnic Mexican community along citizenship. As a result, ethnic Mexicans engaged in a place reconstruction of the Lower Rio Grande Valley from a Mexican place to an American place by the late 1920s. These structural changes, both material and discursive, created an environment ripe for change concerning ethnic Mexican identity construction. Thus, the emergence of the México Americano identity by a small group of World War I veterans, coupled with these structural changes, created a situation suitable for the process of identity reconstruction to expand to the larger México Texano community.

México Americano veterans began civil rights organizations throughout Texas that reflected their identity during the 1920s. Organizations such as the Order Sons of America (OSA), Order Knights of American (OKA), and League of Latin American Citizens (LLAC) embraced United States nationalism and citizenship as important components for advocating civil rights. The first two organizations began during the early 1920s, while the last group began in 1927 at the Harlingen Convention. The convention was an effort to unite the OSA and OKA into a unified statewide civil rights organization. Instead they remained divided, and the LLAC was formed as a third group with chapters predominantly located in the Lower Rio Grande Valley. The convention was a key turning point concerning relations between México Americanos and Mexicanos, and it receives detailed attention below. Eventually some chapters of the OSA, OKA, and the LLAC merged in 1929 to form the League of United Latin American Citizens (LULAC), which became the first statewide and national México Americano civil rights organization. Mexican citizens were excluded from LULAC (Orozco 1992).

Simultaneously during the 1920s, the Mexican government created two organizations within the United States to protect its citizens and promote Mexican nationalism. The *Comisión Honorífica* and the *Cruz Azul* were formed during a Mexican consular convention held in San Antonio in 1921. Both organizations excluded non-Mexican citizens from participating. The *Comision Honorificas* dealt with providing legal protection for Mexicanos, and the *Cruz Azul* provided access to health care resources. The *Cruz Azul* also organized Mexican national celebrations and supported educational efforts, such as the creation and maintenance of Mexican private schools. Local consuls organized and oversaw these *mutualistas* (Franco n.d.:42–49, 121–127). It is unclear whether México Texanos and México Americanos received aid from these organizations despite their exclusion. In all probability, México Texanos and México Americanos did at least benefit from the creation of Mexican schools, Spanish language libraries, and celebration of Mexican cultural events. However, it is clear that the *Comisiones Honorificas* and the Mexican consul only provided legal protection for Mexican citizens (Franco n.d.). Prior to the 1920s, the Mexican government provided protection for México Texanos even though they were not Mexican citizens. The Mexican government's shift from protecting ethnic Mexicans in general to only Mexicanos affected México Texanos and México Americanos directly. This structural change represented a new emphasis on citizenship by the Mexican state at the same time that the United States restricted voting rights to citizens only.

Alien voting rights were eliminated for all elections in the United States by 1926. Prior to the 1920s the right to vote was seen as a natural right not limited by citizenship. Alien residents who intended to become citizens could vote. As a result of the changed voting regulations, Mexicanos were barred from participating in the electoral process and, therefore, could no longer operate as political allies for México Texanos in the United States. The act of Mexicano alien residents living on either side of the border and crossing freely to participate in United States elections ended by the 1920s. The policing of the river and the restriction of voting rights effectively closed the border both materially (armed force) and discursively (citizenship). Likewise, the Mexican state's new emphasis on only protecting Mexicanos left México Texanos and México Americanos in a precarious position.

In 1927, México Americano and Mexicano activists met in Harlingen to form a state-wide civil rights organization. The last attempt to form such an organization occurred at *El Primer Congreso Mexicanists* in 1911. At that congress, ethnic Mexicans united based on their ethnicity and Mexican nationalism. At the Harlingen Convention a contentious debate broke out among ethnic Mexican activists over the issue of citizenship. A small but prominent group of México Americanos led by José Tomás Canales, Alonso S. Perales, and José de la Luz Sáenz forced a motion through the proceedings that their new civil rights organization, League of Latin American Citizens, be solely composed of United States citizens (Orozco 1992, esp. chapter 4). As mentioned already, the original intent of the gathering was to unite the OSA and OKA into one civil rights organization. The issue of citizenship ruptured internal ethnic Mexican relations at the conference, with more than half the delegates storming out in protest. Prior to 1927, and particularly before World War I, ethnic Mexican civil rights efforts never depended on the principle of citizenship. Instead, these earlier efforts focused on a Mexican liberalist ideology of natural rights and ethnic unity. A rationale for excluding Mexicanos from the new civil rights organization, according to Perales and other México Americanos who attended the convention, rested on the tactical decision to use the vote as a political weapon. México Americano leaders found the continued strength of Mexican nationalism among Mexicanos prevented them from becoming United States citizens with voting rights (Orozco 1992:230–231, 242–245). The Harlingen Convention represented a defining moment for United States conquest, colonization, and the closing of the United States/Mexico border.

Thus, the divide created by the convention did not solely occur because of México Americano desires to be patriotic United States citizens. The Mexican state's shift concerning providing protection to Mexicanos only created this divide as well. México Americano leaders pointed out that Mexicanos had the *Comisión Honorífica* and the *Cruz Azul*, while México Texanos and México Americanos had no such protective organizations (Orozco 1992:246–247). The division at the Harlingen Convention represented the choices México Americanos made in relation to the changed structural world of increased United States and Mexican nationalism, emphasis on citizenship, and a closed border. Emphasis on citizenship by both countries left México Texanos and México Americanos in a state of limbo.

In response to the exclusion of Mexicanos from LLAC, an editorial from *El Cronista del Valle* lamented the loss of ethnic unity. The editorial blasted the LLAC for excluding Mexicanos. While supporting the league's efforts at pursuing civil rights in general, the editorial stated, "To feel humiliated because we are not considered members of said league is an aberration, because this exclusion implies that the rights extended to Mexican citizens and to American citizens of Mexican descent are disregarded" (my translation, *El Cronista del Valle*, October 12, 1927). Thus, the Harlingen Convention and its aftermath represented the choices ethnic Mexicans made in response to the macro processes of a closing border. While some México Texanos and Mexicanos continued the discourse of ethnic unity to the 1930s, it eventually declined. As the Río Bravo/Rio Grande truly became an international division, a community once united across the border through expressions of Mexican nationalism and ethnic unity during the early 20th century divided itself based on citizenship into what David Gutierrez described as a world of "walls and mirrors" (1995). The wall of citizenship and the mirror of a similar socio-cultural past became the norm for the 20th-century world of ethnic Mexicans living along the river as their political-economic situation evolved along different paths depending on what side they lived on.

Conclusion

By the late 1920s, the México Texano, Mexicano, and México Americano group identities existed within the ethnic Mexican community in the Lower Rio Grande Valley. The closing of the border and the choice to reconstruct an identity from México Texano to México Americano represented an intertwined process of macro- and micro-phenomena – hybridity. The border as a material and discursive location changed over time as a result of structural forces emanating from the nation-states of the United States and Mexico, and local responses. While the focus of this case study is an examination of the emergence of the México Americano identity as hybrid in a particular space and time, the use of a meso-level analytical lens to examine the process of hybridity, group identity, and the border is something historians should consider as an alternative to postmodern methodologies that emphasize deconstruction. Deconstruction, while important for analyzing systems of power, results in the presentation of hybridity, group identity, and the border as solely discursive phenomena. A meso-level analysis of hybridity, group identity, and the border, on the other hand, allows for an examination of structural forces that affected people and their shared responses – thus centering people as agents in their lives even if restricted by outside forces.

Chapter Eleven

Neither Black Nor White Enough – and Beyond Black or White: The Lived Experiences of African-American Women at Predominantly White Colleges

Sharlene Hesse-Biber and Emily Brooke Barko

Introduction

> I never really had a strong connection to black people, or people of color...not that I couldn't relate to the people of color in my university, but those students of color here got this image from me and completely shut me out. They were thinking, 'Oh, that girl thinks she's white, why does she want to join our group?' I don't have the same stereotypical kind of black background as they do, and I often resent when they say 'Oh, you're white.' Then you start to think about it, and then I will ask them: 'What is white?' And they respond, 'Oh, you talk white.' I speak like an educated person, but that doesn't mean I'm white (I, 18).

This excerpt is from a recent interview conducted with a woman of color who currently attends a predominately white northeastern college. While she identifies herself as a black woman, the black community at her college does not fully accept her. She comments on her torn emotions: "I don't under-stand why I'm forced to have to choose one side or the other, the left or the right, black or white…why can't I be both, or even, why can't I just be the way I want to be, you know?" Among her white friends, she often feels she is not "white enough." This is a recurring feeling among these African-American women, and it guided much of our research in this study. In particular, our research explores a conception of "double consciousness" (DuBois 1903), in which someone experiencing double consciousness is advantaged and disadvantaged – able to negotiate multiple spaces, and yet not a member of either group or world. In DuBois's words, such a person is "always looking at one's self through the eyes of others" (1903:3).

Background and Research Problem

While colleges seek to achieve diversity, perceptions regarding the goal and meaning of diversity often miss the impact of cultural and racial/ethnic factors on the minorities' racial identity and self-esteem. There remains a lack of attention to minority students' experiences, expectations, and satisfaction once they come to college. While affirmative action, initial academic support, and enrichment initiatives created a positive impact on equalizing access, these policies also nurtured a climate ripe for backlash on the part of majority students toward minorities they perceived as being given special treatment and admission, not based on their merit, but on their minority status (Feagin and Picca 2007).

Persons of color who attend historically white colleges often live within diverse social worlds. They are bound by the macrocosm, the larger popular American-white culture, but they also racially identify with a specific subculture. This dual identity presents these students with a very unique role-conflict; they are simultaneously "insiders" and "outsiders," and there is the challenge of to what extent they integrate aspects of these different cultures. In addition, some students of color, like the woman cited earlier, remark on identity dilemmas stemming from differences in social class upbringing that make them appear "too white" to certain groups of color and not "white enough" for their white peers. These conundrums often affect their sense of racial identity.

Research Focus and Inquiry

We are particularly interested in the lived experiences of African-American women attending predominately white colleges. African American-women comprise a statistical majority among female minorities (US Department of Education 2006). African-American women's enrollment in college far outnumbers their male counterparts, where they continue to earn two-thirds of all African-American bachelor's degrees awarded yearly (*Journal of Blacks in Higher Education* 2007:1). As women and minorities, they experience "double jeopardy" with regard to their racial background as well as their gender status; and "triple jeopardy" if their social class places them "outside" the dominant group. They must also deal with a growing minority student gender imbalance.

This research project provides a mixed-methods approach (Creswell and Plano-Clark 2006) to understanding the lived experience of African American females, especially with regard to issues of self esteem and racial identity, as well as ascertaining those factors within their pre-college and college environments that might make some women of color vulnerable to racial identity and self-esteem dilemmas in college.

Participants

We conducted a snowball sample of in-depth interviews with African-American women at one predominantly white northeastern college. We followed up with interpretative focus groups of three to five individuals who were part of our in-depth interview protocol. Subjects (aged 18 to 21) came from working-middle to upper-middle class families and volunteered for interviews, giving their written consent to be asked questions concerning their experiences as related to the study. All respondents were aware of strict confidentiality and could decline to answer any questions asked.

The primary investigator, a white female professional, conducted most of the interviews. Her characteristics might have had both positive and negative effects on the interview process, but this study asserts that qualitative research is a reflexive process in which both subject and interviewer can learn and share with one another based on both their commonalities and differences. Interviewer-interviewee diversity in many instances leads to rich and provocative results (Edwards 1990).

Data Analysis

Data was analyzed using a qualitative "grounded theory" approach (Charmaz 1995). Through the methods dictated by this technique, preliminary analyses of the interviews were conducted as the interviews were being collected. Interviews were then coded thematically and reviewed, evaluated, and reevaluated through the memo-writing process. Grounded theory develops theory during the research process through a continuous interplay between analysis and data collection. It is rooted in the perspective that data interpretations include the perspectives and voices of the people being studied. It differs from more deductive types of general theory because it is generated and developed through data collection and actual research. Inductive methods start with individual cases and develop more conceptual categories to synthesize and understand data patterns. Levels of abstraction are built upon the data to be refined by gathering further data. The investigator must then study the meanings, intentions, and actions of the research participants.

The first step in our grounded theory approach was coding, which was the link between collecting data and developing an emergent theory to explain it. Initial coding was conducted with a line-by-line examination of the data and defining the events occurring in it. This helped build the analysis from the ground up without becoming wedded to a preconceived theoretical perspective. We then conducted focused coding, which uses earlier codes that reappeared in initial coding to sift through large amounts of data. It is more directed, selective, and conceptual than line-by-line coding. We clarified our categories with focused coding by examining all of the data covered and identified the variation within and between the various categories.

Memo-writing was the intermediate step between coding and drafting our analysis. Preliminary unstructured memos helped sort data into topics, define how categories are connected in the overall process, and note interesting ideas and excerpt interesting data. Memo-writing led to theoretical sampling, where we collected further data in our research. Memos simultaneously analyzed previously collected data while shaping future research questions in a reflexive and co-evolving process. We extracted theory directly from the respondents' experiences by allowing the respondents to drive the research and our findings. Through grounded theory, we can become translators presenting respondents' experiences to the world in their own voices.

African-American females attending predominately white northeastern colleges experience a series of identity conundrums depending on their degree of "perceived belonging" to white and black communities prior to college. Our grounded theory analysis uncovered three distinct categories of women whose narratives, for the most part, demonstrate different racial identity scenarios.

Group One consisted of women raised in primarily white communities where their sense of being "different" was a non-issue. They negotiated their first racialized identity in college and experienced being neither "white enough" (skin too dark to sun-bathe with friends, body too big to wear trendy "white" attire, and appearance too black to meet parents of a white boyfriend) nor "black enough" (skin too light, language and dress "too white," and music and social engagement selection decidedly not "black").

Women in Group Two racially self-identified as black prior to college and found that their experiences with whites' negative stereotyping in college strongly aligns them socially and politically with the black campus community. Group Two women eschew those black women who do not identify strongly with the black community (e.g., those with white boyfriends, those who socialize with white friends), perceiving them as outsiders who are "too white" and without allegiance to their racial group.

Women of Group Three have a racial identity aligned with a diverse community prior to college. They are less likely to identify with any specific racial group in college but select from a range of peer groups based more on their compatibility and general interests. Their racial identity is just one of many different aspects of who they are.

We will examine the lived experiences of each group in detail.

Group One: Neither Black Nor White Enough

For this group, difference is a non-issue in childhood. This creates a strong sense of identity in a world where racism seemingly does not exist; however, the consequences of this background in college can be calamitous as respondents often find themselves in a place of liminality or in "no-(wo)man's land," where they do not quite fit into groups of black or of white.

Interviewee 005: Becoming White in College or Being Just Who She Is?

Interviewee 005 is the primary example of Group One's characteristics. She comfortably aligns herself with the white community but feels subtle reverberations that she might not wholly belong in a white group. She grew up "colorblind" without a cognizance of race until entering college.

Growing up, 005 did not feel different from other people. She says, "I just never thought I was different from anyone. I'd never saw, I knew I was black, but I didn't see...it wasn't a problem then" (V, 5). She still socializes with white friends on campus, but this is not because of race; 005 exclaims, "I've always just seen it to be friends with the people that I share similar tastes and dislikes with" (V, 4). She adds, "I've never been able to have a predominantly black group of friends. I think it's just the people I've been around, it's like difficult sort of...I just think I don't fit this stereotypical black form, not form, or personality, character" (V, 4). She adds that she does not listen to black music or dress "black" (V, 5), reiterating, "I'm just not that stereotypical black girl or person" (6).

She must decide if she is black or if she will choose to be black upon coming to school, but she is uncomfortable with such a choice. It's not until 005 encounters diversity and feels she has to make a choice that she finally feels different or unaccepted, stating, "I wasn't used to not being accepted by people because I'm a certain way" (V, 6). She recalls the specific situation when she lost her color-blinds, stating, "Well...freshman year you go into [the dining hall] and you'll see certain tables. And I would find myself confused because there was an all-black section and Asians, and then it was like whites" (V, 6). Subsequently, rather than choose a table based on race, 005 decides, "With my friends, I was just always the only black person there...I didn't feel different in that group, but I felt I would feel different if I was with all of the [black people]" (V, 6).

She feels a little uncomfortable around groups of black people in college because "no one was really like [her], they didn't like the same music [she] did, didn't speak the way [she] did, didn't come from the same background that [she'd] come from" (V, 7). She lives with other black girls, but she is adjusting to feeling comfortable around them. Indeed, when asked if she is going to try to move toward the black community in college, 005 responds, "I'll probably stay where I am, just because it's all I've really known (V, 9)." She yearns for a nonexistent middle-ground when it comes to "picking sides";

she would not like to be solely aligned with the white community, and though we see she tends toward a midpoint between black and white communities, she is clearly leaning toward the latter.

She does not think she will "have to move over [to the black or white side]" (9), but understands her upbringing could help illuminate this decision. We get the sense that 005 has ostensibly grown up with some of the privileges of whiteness, including the ensuing privilege of seeing oneself as raceless. She argues that she is not a stereotypical black person, and while she is reluctant to talk about relationships in terms of skin color, she does, in fact, understand predominant notions of blackness.

It is not until college that 005 begins to feel different when she is with other black people who are unlike her. When confronted with race and choices of diversity, 005 chooses to comfortably "stay white." We might deduce that this is why she does not feel compelled to choose between black or white (as do most of our respondents). However, there is unspoken tension here as 005 talks about feeling both comfortable and "in the middle" when she is with the white group. 005 is an exception, for most of our respondents are left in a netherworld that is not black or not white enough.

Interviewee 013 also became cognizant of her racial identity upon entering college. She recalls, "I was friends with mostly guys in high school, and they were all white except for one who was half African-American and half Irish, so [my minority status] would enter our conversations in a joking fashion...It wasn't really until I got to this [predominantly white] college where something, people talk about it all the time here, that I started really having to think about it because people are always like...it's always being talked about at [this college], the difference between being a minority at [this college] and being a white student at [this college] and how that all plays out" (VIII, 1). Race was once a non-issue for 013, but things changed when she entered college. She says:

> I felt that you had to take sides...I came in with a lot of views, political views and race views that are very different from most of the other minority students here, I feel, so when I became more politically active on campus and people would say to me, 'But you're black, you're supposed to approve of this, this is what you do as a black woman of color. Affirmative action helps you, this is a good thing,' and I said, 'No, there's nothing to do with it. Race doesn't play a role in that.' So I think it was kind of, there was a

forcing, you were on one side or you were on the other of this 'how does race play' (XIII, 2).

Unlike most "colorblind" respondents in Group One, 013 holds onto her racial blinders and refuses to acknowledge any differences or privileges that may be maintained or withheld based on race. She states, "I'm vocal in my disapproval of the more extreme views that [race] was a huge problem and that race was this defining characteristic that made or [broke] your experience here at [this college], and if you were black you had one experience, if you were white you had a different experience" (XIII, 2).

Negative Case Examples of Group One

Unlike 005 and 013, many within this group struggle with feeling not black or white enough. We call these "negative case examples" because respondents have dealt with issues of difference before and throughout their college experience. Taken as a whole, these interviewees can be characterized by feeling different from the very beginning, growing up in tandem within an environment that lacks diversity and leads to a feeling of being not black or white enough. For example, 002 recounts being called "Oreo" and other times a "Huxtable," and 010 is often deemed "white girl" and, like 002, an "Oreo." As a consequence, many of these interviewees try to either achieve whiteness or to prove blackness in order to find some fit among their peers in college.

Feeling Difference in (Non)Diversity

Respondents in this group share memories of always feeling different because of skin color. For example, 001 states, "I've always been the lone black girl, you know, in my group of white girlfriends...there were probably like three African-American or just AHANA kids in my class" (I, 3). She recalls her surprise at hearing one of her classmates declare that she could not play the role of her sister in a school play because she was black. Difference is always an issue in an environment lacking diversity.

Similarly, 003 explains, "Most of the time in classes I've been the only African-American person or woman most of the time, graduating as one of only three black students in a class of 46" (III, 1). She explains, "It feels isolating...It just feels like I don't know what to say, or how to feel part of the group, because it will come out that I'm different, like I'm hiding it, but it's like...there's like a moment where it's like, 'Oh, she's different'" (III, 10).

She faces ominous fears that she will be found out or forced to "come out" with her difference in time.

Body compositions also play a role in marking difference. One respondent discusses how her changing body received varying responses depending upon which cultural world she was inhabiting – black or white. Interviewee 018 recalls thinking:

> Okay, I am different...[During puberty] one of my friends was like, 'Wow, you have big boobs,' and I'm like, 'Okay, is that bad?' And my family...looked at me like I'm weird, but when I went back home, having a bigger top is actually, you're thought of as being mature. So I was like...two different worlds...and I felt like one world embraced my figure and another world didn't. (XVIII, 3)

Skin color, hair, speech, and body shape highlight difference at an early age for respondents growing up in non-diverse settings, and understanding speech and appearance in terms of black or white entails connotations of good or bad that are contextually in flux.

Not Black or White Enough: Making a Choice

These respondents feel ostracized from both groups. For instance, 001 exclaims, "I feel like I kind of wasn't myself with either of the groups. Because I was always too white for the kids, the neighborhood friends, who were like, 'Oh, she's white, dah dah dah dah,' and then my friends in my class was kind of like guarded against, because I couldn't have them over...just the contrast between my white public school friends...I felt like I wasn't as good as the other [white friends]" (I, 6). Subsequently, when asked about her relationship with the black community on campus, 001 describes this relationship as "bordering on nonexistent" (I, 18). She adds:

> I never really had a strong connection to black people, or people of color...the students there got this image from me, you know, and completely shut me out of it...[The people in the group] were probably like, 'Oh that girl thinks she's white, why is [she] here,' that kind of image. (I, 18)

Once again we see notions of stereotypical blackness alongside feelings of an identity divide, as the respondent does not see herself as the stereotype. Conceptions of what is stereotypically black create a sense of otherness, where the respondent is not like that – not like them and not like the others.

Later, 001 states, "I think I see myself in terms of [how] other people see me...I can only identify myself through the eyes of other people...So I feel like you can only identify yourself as society identifies you" (I, 20–21). She tries to reclaim her identity and states, "I can only identify myself in reflection of who I was and who I am now." When asked if she considers herself white, she adamantly exclaims:

> No, no, I definitely don't consider myself white in any way. I often resent that...when people...are like, 'Oh, you're white.' I get very offended by that...It upsets me a lot, I don't know. Then you start to think about it, like I asked the kids I work with, 'What is white?' Is it, 'Oh, you talk white'? I speak like an educated person. That doesn't mean I'm white. (I, 21–22)

The black community does not accept her claims of being a black woman, but 001 argues that this is "[be]cause there's a stereotypical way of how black people should be that's portrayed by the media and things like that, you know, and maybe I should wear like a belly shirt and have my nose pierced, and have extensions in my hair, fake nails, and things like that, but that's not how all black people – women are" (I, 22). She resents that she must choose between two exclusive options.

Later, 001 exclaims:

> Just through my upbringing and my socialization into society with friends...I'd probably be uncomfortable anywhere else [as well]. There used to be a point where I was uncomfortable being in a room with all black people because I felt that they were looking at me and judging me...because I was so used to being with white people. But at the same time, when I came to...orientation, I don't think I'd ever seen so many preppy white people in my entire life, like ever. I felt like I did stick out because I was a black girl in a crowd of white people, but there I was with my dad, who's wearing his oxfords and khakis, I'm wearing nice jeans and a designer purse, so I was like, 'Shit, which side do I go to?' You know what I mean? (I, 23)

Thus, skin color pushes her toward one side, but the ("white") garb she wears pushes her toward the other.

Interviewee 003 laments not being black or white enough; she says, "I used to be made fun of all the time, I was told I was an Oreo...because they said that I was black on the outside but white on the inside." Subsequently, 003 recalls, "I've even been called a Huxtable, like a Huxtable kid, because of 'The Cosby Show,' those kids were like uppity I guess. [But] so I'm like...you can't judge me" (III, 13). She adds, "It's hard to see yourself when you can't see yourself, like in magazines" (III, 2). In accord, 003 states:

> Like I don't see myself, I can't...I don't see a physical representation of myself...I feel like there's not a good, beautiful black woman, because she's always associated with a white person. Like she's more like a white person...[for example] Tyra Banks, she always wears fake hair. Halle Berry, she's mixed. Mariah Carey, mixed. Like there's nowhere that like...when they're like 'strong, black woman,' like I don't fit. I don't have a big butt, I don't have that. I don't have ginormous breasts, I don't have what people associate with black women...I don't have that [black beauty]...I clearly don't have white beauty either. (III, 3)

Like the previous respondents in Group One, 003 fits neither paradigm of black or white, and she is rendered invisible since there is no model for her to emulate, just as there is no model to represent and/or validate who she already is.

Interviewee 010 wanted to be a part of the African -American group, but she was not black enough for them (X, 9). It was not as difficult with the white group because 010 did not feel she needed to prove her blackness. Yet, even if in the periphery, there were always overtones of not being black enough and undertones of not being white enough. There is an increasingly narrow window of what legitimately constitutes black or white, and such constitutions are contextually dependent; what is too black or too white depends upon whether it is the white or black community that is serving as the judge.

Hanging out with white peers challenges the little identity left in 010's life that might be deemed black. She agrees that she can and does embrace groups of white friends, but this is not done without consequence. She states, "I don't think there's no problem having white friends or just even trying to hang out with them, but occasionally the way you see the person, the one black with the group of white friends you kind of call him, he's the 'Oreo,' he's the black guy who's actually trying to be white...And I've [even] caught myself saying that once or twice" (X, 25). She is stuck with the resentful label of Oreo and the choice to be black or be nothing at all (X, 28).

Choice is a recurring theme in the interviews. Upon coming to college, 014 thought, "Whoa, I am this. I am black or I have to have black friends" (IVX, 2). She adds:

I feel like I've divided and have to, like, choose where I want to go...[Here] people always try to put me into different boxes, like how I should look and how that matches up with where I should be from...you can't be part of two cultures. You have to be part of either this culture or that culture. (IVX, 2–4)

When asked about choice, 014 responds, "I think partly it's culture. I think people are just really ingrained on having two separate worlds within one big [one]" (IVX, 10).

Proof of Whiteness and Passing as Black: 003, 010, and 018

Interviewee 003 discusses her longing to find a fit somewhere: "I don't have any connection, and there's no solid evidence [that I'm black]...I'm either acting too white for black people or I'm just acting black," she says (III, 11–12). She discusses how she can pass to white people but not with blacks, for it is the black people who will question the degree to which she is received as "authentically" black (III, 12). Indeed, 003 recalls:

[Black girls] will be like, 'Oh, you're different. Oh, why do you talk like that?' And since I've [just recently] been with only black people, or only black girls, they think my clothes are weird...It's totally different cultures...Why does it have to be such a division? Why can't I just like those clothes, you know what I mean, why can't I just like J. Crew? Why can't I just like the Gap? (III, 12)

Indeed, 003 describes herself as almost a white imposter yearning for validation that she is/has a race. She feels like she is acting race and that she should have the choice to do as she likes without those decisions reflecting the race she is attempting to enact.

In parallel to 003, 010 often feels unaccepted by black peers (X, 3). She states:

It was like proving myself, proving that I had basically street credibility, you know, just, 'Oh, can she dance the way we dance? Can she – does she know the songs that we know? Does she know rap music the way we know rap music, or does she wear the outfits that we wear?'...The black students, at the all-black school, it was like I had to keep proving myself, had to listen to stuff I didn't want to listen to. (X, 3)

Greater proof of racial identity becomes a prerequisite for black (not white) solidarity and to establish the "credibility" of identity.

This is not to say that unquestionable acceptance into white culture is only achieved at the cost of painful accounts of assimilation. Interviewee 018 recalls:

> I remember I had a summer internship at a pharmaceutical company...and in my department I was the only black person in that company, period...There were certain groups that were being joked upon [during lunch breaks], and I feel like I have to laugh just to be a part of the scene, listening to them just like ha ha...I feel like I sometimes have to [laugh] just to fit in, even though it's probably not funny. (XVIII, 18)

Her authenticity of blackness is not being called into question by white peers, but she must seemingly take on the racist attitudes of her peers to keep her blackness in check and unmarked among whites.

Achieving Whiteness in Thinness: 001

Interviewee 001 admires the stereotypical "white" girl body. She states, "I think I started to feel like more aware of my body, like 'Oh maybe I should diet,' 'cause the other kids were doing it too. And looking back, I definitely didn't need to do it, but kind of to go with the crowd" (I, 11). She likes to be "admired by [her] white friends for being so skinny" (I, 15). She states that she does not attach color to thinness (I, 16), yet she also argues, "But when I do think of a rail-thin person or a skinny person, like someone that I would admire, I would think of a white person, because that's what I'm used to seeing" (I, 17).

She elaborates on her discontent with not being black enough, but she focuses on her reverence for thinness that makes her "more white." Excommunicated from black groups, 001 learns that she can become "more white" or accepted among white groups by gaining admiration for her thinness. Thinness becomes a means of mobility in an environment where 001 is not black enough but where white beauty prevails.

Achieving Whiteness in Upper-class-ness

Whiteness can also be achieved through perceived upper-class-ness. Many believe that blackness equals lower class, so anything else would connote whiteness. In speaking of the common relation of blackness to lower socio-economic class, interviewee 014 attests, "I think a lot of people assume that if you're black, then you're on federal aid, you got here through affirmative action, you may not be as smart as everyone else, there are those stereotypes, which are hard because the school's predominantly white, so it's hard to dispel those myths" (IVX, 7).

Similarly, interviewee 018's socioeconomic class and working status make her feel more separate from her white peers (XVIII, 9). Class differences, for example, force her to work as opposed to taking vacation breaks with her peers. This class difference also makes 018 uncomfortable with affluent African-Americans who are not like her (XVIII, 11). She remarks:

> I feel like [the affluent African Americans there are]...very different from the African Americans I've been around in terms of culture, they're snobbish...And they're very, they set their own culture [and] they don't want to embrace other cultures at all...I feel like their parents in terms are well off...where I came from like a low-income family...I wouldn't feel comfortable in that group. (XVIII, 11)

Class not only divides white and black peers, but also creates difference in black communities.

Group Two – Black Enough

Women in Group Two self-identified as black prior to college and because they experience negative stereotyping by the white majority in college, strongly align with the black campus community. These women are "black enough" and do not have to engage in a "not black enough/not white enough" struggle akin to those interviewees in other groups, nor are they enticed to "move beyond their blackness" for transcending racial-ethnic iden-tification, like those interviewees we shall see in Group Three. Thus, Group Two individuals would perceive Group One and Group Three individuals as outsiders who are "too white" and/or without allegiance to their racial group, as denoted by the core black group that has come to epitomize our category named Group Two.

Interviewee 034 confirms that she thinks that many people are pretending a certain black identity, but we asked her why she thinks some people are so compelled to assert their blackness (XXXIV, 16). To this query, 034 replies, "There's not just racial pressures from people outside of the race; there's racial pressures from *inside* the race" (XXXIV, 16, emphasis added). Thus, an expected role or act can stem from the black community itself. We can imagine that many people were not acting out stereotypical blackness prior to coming to a predominantly white college, so it was not until arriving at college that such individuals assumed the role of what they perceived as the proper way to act their race or assert a form of blackness that they imagined should be their (new) role.

When asked about the root of this black stereotype, 034 adds:

> A lot of us are coming from th[ese] major white areas, and we come here and we want people to know that we're black. I'm proud to be black; I wouldn't change it for the world, but this is who I am. I'm not going to come here, dress a certain way, talk a certain way, wear my hair a certain way so people will know that. If you don't know that then whatever; I go to bed and I wake up this color…I can't be anybody else; it's just too much energy, but I feel like a lot of people in high school and here put on this role of acting their race, and I don't think they understand that you can't act it out. It just doesn't happen that way…This whole division is really heart-wrenching because you want to reach a sense of solidarity with people who are like you, people with the same background as you, but who aren't going to accept you because you come from this place they're trying to shun off…Talking a certain way, dressing a certain way is not going to make you into a race…To be rejected by your own people is like being rejected by your own family…So here at [college] I'm just kind of done with [affiliating with this core black group] because [they] want to push us forward but [they're] actually keeping us behind, keeping this negative image for us that not many black people fit into. (XXXIV, 15–17)

Another respondent from Group Three describes this core black-identified group as one that questions blackness and makes you prove it through choices that would seem to affirm blackness. Interviewee 024 remarks:

> The black community isn't as cohesive as I thought…I quickly learned not to trust everyone you meet, in terms of like, the black community is very cliquey. And everyone talks about everyone. Like everyone's in your

business and...[people might wonder] 'Why is she hanging out with white girls? Oh, she thinks she's white.'...That was really shocking to me at first, because I had always had white friends and I never had to choose, you know? And I felt like I had to make a decision...And I get really frustrated, like as I said, with the black community and, like, having these dogged ideas about what it is to be black, and, like, what people must do, and black people, what should be your interest as a black person. (XXIV, 5, 23)

In sum, we see that some respondents feel that members of the core black group are acting out to fit an image of blackness that is expected by the black community on a white college campus. Some black students feel excluded and disheartened by the divisiveness of this faction. They also feel that their identities are being questioned and criticized by the core black group. Yet, as we will see from the next respondents, many outside of this group do not have a completely accurate image of it.

Joining the Black Family

Unlike 034, there is a core group of black respondents who do not feel that they are a group of unambiguous exclusion (as individuals from Groups One and Three might purport). For instance, 019 discusses how all of her friends were black and she was in black organizations when she came to college (IXX, 39). She states:

> I feel like that was a kind of cushion for me, because after my freshman year...I started to hang out with a lot more white people. Not a whole lot, but there were times when I'd go to a white party instead of a black party, and I don't think anybody would look at me weird for that, just because I feel like I've established myself when I came into [this college], and [if] I hung out with people who I hung out with now, I might have been labeled a little different[ly]. (IXX, 39)

She could cross bridges outside of the core black group by establishing allegiance to this group and establishing where she stood within it (IXX, 39).

Respondent 025 recalls, "From the moment I set foot on campus I made sure that it was known that I was African-American and that there were no, there were no mistakes, no one thought that I was white or, and again I got the questions about being mixed and things like that" (XXV, 5). The key to gaining admittance and sustaining acceptance to the black group is a clear declaration of allegiance to the black group; clearly first impressions matter to the black group on the predominantly white campus. She aligned herself with the black community upon entering college because of her light skin tone, which had called her race into question while growing up. She states, "People kind of doubt I guess your race. I, I'd always get the question from people, 'Are you mixed?'...It was just, I felt like I always had to prove that I was black" (XXV, 3). Therefore, 025 strove to prove her blackness to compensate for physical whiteness, and she was propelled her into a hyper-black allegiance with the core black-identified group on campus that made it clear from the start that she is black.

Too White Equals Self-Hate

Another important element in joining and being accepted by the core black-identified group is demonstrating that you are *not* a white caricature, and secondly, that you are proud to be black (as acting too white would indicate the converse).

For instance, straightening one's hair within this community is equated with whiteness and self-hate. Interviewee 033 recalls:

> I knew from an early age, even though my mother refused to straighten my hair...I don't [even] think I [would have asked to have my hair straightened] because I was afraid and I felt like I was committing treason against the black community, my African ancestry if I were to ask to straighten my hair...[and in] my school you literally could not straighten your hair. It was against the rules...I was taught that it's assimilation. It's self-hatred...[taught] by my school and my family...I mean, I think that it's still to a certain degree a manifestation of um, self-hatred, but self-hatred to like the fact that, that black beauty is hated in our society, so we just take it on. (XXXIII, 13–14)

We asked 019 if she thought that some black people were shunned by this core black community for acting too white. She responds:

> I'm sure it happens, but I feel like there's a difference...there are people on this campus who – I'm not talking about talking properly, I'm talking about speaking 'valley girls,' just go – like, you can tell the difference between somebody who's just really white-acting but doesn't really hate themselves

because they're black and don't want to be associated with that community at all...you're not gonna fit in if you're too white; at some point people are going to be turned off by that, but I still consider those people a part of the black community because everyone knows that they are. (IXX, 38)

Interviewee 020 also exclaims:

We have Oreos, we don't like them. They try to be something that [they]'re not. Like, embrace who you are and take it from there; I'm not saying that because you are black that you can't be 'whitey.' We can all speak properly, we can all do the things that are acceptable by the 'whites,' acceptable by predominantly whites, and still be black, but there are those who feel that...[they] say that discrimination doesn't exist or race doesn't really exist, just this world isn't perfect or something. And to them, when they finally realize that it's not like that, they don't understand why, and it's like they have to be re-taught to realize what people have said in the history books. (XX, 14)

When asked if these people get cast aside or lost in the mix, 020 replies, "They have no place" (XX, 14). These individuals are not white enough or black enough for either group and adds, "There are some blacks who ostracize themselves from the blacks, and that doesn't get you anywhere because when you're discriminated by the whites, where are you gonna go? You already made your enemies with the blacks" (XX, 15).

There are varying degrees to which an individual can be ostracized from the black community, but it's important to note that some of the members of this black community are unsure as to what black even means. Indeed, 020 mulls over understandings of blackness and asks:

Truly, what defines black? What is black? Is it an actual complexion, is it a culture, and truly can you sit and say that things that are culturally acceptable from blacks such as our music, our clothing sometimes, cannot be integrated with whites? (XX, 15)

Nonetheless, for the majority of respondents in this black-identified group, a strong notion of blackness allows interviewees to attest that "race has always been an issue" and believe that blackness allows one to:

...know who I was and where I came from. So...there's never been a point where I never thought about, that my identity is that I'm black...I decided that I was going to be black and female all the time...[and] understand the ways in which black females do things...[it's about], like, reveling in that tradition. (XXXIII, 5, 15–16)

Group Three: Beyond Black or White

Members of Group Three grew up in a diverse environment that did not make them feel the necessity to neatly or completely fit into a black or white social "box." For this group, identity surpasses any sense of "racial" identity, and "race" is just one of the many perceived attributes that makes these respondents who they are. Most respondents in Group Three had upbringings where diverse environments affirmed the values that they now hold for themselves and others that transcend notions of racial identity.

Growing Up Diverse

Interviewees 004, 008, and 009 are key examples that demonstrate the characteristics of Group Three. In high school, 004 notes that there were "enough groups of people that you can interact with that you felt, 'Okay, I'm part of something.'...Not necessarily a group, you didn't have to be in a group" (IV, 3). Clearly, 004 does not feel compelled to neatly fit into a social or racial box like the Group One respondents.

Interviewee 009 attended a diverse grade school. She says, "White people [got] along with black people...and there was no difference between each other...So I always felt open to talk to people of other races because...I had grown up that way" (IX, 9). When separate black and white groups emerged in high school, this respondent continued to experience diversity by using her cheerleader status to become a "floater." She describes the term: "I never really associated myself with anybody in particular. I had my friends who were my friends, and we were just friends, and then I talked to everybody, so it was one of those, you know, 'I can hang out with the white kids, I can hang out with the black kids, I can hang out with Hispanics and the Asians, and everybody'" (IX, 5). Her status as a floater brings its complexities:

It's a little difficult because there are some people who...are like extremes. So they're black people who are just like, 'Why are you talking to them?'...And it's like, 'Why not, why not talk to them?' And they're like, 'You talk white, or you act white,' and I'm like, 'I'm sorry I talk properly.'...And so then you had your black people that were like that...and I was on the cheerleading team...[which gave me entry into the white community]. (IX, 7)

In reflection, 009's ability to float amid the two groups entices her to look beyond static categories of blackness or whiteness.

Beyond Black

Respondents in Group Three prioritize attributes other than race to center their common collective. Interviewee 008 moves beyond blackness by way of her experience at a multi-ethnic high school and describes her friends as "a racial rainbow of people" (7). She adds:

> We kind of learned through each other...We buil[t] off each other a lot when it came to race and whatnot...We kind of grew kind of like a family, kind of like a close-knit family of, like, different races...all coming from different backgrounds...And we saw each other for people and not for races and whatnot. (VIII, 7, 8)

Her diverse experiences expose her peers as human beings with qualities beyond race (and beyond class).

Interviewee 008 does not take narrow-minded and ignorant criticisms to heart. She would tell judgmental peers not to "judge a book by its cover" and suggests that they "walk a day through my shoes and what I have experienced as an individual" (VIII, 17) to understand her experiences. She also looks for groups of people who are not "trying to, in a way, prove their blackness" (VIII, 18). And although 008 is still searching for the right fit on campus, this fit is not race-based. She says, "I'm looking for kind of a group that...their number one issue would not be race, that their number one issue would look outside, above and beyond it, and kind of judge someone on the content of their character. I'm looking for a group of people that...don't need to prove themselves so much socially but maybe academically" (VIII, 18–19). Overall, character takes precedence over racial identification or racial allegiance for 008 when it comes to finding a college niche.

Interviewee 009 also looks beyond racial boundaries for the friends that she keeps company with in college (IX, 13). She suggests that sharing "skin color doesn't mean that your goals, your morals, and all that stuff are the same" (IX, 13). Instead of using racial qualities to describe herself, 009 uses labels such as "leader," "intelligent," "focused," and "determined" – and later, "Christian," "child of God," "determined," "smart," "outgoing," and "African-American female" (IX, 18, 21). She states, "Even though I take pride in who I am and the race that I am, it doesn't make me." She adds, "I don't identify myself with a black person just because we're black" (IX, 21, 19). She floats without special allegiance to either racial group, nor does she look for friends of a certain racial group. Diversity, for 009, transcends limited notions of race.

Finally, in similar fashion, 024 calls attention to the concerted effort that she makes to resist being held to any particular notions of identity. She says, "I've always been the type of person that wouldn't classify myself in particularly one group. Like, I pride myself in being able to float in-between groups...I would say, like, yes, I am part of the black community, um, however, like, I don't see that as my only community at [this college]" (IVXX, 8–9). We hear the core black-identified group described as very self-interested. For the majority of respondents, it feels impossible to be accepted by a self-interested group when respondents believe that this core group sees and treats them as Other.

Negative Case Examples of Group Three

There are also many negative case examples within Group Three, including interviewees 007, 002, and 006. Interviewee 007 comes from a diverse background but yearns to find a racial fit; 002 and 006 do not come from diverse backgrounds but they search for a fit that is beyond black (or white). There is a negative relationship between a past and a present of diversity and lack thereof. In the case of 007, diversity predicts conformity.

Diversity to Conformity: 007

Interviewee 007 comes from an environment of diversity and acceptance but seeks a category (most qualified by) of color through her college experience. Self-described as a multi-ethnic "mutt" with a rich heritage, 007 had many friends in high school, which were "just one big diverse conglomerate." In college, 007 says, "I had a hard time adjusting because I wasn't black enough to hang out with the hardcore black people, but I wasn't white so I didn't hang out with the white people anymore" (VII, 3).

She initially embraced different communities at college (e.g., AHANA [African-American, Hispanic, Asian, and Native American] friends and white friends) to fill the void left by her diverse high school friendships, but these groups serve different social purposes. She states that her groups of friends are "very much separate...and [her black] friends aren't the go-and-get-drunk kind of people, whereas [her] Caucasian friends were, so [she] just did different things with them" (VII, 9–10). Hence, 007 has found unique groups to fill different needs in her life.

Overall, we see that as diversity becomes segregated in college, separate facets of 007's personality are satisfied in different groups in separate social moments, unlike her earlier experiences when she was part of "one big conglomerate" of peers. She finds an alternative in an off-campus sorority whose members closely resemble her personally, politically, and aesthetically. Once her former conglomerate of diversity is dismantled in college and 007 is only able to experience diversity in fragments, 007 instead turns towards a group that most holistically represents her.

Uniformity to Diversity: 002 and 006

Interviewee 002 comes from a background where she was the only black student to graduate from her school (II, 1). She never felt different from other children growing up but had some awareness that her skin color was different (II, 2). She is told she is "the whitest black girl [her peer has] ever known" (II, 2), but she shrugs such comments aside, recognizing that she always felt the freedom to "just d[o] the stuff [she] liked to do, what interests [her]" without feeling different, even amidst standing out as the "whiter" black girl.

In reflection, part of 002's acceptance of diversity is due to her multiethnic background. She is proud of her mixed heritage when asked if there has been any shift in her identity since making the transition to college. She notes:

> There's definitely been a shift...I've always said when someone asks you, 'What are you?' I would always tell them just because it's so unique: I'm half bohemian, I'm a quarter Filipino, an eighth French Canadian, and an eighth Irish, and before it was just kind of like I'd just spewed it all off 'cause I knew it, and now I just spew it all off cause I'm proud of it. (II, 5)

Hence, we see that while 002 does not come from an ethnically diverse background, her diverse sense of self frees her from perceived needs to be aligned with a fixed group. She states:

I feel like I don't have to choose [between the Caucasian community and her multiethnic friends]...'cause I have really good friends in both, and they know me for me, like I don't hide my personality from one group to another, even though I may slightly change the language or shift things, but I dress the same way, I act the same way, I'm just as outgoing with both, I try to get people to do whatever [I'm doing]...I've never felt like I haven't belonged, either. (II, 7)

Further, 002 believes that "each culture has something to offer each other," and she doesn't buy into exclusive adherence to African-American culture ideology (II, 8). When asked what allows her to be so open to mixed heritage, she replies, "I think part of it has to do with the whole, the fact that I myself am not just one specific race...I just love people for their personality...you just need to love them for who they are and be open to new ideas and new things, and you just can't judge a book by its cover" (II, 8). Overall, we see that pockets of diversity, stemming from such things as her family heritage and her church group, help her to find pride and acceptance in her difference.

Interviewee 006 discusses how a lack of diversity made her grow up feeling different. Like 002, 006 looks beyond blackness (or whiteness) to find greater humanity in her college peers. Yet, 006 does not begin at this point. She recalls "always [having] felt different...a feeling about people perceiving [her] as different" (VI, 2, 7). Like a number of other respondents, 006 has mostly white friends and was often the only black person in her grade (VI, 2). Even in terms of appearance, 006 came to believe that she was less beautiful than other girls, thinking that "white girls are more beautiful than black women" (VI, 7). This raised feelings of inadequacy and difference for 006.

However, once she arrived at college, 006 let go of the need to fit into a linear mold. She has a core of multiethnic friends, but she still has some hostility toward both white groups for their arrogant white privilege (VI, 13) and black groups for "white-washing" her (deeming her too white to be black) (VI, 14). She makes sense of this tension upon entering college (VI, 13-14).

She is able to put social constructions of beauty aside to see herself as beautiful, as she further recognizes "that the standard of beauty is Eurocentric." She adds, "I do not fit in that, but that doesn't necessarily mean that I'm ugly but, rather, that the standard is messed up" (VI, 15, 18). Correspondingly, 006 seems to gain cognizance that a fixed linear box of racial allegiance is absurd. Indeed, when talking about her current friends, who are "very mixed as far as the group goes," she adds, "I think a lot of our bonding [is] based just on personality and values, rather than just, like, 'Oh, you're black, and I'm looking for another black friend'...Like when I got here, I was like, 'You know what, if I meet another black person, then I do. If I don't, then I don't" (VI, 19). Thus, here we see that personalities and values come to take a higher importance than blackness.

Subsequently, 006 has identified with others who have felt ugly because they are not white, because she too has felt the same self-disgust (VI, 19). She offers the example of being able to identify with a white girl because they both share the same passion for reading (VI, 19). Taken together, we see that 006 connects with others based upon shared aspects of life that reach beyond skin color to which she can relate (VI, 20). Instead, for 006, it comes down to respect and values, not skin color. In effect, not fitting in and not coming from an environment of diversity serves two purposes. First, 006 decides that she is not going to fit in, but that this is not the result of her inferiority. It is rather the effect of meaningless (seemingly fixed) social categories in which she is always too white or too black too fit. Secondly, 006 creates a new boundless category transcending race that is sustained by shared values and life experiences.

Discussion

Much can be said about racial identity in terms of social context. Firstly, for a majority of respondents in Group One, growing up in an environment of difference propelled them toward a future where they do not quite fit, leaving them in the liminal position and oscillating double consciousness of not being white enough or not being black enough. Many respondents feel compelled to choose blackness or whiteness, even though they do not feel they fit either group. In fact, most Group One respondents' endeavors are judged as disingenuous acts. They constantly struggle to achieve whiteness or prove blackness. The major themes driving Group One are matters of difference, failure to be black or white enough, and compulsions to prove blackness or achieve whiteness.

Group One respondents remind us that we must consider the degree to which a respondent is cognizant of and/or hampered by notions of difference growing up, the perceived sense of failure or powerlessness a respondent feels for feeling forced to dwell in a netherworld of not-white/not-black enough, and the extent to which a respondent's present life is captured by compulsions to "do" whiteness or blackness. In the majority of cases within Group One, there is a positive relationship between growing up in a non-diverse setting with strong sentiments of difference and an outcome where one is left seeing oneself and being received as neither black nor white enough.

Group Two includes women who self-identify as black prior to entering the college environment and who come to comprise the "hardcore" black community on campus. What is clear from this group is that they self-identify as black through a hyper-awareness of their historical black heritage. Interviewee 033, for example, grew up in a predominantly white community but attended an African-American-centered school as a way of "countering traditional narratives of education...I didn't know any American history growing up. I knew African history" (XXXIII, 1). While Group 2 respondents celebrate their African and/or African-American heritage, they assert their blackness, which becomes a political position as the individual takes responsibility for uplifting and promoting the interests of the black community. Interviewee 033 notes that her political consciousness began in high school, which was "when I started to kind of understand my identity, um, as, as one that could imply political power...I stopped thinking about being black as just being black like when you're born...but as your responsibilities and what's going on in the black community, and that to me started to form, 'What's black enough?' versus...how I spoke, how I dressed" (XXXIII, 6). Issues of appearance can also become sites for political resistance, and outward appearance like the decision to straighten one's hair can assume political significance. Thus, respondents in Group Two do not struggle with the same extent of double consciousness and liminal positionality as do women in Group One, given that Group One is primarily concerned with exclusively identifying as black and with seeing oneself through the eyes of others no more than within this "hardcore" black community.

For the majority of respondents in Group Three, we discover that diverse upbringings entice respondents to look beyond blackness when it comes to self-affirmations and quests for fit among peers in a college environment. For the majority of respondents in Group Three, diversity transcends racial identity as respondents look for social fit among peers with similar life experiences, interests, and values. In short, the two primary themes that drive Group Three are notions of growing up within diversity and moving beyond boundaries of blackness. These respondents reveal the importance of considering the extent to which an individual has experienced diversity prior to encountering a predominantly white environment and the degree to which this upbringing impacts one's perception of blackness within oneself and others. For most of Group Three's cases, we find a positive relationship between a diverse childhood and an outcome where identity is affirmed and shared in transcendent ideas of diversity.

A key variable in predicting fit for respondents when they arrive at college is having had experience in environments where difference is valued and race is not paramount to individual identities, values, or social hierarchies. As a result, individuals from diverse environments feel less pressure to do, achieve, prove, or pass as a race. As an alternative, race becomes one of the many characteristics that make respondents who they are alongside who they perceive their peers to be.

These data raise important issues concerning the plight of those students who feel, as one respondent from Group One notes, "floating between groups" or feeling a sense of isolation, where there is no group of students with whom they can identify. This research raises important questions concerning how diversity is achieved on a predominantly white college campus. How can one achieve a status of being "black enough" when the lived realities of so many respondents in our study includes experiences of not enough of whiteness or blackness? What constitutes unwavering blackness, and what are the prerequisites for obtaining this identity? Can blackness ever be achieved, or is blackness, like gender, a reiterative practice that must constantly be performed?

Group Three presents us with a new way of thinking about differences in terms of "diversity," whereby racial identity is but one of many different identities that are embraced by students of color. Respondents here do not experience "double consciousness" in the sense of DuBois (1903), but rather occupy and embrace multiple, comparably valued, consciousnesses. Indeed, we know that those women who embrace a diversity model of identity in our study have had successful diverse experiences prior to coming to college, and their experience of diversity speaks to the importance of linking diversity initiatives at the pre-college level with those at the college environment level.

The experiences of all three groups of women points to the need for researchers to take into account the different social contexts that women of color bring with them to their colleges or universities. They bring different life experiences with regard to race and how they incorporate their sense of their racial identity while transitioning into their college years. Women of color are not all the same; they differ with respect to their class position, social location, and their degree of racial/ethnic identity. Some grow up in all white neighborhoods prior to coming to college, where having a sense of racial identity is not central to their sense of self. Other students of color express a deep connection to their racial/ethnic history, having grown up in a community of color. Still others come from very diverse backgrounds, where there is a great deal of attention paid to navigating a variety of racial differences within their school, neighborhood, and family life.

Our research findings also reveal the need to explore in more detail how differences in racial identity formation in college impact black women's perception of body image (hair color, weight, figure). Some research suggests that African-American women who enter predominately white colleges with a negative or weak racial identity and self-esteem are especially vulnerable to internalizing white, Western norms of beauty, which places them at greater risk for developing body image issues and eating disorders (see: Hesse-Biber 1996; Root 1990; Stice, Schupak-Neuberg, Shaw, and Stein 1994; Stice and Shaw 1994).

Chapter Twelve

Creating Place from Conflicted Space: Bi/Multi-Racial *Māori* Women's Inclusion within New Zealand Mental Health Services

Tess Moeke-Maxwell

Introduction

I was a 16-year-old college dropout when I got pregnant. I married the following year and had a couple more children before I got divorced at age 22. At 29, and financially reliant on a Domestic Purposes Benefit, I decided to embark on a university education. In preparation, I attended a bridging course for women. I was filled with a mixture of fear and excitement. On the first day, participants were given the option to stay in the main group or join a Maori women's group. I really wanted to join the other Maori women, but there was a problem; I was white, and I assumed the class would be taught in *te reo Māori* (indigenous language), and I was far from fluent. I felt torn. My heart wanted to be in the Maori group, but I imagined the other women staring at my white face thinking "What's she doing here?" So I stayed in the mainstream group. But I never quite belonged there, either.

What this does not tell you is that I struggled through my adolescence and early adulthood with great dispiritedness resultant from a number of social and environmental factors. Twice, the sense of isolation and hopelessness became overwhelming, and

I was admitted to the hospital. In the early 1980s, mental health services treatment completely lacked a cultural focus, and staff were inept at helping me understand my "mixed bag" of life experiences, which included being a fair-skinned bi/multiracial *Maori* (indigenous) and *Pakeha* (European/New Zealander) lesbian trapped in a heterosexual relationship. The climate was changing from monocultural nationalism to biculturalism. Highly politicized Maori ethnicities were employed in Maori sovereignty struggles, which strategically reproduced the notion of an essentialized Maori identity. Juxtaposed neatly against a discrete, finite, and stable Pakeha identity, the Maori/Pakeha cultural binary was reproduced. With respect to my racial corporeality, I was constructed by mental health services as Pakeha, in binary opposition to Maori. This was irrespective of the fact that my mother is a "brown" indigenous woman. I was white, and I was Pakeha. End of story.

Based on my personal engagement with the mental health sector, as both a user of services during the early 1980s, and much later as a mental health clinician and researcher, I am of the opinion that there is a blind spot in current articulations of Maori identity within cultural assessment and intervention frameworks. Simply put, there is amnesia about the historiography of the 'place' of race within theoretical articulations of Maori diversity. There is also a lack of information and utilization of a Maori hybridity concept within configurations of Maori subjectivity. The definition of hybridity I utilize in this chapter is informed by the work of Homi Bhabha:

> The importance of hybridity is not to be able to trace two original movements from which the third emerges, rather hybridity…is the 'third space' which enables other positions to emerge. This third space displaces the histories that constitute it, and sets up new structures of authority, new political initiatives, which are inadequately understood through received wisdom…The process of cultural hybridity gives rise to a something different, something new and unrecognisable, a new area of negotiation of meaning and representation. (1994:211)

Maori bi/multi raciality and ethnic diversity is clearly increasing; however, there is lack of robust research on the social construction and discursive performance of the raced and gendered Maori subject. Bhabha's concept of hybridity is useful in that it provides a space to think about Maori subjectivity in a way that takes into account the new subjectivities that are formed from the presence of more than one biological lineage and ethnic identity (Bhabha 1990, 1994). However, I am not proposing an altogether new subjectivity, or one that claims to be superior to an indigenous or settler/Other identity in the way that was theorized by Gloria Anzaldúa (1987). Rather, I argue for a space where the unique identities of bi/multiracial Maori women who identify with more than one ethnicity can claim a space within articulations of Maori identity within mental health services. I suggest a space must be forged to theorize and develop meaningful and robust research on Maori women who live on the cultural margins of Maori and Pakeha/Other land-scapes. Research is needed on Maori women who embody their bi/multiracial corporeality and ethnic diversity. I suggest this narrative of Maori identity is one that responds to the fluidity of Maori and Pakeha culture and, as such, is constantly in flux and negotiated.

Grounded in my own experiences, and informed by my PhD research on Maori women's cultural hybridity, I claim a space for the inclusion of the raced and gendered Maori women's subjectivity within the theoretical development and application of assessment and intervention frameworks (Moeke-Maxwell 2003). More specifically, this chapter argues for a space to include ethnic pluralism and racial corporeality in the development and implementation of assessment and intervention frameworks within the discourse of mental health. According to Durie (2001), "The purpose of cultural assessment is to not only assist in reaching a conclusion about the client's mental state but also to plan treatment and rehabilitation programs that are relevant and motivating" (236). I suggest that the advantages and disadvantages associated with Maori women's bi/multiracial corporeality and plural ethnicity should also be theorized and included within mental health services assessment and interventions. This is an attempt at representing women who live with the ambiguity of being positioned with Maori, Pakeha, and/or Other *whakapapa* (genealogy), ethnic identities, and a heterogeneous array of overlapping and often contradictory cultural values, beliefs, and practices associated with their unique cultural specificities.

Bi/multiracial Maori women's "difference" can be included within the landscape of New Zealand mental health services through raising the clinician's awareness and understanding of Maori women's plural ethnicity and bi/multiracial corporeality. Her unique multiple subjectivity and discursive positioning is occluded within current "cultural diversity" narratives and obscure the difference her raced and gendered corporeality and unique historiography inscribe on her body and psyche. Naming Maori difference as "cultural diversity" obscures a rich potential of information pertaining to the bi/multiracial woman's embodied performance as both the raced and de/raced subject. I introduce a popular indigenous health framework, Te Whare Tapa Wha, and an operationalized version, the Meihana Model, to explore the "blind spot" within current articulations of cultural assessment and intervention frameworks (Pitama, Robertson, Cram, Gillies, Huria, Dallas-Katoa 2007). Some suggestions are made toward extending Maori health models to become more inclusive of bi/multiraciality and plural ethnicity.

Maori Ethnic Diversity

In 1986, the New Zealand Census classification of Maori shifted from racial quantification to choice of ethnic origin. This was adapted in 1991 to choice of ethnic group, and in 1996 the choice of plural ethnicities was included. In 2001, the Census also included a non-biological ethnic group identification classification as well.

In 2006, Maori were counted in two ways in the New Zealand Census: through biological descent and ethnicity. According to the 2006 New Zealand Census, 643,977 people, equivalent to 17.7 percent of the total New Zealand population, self-identified with Maori descent, although within this group, 102,366 people did not know their *iwi* (tribal group). In terms of ethnicity, 42.2 percent of Maori stated that they identified with European ethnic groups, 7.0 percent with Pacific Peoples' ethnic groups, 1.5 percent with Asian ethnic groups, and 2.3 percent also gave "New Zealander" as one of their ethnic groups (Statistics New Zealand 2007).

Despite the move toward recognizing ethnic diversity, little has been done within mental health services to provide assessment and interventions that reflect the unique life experiences and meaning of ethnic diversity for Maori who identify as having more than one racial and/or ethnic identity. Given the ethnic composition of Maori, it is apparent that more research and development needs to be undertaken on health initiatives that reflect this ethnically diverse demographic. For example, by 2051 the number of people who identify as Maori is likely to increase to 22 percent of the population, or one million people. Nearly half of New Zealand's population will be non-European.

Arguably, the ethnic composition of Maori will continue to change dramatically due to continuing immigration and global vacillation, leading to an increase in cross-cultural interfacing that will no doubt contribute to our increasing fertility rates and bi/multiracial, ethnically diverse offspring.

"Culture" – Linked to Health Gain Initiatives

Demographically, *tangata whenua* (indigenous peoples/people of the land) are the largest minority group. Maori continue to be overrepresented as consumers within mental health services in contrast to pre-colonial *tangata whenua*, who enjoyed a high level of health pre-colonization (Kingi 2007). Maori generally access services later and, consequently, experience more acute symptoms, co-morbidity issues, and diagnostic classifications in contrast to their non-indigenous counterparts (European/Pakeha, the dominant white cultural group descendant from *tauiwi* [immigrants/colonial settlers], and other non-indigenous peoples) (Durie 1994a, 1994b, 2004; Oakley Brown, Wells, Scott (eds.) 2006). Discursively critiqued for its monocultural scope and practice, the health sector is beginning to make changes to enable it to respond appropriately and effectively to Maori health needs (Ministry of Health (MoH) 2001a, 2001b, 2002a, 2002b, 2006; Te Rau Matatini 2006a, 2000b). Political arguments have generally positioned Maori health within the context of Maori colonization, marginalization, and disenfranchisement (Walker 1987, 1990; Smith 1998). If an economic determinist argument saw Maori health disparities through a cultural lens of vulnerability and oppression, its antithesis was, not surprisingly, focused on a cultural lens of empowerment and emancipation to ensure health gains.

A strategic move to instate the rights of New Zealand's indigenous peoples within appeals to *tino rangatiratanga* (Maori sovereignty) has often been used in political arguments to redress Maori disparities (Awatere 1984; Walker 1987, 1990). These appeals to Maori inclusivity evoke the spirit of partnership, participation, and protection guaranteed to Maori by the Crown via the nation's founding treaty, the Treaty of Waitangi (1840) (Kelsey 1984; Orange 1997; Pearson 1990, 1991; Smith 1998; Walker 1987, 1990). Simply, the Crown has a responsibility to uphold the cultural and human rights of Maori. More recently, evidence of the link between culture and health gains was effectively argued during the 1980s by the New Zealand Nursing Council, who sought the inclusion of cultural safety practice within nursing education and professional registration (Durie 2001). A revised nursing protocol educated nurses to the concept and value of culture and aimed to increase awareness and understanding of culture as it pertained to the nurse's identity as well as the patient's.

For the first time, New Zealand nurses were required to look introspectively at their own cultural identity in order to gain awareness and increased understanding of Maori cultural identity. For the first time, culture was advocated as a positive resource in nursing training. Hence, cultural philosophies and protocols were integrated into nursing practice to ensure cultural safety for indigenous peoples. Following this achievement, a shift toward the implementation of cultural competencies, and, more latterly, dual competencies (including both clinical and cultural expertise) have been introduced to provide culturally appropriate and meaningful assessments and/or interventions for utilization with Maori. This agenda is underpinned by the need to provide robust, evidence-based services capable of responding appropriately to Maori consumers' needs, leading to better health outcomes for *tangata whenua*.

Cultural Assessment and Intervention Models

In its Maori health strategy, He Korowai Oranga, the Ministry of Health documented what Maori need in order to achieve *whānau ora* (optimal wellness for families). They stated:

> Maori want to be able to express themselves as Maori in Aotearoa. This pathway supports whānau (including tohunga [specialists in spiritual matters], kaumatua, Maori healers, health specialists, and researchers) to develop services that reflect Maori cultural values. Therefore, extending opportunities for health services to practice Maori views of health and healing (while recognising the diversity of whānau) will be fostered in order to progress whānau ora outcomes. (2002:12)

Consistent with the above, the purpose of cultural assessment is to provide a service or treatment plan that is as congruous with the person's normal cultural life experiences as possible. The affirmation of positive, healthy cultural beliefs and lifestyles is central to this objective. Durie states, "A cultural assessment will at least provide a basis for understanding for the patient and may lead to a cultural formulation of the problem, to compliment a DSM-IV diagnosis" (2001:236). Although a number of indigenous health frameworks have been developed, it is beyond the scope of this chapter to address them all. However, in order to demonstrate the blind spot in current configurations, I turn to one of the most widely recognized Maori health frameworks utilized in mental health services policy and practice by Maori and non-Maori services and clinicians.

First documented in 1984 by Mason Durie, the Whare Tapa Wha framework was introduced publicly (Durie 2001). The term literally refers to a four-sided house, with the inference that four major cornerstones contribute to a sense of well being for the individual. The four cornerstones are metaphorically linked to elements that must be in balance to achieve a sense of well being. The model's usefulness resides in its ability to formulate a broad range of information about an individual, utilizing a cultural and clinical lens to explore the individual's cultural status and *whānau* (family) perspective. According to Durie (2001), the four sides of the *whare* (house) pertain to specific elements that can be measured or assessed for balance. For example, the Taha Wairua element refers to the individual's cultural and spiritual values and belief systems and involves an exploration of Maori identity. Taha Hinengaro is concerned with the client's psychiatric history and substance use. The individual's level of knowledge and information and ability to control behavior is also noted. In terms of the Taha Tinana element, this assesses the individual's sleep patterns, sense of body image, and activity levels. Its primary concern is with physical health. The Taha Whānau element involves exploring significant family relationships and personal history linking the individual with their family and the wider social and environmental institutions (Durie 2001).

By 2007, the Whare Tapa Wha model evolved and was operationalized by a wide range of mainstream and iwi services, and by Maori and non-Maori clinicians. For example, the Meihana Model was recently published as a clinical assessment and intervention framework that endorses the original four cornerstones (Taha Tinana, Tahi Wairua, Tahi Hinegnaro, and Tahi Whānau) and includes an addendum of two elements: Taiao and Iwi Katoa (Pitama et al. 2007). The first, "Taiao," refers to the physical environment of the service and is linked to "accessibility and acceptability of the service," while the second, "Iwi Katoa," refers to the inclusion of the "social structures that impact on the capacity of the organization to work alongside client/whānau." This practice model has been designed to be used alongside Maori beliefs, values, and experiences "to guide clinical assessment and intervention with Maori clients and whānau accessing mental health services." The authors claim the model provides a "more comprehensive assessment of clients/whānau" (Pitama et al. 2007).

A major strength of the model is that it seeks to uphold Maori beliefs, values, and experiences in an effort to minimize cultural assumptions and expectations and to build greater consideration of individual client's cultural needs and wants. The Meihana Model seeks to identify Maori beliefs, values, and experiences that overlay the six dimensions of the framework. With regard to Maori identity, special care was taken to:

> ...avoid defining and constricting Maori clients/whānau on a continuum or spectrum of 'Maoriness'...the Meihana Model works on the assumption that any client/whānau that self-identifies as Maori is Maori, regardless of the degree to which this is evident to the clinician. (120)

The authors also stated that:

> The role of the clinician is not to determine 'how Maori the client is,' or their level of 'Maoriness.' It is instead to identify their beliefs, values, and experiences within a Maori context, both currently and in the past. This allows the clinical team to explore how these factors influence and impact on presenting issues and how they may impact on potential intervention plans. (120)

The Meihana Model is inclusive of Maori cultural beliefs, values, and experiences and is designed to assist the mental health service/worker to enable the clients to define their experiences in a way that is congruous with their experiences. Although the pilot is still underway, initial results are promising. However, there are limitations with the model, which I will now address.

Exclusion of Maori Women's Bi/Multiracial Corporeality and Plural Ethnicity

Assessment and intervention models, like the Meihana Model, which seek to avoid classifying and homogenizing Maori as a unified group, correctly resist normative and linear models of identity. They avoid the prescriptive assumptions and expectations underpinning continuum identity narratives.

These models assume that people of Maori decent who have not been sub-jectivized with a singular Maori cultural identity (ethnic identification and a sense of belonging to a Maori whānau, iwi, and hapu and related shared values beliefs and practices) will naturally seek out a "traditional" or quintes-sentially Maori identity (Moeke-Maxwell 2003, 2006, 2007). Identity continuum arguments tend to assume that obtaining an authentic or quintessential Maori ethnicity is not only easily obtainable but contingent upon *matauranga* Maori (learning about indigenous knowledge, including whānau histories and cul-tural traditions, and *whakapapa*, cultural values, beliefs, language, and spiritual beliefs and customs). It also assumes participation in familial, social, cultural, and/or political endeavors associated with Maori culture. Further, identity continuum narratives do not support plural cultural experiences (different cultural "truths" Maori have about themselves), and they also function to lock Maori and Pakeha/Other into an "us" and "them" binary opposition, fore-closing the possibility of other postcolonial New Zealand identity narratives.

I have argued elsewhere that dominant narratives of Maori identity are informed by, and inform, essentialist driven constructions of a *tuturu* (tradi-tional/authentic) Maori identity associated with national identity formation (Moeke-Maxwell 2003). I have argued that a continuum model of ethnicity is identifiable at one end by an axis that functions as "lack" or "cultural deficit." The identity narratives associated with this axis are stereotypically narrated as either colonized (read: disenfranchised, criminalized, and/or pathologized) or assimilated – the ultimate conclusion of colonialism and subjugation of race/difference to the national requirement of unity/community epitomized in the formation of a monocultural nationalism (Moeke-Maxwell 2003). The national imperative to create a unified, homogenous community was real-ized in the early 1900s and influenced the social construction of Maori and Pakeha identity (Belich 1996, Sinclair 1986). At the other end of the identity continuum axis is the desirable quintessential or tuturu identity signified by cultural markers of Maori difference (*te reo*, cultural beliefs, values and norms, association with *whenua*/land). In short, the underlying imperative within descriptive continuum models prescribes people with Maori ancestry as "on their way" to becoming more Maori. By extension, it implies that as one becomes "more" Maori, one becomes "less" of something else. The struggle with this ethnic polarization has been documented in recent years (Collins 1999; Meridith 1999a, 1999b, 1999c; Moeke-Maxwell 2003, 2005, 2006).

The health models (Whare Tapa Wha, and the Meihana Model more spe-cifically) have the capacity to provide an exploration of the client's identity through the cultural lens of the client and their whānau. As stated previ-ously, the clinician's role is to enable an identification of the client's values, beliefs, and experiences within a Maori context to enable an exploration of the way these factors impact the presenting issues and intervention initia-tives. But herein lies the problem, and it is twofold. First, the clients may not be able to articulate sufficiently their unique ambivalence and multiple positioning. They may have little understanding of the way in which their plural ethnicity and bi/multiracial corporeality, gendered subjectivities, and multiple spatial positioning (associated with their respective cultures) create contradictions and instabilities that position them discursively in the nation. A new language is required to enable bi/multiracial people to understand how subjects are called into being via their gendered and racial corporeality within the nation and how they resist the call to a singular ethnicity (Foster 1996, Hall 1997).

Secondly, given the lack of research on Maori identity with respect to plural ethnicity and bi/multiracial corporeality, and an absence of health frameworks that take into consideration bi/multiracial corporality and eth-nic plurality, mental health clinicians are poorly positioned to facilitate the exploration of diverse ethnic narratives. Nor is enough known about the way power discursively works in the nation to privilege or disadvantage Maori based upon white and brown corporeal bodies within the postcolo-nial nation (Moeke-Maxwell 2003, 2005, 2006). Irrespective of the recent shift from biological quantification to ethnic diversity, "brownness" still func-tions metonymically as Maori "difference" in the postcolonial nation. Race, or the symbolic value attached to brownness (and in binary opposition to whiteness), has consequences for how subjects are discursively positioned in material ways in the nation. "Space" is not innocent; it is always loaded with cultural meaning (Friedman 1998, McDowell 1999, Mohanram 1999, Yeat-man 1995). Therefore, racial corporeality must be taken into consideration in articulations of Maori subjectivity. Further, women are socially constructed in highly specific ways, which needs to be included within the exploration of subjectivity (Butler 1990).

Having a deeper awareness and understanding of bi/multiracial corpo-reality and ethnic diversity will contribute to successful assessments and interventions through exploring the rich narrative context of individual bi/multiracial women. For example, within the dimension of "Iwi Katoa," the authors of the Meihana Model discuss the place of "attachment" for Maori clients accessing health services. The authors state that a high level of attachment is important for a client to establish rapport with the service and clinician to ensure a sense of safety. However, I suggest that this is compromised if clinicians continue to hold dominant identity narratives about Maori identity irrespective of how Maori narrate their life experiences. Clinicians could benefit from cultural competencies training and health models that engender an exploration of the complexities associated with being bi/multiracial and with identifying with more than one ethnicity. This would allow for a deeper understanding of the client's issues and could be useful in informing relevant and meaningful interventions. Further, it is not just consumers who are becoming increasingly more diverse, but the Maori workforce is also becoming multiply subjectivized and discursively inscribed reflecting diverse realities and experiences. The mental health sector must focus on creating landscapes of inclusivity to honor the *tino rangatiratanga* of every individual; client, whānau, and clinician. The trick is not to throw out the pearl with the oyster shell.

Including Bi/Multiracial Corporeality and Plural Ethnicity

As highlighted, Maori models of health incorporate a holistic perspective that includes contextualizing the individual's sense of self and life experiences within the broader whānau identity and environment in an effort to achieve an integrated approach to health care. The Meihana Model attempts to address each dimension of a client's life through a cultural lens. If we extend upon this to look at the client through a bi/multicultural lens, we will see that a number of lenses are needed to view the individual to make sense of his or her life experiences. Without cultural competencies in plural ethnicity, informed by the subject's bi/multiracial subjectivity and heterogeneous/shifting spatial positioning, an unprepared clinician could miss valuable opportunities to explore the client's unique life experiences. The ways bi/multiracial women resist or mediate their ambiguous and often culturally conflicted identities as they resist the call to authenticity or its marginalized counterpart could provide information about resiliency, for example. Given the desire to see services providing best practice and quality services for Maori service users, informed clinicians could support bi/multiracial women to make sense of, and develop new meaning about, their identities and life experiences.

Previous research on this subject provided me with some insight into the social construction of the bi/multiracial subject (Moeke-Maxwell 2003). This led me to think about how the subject becomes inscribed with identity through the nation's call to inclusivity in the bicultural nation. The bicultural nation discursively calls its subjects into being as either Maori or Pakeha via the corporeal presence of individual white or brown bodies. Through their respective *whanaungatanga* (family ties, connections, and relationships) and historically specific life experiences, the call to "being" is either sanctioned or disavowed. This "difference" produces an anxiety that is constantly in flux, mediated, or repressed. The anxiety is produced through tensions that emerge as a result of the bi/multiracial woman's presence on the cultural margins. As the subject of difference, she is both familiar and feared; neither brown nor white, she is the excess of the Maori/Pakeha colonial relationship.

Bi/multiracial women are likely to be positioned on the bicultural interface between indigenous and Western landscapes as cultural interlocutors in spaces that often produce bicultural hot spots (places of cross-cultural disjuncture) that have real implications for the bi/multiracial woman (Moeke-Maxwell 2003, 2006). Bi/multiracial women may even be exoticized or experience different forms of racism dependent on their phenotypes and their spatial positioning within the nation. My previous research indicated that space (read: landscape) is symbolically loaded with cultural meaning. Symbolically, brown bodies function metonymically as Maori cultural landscape and Pakeha as non-Maori cultural landscape; Maori belong in brown spaces, and white bodies belong in white places. Brown bodies in symbolically designated white/Pakeha spaces, or white bodies in symbolically designated brown/indigenous spaces may provoke an uncanny anxiety in the nation's psyche, which produces neocolonial forms of racism toward the newly excluded other, the bi/multiracial woman. In turn, new configurations of contestation and resistance are formed as bi/multi women resist the call to be relegated to either brown or white landscapes. Wen Shu Lee provides a definition of colorism:

> Awareness of the ideological operations of color codes challenges aesthetic values associated with different colors. One may argue that black pearls

are as beautiful as white pearls, and white swans are no more elegant than black swans. When color is used to mark a group of people away from another group of people, and such a marking becomes the basis for one group's inferiority to another, color becomes 'colorism' and is co-opted into as system of privilege and oppression, a hierarchy. Blackness and whiteness are no longer innocent, an abstract, aesthetic matter. They become markers used to explain and justify concrete material gain and loss, privilege and the lack thereof. (1997:283)

Gender is linked to cultural norms and regulations (ways of behaving) that impact the subject's performance as the raced or de-raced gendered subject. Having more than one gendered code can cause conflict, contradiction, and uncertainty, which need to be supported and managed. Linda McDowell states:

Instead of identities of 'oppositional' or 'minority' groups being constructed as different from a 'norm,' it is now asserted that all identities are a fluid amalgam of memories of places and origins, constructed by and through fragments and nuances, journeys and rests, of movements between. Thus, the 'in-between' is itself a process or a dynamic, not just a stage on the way to a more final identity. (1999:215)

Mental health professionals, with the appropriate knowledge, can support Maori to gain a richer understanding of their cultural identity/ies and ethnicity/ies and movements "in-between" to ensure health gains are maximized.

To be more specific, I return to the blind spot in current health models. I argue here they subjugate "race" to "culture." In a nation where raced and de-raced bodies are called into being and positioned discursively in the nation with material advantages and disadvantages on the basis of color (phenotypes), health models should be amended to examine the configuration of the raced and gendered body in explorations of client subjectivity and historically specific experience. The clinician should be mindful that the individual's life experiences and reality may be quite different to his or her family's identity formation. For example, if an individual's mother is Indian and her father is Maori, the bi/multiracial subject will arguably have a different subjectivity to her family based on her dual cultural templates and biracial corporeal presence and performance. This will no doubt produce different knowledge and experiences than that which is available to the parents. The bi/multiracial subject exceeds the "difference" of either parent. She may have more than one *turangawaewae* (place of belonging/home) and an assortment of different *tikanga* (cultural values, beliefs, and practices) dependent on her genealogies.

Extending Maori Health Frameworks: Bi/Multiracial Maori Inclusivity

Who Maori are, how Maori make sense of their lives, their singular (Maori) worldview, or their dual or multiple cultural experiences and worldviews are important if Maori are to achieve optimal health gains. The health environment must be culturally accessible and responsive to ensure Maori feel comfortable accessing health services. It is every individual's right to develop and maintain a healthy image of himself or herself, to have good self-esteem, and to have relationships with mental health services and clinicians who include their whānau and who understand the complexity of Maori identity. Maori health frameworks, like the Whare Tapa Wha model and the Meihana Model, could be extended by ensuring the clinician becomes more aware of the social construction of bi/multiracial women's subjectivity and plural ethnicity. The following suggestions contribute an example of how health professionals might begin to think more laterally about Maori identity.

Suggestions for Mental Health Assessments and Interventions

- Every person has the right to make decisions concerning their identity/ies without being obstructed or limited in any way.
- Every person of Maori descent has the right to expect mental health treatment that supports the person's ethnicity or helps the individual to develop and maintain his or her unique sense of ethnic identity.
- Individuals have the right to define themselves ethnically in whatever way they feel best explains their particular set of circumstances (histories, biological descent lines, etc.).
- Every person has the right to express how he or she feels about his or her ethnicity without the mental health professionals assuming they know best.

- "Meaning" about one's ethnicity will be varied in accordance with the diversity of descent lines, corporeality (phenotypes), and ethnic alliances. Mental health professionals will accept that Maori identity can be diverse, complicated, and subject to change.
- Mental health professionals should take care not to pathologize people who have more than one cultural/ethnic and biological identity. The health professional has a responsibility to normalize diverse ethnic self-identifications to enable Maori consumers to makes sense of, and manage, any notable tensions their plural ethnicities and bi/multiracial genealogies present.
- People who do not have a clear understanding of their ethnicity have the right to non-biased information about Maori ethnic diversity and bi/multi-raciality. Where appropriate, and in consultation with the individual and/or his or her whānau, this may include the provision of appropriate cultural resources (including *kaumatua*, *tohunga* (spiritual experts), and culturally competent health experts) or support.
- Having more than one cultural ethnicity does not reduce the "value" of what it means to be Maori. Maori clients will experience themselves, and express themselves, as Maori in a variety of different ways. It is important that clients' experiential awareness and understanding of themselves as Maori is not diminished by the presence of other ethnic experiences and identities or racial embodiment.

When working with Maori, it might be a useful to consider the following:

- Does the client have more than one set of *whakapapa* (Maori, Pakeha, Other), cultural histories, or cultural experiences and ethnicities?
- How does the client define himself or herself phentotypically, and does this inform the client's cultural and ethnic identification/s or the way the client is perceived ethnically?
- Do you assume a client is Maori because he or she is brown or not because he or she signifies as white?
- What does the consumer think and feel about his or her body (proud, ashamed, confused, angry, happy, etc.)?
- Has, or does the bi/multiracial client experience being exoticised?
- How does the client make sense of his or her bi/multi-raced body and plural ethnicity?

- If the bi/multiracial woman is white, or brown, or signifies phentotypically with Asian or Chinese corporeality, for example, what types of narratives might this produce and what meaning does the client have about herself and her presence in her whānau, iwi, and society in general?
- Does the individual's gendered and racial corporeality impact the client's construction of himself or herself as Maori and Jewish, or Maori and Chinese, or Maori and Samoan, or so on?
- Are there any overlaps or spaces of synthesis or disjuncture caused through being multiply subjectivated, and by extension, multiply positioned spatially within the nation?
- Are there any problems caused through their cultural vacillations as they travel to their respective homes/roots and places of ethnic specificity? How might these constant journeys impact them?
- What are the risks and rewards if one is brown or white or signifies as someone Other than Maori and Pakeha New Zealander?
- How might racism impact people who live with the ambiguity of straddling and mediating two or more ethnicities and cultural realities/lifestyles that produce experiences that may be different to Maori (e.g., those who not only signify as Maori but also identify solely with a Maori worldview)?
- How does internalized racial stigma and discrimination impact people?
- What is the whānau's narrative about the individual's identity, and how might this align with or differ from the client's story?
- How does the client "perform" his or her ethnic plurality?
- How does the client manage or mediate his or her plural ethnicity?
- Do the client's ethnicities conflict or complement each other?
- Is there a unifying narrative that enables subjects to mediate the tensions that accompany their plural ethnicity and corporeality as they culturally vacillate across shifting landscapes?
- Does the client experience being in flux as he or she engages with conflicted space?

To this end, thinking about Maori women's identity in a way that incorporates the corporeality of the subject, as well as her plural ethnicity, will go some way toward providing relevant and motivating assessment and treatment plans.

Conclusion

Further research on Maori women's plural ethnicity and bi/multiracial corporeality needs to be undertaken if culturally meaningful health frameworks are to be developed and implemented within mental health services. This will go some way toward mental health services being able to respond effectively to those who identify ethnically as Maori. Through extending the workforce's clinical and cultural competencies, their capacity to engage with, and respond to, the bi/multiracial woman in a more meaningful and useful way will hopefully assist health gains. By way of example, I suggested that mental health services and practitioners must foster a greater awareness and understanding of bi/multiracial Maori women's subjectivity within assessment and intervention frameworks to ensure a more in-depth process can be undertaken. An exploration of the individual's understanding of the social construction of her identity, within the context of the whānau identity, will no doubt promote a deeper narrative about her experiences. This rich contextual information could provide a wealth of information about the bi/multiracial subject, which could support the health worker to promote health gains. If health initiatives take into account the rich wealth of information about the Maori client's values and beliefs about plural ethnicity and bi/multiracial corporeality, an opportunity exists to support recovery.

Maori are a diverse group of people who have a shared history and cultural traditions. Maori are increasingly becoming more racially and culturally diverse. Ethnic identification with more than one culture and history, and participation in the cultural experiences that accompany these, exceed the available narratives of Maori identities that inform current assessment and intervention models today. Not to look more critically at the discourse of Maori identity (and, within this, the exploration of self-constructions of identity that are informed by bi/multiracial genealogy, ethnic plurality, and the multiple cultural positioning that stem from the client's respective subjectivities) runs the risk of throwing out the pearl with the oyster shell. In this chapter, I proposed some suggestions that might be a useful starting point for actually engaging more closely with cultural diversity in terms of the process of engagement with respect to assessments and intervention initiatives with bi/multiracial women. How people make sense of their "difference" and "sameness" via their respective Maori and Pakeha/Other corporeal embodiment will provide useful information that will contribute to health gains.

These suggestions may enable mental health professionals to include Maori women's bi/multiracial corporeality and ethnic diversity within assessment and intervention strategies in more depth. Health frameworks that can equip clinicians to understand how bi/multiracial Maori women become named, and simultaneously answer the call to identity, is hugely important if mental health services are to respond meaningfully to her unique life experiences and assist her recovery journey.

Epilogue

I return to the opening story to conclude. At the end of the bridging course, both the Maori and Pakeha groups came back together to form one group. A *kaumatua* (respected Maori leader) was invited to speak to the class. He presented us with a *wero* (challenge) when he stated:

> When Maori come to university they are happy to get a C grade on their assignment, and they think 'Ka pai, I've passed!' But, I'm telling you Maori students, don't settle for the C mark—go for the A. Play hard and work hard; but no matter what, aim for excellence to help our people.

After the bridging course, my three children and I left our whānau and moved towns so I could study. By the time my PhD was conferred in 2003, I had been awarded numerous scholarships/awards for my academic achievements.

Yes, I am white. And I still do not have a great command of *te reo*. But somehow, this white girl heard the *kaumatua*'s call.

Glossary of Maori Words

hinengaro: mind; heart; conscience

hui: gathering; meeting

iwi: tribe; extended family group; people

Maori: New Zealand indigenous person

marae: meeting ground; traditional infrastructure

Ngati (Nga/Ngai): people of (used with tribal names)

Pakeha: New Zealander of European/British ancestry

tangata whenua: indigenous person/people; "people of the land"

tauiwi: white colonial settler; foreigner; immigrant

te reo Maori: the Maori language

tikanga: indigenous knowledge/practice; traditional custom

tinana: body

tino rangatiratanga: total self-government; national independence

tohunga: priest

tuturu: authentic; original

wairua: spirit

wero: challenge

whakapapa: ancestry; genealogical links

whānau: family; community

whanaungatanga: kinship systems/relationships; relative; kin

whare: house

whenua: land; placenta

Chapter Thirteen

Women Occupying the Hybrid Space: Second-Generation Korean-American Women Negotiating Choices Regarding Work and Family

Helen Kim

For children of immigrants, the task of incorporating two or more cultures to create a hybrid culture and identity is an inextricable part of everyday life. Second-generation Asian-Americans, for instance, often confront the challenges of negotiating the norms, beliefs, and behaviors associated with a specific ethnic/cultural background (e.g., Korean, Japanese, Indian) distinct from those located within mainstream American society. Thus, arriving at a "hyphenated American" identity is often the result of these negotiations, whereby children of immigrants are able to fuse elements of seemingly distinct cultural backgrounds to comfortably self-identify as a hybrid.

Carving out a hybrid identity, especially for second-generation individuals of color, is more nuanced than merely combining distinct ethnic/cultural backgrounds. This process necessarily calls into question how individuals navigate interlocking systems of privilege and oppression, which are inherently gendered and racialized. For Americans of Asian descent, long-standing racialized images continue to paint this population as "other." Most often,

Asians are depicted as "forever foreigners" – unassimilable and sometimes threatening to the social, economic, and political security of mainstream white America. These racialized images are also gendered. Asian-Americans are repeatedly portrayed as both masculine and feminine at the same time that they are neither masculine nor feminine. Asian-American women, for example, are depicted as hyperfeminine, submissive, and sexually available to men at the same time that they are masculinized as scheming, treacherous "Dragon Ladies" (Espiritu 1997). These "controlling images" (Hill Collins 2000) may potentially result in the internalization of racialized and gendered stereotypes to the point where members of the second generation may reject their particular racial and ethnic/cultural identity in favor of one more closely associated with the white mainstream.

The task, then, for second-generation Asian-Americans in carving out a hybrid identity involves a complex web of negotiations not only with different cultural backgrounds that assume different ethnic and gender norms but also with mainstream racialized and gendered images that paint Asian-Americans as foreign and other. Indeed, for members of the second generation, arriving at a hybrid identity involves maneuvering social hierarchies based on intersections of race, ethnicity, and gender in addition to shifting norms that signal difference.

The notion of hybridity based on intersections of race, ethnicity, and gender is especially salient to our understanding of the social construction of gender (Kessler and McKenna 1978, Lorber 1994, West and Zimmerman 1987). Especially as women move among numerous arenas governed by different racialized gendered norms, "doing gender" may vary across social locations. For example, second-generation Asian-American women attending college constantly transition within different social contexts (e.g., school, family, peer group, etc.) that may be dictated by multiple and sometimes conflicting norms and expectations and, as a result, may change their gender performances accordingly. Furthermore, these women may utilize various strategies to realize these shifts.

At the empirical level, a fairly new and growing body of research has analyzed how Asian-American women "do gender" as these performances reflect dominant and subordinate femininities (Pyke and Johnson 2003). Investigations into the ways members of this population negotiate these hierarchies can shed light on some important questions regarding the everyday construction of gender for racially and ethnically marginalized women. For example, how do the choices Asian-American women make regarding career and family life reflect privileged and lesser femininities? What meaning and value do Asian-American women attribute to the various femininities with which they interact? How and why do these women actualize and distance themselves from multiple racialized femininities?

This chapter addresses some of these questions and issues by looking at how a sample of 20 second-generation Korean-American women attending a prestigious Midwestern public university negotiate multiple dominant and subordinate femininities in the everyday construction of their gender identities. More specifically, I argue that interviewees' aspirations to fulfill certain academic and career paths reflect numerous racialized gender ideologies, especially regarding beliefs surrounding white femininity, which are privileged over those associated with Asian femininity. Furthermore, I demonstrate that in interaction with these multiple femininities, informants attempt to carve out a hybrid identity based on a racialized femininity that does not cast their position as inferior to whites. In these attempts, informants identify their choices regarding future roles as Asian/Korean-American women as a way of preserving a positive sense of race/ethnicity as well as gender.

To frame my analysis, I draw on the scholarship regarding the intersections of race/ethnicity and gender, which posits that images of femininity most closely associated with white upper-class women are privileged over those connected to women of color from different class backgrounds. As a result, racialized femininities, such as those associated with Asian-Americans, are subordinated. To understand my informants' responses to dominant and subordinated femininities, I also describe various "controlling images" (Hill Collins 2000) that mainstream society has perpetuated of racially marginalized women, with attention paid to those regarding Asian women.

In addition, I detail some of the research on gender dynamics among Asian-Americans, particularly as gender arrangements and conceptualizations of women's roles have shifted with the transition from one's country of origin to the United States. This background information is important to understand since most of my informants referred to these in their conceptualizations of Asian femininities and, more broadly, what it means to be an Asian/Korean-American woman.

Literature Review

Within the sociological literature, recent work has emerged to illustrate how women construct their gender identities within a system in which racism and sexism operate simultaneously. In particular, some feminist scholars have argued that a dominant femininity operates to privilege white upper-class women over racially marginalized women. While gender analyses have relied on a longer tradition of investigating the ways in which men's domination of women and hierarchies among men have operated (Chen 1999, Connell 1987, Pyke 1996), much less attention has been paid to how certain femininities and groups of women are privileged over others.

Recent scholarship on the intersection of race, gender, and class has focused more actively on dominant and subordinated femininities. Much of this work focuses on "controlling images" that normalize an image of femininity associated with white upper-class women and simultaneously devalues other femininities located among racially marginalized groups. A prominent example of this type of scholarship can be found in Patricia Hill Collins' (2000) work on mainstream society's images of black women. Hill Collins argues that dominant white society perpetuates depictions of the overly aggressive black matriarch to fault women for poverty, declining marriage rates, and the absence of black fathers among this population. Hill Collins also argues that these images become internalized among women of color so that they continually reinforce white femininity as an unproblematic standard at the same time that they limit the possibility of identification on one's own terms. Thus, racially marginalized women draw upon these images to make sense out of their everyday construction of their racialized gender identities.

Work concerning Asian-American women also demonstrates the significance of controlling images that shape the construction of gender for members of this population. While mainstream society has depicted black women as domineering and aggressive, women of Asian descent are predominantly seen as hyperfeminine. Controlling images also paint Asian and Asian-American women as passive, submissive, sexually exotic, and always available for men (Espiritu 1997). Similar to the ramifications of dominant images of black women, such depictions often limit the possibility of positive self-identification among Asian and Asian-American women while simultaneously privileging white femininity as superior.

Just as Asian-American women's conceptualizations of femininity may be informed by mainstream controlling images that are internalized, women's everyday construction of gender also reflects dominant gender ideologies and arrangements as they are rooted in lived experiences. Especially for children of immigrants, movement between arenas with different and sometimes opposing ideologies can result in substantial conflict concerning issues related to gender (Zhou and Bankston 1998). These individuals may negotiate between gender norms that they perceive to be located within the mainstream and/or those they more closely associate with their race/ethnicity.

Scholarship on Asians and Asian-Americans argues that gender ideologies and arrangements are rooted in longstanding patriarchal systems but also recognizes some important shifts currently underway. Countries like Korea are informed by a Confucian moral code in which men are granted authority and power over women in all social arenas, ranging from the family to economic and political spheres. While men occupy positions of power outside the domestic sphere, women's identities are wrapped up in their role as homemakers expected to be in service primarily to a household's male members. Furthermore, the Confucian family structure in Korea encumbers women with the responsibility of caring for their husbands' immediate and extended family. Traditionally, these expectations have meant that Korean women live with their in-laws, abandoning their own families of origin. More recently, living arrangements and duties assigned to women have shifted, with couples living independently from their parents and extended families. Yet, Korean women are, in large part, expected to assume domestic responsibilities including child care, household maintenance, and care for their own relatives and in-laws (Abelmann and Lie 1995). While these conditions are most closely associated with the lives of first generation women, members of the second generation interact with and are impacted by this ideology, most closely in everyday family and home life.

However, the most dominant ideologies and systems are not immune to resistance or redefinition, and the experiences of Korean immigrants to the US provide examples of such change. With migration to the United States, first-generation Korean-Americans have undergone dramatic changes in gender arrangements, especially as Korean men have witnessed losses in their economic power upon arrival and have increasingly depended on their wives' earnings (Lim 1997, Min 1998). Along with their participation in the paid labor force and accompanying economic power, first-generation women have experienced increased autonomy and diminished ties to the domestic sphere. Nevertheless, Korean women have not completely abandoned an ethnic patriarchal system, especially as it confirms their parental authority and supplies a familiar structure to confront the social expectations, discrimination, and economic insecurity of US society (Lim 1997). Thus, actual shifts in male-female arrangements do not preclude the continued pervasiveness of traditional gender ideologies located in one's ethnicity coupled with mainstream controlling images pertaining to women of Asian descent. In this sense, first-generation Korean-American women, on an everyday basis, assume a hybrid identity to begin with. Through their participation in the US workforce and their local ethnic communities and families, immigrant women simultaneously embody Korean and American identities as they adopt differing cultural norms according to shifting social locations.

Privileged and subordinate racialized femininities, especially as they juxtapose white women to Asian-American women, emerged quite prominently throughout this project. In the following sections, I demonstrate how these issues played out for my informants in the social realms of work and family. More specifically, I discuss how their decisions to pursue either the domestic sphere and/or the paid labor force post-college reflect their sense of being able to actualize a certain kind of racialized femininity. My focus on these arenas reflects respondents' efforts to make sense out of their positions as second-generation Korean-American women attending college, poised to make choices about entering the paid labor force and/or the domestic sphere. While I did not anticipate hearing as much as I did about their future goals as they related to work and family, it became quickly clear that their constructions of gender heavily revolved around their career and family aspirations.

Research Method

Over a six-month period from March to October 2003, I conducted in-depth, semi-structured interviews with 20 second-generation Korean-American women attending a major Midwestern public university. All the women in my sample self-identified as Korean-American and Asian-American. Ranging in age from 18 to 24 with an average age of 19.5, interviewees were either in the midst of their college education or had just received their bachelor's degree. Those who had recently completed their undergraduate education were waiting to start full-time jobs in fall 2003 or were taking time off to decide what to do next. Among my sample, 17 women were of the true second generation, having been born and raised solely in the United States. The remaining three were born in South Korea and emigrated to the US at or before the age of three.

Rather than conduct interviews on a one-time basis, I wanted to talk to women multiple times for various reasons. Foremost, I was interested in gaining participants' trust, especially over the course of a discussion that delved into fairly personal subjects such as racial/gender identity. Multiple interviews allowed me to ask introductory questions to establish a rapport and subsequently follow up with questions that were more sensitive in nature and that incorporated responses from the previous interview(s). This allowed time for reflection between interviews for myself and the interviewees. In addition, the wide range, depth, and seriousness of questions did not seem suited for a one-shot one- to two-hour period of time. Along with concerns of not being able to establish a comfortable level of trust during one session, I was concerned that participants would feel overwhelmed and tire easily during a single long interview session.

First interviews consisted of questions and responses revolving around background information such as childhood and adolescent experiences, daily activities, academic interests, and future goals and priorities. During many of the interviews, I did not need to prompt women to talk about the intersections of race and gender according to their experiences. Rather, they freely discussed conceptualizations of Korean-American/Asian-American women as part of their growing up, their current day-to-day experiences as college students, and the diversity of contexts within these environments. Second and final interviews served as opportunities to focus more specifically on racial/gender conceptualizations brought up by the interviewees themselves during initial interviews. Furthermore, discussions centered on racialized beliefs about gender behavior as they demonstrated responses to mainstream society's depictions of Asian-American women in relationship to racialized gender imagery of other women. These conversations heavily revolved around future goals and choices regarding career and family after college.

Negotiating Choices Regarding Work and Family: Incorporating Dominant and Subordinated Femininities

As a backdrop to a discussion of gender identity pertaining to women's aspirations, it is important to highlight how respondents conceptualized Asian and white femininities especially as they are reflected in their career and family goals. First, Asian femininity and Asian women were generally viewed in terms of dominant stereotypes. Informants negatively remarked on characteristics of the "typical Asian woman" or the "typical Korean woman," who was commonly described according to dominant stereotypes associated with submissiveness and passivity. More concretely, participants referenced first-generation Asian women in these depictions. This population was often negatively portrayed as composed of stay-at-home moms whose primary functions were to maintain the household through domestic tasks such as cooking and cleaning. By describing these women primarily in a derogatory manner, informants attempted to distance themselves from this image. In addition, first-generation Asian women, such as the informants' own mothers or female relatives, were described as the "typical Asian woman" or the "typical Korean woman" even though they were largely recognized as economic contributors to the household income. That they assumed domestic roles in addition to their paid labor cast them in a negative light in which they were seen as subservient to men. Often, interviewees referenced their own mothers in this fashion, commenting on the power differentials between fathers who generally did not assume domestic roles and, therefore, had more leisure time for individual pursuits. Even though some informants recognized their own mothers as personal role models for the economic and domestic sacrifices they made for their families, they were simultaneously depicted and denigrated as subservient to men. Moreover, first-generation mothers were seen as absent from disciplining children, while fathers were viewed as the primary enforces of rules and standards in the home.

In contrast, images of white gender arrangements were viewed as much more egalitarian. Pertaining to the domestic sphere, for example, "in American families the wife will cook and the husband will do the dishes" (Lani). This view of gender roles among whites was also reflected in observations on attitudes toward achievement. In general, white women were regarded as having more choices available to them because of a greater emphasis on individual power and freedom. Many interviewees reflected on these options with a sense of envy and perceived their own lives as devoid of any personal choice. However, as I will discuss, informants revealed various elements of individual choice regarding their goals and aspirations as they engaged with multiple expectations concerning their position as Asian/Korean-American women.

For many of my interviewees, their aspirations as college-educated Asian-American women revolved heavily around decisions to enter and remain in the professional world vs. the domestic sphere. These paths were predominantly seen on two ends of a spectrum with the choice of one role precluding the possibility of fulfilling the other simultaneously. While the literature on women and work has long emphasized similar concerns inherent in these options for women of diverse backgrounds, informants centralized particular racialized and ethnicized conceptualizations of women's responsibilities and femininity in their discussions of these future roles. More specifically, women highlighted their ambitions using a lens through which the importance of realizing their future professional and/or domestic roles reflects the actualization of a certain kind of femininity wrapped up in their position as second-generation Korean-American women. As I detail further, my interviewees' choices as Korean-American women predominantly reflect numerous tensions surrounding the preservation of some level of ethnic authenticity (Tuan 1999, Kibria 2002) that cannot be divorced from certain gender dynamics and notions of femininity. In more concrete terms, the pressure to fulfill the model minority image, and therefore maintain a sense of racial and ethnic legitimacy, emerged as a reflection of the position of women, especially in the historical context of Korean immigrant women's participation in the US paid labor force and the perceived effects of first-generation women's work on second-generation daughters. Furthermore, the available options women identified were also depicted in terms of how these compare primarily to other white women who embody a more dominant racialized femininity. These discussions are critical to illuminate not only because they appropriately fuse gender with race and ethnicity but also because they identify the strategies women employ to conform to and resist various forms of dominant and subordinated femininities.

The importance of academic and occupational success clearly emerged as a launchpad from which many of my interviewees shaped their sense of racial, ethnic, and gender identity. Consistent with previous scholarship, assumptions of high academic achievement and professional status among this population appear gender-blind, with success open to men and women alike. On the surface, this perspective rang clear repeatedly throughout my conversations with informants who openly stressed the intense pressures they felt to achieve. More specifically, women talked about the importance of high academic achievement in college as a necessary stepping stone toward doing "the typical Asian thing" or "the typical Korean thing" – by working hard and getting good grades, one can secure stable and well-paid employment upon graduation and ensure a stable and prosperous life beyond school. In this sense, it appears that the belief in a meritocratic system open to Korean-Americans and Asian ethnics alike emphasizes the possibility of achievement regardless of one's gender.

However, the more I talked with women about what it takes to succeed, the more certain gendered expectations necessary to enact these strategies emerged. Informants extensively discussed academic and occupational achievement as the product of participation in a highly competitive atmosphere characterized by traditional masculine traits such as aggressiveness and individualism. These depictions of the Asian-American model minority contrast what little scholarship addresses the gendered dimensions of this image, namely as one associated with docility and passiveness as ingredients of success. To be the "typical Asian" for many interviewees is to actualize the standard of a high-achieving woman who relies on more masculine strategies to attain success that upset traditional notions and images of Asian femininity, which monolithically depict Asian women to be hyper-passive and subservient. In this sense, achieving "model minority" status emerges as a type of hybrid identity, as it is seen as an expression of female and male characteristics. In terms of how gender intersects with ethnicity, this hybridity can also be interpreted as an identity that informants assume as a means for them to retain that which they see as ethnically Asian or Korean within American society.

Informants like Angela, a first-year student who identifies ambitions of going to medical school that are not completely her own, elaborated on various gendered dimensions of academic rivalry among co-ethnics in the context of parental expectations to succeed. Additionally, she discusses these dynamics in the context of other options to competition that she sees available to her:

> Helen: When you say you talk about competition with your Korean friends, what are you competing about?

Angela: We talk about competition and pressure, like what our parents expect of us. Our dad, his dream was for the five of us (Angela and her three sisters and brother) to be doctors and right now it's zero. I don't know if I want to be because of him, because he said something or because he hasn't. And I know I want to, but my best Korean friend, Jennica, is actually...she's an only child and so she and I are kind of in the same boat because we are our parents' last hope. We always talk about the pressure and how we don't necessarily know if it's worth the competition between our friends and just in this university or wherever we go to do something that we don't necessarily have the same passion for as our parents or as our other friends. We talk about our other friends who are in business school or are pre-law. It's amazing how competitive our friends can be. It's just something we never understand.

For women like Angela and Jennica, the demands of competition that come directly from one's parents and more broadly from dominant society indicate a gender ideology that resists conventional notions of Asian/Korean patriarchal demands on women. As their parents' "last hope," it appears that Angela's and Jennica's potential successes reflect gender-neutral positions as children of Korean parents who emigrated to the US to ostensibly provide better educational and occupational opportunities for their families. Yet, achievement largely hinges on being able to invoke a hybrid identity. In other words, informants view their success as dependent upon their ability to de-emphasize more conventional aspects of Asian femininity to be able to survive in a masculinized, cutthroat environment that includes Asian-American men and women.

Moreover, while this competition is most directly felt within informants' peer groups, which predominantly include other Korean-American students, these women are undoubtedly competing within a larger population encompassing students across various racial/ethnic and gender backgrounds. Thus, their success within the broader campus context further depends on being able to display a racialized gender performance that does double duty, intra-ethnically and among diverse groups.

Jennica, Angela's "best Korean friend" also talked to me about the parental demands regarding academic and occupational achievement and broader society's expectations of fulfilling a model minority status as an Asian-American college student. Amid these depictions, Jennica elaborates on the racialized/ethnic gender dimensions of these pressures as integral to her position as a Korean-American woman, and thus, as someone different from whites.

> Helen: How would you say that your parents raised you?
>
> Jennica: Well, they disciplined. My dad is (the disciplinarian), because I'm an only child, and my mom was really passive. So my dad took on that role. He was very strict, a very old-school Korean father, military-like, very, very disciplined. So, I'm not really used to, you know, when I hear some of my Caucasian friends, and the whole idea of, 'Oh, you can do whatever you want, go to college to have fun.' That's not my parents. My parents are like, 'Make sure you get into med school, make sure you get a job, so how'd you do on your last exam?' The stress level's very different. I know a lot of my Caucasian (girl) friends (from home) tend to really, I mean, they care about their grades, but if they don't do so hot, it's not the end of the world for them. And the sense of 'It's college, don't worry about it. You'll do fine next semester.' But to me, if I do poorly on an exam, then damn! I'm going to hear it from my dad and then hear from my mom, and then other Korean people are going to know. And then it's hard when my Caucasian (girl) friends are like, 'Don't worry about it! I'm sure your parents will understand.' And I'm just like, 'You don't understand, because my parents won't understand.

Distinct from the more relaxed attitude and perspective about achievement she locates among her white girlfriends from home, Jennica connects very strict expectations to succeed as something that is part of what it means to be a second-generation Korean-American. Jennica and other informants constructed whiteness and white femininity as devoid of pressures to achieve highly and, therefore, to assume fierce competition among one another. Interviewees talked about envying white female peers, in particular, for having a more relaxed and laissez-faire attitude toward academic and occupational accomplishment, in large part because their experiences were seen as devoid of parental and societal pressures to achieve. Additionally, Jennica and other informants constructed a certain level of personal and social security among white women that is seen as unavailable to Korean-American women. That Jennica stresses the impossibility of her white girlfriends' ability to understand the pressure to get good grades emphasizes these conceptualizations and positions them as desirable. Moreover, these comments point to the impossibility of Asian femininity mirroring white femininity and, as such, reinforce white femininity's position over other racialized forms. In addition, the comparison with white femininity perpetuates longstanding notions of a subordinated Asian femininity. Again, this kind of rationalization demonstrates an expression of hybridity through which women are able to retain their ethnic distinctiveness in American society. As Jennica and others framed their academic and career choices, most of which were approached with ambivalence and an absence of passion, as something forced upon them by parents, more traditional conceptualizations of Asian femininity were invoked. Informants' possible fulfillment of these roles reinforces these ideologies as they speak to the importance of filial piety and women's obligations to their own parents.

Just as informants spoke of the undesirability of competition among co-ethnic peers, they also constructed strong notions of tenuousness surrounding achievement in college and beyond. In this sense, women indirectly refuted popular notions of the Asian-American model minority who, because of hard work and diligence, is guaranteed success regardless of one's race, ethnicity, and/or gender. Thus, at the same time that interviewees normalized achievement intraracially and intraethnically, their personal sense of doubt and frustration challenges assumptions of security commonly held by co-ethnics who uphold the value of the model minority image.

More concretely tied to the racialized gender elements of Asian-American meritocracy, some interviewees spoke of their diminished sense of security in terms of their position as racially marginalized women. In our third conversation, Jule offered the following reflections on being a Korean-American woman:

> Helen: How do you feel being a Korean-American woman?
>
> Jule: I think there are probably more pressures than with white Americans because not only do you have to be a woman and put up with the same pressures of just looking a certain way, just looking the ideal, but because you're a minority it's more pressure to make a name for yourself. And to prove that although you are a minority, you are equal and that you can do the same or better career-wise as an Asian-American woman. So, there are the same pressures but more because you're a minority.
>
> Helen: Okay. What sort of advantages do you think there are to being a Korean-American woman?

Jule: That when you do accomplish your goals, it's more of a big deal. Like if a Caucasian woman made it in this world, it's like, "Wow. Okay, she's a woman; she made it." But then if she's a Korean-American, it's like, "Whoa!" Even more of a big deal.

What, then, does it mean for Korean-American women to choose to achieve in these ways, given the undesirable environment in which they feel they have to place themselves combined with their doubly marginalized position as Asian/Korean-American women? In addition to the societal and parental pressures that prevailed in our conversations, many informants talked specifically about the influence and histories of their first-generation mothers on their efforts to succeed academically and occupationally. Many interviewees described mothers who immigrated to the US not expecting to have to work in the paid labor force in addition to assuming the role of homemaker in the domestic sphere. These mothers were depicted as feeling trapped in dysfunctional marriages, especially because of a financial dependency on husbands due to their lack of education and immigration status. Interviewees talked about how their mothers have emphasized the importance of achievement in college as directly linked to individual freedom through financial independence and elimination of the need to rely on men for support. In this sense, women's notions of commitment to academic achievement are also colored by these experiences at the same time that they are seen as not guaranteed.

To negotiate these uncertainties and to foster a sense of ownership over something that was not the product of parental pressure, many informants talked about pursuing more domestic roles as alternatives to the pursuit of academic and professional success in an aggressive environment. Revisiting her pursuit of medical school in our third interview, Jennica talked to me about eventually wanting to become a housewife for numerous reasons that reflect a particular racialized femininity:

> Helen: The first time that we talked, you talked about how you were on the sort of pre-med track, and that you were thinking about it, but you really wouldn't mind just staying at home…
> Jennica: Right.
> Helen: …with the kids. What are your thoughts on that nowadays?
> Jennica: Pre-med's not really my thing anymore., I'm still…I'm taking Organic Chemistry II right now, but I think I'm gonna try pre-law. The thing is, personally, I just want to be a housewife. I'm just convinced that…I

guess it all depends who my husband is, but if he's someone that is really stressed out, then having two people have careers rips two people apart. And I'm very old school, very conservative, very anti-feminist. I'm very into the whole idea that he'll come home, and have his problems, and you're just there to be able to say, 'Oh no.' Talk to him, and just listen to him, that kind of thing. And I'm really big into family. I want that really tight home unit. Everyone says I'm wasting my time coming to the (University) to try to get an education in something I'm not even gonna do. But it's kind of like one of those things. My parents keep telling me, 'Well, you have to get an education, you have to get an education. What if you get married, and then your husband dies? And then you got nothing.' It's probably a good idea because you can only really be a housewife for so long because your kids go to school, and then there's really nothing to do at home. So it's good to have something to fall back on. And maybe just in case times get hard. And it's always good to have some kind of gift. I guess that would be a waste for me if I didn't pursue something.

Helen: What's appealing about being a housewife?

Jennica: I guess, I would say because my mom couldn't be one. So it's kind of like being able to take care of people, and not being so focused on work. When I was growing up, because my parents worked so much, I was very turned off by work. If I have to work, I'm a very hard worker. But in general, I don't like to be around making money. Even if I become a doctor, I really don't want to get paid for being a doctor. I would rather just work at free (clinic). That was my dream, which I don't think is gonna happen. But just to open up a free clinic. I'm not really into, like, making money. I think you tend to get too caught up in it, and especially when you do something like become a lawyer or a doctor or a business person, you get so caught up in the beginning. You're like, 'Oh no, no, no. I'm just doing it so I can get by.' But then you get so caught up in it, and then you forget what you're doing, you know, before you know it, you're like caught up in all this junk. But I don't like the whole idea of making money. And then secondly, if I was a housewife, I'd probably just be painting, which is my dream anyways – to just stay home and be able to just draw and paint.

Though Jennica doesn't abandon the possibility of having a professional career sometime in the future, she and others powerfully identify with desires to become housewives and lead domestic lives. This tension and the option to pick and choose highlight numerous aspects of a particular kind of racialized femininity they and other interviewees aspire to. First, situating the decision to become a professional as necessarily in conflict with being a mother and housewife precludes the possibility of assuming both roles simultaneously. Interviewees like Jennica expressed strong interest in eventually rejecting the path toward individual professional achievement as Korean-American women and, indeed, question whether or not "it is worth the competition" to succeed in light of domestic options available to them. In this sense, it seems that many interviewees are also rejecting a certain gender identity located among model minority Korean-American and Asian-American women who are successful as a result of maintaining a competitive edge. Instead, they are interested in realizing a type of femininity marked by supporting roles within the domestic sphere.

Another element of these negotiations, which illuminates a certain racialized/ethnic femininity, is the importance placed on the racial/ethnic background of one's future husband. Almost all of my interviewees placed great emphasis on the importance of preserving one's ethnic ties and identity through marriage, especially to a fellow second-generation Korean-American man who is well-educated and on a path toward a high-status professional job after college. Ideally, through marriage and parenting, various elements of one's ethnic background would be preserved and passed on to one's children. However, to realize the possibility of maintaining a sense of ethnic identity, women simultaneously identified the impossibility of assuming certain roles as Asian/Korean-American women because they would upset specific gender and power dynamics they situated within their own ethnic group. Thus, the option of a dual professional-career household was met with great skepticism by women who envisioned this path as a threat to the stability of a Korean-American partnership as well as to one's sense of gender identity.

Finally, the importance of choosing the domestic sphere over a professional career is clearly wrapped up in the presence of their own mothers in the home during their own childhood and adolescence. As statistics on Korean immigrant women's paid labor force participation in the US indicate, the presence of first-generation mothers in the home has not been strong since much of the economic survival of Korean immigrant families has depended heavily on women's wages. This absence was certainly evident in my informants' experiences and emerged as a point of discomfort and conflicting emotions in reflections on their upbringing. So, while interviewees recognized the important financial and emotional sacrifices their first-generation mothers made, they also were somewhat resentful of their mothers' absence in the home. In embarking on their own adulthood and the possibility of entering the working and domestic world, women like Lani and Jennica placed much greater importance on staying at home to ensure that their future husbands' and children's lives include the constant presence of a wife and mother.

Perhaps, then, one's position as a second-generation Asian/Korean-American woman incorporates these tensions. While some interviewees were interested in maintaining a traditional notion of Asian/Korean femininity, they expressed a desire to reclaim this in a more positive light that reflects their position as distinct from the first generation yet also tied to one's ethnic roots. Thus, while notions of the "typical Asian woman" were denigrated, informants were, indeed, drawn to the eventual possibility of actualizing this femininity, especially in light of the demands they encountered as college students. Especially as they locate the importance of preserving ties to their ethnic group through partnerships with second-generation Korean-American men, informants stress the need to actualize a particular kind of racialized/ethnic gender identity. In their everyday construction of gender, then, they reject a dominant femininity that privileges white women while they incorporate a subordinated femininity as it makes sense in their own lives. However, as informants reclaim this femininity, this choice plainly hinges on their conceptualizations of male desires, which may not completely correspond to their own.

Clearly, the hybrid identities adopted by my informants are ones chosen in the here and now. As they transition out of college, numerous questions regarding the stability of these hybrid identities come to mind. For example, with immersion in the paid labor force and/or the domestic sphere, how will these hybrid identities play out? Will they shift with differing social locations or will they remain similar? How might these hybrid identities play out in intimate relationships with men of similar or different racial and ethnic backgrounds? Future investigations may reveal greater insight into a wider range of conditions under which women who occupy the hybrid space maintain and shift these identities.

Discussion

In this chapter I have shown how my informants' discussions of work and family reflect their position as racially marginalized women who simultaneously construct an everyday sense of their gender identity according to dominant and subordinated femininities. Throughout, interviewees primarily emphasized the importance of conforming to the standard of the model minority, especially as these pressures were communicated by their immigrant parents. However, in contrast to much of the existing literature, the relation of Asian-American women to this marker has largely been overlooked, serving to further homogenize the experiences of all Asian Americans, regardless of gender. My informants' discussions of their relationship to this standard indicate their attempts to carve out a hybrid identity. Participants' position as second-generation women who are currently experiencing the pressures of conforming to a racialized standard that is often in conflict with more dominant conceptualizations of Asian femininity illuminate the struggles in arriving at a hybrid sense of self – one that stresses embodying gendered norms located within one's ethnicity while simultaneously requiring the discarding of their femininity as women of Korean descent.

The larger implications of such conversations are numerous. These findings illustrate the powerful back-and-forth between dominant and subordinate forms of femininity. As my interviewees drew on stereotypical assumptions of Asian/Korean femininity as inherently oppressive of women at the same time that white femininity was depicted as a sea of gender equality, they indicated that Korean-American women will only find gender equality by rejecting their ethnicity. For them, the possibility of maintaining some sense of connection to their ethnicity can only be realized by choosing to hold onto and actualize a subordinated femininity that they, on some level, criticize. Not only does this reduce white femininity to an empirical unreality, but it also suggests that resisting stereotypical Asian or Korean gendered norms would mean the loss of one's ethnicity. These attitudes obscure differences in ethnic gender practices. If one looks at these women's reactions to their mothers, they are criticized for not having been there as mothers or having played more "passive" roles in the home but are not recognized for their strength in their contributions to making immigration possible in the first place because of their financial contributions to their household.

On a more structural level pertaining to the dynamics of gender, work, and family in the United States, findings reported in a 2005 *New York Times* article discuss an apparent trend among well-educated, young women who are choosing to put aside their careers in favor of raising children. Laura Wexler, a professor of American and women's and gender studies at Yale, posits that "Women are still thinking of this as a private issue; they're accepting it...Women have been given full-time working career opportunities and encouragement with no social changes to support it." Thus, well-educated women across multiple racial and ethnic backgrounds may exercise a primarily private choice to raise a family over participating in the paid labor force. However, this phenomenon arguably has an additional layer for women like Jennica, Lani, and Kerry, whose choices may reflect a desire to hold onto their ethnicity through their gendered choices. For women who occupy a hybrid space, such as my second-generation Korean-American informants, these decisions certainly reflect what is often an uncomfortable space to occupy as race, ethnicity, and gender collide. Critically, though, one cannot turn a blind eye to how most of my informants' choices are potentially problematic attempts to realize a very limited and uneasy vision of what it means to be a Korean-American woman in the early 2000s.

Chapter Fourteen

Hybrid Identities in the Diaspora: Second-Generation West Indians in Brooklyn[1]

Bedelia Nicola Richards

How does ethnic identity manifest among contemporary second-generation West Indian youth?
In this essay I argue that the ethnic identities of
post-1990s second-generation West Indian youth in
Brooklyn are best characterized as "hybrid identities." Diaspora communities like the one created by
West Indian immigrants in Brooklyn provide ideal
conditions for the development of hybrid identities,
the fusion of two or more cultures coexisting in a
single individual (Iyall Smith and Leavy 2008). In
addition to the question already posed, this paper
will explicate how second-generation West Indian
youth experience, make sense of, and express the
inherent complexity of identities that emerge from
living in a hybrid cultural space. My analyses are
based on the premise that there is something new
and different about the way in which second-generation West Indian youth today conceptualize their
ethnic identities (Richards 2007) as opposed to their
representation in publications based on the Brooklyn

[1] I would like to thank Milton Vickerman for reading and providing feedback
on an earlier version of this chapter. I made this request during a busy time of the
semester and close to the holiday season, so I appreciate that he was so generous
with his time.

West Indian experience in the 1980s and early 1990s (Waters 2001, Zephir 2001). Most prominent among them is the work of Waters (2001), who described a cultural disconnect between most working-class West Indian youth and their immigrant parents. Waters (2001) and others predict that the greater salience of ethnicity among middle-class youth would rapidly erode, much like their working-class counterparts, as racial discrimination became a more prominent fixture in the lives of these young people (Waters 2001; Portes and Rumbaut 2001; Kasinitz, Battle, and Miyares 2001).

I am in agreement with Vickerman (2001) and Butterfield (2001), who point to more fluidity in the ethnic identities of West Indian adolescents, rejecting the notion that second-generation West Indian youth necessarily choose between a "racial" and an "ethnic" identity. Notwithstanding these objections, rarely has anyone challenged directly the idea of an inevitable and indisputable ethnic decline among second- (and later-)generation black West Indian youth. I, too, recognize that the ubiquitous nature of black-white racial divisions in the United States poses a challenge to the persistence of ethnicity among children of black immigrants from Haiti and the English-speaking Caribbean islands (Vickerman 2001). Yet, my data suggests that the social reality of 21st-century Brooklyn West Indian youth is quite different from those who came of age in New York City in the 1980s and early 1990s. Specifically, contemporary second-generation West Indian youth in Brooklyn place a high social value on identifying as West Indian ethnics and are likely to identify ethnically regardless of the social class backgrounds of their parents (Richards 2007). I attribute this high social value to the objective reality of living within a predominantly West Indian environment. I elaborate on these issues in the current chapter using data collected primarily from interviews with 24 second-generation West Indian youth who were 10th graders when I interviewed them. My analyses are also informed by eight months of participant observation in two Brooklyn high schools, where I recruited these students for a research project with a more comprehensive agenda.

Hybrid Identities in Social Context

William Yancey and his colleagues (1976) have influenced how I think about the survival of ethnicity among today's second-generation West Indian youth. In their essay "Emergent Ethnicity: a Review and Reformulation," Yancey and his colleagues challenge the assumption that ethnicity among American ethnic groups is rooted in these groups' cultures of origin rather than in the ethnic communities that they recreate in the United States. Instead, these scholars propose that ethnicity is an "emergent phenomenon" that changes and fluctuates depending on the structural conditions to which immigrant groups are exposed. Yet, they do agree that it is possible for immigrant culture to reconsolidate in the US context under certain circumstances. They assert that ethnicity is likely to remain vibrant among immigrants who live in the same residential areas and share common social institutions such as churches, schools, and workplaces where kinship and friendship networks are strengthened and maintained.

Massey (1995) arrives at a similar set of conclusions about how social conditions within the United States ultimately shape manifestations of ethnicity among American ethnic groups. He asserts that the continuous influx of immigrants into the United States since 1965 and their geographical concentration in particular cities and neighborhoods is likely to retard the process of cultural assimilation so that "rather than a slow, steady, and relatively coherent progression of ethnicity toward twilight, it will increasingly stretch from dawn to dusk" (645). Within this framework, the salience and persistence of ethnicity among second-generation children of West Indian immigrants is not unusual. Anglophone West Indians as a whole are the largest immigrant group in New York City, and are estimated to comprise close to one-third of the city's black population (Foner 2001). Therefore, I suggest in this chapter that patterns of ethnic self-identification that I have observed among West Indian youth are associated with what other scholars have labeled the "Caribbeanization" of New York City (Kasinitz 1992, Waters 2001, Zephir 2001). In particular, because Brooklyn is the borough with the highest concentration of recent West Indian immigrants, it facilitates identification with West Indian culture (Kasinitz 1992, Palmer 1995).

Brooklyn: A Bona Fide Caribbean Island

Some scholars attribute the persistence of ethnicity among recent immigrants and their children to their transnational ties to extended families in the Caribbean and elsewhere (Waters 2001, Rogers 2001). It is likely that transnationalism does play a role in shaping ethnic identity among children of immigrants who travel regularly to visit family in the Caribbean. However, many of the students whom I interviewed had never been to the Caribbean and did not have meaningful relationships with family members who lived abroad. While these students saw American culture as an omnipresent force that had some influence on them, they still identified ethnically, based on the nationalities of their parents or as hyphenated ethnic Americans. As a result, following Yancey and his colleagues (1976), I also find it useful to think about the ethnic identities of my respondents as an "emergent phenomenon" cultivated from the unique social position of Brooklyn as the epicenter of West Indian culture in New York City and the United States as a whole. Consequently, I do not regard patterns of ethnic self-identification reported here as mere artifacts of the successful intergenerational transmission of West Indian culture from immigrant parents to their second-generation offspring.

Rooted as it is in the American context, Brooklyn itself is a fusion of West Indian and American cultural influences. Accordingly, I consider the ethnic identities forged among my second-generation respondents as hybrid identities, reflecting these dual influences regardless of the ethnic labels that they use to identify themselves. These youngsters can be exposed to American culture even if they rarely socialize with individuals outside of the ethnic community. Still, I concur with Yancey and his colleagues (1976), as well as Massey (1995), that ethnicity can survive into the second generation and beyond, but it does so in a form that is adaptive to the American context. As such, second-generation West Indian youth do not need to leave Brooklyn in order to become immersed in island ways and customs. In fact the economic situation in Haiti and most Anglophone Caribbean islands have made migration an economic imperative for many. As a result, Caribbean peoples have had a long history of migration to places like New York (Palmer 1995, Kasinitz 1992), Toronto, and London (Henry 1994), and have formed ethnic communities where they settle. Among these diaspora communities, New York City stands out as the location where West Indian cultural influences remain the most visible and vibrant, especially in Brooklyn (Palmer 1995).

My own experiences living in Brooklyn has provided me with additional insight into the peculiarity of the Brooklyn West Indian experience. It is treated by West Indians at home and abroad as if it were a sister "island" in the North American context. In addition, my interactions with West Indians who live in other areas of New York City with a strong West Indian presence lead me to believe that despite what these neighborhoods may have in common, the Brooklyn experience remains distinctive. You see, West Indians in New York are just as attached to their identities as New Yorkers as they are to their identities as West Indians, and West Indians from Brooklyn attach even further significance to being from Brooklyn. For example, on a trip to the Washington DC West Indian American carnival parade in June 2005, I wagered that the majority of the folks dancing in the street were Brooklyn West Indians who traveled to such events religiously wherever they were held in the United States. My unscientific prediction was realized throughout the course of the carnival parade during the various call and response "roll calls." Roll calls are used by music selectors to energize the crowd in a party by appealing to the nationalistic sentiments of partygoers. The music selector usually asks the crowd "anybody from..." and proceeds to name as many of the Caribbean islands as he can. The crowd responds on cue by boisterously waving their island flags from left to right or in circles above their heads, flamboyantly competing to see who can best "represent" their island nations. Indeed, throughout the course of the parade, Brooklyn appeared to be the most popular island. The selectors inquired more about whether anyone in the crowd was from Brooklyn than they did any of the Caribbean islands, including Jamaica and Trinidad, the two most well-known. I recognize, therefore, that the ethnic identities of my respondents are embedded within a social context that is itself an amalgam of American and West Indian cultural influences. So I am not surprised that many of my second-generation respondents continue to see themselves as West Indian ethnics even when they acknowledge these dual cultural influences.

Ethnic Performances: Lights, Camera, Action!

In his book the *Presentation of Self in Everyday Life,* Erving Goffman (1959) approaches the study of human behavior using a conceptual framework that treats life as a stage where each person takes on a role, and social interactions between individuals are characterized as performances. Goffman (1959) further distinguishes between the persons who give sincere performances and those who wish to mislead their audiences in some way. Although he concedes that there is more variation between these two extremes, he contends that the sincere individual is one who "can be fully taken in by his own act; he can be sincerely convinced that the impression of reality which he stages is the 'real reality'; in contrast, the individual at the opposite end of the sincerity continuum is one who "has no belief in his own act and no ultimate concern with the beliefs of his audience" (1959:18).

In addition to Goffman's (1959) conceptual framework, I make use of Zephir's (2001) distinction between monocultural and bicultural ethnics. In her work, the monocultural and bicultural designations align respectively with those who identify with a single national origin group relative to those who identify with hyphenated American ethnic labels. In my sample, I have used the monocultural and bicultural designations to describe individuals who refer to themselves using single national origin or pan-ethnic West Indian labels. However, I apply the term monocultural ethnics to students who assert that they are influenced primarily by the culture of a single West Indian nationality group, and I use the term bicultural ethnics to describe individuals who think of themselves as influenced by both American and West Indian cultures. Ethnic Americans see themselves as a product of these same dual cultural influences, but their use of hyphenated ethnic labels signifies greater acceptance of this fact. At the end of this spectrum are students who identify as American because they see their American nationality or the African-American community as a more significant influence on them than their parents' ethnic origins. Only one of my 24 interviewees fell into this category, a finding that is consistent with evidence from my eight months of observations in the two Brooklyn high schools where I conducted my research.

From a Goffmanian perspective, students whom I categorize in this document as monocultural ethnics gave the most sincere ethnic performances relative to students whom I categorized as bicultural ethnics or ethnic Americans. They "wore" their ethnic identities with the greatest level of comfort and ease. Monocultural ethnics were more deeply immersed and involved in their ethnic communities than other youth. As a result, they expressed the greatest level of confidence in their performances as West Indian ethnics. Their extensive involvement in their ethnic communities led to what I refer to as a high level of "cultural competence," and this is why monoculturals perceived their own ethnic performances as natural. Conversely, biculturals and ethnic Americans provide a more visible presentation of the self-conscious ways in which ethnic identity is constructed, because there is often a disjuncture between their levels of cultural competence and the image of themselves that they wish to convey in their performances as West Indian ethnics. The rest of this essay provides an in-depth discussion of these three ethnic identity types and how students who fall into these categories make sense of having both "West Indian roots" and "American branches" (Richards 2007).

Monocultural Ethnics

I began my student interviews with light conversation and pleasant banter to gain the confidence of my study participants and deflect attention away from the formality of the tape recorder. When my respondents were Jamaicans, I emphasized our shared nationality. In an effort to bond, I would ask common questions such as "what part of Jamaica is your family from?" My strategy worked with Omar, who was reserved, but not uncommunicative. In fact, I learned that his father still lived in the parish of St. Elizabeth in Jamaica. Throughout the course of our conversation, I became impressed with Omar's knowledge of Jamaican geography and culture. I had encountered a number of second-generation West Indian youth for whom identifying as West Indian ethnics was important, but who knew little about their parents' countries of origin. Omar was different. He had been spending summers in Jamaica "ever since he was a baby." Over the years, Omar had the opportunity to visit his sister, who lived in Mandeville. More often than not, however, his time was shared equally between St. Elizabeth, where his father lived, and Spanish Town, where his mother's family resided. I categorize students like Omar as monocultural ethnics because of their high level of involvement in the everyday life of ethnic communities in Brooklyn and the Caribbean.

As my conversation with Omar continued to unfold, I realized that storytelling is a powerful medium for creating and maintaining ethnic group consciousness. I began to see ethnic group consciousness as the stories we have in common about ourselves and about the community to which we belong. These stories, and our shared interpretations and emotional responses to them, are the basis of a collective identity that links the historical past to the present. The story of Hurricane Gilbert links both Omar and me to Jamaica though, ironically, neither of us experienced it personally. As a category-four hurricane, Gilbert devastated Jamaica in September 1988. It was the same year that my mother, uncle, and I migrated to the United States. When others recounted their stories of hurricane Gilbert, I had no memories to share. I did not remember zinc roofs flying, water up to my knees, or the painstaking recovery period that survivors of the hurricane describe in such vivid detail. But the story has been told so many times by my Jamaican relatives and friends that I can give an account of this catastrophe from multiple perspectives as if I had experienced the events personally.

I discovered during my interview with Omar that he too had a Hurricane Gilbert story. Omar's mother was pregnant with him when she visited Jamaica in 1988. She almost gave birth to Omar in Jamaica because Hurricane Gilbert forced her to extend her stay. When the hurricane came to an end, she returned to Brooklyn and gave birth to Omar one week later. The details of Omar's Hurricane Gilbert story represent one dimension of cultural competence that serves as a metaphorical bridge across generations, whether this knowledge is acquired from direct experience or through the oral tradition of storytelling. In this case the Hurricane Gilbert story links Omar to his mother and connects them both to a specific event in Jamaican history. Omar now had ownership of a piece of Jamaican collective memory that he was likely to pass on to his own children whether or not they become as personally involved in Jamaican culture as he has. Moreover, just as his personal experiences helped him to bond with me, it will facilitate developing relationships with other co-ethnics whose personal experiences complement his own. These relationships are the bridges that link one generation to the next and are a key mechanism for cultural transmission and preservation.

Ethnic group consciousness develops in part from the telling and retelling of these stories. I was not surprised, therefore, that despite his American nationality, Omar described himself as "Jamaican" and asserted that he was influenced primarily by Jamaican culture. His explanation for this is represented in the following excerpt from our conversation that day:

> Interviewer: So, um, you said that both of your parents are from Jamaica, right?
> Omar: Mm-hm.
> Interviewer: And you were born here. What does that make you?
> Omar: I say I'm still Jamaican, anyway.
> Interviewer: I still have to ask. [LAUGHS]. Um, okay, so one of the things I'm trying to get at is, that you know, there are other folks just like you, both their parents are from Jamaica or in the Caribbean, and they're born in the US, but they're like, I'm American.
> Omar: Yeah, I know,

Interviewer: So I'm trying to figure out how these folks are different from you.

Omar: Me, I just feel like...since I'm always around them, I feel like I'm one too, I know all of the, like, they have sayings, and with food and everything, I am just used to it, so I just say I'm Jamaican. Also, 'cause American is like a whole different culture, you know. And you're not around that every day.

Omar achieved a deep immersion into Jamaican culture from his frequent trips to the island every year. However, it is the existence of a strong Jamaican presence in Brooklyn that makes it possible for Omar to dismiss American culture as something that he is "not around...everyday" and ultimately does not define him as a person. He was unable to relate to stories about West Indians who grew up in Brooklyn 15 or 20 years ago who were afraid to publicly acknowledge their ethnic backgrounds. Omar was certain that this was a relic of the past, as he explained "I think that that time, that's a long time ago, but now, New York, as you can tell, is full of Caribbean people, everywhere, so, it's like, it's different, 'cause you're always around it [West Indian culture], especially if you live in Brooklyn, not like Manhattan or something like that. Like, if you live in Brooklyn, Caribbean people are [always] around you...Actually, we have a lot of Jamaicans. We have a lot of Jamaicans in Brooklyn, too." Other American-born monocultural ethnics were more willing than Omar to concede being influenced to some extent by American culture. Still, like Omar, they did not think of American culture as having a tangible impact on them as individuals.

Bicultural Ethnics

The visibility of West Indian culture in Brooklyn and the frequency of interaction among co-ethnics makes identification with West Indian culture an accepted norm among second-generation youth. As a result, bicultural ethnics admit that they are influenced in a broad sense by American culture, but because they feel a deeper connection to their Caribbean roots in their everyday lives, they still do not think of themselves as Americans. In spite of this, biculturals were aware of their estrangement from island-based West Indian culture. From the perspective of Goffman's performance analogy, I think of the ethnic performances of bicultural ethnics as less sincere because they intentionally de-emphasize their partial alienation from West Indian culture. Bicultural ethnics realize that they lack a certain level of cultural competence that is naturally enacted by recent or first-generation immigrants. They are often insecure in regard to the authenticity of their performances as West Indian ethnics in situations where their ethnic identities are challenged. I illustrate the inner struggle that makes the bicultural ethnic performance potentially insincere through the analyses below where I spotlight Wayne. He understood intuitively that he represented a blending of two cultures, but he wrestled with how to best convey the duality of his ethnic identity.

> Interviewer: What do you think of yourself [culturally]?
> Wayne: Like, um, I'm a Yankee. Um, let's see, I'm half Jamaican and half Grenadian. It's like everything put into one. That's me right there.
> Interviewer: You're half Jamaican.
> Wayne: Half Jamaican.
> Interviewer: Half Grenadian. You say you're a Yankee too?
> Wayne: Yeah, I'm a Yankee, but don't add that. [chuckle]
> Interviewer: Okay, when your friends are talking to you and they're like what are you, what do you say?
> Wayne: I be like half Jamaican
> Interviewer: That's what you tell them?
> Wayne: [and] Half Grenadian. Yeah.
> Interviewer: Alright, alright cool.
> Wayne: Me personally, I be like, I'm from Brooklyn.

In the beginning of our dialogue, Wayne refers to himself first as a "Yankee" in part because he knew that he was estranged from Jamaican culture as it was practiced on the island, and because he knew that his Jamaican relatives thought of him as an American. As he explained it: "a Yankee is just American. Like Brooklyn, New York, that's a Yankee. Somebody that's not from the Caribbean. That's what they call me when I go to Jamaica." Wayne partially agreed with his Jamaican relatives that he was a Yankee: "That is how they see me [but] that is also how I see myself because it's true." However, because Wayne's frame of reference is Brooklyn, he felt equally connected to his Jamaican and Grenadian ethnic backgrounds. In fact, Wayne's hybrid identity is captured spectacularly in the very last line of our dialogue when he suggests that the identity that is most meaningful to him "personally" is that he is "from Brooklyn." Like Brooklyn, Wayne saw himself as an amalgam of West Indian and American cultural influences, so identifying with his neighborhood was a simplistic way of recognizing that he is "everything put into one," American and West Indian at the same time. Given that this is so, one would expect Wayne to select a hyphenated ethnic label to describe himself. Yet, despite his internal struggle, Wayne ultimately identifies with the national origins of his parents in part because, in Brooklyn, a higher social value is attached to identifying as West Indian than American. For this reason, Wayne and others like him deliberately elevate their West Indian roots above their American nationality.

Eddie is a bicultural ethnic who represents a less problematic approach to constructing a West Indian ethnic identity that acknowledges American cultural influences. He migrated from Grenada to the United States as a child but refers to himself as a "Caribbean." "I say I'm from the Caribbean," he told me, "but...I'm from Grenada." My evidence suggests that Eddie refers to himself as a Caribbean because other second-generation youth serve as his primary frame of reference, not Grenadians back home or even first-generation Grenadians like his mother and grandmother, who live in Brooklyn. Note that all of Eddie's childhood friends have roots in the Caribbean: "Yeah. Everybody, all my friends are from the Caribbean...Like half of my friends are from Grenada, half of them are from Jamaica." Identifying as Caribbean signifies that Eddie attributes a common culture to individuals who originate from the various islands in the Caribbean and that he perceives these commonalities as more significant than the ways in which individuals from each island are different.

At the same time, identifying as Caribbean did not preclude Eddie from acknowledging that, unlike first-generation immigrants like his mother, he was more comfortable and familiar with how life is structured in the United States than with the rhythm and flow of day-to-day life in Grenada:

> I don't know. It's like I was born up here, 'cause I been up here for so long. And I just went to Grenada in the eighth grade. I mean, ninth grade. That's the last time I went in nine years...'Cause I've been up here, and I've adapted to this environment, and now, if I'm there [it is] for a little bit of time. So I don't really know that much about – I know where my family's from, I know from memory, but I don't really know that much about down there. Up here, I could tell you everything. But I don't know that much [about] down there.

Eddie also chooses to call himself a "Caribbean" instead of a "Grenadian" in order to distance himself from negative characteristics of Grenadians that embarrass his American sensibilities:

> Eddie: I don't talk like a Grenadian. I mean...the way I dress, I don't dress like they do.
> Interviewer: How do they dress?
> Eddie: They dress – tacky.
> Interviewer: Describe it to me. Describe what [is] tacky.
> Eddie: Like, they wear like old clothes and messed-up clothes and everything. I don't dress like that...
> Interviewer: ...So, I'm, trying to figure out if you were just talking about people on the island dressing tacky, or your [Grenadian] family here, too.
> Eddie: No! People on the island.
> Interviewer: Oh, okay. So not your family [in Brooklyn], then.
> Eddie: No, my family don't dress tacky.

Eddie's estrangement from Grenada helps to explain why he would interpret manifestations of relative economic disadvantage in his Grenadian relatives as attributes of Grenadian culture on the island. In reality, then, Eddie identifies as Caribbean in part because of his desire to identify with a group that embodies positive characteristics. At the same time, although Eddie feels culturally disconnected from Grenada, he is able to comfortably identify as "Caribbean" because of multi-layered opportunities to interact with co-ethnics within the West Indian diaspora community in Brooklyn. His Caribbean identity has been nurtured from living in a predominantly West Indian neighborhood, from attending neighborhood schools in his formative years where most of his teachers were West Indians, and because all of his friends have roots in the Caribbean.

Eddie also constructs a Caribbean identity for himself by drawing rigid ethnic boundaries between his Americanized Caribbean collective and his African-American peers. He was one of the only students who perceived cultural differences between African-Americans and students with a West Indian background as a source of tension and potential conflict between the two groups. Eddie explained that at his school, "most of the people who are from the Caribbean are from East Flatbush," and that "most of the Americans is from Coney Island...and sometimes they don't combine [get along]." When asked to elaborate, he explained that in the lunch room at his school

"Caribbean kids" were more likely to amuse themselves by "banging on the walls and...dancing [to reggae music]," but that the "Coney Island people" did not understand why they did this. Instead, Eddie explains that African-American students "would take a bottle, and they'd start playing basketball, [then] we're like, what are they doing?"

Eddie used a tripartite frame of reference to construct his identity as a Caribbean. When his frame of reference was his first-generation parents or island-based Grenadian culture, Eddie was aware of the various ways in which he was more American than West Indian. In these cases he ascribed a positive value to his "Americanness" because it was associated with first-world consumption patterns and a lifestyle of material comfort relative to the life of hardship that he associated with life in Grenada. In contrast, when Eddie's frame of reference was his African-American peers, he drew sharp ethnic boundaries that emphasized the ways in which he was more Caribbean than American. In the narratives above, these boundaries are drawn based on Eddie's participation in West Indian social activities such as his enjoyment of reggae music and dancing. These activities contributed to Eddie feeling more like a "Caribbean" in comparison to African-American peers, whom he perceived as more interested in playing basketball. Further, when African-Americans were his frame of reference, Eddie was more likely to emphasize the positive characteristics attributed to being West Indian, such as a strong work ethic. However, the third and most important prong in this tripartite comparison were other second-generation peers, some of whom were born in the United States and others who migrated as young children like Eddie.

Symbolic Ethnicity and Weak Social Ties

A number of scholars have used the term symbolic ethnicity to characterize European-American ethnicity in the third generation and beyond. This form of ethnicity emerged just as European ethnics achieved middle-class status and positions of power previously unattained by their parents and grandparents (Gans 1979). Yet Gans suggests that third-generation European-Americans continued to think of themselves as ethnics even as their everyday lives increasingly became divorced from the social practices that defined ethnic group membership among first- and second-generation immigrants. He describes symbolic ethnicity as a force that "takes on an expressive rather than an instrumental function in people's lives, becoming more of a leisure time activity and losing its relevance, say, to earning a living or regulating family life" (Gans 1979:9). Taken as a whole, emergent forms of ethnicity among today's second-generation West Indian youth do not conform to this notion of symbolic ethnicity because of how easily social ties to the ethnic community can be maintained in Brooklyn. Despite this overall picture, however, each individual has a different relationship to the social institutions in the community that reinforce ethnic group membership and affiliation. Thus, there are second-generation youth who live in Brooklyn, but their ties to the ethnic community are weak and their levels of cultural competence are low. For these individuals, ethnic identity is best expressed in symbolic form.

Ironically, a couple of the students placed in this category applied a single national origin label to describe themselves. Yet, if such a high social value were not attached to identifying as West Indian ethnics among Brooklyn's second-generation West Indians, it is likely that these students would simply have identified as "American." For, as Gans (1979) suggests, symbolic ethnicity is likely to arise under conditions where there is no social cost to identifying ethnically. This explains why young people like Silvia and Christopher, who are marginally invested in being identified as West Indian ethnics, choose nonetheless to identify as "Jamaicans." For example, when I asked why he identified as Jamaican, Christopher's response was: "If you're Jamaican, you're Jamaican, you know. I like my parents' nation. God knows I love their food, you know, I really like West Indian culture." On the one hand, Christopher's flippant response to my question signifies detachment when he speaks of Jamaica as his "parents' nation," and Jamaican food as "their food." On the other hand, his symbolic attachment to Jamaican culture compels him to publicly associate himself with other Jamaicans and with aspects of Jamaican culture that he values. Yet, unlike Wayne, Christopher does not ponder whether the Jamaican label accurately reflects his involvement, knowledge, or competence in Jamaican culture.

Silvia expressed a similar sentiment when she told me in our interview that she was "half Jamaican, half Indian, and half Chinese," but that of the three she identified most with being Jamaican. She thought of herself as Jamaican "because my whole family is Jamaican. Only like two people in my family are American. So I'm more Jamaican because my mother is Jamaican and she is half Chinese and my father is Jamaican and he's half Indian." Yet Silvia admitted that being Jamaican was really not that important to her. It's "not a big deal," she told me. "Nobody [at school] ask, nobody know I am

Jamaican...They don't ask, and I don't tell them nothing." For students like Silvia and Christopher, a single national origin label does not necessarily point to a more meaningful connection to Jamaican culture. They do so in part because identifying ethnically is about ancestry more so than it is about cultural involvement, and because identifying as Jamaicans bestows a higher social status among their peers than identifying as American.

Ethnic Americans

Ethnic Americans are similar to bicultural ethnics in that both believe that they are influenced by American and West Indian cultures. However, choosing between their American nationalities and their West Indian roots was a more difficult task for ethnic Americans than their bicultural counterparts. I distinguish ethnic Americans from bicultural ethnics because they elect to use a hyphenated ethnic label to signal that they place equal importance on the culture associated with their parents' national origins as well as the culture associated with their American nationality. Applying Goffman's performance analogy here, ethnic Americans appear at first glance to give a more sincere ethnic performance than biculturals because the hyphenated ethnic label is a more accurate representation of how they view themselves. However, in this context most ethnic Americans are Haitians who identify as hyphenated Americans in part to minimize the stigma attached to being Haitian. As a result, the ambivalent feelings they share in regard to identifying as Haitian also undermine the sincerity of their ethnic performances.

Although ethnic Americans use hyphenated ethnic labels as a way of acknowledging the hybridity of their ethnic identities, some of them still struggled with how to convey the complexity of their dual identities. For example, Naomi thought of herself as a fusion of Haitian and American cultural influences, which is why she calls herself a Haitian-American. At the same time, because she felt a meaningful connection to both cultures, she saw no contradiction when she described herself as Haitian-American in one instance and as Haitian in another during the same conversation.

> Interviewer: Where are your parents from?
> Naomi: They're from Haiti.
> Interviewer: Okay, and were you born in Haiti or were you born here?
> Naomi: No, I was born here.
> Interviewer: Okay, so what does that make you?

Naomi: Um, a Haitian-American.

Interviewer: Okay. When people ask you what you are, is that what you tell them?

Naomi: Uh-huh.

Interviewer: Okay. What does that mean to you?

Naomi: I am totally proud to be Haitian. I just tell them, like if somebody says, 'Um, where are you from?' I'm going to be like 'I'm Haitian.' But sometimes I tell them I'm Haitian-American, I'm Haitian.

Previous research on ethnic identity among second-generation youth would suggest that immigrant youth who identify with a single or hyphenated national origin label such as Haitian or Haitian-American, respectively, as identifying to some degree with the immigrant experience (Portes and Rumbaut 2001, Waters 2001, Zephir 2001). As a result, when Naomi used these two terms interchangeably it was not necessarily problematic because they indicate degrees of attachment to her Haitian background. However, the exchange that follows indicates a greater level of fluidity than previous research has accounted for when Naomi reported seeing no difference between these two "ethnic" labels and identifying as an unhyphenated American.

Interviewer: So is that basically what you [told people] when you were younger? Or just now?

Naomi: I told them that I was Haitian-American and that my parents are Haitian. And then, you know I'm full Haitian but you know, I just told them that.

Interviewer: Right.

Naomi: Because at least I'm American but my parents are Haitian.

Interviewer: Okay, so, um, I just heard two different things and I'm trying to make sure that I get to understand what you mean. You just said, well 'I'm American.'

Naomi: Uh-huh.

Interviewer: But before you said 'I'm Haitian-American.'

Naomi: Uh-huh.

Interviewer: Um, which one is it – do you use those interchangeably? I'm trying to figure out what you mean when you say that.

Naomi: Sometimes, like, well most of the time I say I'm Haitian-American, most of the time. And to me it's like, I really don't know, it's like the same thing to me. Like, American, Haitian-American. Because the fact that I was born here, that makes me American, and the fact that my parents are Haitian that makes me Haitian-American. So it really, to me it really doesn't make a difference.

Interviewer: So when people ask you, what do you usually say?

Naomi: Most of the time I say Haitian-American.

In the beginning of this second dialogue Naomi suggests that when she was younger she routinely described herself to others as Haitian-American when in reality she thought of herself as "full Haitian." In the very next statement, Naomi seemed to contradict herself when she suggests that she thinks of herself as American, and it is really her parents who are Haitian. By the end of our conversation, however, we see that Naomi has a clear preference for the term Haitian-American to describe herself because she sees herself as a mixture of both cultures.

Naomi: Um, actually, like, I consider myself Haitian but at the same time American because I was born here.

Interviewer: Okay, so which one – if you had to choose, would you gravitate more toward one of these labels than the other? Do you feel more strongly toward one of these labels or do you feel like they're, like, you are like both at the same time?

Naomi: I feel like I'm both at the same time. Yeah.

Ethnic Americans like Naomi see themselves as Americans in part because they recognize that, while everyday life in the United States might be structured within a predominantly West Indian context, they have no direct experience of life in the islands:

Um, what makes me feel like I'm American? Hmm. I'm adapted to my environment. Because of the school that I go to, like in Haiti the schools are much different…Well the [Haitian] church that I go to…most of us are born here, so it's like we're starting the new thing. And um…because I'm in America. And I was born here, like I never lived in Haiti before, so it's like I've been here for 16 – almost 17-years, so I feel like a part of me is American. I feel like a part of me is American from the fact that I was born here and I never lived in Haiti before. I don't have the accent, you know.

Even so, despite the omnipresence of American culture, Naomi feels a meaningful connection to Haitian culture through her involvement in the

American-based Haitian community in Brooklyn, and this prevents her from seeing herself only as American. She explained it to me this way: "I speak Creole very well, um, my parents are Haitian. I eat the Haitian food. I know how to make the Haitian food. Well, I don't know how to make it, but I know the recipes. Um, I'm in a Haitian church. I've been in a Haitian church all my life. My family is Haitian, so that makes me – my family makes me kind of Haitian." Similar to bicultural ethnics, Naomi used other second-generation Haitians in her peer group as her primary frame of reference for constructing an identity as Haitian-American. For example, Naomi identified her Haitian church both as an institution that fostered an attachment to Haitian culture and simultaneously as an institution that was Americanizing her. Attending a Haitian church provided Naomi with the opportunity to practice Creole and to interact with other Haitians over a prolonged period of time. However, most of her peers at this church were American-born Haitians like herself and together she saw them as "starting the new [American] thing."

Establishing the Case for Anti-Haitian Prejudice

All except one of the students whom I categorized as ethnic Americans were Haitians, and all of these Haitian students were ambivalent about identifying as Haitian. Similar to Naomi, these students described a meaningful connection with and pride in their Haitian ethnic origins because of relationships with their families, as well as their involvement in the Haitian diaspora community in Brooklyn. In fact, ethnic Americans with a Haitian background were more involved in the Haitian community than students like Christopher and Silvia, who identified using a single national origin label. So, we can no longer assume that an unhyphenated national origin label signifies a greater connection to the immigrant experience or that a hyphenated label necessarily signifies less active involvement in the culture. Rather, I suspect that students who identified as Haitian-American did so in part to distance themselves from the stigma associated with identifying as Haitian relative to other Caribbean nationalities. For example, my respondents agreed with Terry Ann, the only student who identified as American, that Jamaicans were the most popular Caribbean nationality group: "Yeah, like especially if you're Jamaican. To be Jamaican or something like that, it's like if somebody…says yeah, I'm Jamaican, [then another person will say] yeah, I'm Jamaican too, and then everybody wants to be Jamaican. Everybody wants to be from the Caribbean, but especially from Jamaica."

The popularity of Jamaicans is a stark contrast to the stigma attached to being Haitian. As a result, Henri, who identified as Haitian-American, asserted that he felt more marginalized as a result of his Haitian ethnic background than for being black:

> So, like, I was mostly made fun of for being Haitian than for being a black man. I never heard somebody say like 'Hey, look at that black kid over there. Get out of here black kid.' I've never heard that before. I was surrounded by black people all the time. I was just swimming in black people, you know, practically. And if I were to hear that, you know, it would sound weird. You know, like there's different types of black people. There's a lot – there's a vast majority of black [people] like, it could be like black A, black B, black C, you know? So it wouldn't really be like that [would] affect...me. I'm like yeah, I'm black. What do you wanna do?

In the United States, where racial divisions between blacks and whites are sharp and unrelenting, Henri's assertion that prejudice against Haitians is more problematic for him than being a black male must seem incredulous. For scholars do not often address cultural differences among blacks, but when they do, the trend is to highlight tensions between American blacks and those who are foreign-born (Waters 2001, Rogers 2001). Among my Afro-Caribbean study participants, however, I found anti-Haitian sentiments to be strong, and anti-African-American sentiments to be virtually nonexistent. Henri's dialogue above is representative of the prevalence and potency of xenophobic attitudes against Haitians that I encountered during the course of my research. At the same time, racial residential segregation contributes to the fact that Henri's immediate social reality is predominantly black, making ethnic divisions between Haitians and other Afro-Caribbean nationality groups a more salient concern than black/white racial differences.

Naomi provided a similar perspective in our interview when she explained that "Jamaicans, Trinidadians, Guyanese, and people who are Grenadian, or all of them other Caribbean countries don't really get pressured like Haitians...even if they do make fun of, like, other Caribbean countries, Haiti gets the most. Haitians get the most pressure."

Femi, who was born in Haiti, believed that this stigma emerged from the way in which Haitians are misrepresented in the media. She explained that:

> TV portrays Haitians as like they [are] bad people, like they're dirty – and [it is also because] they'll never show a good part of Haiti on TV. Like, you always see the dirty part where, like, people are on the street dying and, you know, the kids are naked. So when people see that, they think that's where you're from, they think that's how you are, and so they put you in that position where, like, this is you.

Haitian students were aware of these negative portrayals, and so they were ambivalent about identifying as Haitian. As a result, they emphasized their partial American identity in order to soften the impact of identifying only as Haitian.

Deflecting Anti-Haitian Prejudice

Haitian students were caught in a double bind. On the one hand, they lived in an environment where identifying as a West Indian ethnic was valued and encouraged. On the other hand, their particular nationality occupied the lowest status in relation to other Caribbean nationality groups. As a result, during our conversations, ethnic American Haitian students employed strategies for deflecting anti-Haitian bias without appearing as if they were ashamed of their Haitian background. In some cases, Haitian students diffused this bias by emphasizing the ways in which their Haitianness did not define them as individuals. For example, Naomi, who told us earlier that she was proud to be Haitian, had this to say later in our interview: "Like me being Haitian, that doesn't make me who I am. That has nothing to do with my personality. That's what people need to realize, like, a lot of kids are ignorant. They don't want to be friends with you because of the fact that you're Haitian or whatever." Naomi's perception came from experiences she had as a little girl as well as the experiences of her friends. For example, a male friend from her church shared an incident that happened between him and a female friend from Trinidad when they were in junior high school: "The girl [told him] I'm sorry, I can't be your friend because my mom doesn't like Haitians. She said I can't talk to you no more, and I have to wash myself because I touched you and I don't know – they think that Haitians have AIDS, or whatever it is. I really don't know."

I observed a similar strategy with Maxwell, who identified as Haitian-American. Similar to bicultural ethnics and fellow ethnic Americans, Maxwell thought of himself as a combination of American and Haitian characteristics: "The way I dress makes me American. The way I think makes me a little Haitian, a little American. And the way I talk makes me Haitian, or, yeah, makes me Haitian because a lot of people be asking me every time I talk to them if I'm Haitian or not." In fact, although Maxwell was born in the United States, he speaks Creole fluently. He told me, "When I was little, a lot of people I know was speaking a lot of Creole, and that's how I got used to the language and everything. But being American and being Haitian, I don't see the difference." To a certain extent, Maxwell suggests that there is no difference between being Haitian and being American because, as we see from his first set of comments, he thinks of himself as both at the same time. Similar to his contemporaries, such as Naomi above, Maxwell experiences the boundary between Haitian and American culture as a continuum with fluid and permeable cultural markers. Yet, as our conversation proceeds it becomes clear that like Naomi, Maxwell wished to distance himself from the negative stereotypes associated with his Haitian background. As a result, he emphasized that being Haitian did not define him as an individual; it merely signified a category of people who happened to speak Creole like he did. As a result, when I pressed Maxwell to say whether he felt more strongly about identifying as Haitian or as American, he explained: "[I value them] equally, because even though I use one language mostly, I know I'm still an American. I know I'm still Haitian. It doesn't matter what I am. What matters is who I am and what I become."

Ironically, Barrington is a bicultural ethnic with a strong attachment to his Haitian origin. Barrington diverges from fellow Haitians who are ethnic Americans because of his unabashed pride in his Haitianess. Yet, even Barrington attempts to minimize the uniqueness of Haitians relative to other Afro-Caribbean ethnic groups:

> It's very important to me. I really like being Haitian. It just shows that I am independent because Haitians got independence first. And you know many people say Haiti is the poorest country. That is a true account. But being Haitian does not prove that you are poor or anything. Being Haitian just means that you are from the Caribbean. I don't really think that being Haitian makes you different from anybody else because all of us from the Caribbean are black. Even though we don't speak the same languages,

we came from the same motherland. So being Haitian means something to me, I love being Haitian. But it doesn't differentiate me from any other human being.

Some ethnic minorities respond to prejudice and discrimination by becoming even more nationalistic than under normal circumstances (Portes and Rumbaut 2001). Barrington's strong identification with his Haitian ethnic origins helps to explain why he diverges from other American-born Haitians. Yet he was as defensive as his ethnic American counterparts about the distorted images of Haitians, and like them, he employed certain rhetorical strategies for deflecting anti-Haitian biases. Barrington's attempt to prove how similar Haitians are to other Caribbean ethnic groups is indicative of such a strategy:

> Oh. You see Jamaicans and Haitians always get confused. I don't know, I think it's the complexion and we act similarly. We do similar things like the ladies wear the headbands, I mean the head cloth and stuff like that. And they are really dark-skinned...like the first generation...like the grandmothers...they are really dark-skinned, and the fathers, they are really dark-skinned too. In order to really see who is a Haitian or who is Jamaican, is the dark skin. Once you see dark skin you really know that he is Haitian or he is Jamaican.

Intent on convincing me, Barrington elaborates further:

> And the practices too, the religious practices are basically the same. But food and language, if you take away the language and the food, Haitians are just like Jamaicans. If Haitians spoke English with a little accent they would be considered Jamaicans, I think so. It is a language barrier. I think that's what caused the whole stereotype, it is the language barrier...If Haitians could speak English, everybody would get along perfectly. There would be no stereotypes, no dividing boundaries, or whatever, it would just be a big Caribbean family, no difference.

The similarities between Barrington's strategy for deflecting anti-Haitian bias and those of his ethnic American counterparts solidifies my claim that many ethnic Americans construct an identity as Haitian-American in order to distance themselves from the stigma associated with being Haitian. Thus, I do not consider it a coincidence that Barrington speaks at length during our interview about the similarities between Haitians and Jamaicans to further establish that the division between Haitians and other Caribbean nations was artificial. If Barrington can show that Haitians and Jamaicans are virtually indistinguishable from each other; it strengthens his case that Haitians should not be marginalized from other Afro-Caribbean ethnic groups.

The Haitian case also serves to highlight a recurrent theme of this chapter. First, the Haitian case suggests that all of my second-generation respondents construct their identities based on the social value that they attach either to the culture of their parents' national origin group or to a more generalized "West Indian" or "Caribbean" culture. This social value reflects the objective reality of living within a predominantly West Indian community. In this social context, young people like Barrington use second-generation Afro-Caribbean peers to construct their racial and ethnic identities, respectively. For example, Barrington emphasizes the African origin of people from the Caribbean as a unifying trait, but in the end he suggests that if stereotypes against Haitians were not so prevalent, people of African descent from the Caribbean would be one "big Caribbean family." Where does that leave African-Americans? My research suggests an expanding definition of blackness that includes African-Americans as part of the larger black collective. However, my respondents live in a world where ethnicity among blacks is a social norm. In contrast to what exists in mainstream American society, here blackness is not defined in relation to African-Americans because it recognizes that a Caribbean cultural identity can coexist with a racial identity as "black." Also in contradiction to the mainstream view is the fact that within this cultural milieu, African-Americans are used as the standard for measuring one's "Americanness," not European-Americans.

The Future of Blackness

Consistent with Kasinitz's assertions in the concluding chapter of *Islands in the City* (2001), this essay confirms that "at least in New York, 'blackness' no longer simply means African-Americans." In the same edited volume, Crowder and Tedrow (2001) track the impact of West Indian immigrants in transforming the residential landscape of New York City. Based on data from the 1980 and 1990 censuses, they conclude that "by 1980 West Indians had carved out a set of distinct enclaves within larger black sections of... [New

York City], and these enclaves have only solidified over time...[They] view the formation of these distinct neighborhoods as important means through which West Indians maintain and cultivate their ethnic distinctiveness" (82).

This essay has focused on how this growing concentration of West Indian immigrants has affected the identities of the children of black immigrants from Haiti and the Anglophone Caribbean islands. In doing so, I am contributing to our knowledge about an issue that is among "the least researched, but potentially most important aspects of contemporary black immigration to New York" (270). Through the analyses presented thus far, I have identified what I consider to be a new era in the evolution and expansion of ethnic identity within the West Indian diaspora community in Brooklyn, presenting new ethnic options for Afro-Caribbean youth inside and outside of the ethnic enclave.

Thus far, I have argued that the growth and concentration of West Indian immigrants in certain boroughs and neighborhoods in New York City has facilitated the hybridization of the various Caribbean island cultures represented among second-generation youth. The young people whom I interviewed and observed are like their American (African-American) counterparts in many ways. Most of them do not have accents, many of them like hip hop and rap, dress like African-Americans, celebrate Kwanzaa in school, join their school's step team, and discuss issues of race and racism in their Black Heritage Society meetings. None of these young people had a problem interacting with their African-American peers in school or identifying with African-Americans as fellow "blacks." Even so, the majority of students were clear on the fact that they are also culturally Haitian, or Jamaican, or Trinidadian. They certainly would admit that they express a different kind of ethnic identity from their parents. Nonetheless, because most of these students interacted primarily with other second generation West Indians in their neighborhoods, schools, and churches, this reinforced a shared feeling of being ethnically distinct. In fact, having foreign-born parents and relatives from the Caribbean was a source of pride and prestige within these predominantly West Indian peer groups.

I would argue that the social value of the West Indian ethnic identity is likely to spread beyond New York's borders. Based on this premise, this research challenges the dominant view that racial discrimination will necessarily erode ethnic affiliation among second- and later-generation West

Indian youth. Instead, my research findings suggest that a process of cultural hybridization is already underway among my second-generation respondents, and so a West Indian ethnic identity is likely to remain salient among future generations of West Indian youth. For example, while this chapter reveals that Haitian identity remains stigmatized among second-generation youth, in the larger study upon which this chapter is based, there is also compelling evidence that this stigma is growing increasingly weaker. Consistent with Vickerman (2006), I observed what I would characterize as the nascent formation of pan-Caribbean identities. The pan-Caribbean identity allows second-generation youth to identify with their ethnic origins in a way that recognizes that they are different from their parents and co-ethnics in the islands, but that they are also culturally distinct from African-Americans. So while I agree that future generations of these West Indian ethnics will eventually "fade" into "black America," they will likely do so as "Caribbeans" or "Caribbean-Americans," changing what it means to be black in the United States.

Some scholars have pointed to the ways in which African-American youth are being influenced by Caribbean culture in New York City (Butterfield 2004), and so it is just as likely that cultural hybridization will take place among West Indian and African-American groups. Regardless of the scenario, our present definitions of blackness will certainly be challenged and reconfigured in the process. In this regard, my argument might diverge in important ways from current predictions about the nature of black identity among future generations of Caribbean-descended youth. Yet I consider my story to be an extension rather than a refutation of previous research. My story is different, simply put, because the social reality of West Indian immigrants in Brooklyn has changed, and so my findings do not comport with conclusions made on the basis of research conducted from the 1980s up through the mid-1990s. West Indian immigrants have evolved from being characterized as "invisible immigrants" (Bryce-Laporte 1972) to being "invisible no more" (Kasinitz 2001). Now they are well on their way toward getting noticed.

Chapter Fifteen

Hybridized Korean Identities: The Making of Korean-Americans and *Joseonjok*

Helene K. Lee

> I want to say that I'm a third-culture kid, right.
> You're a new type of nationality, where there's
> a mix of outside cultures coming together. And
> for me, being Korean-American, that's basically
> what it is, it's mixing two different cultures and
> putting them together and make who I am.
> (Gloria, 26-year-old Korean-American)

In this chapter, I explore how Korean immigrant communities in China and the US, divorced from the homeland, integrate selective aspects of Koreanness with their "home" culture to create a third identity that is rooted in their local context but connected to the global as part of the Korean diaspora. Rather than seeing diasporic hybrid Korean identities as a fixed, monolithic set of experiences or a simple mixture of "two outside cultures," as in Gloria's opening quote, I argue these third spaces are full of minefields precisely because there are unwritten rules of conduct on being a "third-culture kid." Instead, there are competing claims of authenticity and normalization that are contested and regulated by "structures of authority" in the form of multiple sets of actors who lay claim to this "third space," which Homi Bhabha sees as the location where hybridized third identity is expressed. A comparative analysis offers insights into the similarities and differences within these diasporized hybrid identities and the contestations over authenticity that arise within this third space.

Homi Bhabha's notion of the "third space" argues that the contradictions within it "enable other positions to emerge. This third space displaces the histories that constitute it and sets up new structures of authority, new political initiatives, which are inadequately understood through received wisdom" (1990:211). In this liminal space "in between," Bhabha asks the question, "How do strategies of representation or empowerment come to be formulated in the competing claims of communities where, despite shared histories of deprivation and discrimination, the exchange of values, meanings, and priorities may not always be collaborative and dialogical, but may be profoundly antagonistic, conflictual, and even incommensurable?" (1994:2). Maira echoes a similar concept of the "third place" as "not a fixed location but an emerging set of disparate, sometimes contradictory, experiences and narratives of hybridity and nostalgia in the second generation" (2002:87). Rather than envisioning hybridity to describe an equal mix of two cultures to produce a third uniform experience, this chapter examines the commonalities – but also the conflictual and contradictory aspects – of hybrid Koreanness within Korean-American and Joseonjok communities.

This chapter uses qualitative data collected from semi-structured interviews with 33 *Joseonjok* (ethnic Koreans living in China) and 31 Korean-Americans. These interviews were conducted in Seoul, South Korea, during a 16-month period between August 2004 and December 2005. An analysis of the experiences of diasporic hybrid identities would be decontextualized without an understanding of the ethnic experiences of Korean-Americans and Joseonjok in their respective home countries. It is through their experiences after moving to South Korea and encountering homeland expectations of what it means to be "Korean" that informs their reflections on the multiple meanings of being ethnic Koreans back in their home countries. I begin with a brief overview of the out-migration histories of ethnic Koreans to the US and China.

Migration histories

The Creation of Korean Americans: South Korea to the US

According to the 2000 US census, there are an estimated 2 million Korean-Americans in the US, including both recent and more settled immigrants. Initial migration from the Asia region began in the 1800s with large numbers of mostly male migrants filling the role of cheap labor in the agricultural, mining, and railroad industries. However, the growing "hordes" of Asian migrants fueled the fear of "Yellow Peril" and triggered a virulent reaction against their dramatically different physical appearances, languages, cultural traditions, and foods as compared to earlier European immigrants. These fears led to successive restrictive immigration policies, such as the 1875 Page Law, the 1882 Chinese Exclusion Act, the 1907 Gentleman's Agreement, and the 1924 Immigration Act, that generally held immigration from Asia to low levels until the passage of the 1965 Immigration Act opened borders to an extent previously unseen (Espiritu 2000).

Specific to the Korean context, the presence of American troops in the Korean peninsula has been consistent since the end of World War II in 1945 and played a decisive role during the Korean War (1950–1953). Now, nearly 60 years later, US military personnel remain due to the potentially volatile situation between North and South Korea since the cease-fire agreement was brokered. Additionally, the active role of the US in South Korean affairs in the past six decades has created close relationships between the two countries economically, politically, and socially. During this period, many South Korean women emigrated to the US as war brides alongside their American GI husbands, and through family reunification sponsorships many extended family members of these wives gained entry into the US. Additionally in the post-1965 era, many of the professional, highly educated classes in developing countries like South Korea were recruited to core countries like the US to fill gaps in the labor market.

All of the Korean-Americans interviewed emigrated with their families or were born in the US in this post-1965 context. As a result, the migration experience was a relatively recent one for the Korean-Americans I interviewed as members of the 1.5 or second generation. Fifteen out of 31 Korean-Americans were born in the US or US territories, while of the 15 who were born in Korea or elsewhere, the majority came to the US during their early childhood or infancy with very few concrete memories of living in Korea. For those who left later, all except one came with their immediate family members with little voice in making the decision to migrate. In terms of where they settled in the US, nearly half identified hometowns in California with the second-largest concentration in the northeast, primarily in the New York and New Jersey area. While Korean-Americans, and more broadly Asian-Americans, are generally seen as integrated into mainstream American society through their portrayal in the media as the "model minority," the Korean-Americans whom I interviewed remained strongly committed to their Korean identities.

The Creation of Joseonjok: South Korea to China

Much has been written about the Joseonjok, who also face challenges of "dual identities" as Chinese citizens of Korean ancestry with a long history in the Manchurian region near the border of North Korea (Choi 2001, Piao 1990, Masayuki 1990, He 1990, Jin 1990, C. J. Lee 1986). As will be explored throughout this chapter, the state plays a more explicit role in the lives of ethnic Koreans in China than is seen in the Korean-American context, particularly through the establishment of Yanbian Autonomous Prefecture for ethnic Koreans in China.

According to the 2000 national census, Han Chinese make up 91.59 percent of the population, while the remaining 8.41 percent comprise 55 officially recognized minority nationalities (Choi 2001). Of these 55 minority groups, as of 1999, the Korean population was estimated to be about 2 million. Overall, Joseonjok carry positive connotations and are viewed as "model minorities" in China due to their high literacy rates, high rates of college matriculation, agricultural skills, and strong sense of ethnic identity (Choi 2001:119). Historically, Joseonjok are seen to have played pivotal roles in the resistance movement against the Japanese during China's Liberation War and were instrumental in the building of the new socialist People's Republic of China (Piao 1990, Masayuki 1990). Many Joseonjok I interviewed talked about their out-migration to China as forced, rather than voluntary, due to famine, lack of economic opportunities in the Korean peninsula, and Japanese colonization.

These different migration legacies for Korean-Americans in the US and Joseonjok in China have led to the establishment of relatively stable ethnic

Korean communities abroad. The ethnic Korean populations in the US and China represent the two largest communities of ethnic Koreans outside of the Korean peninsula, making them ideal case studies for understanding the complexities of hybridized Korean identities.

Ethnic Korean Identities as Difference

In this section, I focus on how Korean-Americans and Joseonjok talk about how "difference" structures their lives as ethnic minorities in their home countries. While there was a range in the experiences across the sample, a strong theme that ran throughout all the interviews was a heightened awareness of this difference and the sense that they occupied two different and incompatible worlds: an immigrant, ethnic world and a mainstream Chinese or American world.

Salience of Racial Classification as Asian-American

Race was the primary factor that marked Korean-Americans in the US as "different." Because of their physical appearance, interviewees felt they were immediately coded as "Asian," "Asian-American," or, more specifically, "Korean-American" in everyday interactions. The Korean-Americans I spoke with often talked about the "Where are you *really* from?" question as an explicit way in which they were reminded of their hybridized American identity. When I asked John, a 24-year-old Korean-American, about the difference between being American and Korean-American, he responded, "I think people [Korean-Americans] who say they're American, they're fooling themselves. No one is going to look at you and say, 'Oh, are you American?' [When asked] 'Where are you from?' [I would reply] I'm from New Jersey. 'No, I mean like, originally.' For me, I say Jersey and when they give me a look, I say Korea."

Memories of this type of exchange came up repeatedly in interviews with Korean-Americans and were often told with a wry smile and a tone tinged with sarcasm. For John, deliberately playing with the question was a strategy to deal with the double-edged nature of the query that reemphasized his Asian origins even though he was born and raised in the US. This is in contrast to what Lieberson and Waters found in Americans of European origin who claim an American ancestry and are part of a growing number of "unhyphenated whites," referring to people who "are able or willing to identify themselves solely as whites, and who have little or no interest in or knowledge of their European ancestry or origin" (1988:251). This difference between whites and non-whites did not go unnoticed by Korean-Americans like Maya, who said in frustration, "African-American, Chinese-American, Korean-American. Why do we have to be that and white people are just American?"

Racial theorists like Milton Gordon (1964) posited that early European immigrants were slowly absorbed into dominant American culture in what has been called the "melting pot" metaphor of assimilation. However, non-European immigrants did not adhere to the expected linear model of assimilation. The Civil Rights movement of the 1960s illustrated the history of struggle in the US that communities of color have faced against political, economic, and social repression as exemplified by the Black Panthers, the "Black is Beautiful" cultural movement, the American Indian Movement, the Chicana/o movement, and the Yellow Power movement, to name a few.

With the certainty that new immigrants and US people of color were not going to melt into a homogenous national culture, multiculturalism has gained credence in the decades since the 1960s. The main underlying ideology is cultural pluralism, the notion that individual heritages should be preserved and diversity is seen as strength. It is during this period that hyphenated Americans such as African-Americans or Asian-Americans became part of mainstream vernacular. But at the level of lived experience, many immigrants, like Korean-Americans, are torn between celebrating and protecting their ethnic cultural ties and the pressure to assimilate, to become more "American" and minimize difference.

What cultural pluralism under multiculturalism promotes is what I call "sameness in difference." By pushing color-blind notions of meritocracy in conjunction with the restriction of "difference" through acceptable outlets like the designation of February as "Black History Month" or May as "Asian Pacific–American Heritage Month," difference is celebrated and acknowledged but under the banner of sameness as "Americans." Diversity becomes relegated to the consumption of ethnic foods, performances of traditional dances, and clothing, as well as the celebration of festivals like Cinco de Mayo and Fiesta. In a critique of multiculturalism, Das Gupta argues the state "deliberately promotes a multiculturalism that glides over the actual relationships between and within cultures in contact in the United States" (1997:591).

For example, English-only policies were one area in which Korean-American interviewees felt the intervention of the US state toward assimilation in their lives. The fierce battle against bilingual education in states like California with high immigrant populations, exemplified in legislation like Proposition 227 (the "English for the children" initiative), highlights official state policies that push for assimilation. These "English-only" policies, labeled "pragmatic racism" by Vijay Prashad (2000), exemplify the need within the US to have some common culture and language that solidify what it means to be American. As will be seen in a later discussion of Korean-Americans in the education system, language is a key issue that illustrates the shortcomings of multiculturalism in which diversity for other cultures is tolerated as long as it is not a threat to the larger fabric that ties Americans together.

Difference in Sameness: Cultural Pluralism in the Chinese Context

While diversity in the national population is acknowledged in China as well, differences are not necessarily smoothed over but actively protected. Chinese state policy dating back to the Communist Revolution called for a rebuilding of the nation to promote equality among Chinese citizens along the lines of gender, race, and class. The key difference underlying the majority of Joseonjok experiences is the official policy of the Chinese state toward the 55 recognized minority groups within the country. In the constitution, it is explicitly stated that "[e]ach nationality possesses equal rights in such areas as politics, economy, culture, language, religion, and more. Any one nationality is prohibited from enjoying special prerogatives" (He 1990:3). Unlike in the US, there are national mandates recognizing and protecting diversity within China, as evidenced by the autonomous areas set aside for minority groups. While independence movements such as the situation in Tibet are met with military force, autonomous nationality regions established in 1949, including 33 autonomous prefectures and 104 autonomous counties, allow for minority groups to nurture cultural and linguistic traditions while still retaining allegiance to the Chinese state (He 1990:6).

Most of the Joseonjok I interviewed came from hometowns in the Yanbian Korean Autonomous Prefecture, an area in northeastern China referred to as Manchuria where a majority of the nearly 2 million Joseonjok in China reside. In Yanbian, Joseonjok comprise nearly 40 percent of the population and the official languages are Mandarin Chinese and Korean. Joseonjok schools from elementary levels through high school, as well as Yanbian University, offer instruction in Korean and Chinese, formalizing bilingual education in this area, a distinct difference from Korean-Americans in the US who rely primarily on their family and independent Saturday schools for Korean language instruction.

Because they lived in a region designated by the state to maintain Korean customs and language, Joseonjok were well aware of their identities as ethnic minorities but did not believe this was a large obstacle to their social, economic, and political mobility. As Hee Sook explains, "In China, there are many different races. The nation protects and maintains these cultural differences... Whether or not one was born in Korea, it is understood that Joseonjok have Chinese citizenship but roots in Korea." On official documents and their identity cards, their status as Joseonjok are clearly marked so that their Chinese identities are always modified by their Korean ethnic origins. The state explicitly intervenes in the lives of its citizens, officially classifying people by their ethnic backgrounds, whereas for Korean-Americans, documents denote all citizens as "Americans" without racial or ethnic qualifiers.

Difference as Markers of Inferiority

Many Korean-Americans and Joseonjok struggle with making sense of how their linguistic, cultural, and physical differences locate them in relation to larger dominant society. In the US, the discourse of "color-blindness" has pushed for a disavowal of race as an impediment to upward mobility and equality, including the abolishment of affirmative action policies in states like California, Florida, and Michigan. Some Korean-Americans appear to support these notions of meritocracy and talked about their frustrations with the constant discussion of race in the US. Catherine, a 23-year-old Korean-American, expressed frustration with Korean-Americans who did not acknowledge the privilege of growing up in the US:

> I knew that being Korean was important to me... but I also recognized that I was born and raised in the States and that was a really great privilege... [S]o, actually I get kind of mad when I meet Korean-Americans who... bash America when they don't really try to take advantage of everything that their parents worked so hard for them to try to get.

Going one step further, Maya equated complaints of racism with ignorance, "Koreans [Korean-Americans] are always complaining about racism, we're discriminated against, fuck the white man...Korean power. I was like, 'you're so ignorant, it's so embarrassing. I don't want to be associated with you guys.'"

For some, the fluidity of crossing the boundaries between Americanness and Koreanness was a daily part of their lives. As Daniel explained, "I'm not big on identity. I could be Korean-American one day, I could be American the next." However, he did acknowledge the real effects of racism in the ways his immigrant parents brought him up in the States: "I remember my mom saying I had to study twice as hard, and my English had to be better than other people's English because I was Korean, not white. I had to do everything twice as good because of racism and stuff." Others I spoke with felt that their racial difference as non-whites was an impediment for upward mobility and spoke explicitly about dealing with racism and discrimination. Sang yul, a biracial Korean-American in his 30s, shared his experiences about growing up in a working-class town in Ohio as one of a few non-white residents:

> My brother started a youth football league when he was eight years old. When you start, the coach would put medical tape on your helmet and write your name so he could tell who was who. He wrote everybody's last names on their helmet, except my brother's. On his helmet he wrote 'Chink.' That was what my brother was called from that point onwards, his nickname that stuck throughout high school. That's literally an example of how we were labeled.

Herb, a 26-year-old Korean-American male, also talked about how violence and fights clearly illustrated discrimination operating in his own life as a person of color:

> Growing up in a rich white neighborhood, I mean we used to have race fights in our school. We were outnumbered, one fight there were 10 of us, 30–40 white guys...The cops pick up five of us Asians, including myself and my brother, and one white guy who was tangled up with my brother so he couldn't run away. Makes you think, out of 30–40 white guys fighting and 10 of us Asians, they pick up five Asians and one white guy. It ain't a fair deal.

This is not unlike 36-year-old Joseonjok Chul Kwon's memories of the distinct divisions between Joseonjok and Han Chinese growing up. As he recalled, "When you say Joseonjok in Chinese, it's called *kko-lee-fang-zzeu*. It literally means water from *Goryeo* (name for Korea originating in the Goryeo Dynasty from 918–1392)... [T]hat word has come down from the past when Korea and China fought against each other. If you go to my village in China, there's a Joseonjok village and a Hanjok village, and often the two villages fight." Myeong dae echoed a similar situation in his childhood, "We grew up fighting. We just fought a lot continuously since we were kids. If the Chinese (Han) kids came over, we would always romp around. They would make fun of me because I wasn't Chinese."

Out of necessity, because their parents lacked English fluency prior to migration, many Korean-Americans and Joseonjok found themselves, at times reluctantly, in the role of translators, mediating interactions between the private sphere of the immigrant Korean home and the public sphere of larger American or Chinese society. Herb, a Korean-American, recounted a painful memory from his childhood that equated "difference" with inferiority:

> I had to translate for my mother. The other kids asked if my mom was retarded. They were mostly white. Some of them said my mom was stupid, she can't even speak English. It was so embarrassing – my mom can't talk with other people, you feel inferior too. These white people are better than me. I look different already, now I know that we're valued less.

While these experiences were not representative of all Korean-Americans I interviewed, "American" was nearly always equated with "white" for almost all those I spoke with, both men and women. Regardless of whether their social networks in the US were primarily Korean-American or not, all interviewees talked about an awareness that as ethnic Americans, they were marginalized and not part of the dominant (white) culture.

While issues of "color" and racial classification were the primary markers of difference for Korean-Americans, Joseonjok identified the issue of rural/urban status combined with their ethnic identities as an additional factor of difference in their lives as Chinese citizens. Research done on rural-to-urban migration in China indicates that the geographical differences are distinct enough to create deep divisions between Chinese citizens that may operate similarly as racial divisions do in the US. In her work on Chinese internal migration patterns, Solinger found that "urban Chinese generally view rural Chinese as ethnically distinct" (1990:456).

Urban-Rural Classification: China's Household Registration System

The Chinese state intervenes directly in the lives of its citizens through the household registration (*hukuo*) program. Begun in 1955 as part of the first Five-Year Plan, this program attempted to control the amount of internal migration among its citizens as a "floating population" of illegal migrants from rural areas rose to an estimated 60–80 million peasants in cities searching for work (Solinger 1990, 1995; Yang and Guo 1996; Roberts 1997; Wu and Treiman 2004). According to the household registration system, all citizens are classified as an agricultural household (*nongye hukou*) or urban household (*chengshijumin hukou*), a division strictly enforced by the state (Roberts 1997, Wu and Treiman 2004). Chinese citizens with households in designated urban areas gain access to an urban citizenship denied to those from rural areas. These privileges include "full labor insurance, generous retirement and medical packages, housing, and life-time job tenure. In addition, all proper, permanent urban residents received dwellings at exceedingly low rents; almost gratis public transportation, home heating, and water; guaranteed jobs; and heavily subsidized grain, oil, and other daily necessities (Solinger 1990:464).

For rural residents who wish to migrate, they must apply for permission from the local government as well as temporary resident permits from the urban police. In addition, employers of rural migrants must also apply for legal work permits and secure legal documents of their employees (Roberts 1997). Roberts argues that the status of migrant laborers, regardless of their Chinese citizenship, is akin to undocumented workers in the US, and they are subject to lower wages as well as harassment from authorities (1997: 270). Following economic reforms beginning in the 1980s, there was a slight loosening of restrictions freeing up some rural-to-urban migration, but these workers faced discrimination in the labor market as well as the housing sector as compared to registered urban residents (Wu and Treiman 2004).

Most of the Joseonjok interviewed for this study were from rural areas. Following her college graduation from a Beijing university, Hee Sook, a Joseonjok woman in her early 30s, was required to return to her rural village without the option of finding employment and setting up residence in Beijing. Hee Sook explained how China's domestic policy affected her even though she had left her rural hometown to attend college in Beijing:

> In China, it's where you were born and where your mother lives that counts... [I]f my mom was from Beijing, I'd be from Beijing. It follows your mother. My mom is from Yonggil, therefore I am from Yonggil. Resources are allocated by neighborhood/areas... But you can't change your registered hometown. In the past, I heard that if you had money, you could change it. Now, that's not possible.

While underrepresented minority groups like Joseonjok are given some advantages by the state, such as exemption from the one-child-only reproductive restrictions as well as extra points for college admission, the advantages come with real limitations. This translates to increased opportunities for higher education in urban areas for students from rural areas, but following graduation, these students are not permitted to reside in the cities where most of the economic opportunities and development are located. Upon their return to their rural hometowns, many of these graduates find few economic opportunities to apply their skills. While state-mandated initiatives do benefit minority groups like the Joseonjok, they also underscore the differences between the Joseonjok and the Han majority.

I use a discussion of "difference" in this first section to highlight the ways in which the "third space" is constructed between ethnic identities and national identities. The next section will focus on how competing "structures of authority" such as the family, peer groups, the church, and the state, regulate and monitor these hybrid communities both internally and externally.

Structures of Authority

Family: Older vs. Younger Generation

Parents, and grandparents in some cases, mainly through language and food, transmit the most salient markers of Koreanness identified by both Korean-Americans and Joseonjok. In this way, older generations operate as "authority" figures in defining what is "Korean" and how it is performed by younger generations. Within the home, most Korean-Americans and Joseonjok grew up eating "three square Korean meals a day," with dishes like *kim chee*, a spicy fermented cabbage side dish unique to Korean cuisine, and the particular smell of *duen jjang*, the Korean version of miso, wafting through their homes. In addition to "consuming" Koreanness, many Korean-Americans talked about the primordial links that inextricably made them Korean. As Paula recalled, "My mom and dad are Korean...she [my mother] would always say, your blood is Korean...what's running through you is Korean, but you're American." Conversations with Joseonjok often returned to bloodlines and heritage as explanations of the persistence of ethnic Korean identities in China despite two or three generations of distance from the initial migration experience.

Similar to Korean-Americans, the Joseonjok family became the primary conduit for markers of Koreanness. Chung ae, a 27-year-old Joseonjok graduate student, talked about growing up in Yonggil, a city with a substantial ethnic Korean population. Although there was a mix of Chinese and Korean elements in her third-generation Korean household, there were certain aspects, such as gathering together as a family to perform the traditional Korean bowing ceremony during the New Year's celebration, that were strictly observed. She stated, "It is important to preserve these Korean customs and traditions because we are the same minjok (race or people)...Because we are the same people, until the day when reunification happens, traditional ties are necessary to bind people together." However, as Kyeong mi, a 29-year-old Joseonjok woman, explained, elements of Korean cultures were also modified by the local context in China: "Since we are Joseonjok, we had Korean customs. But since we are not completely Korean either, we also had some Chinese customs. You can just look at it as half and half." While it was generally accepted that there would be changes in traditional practices in hybrid cultures, both Joseonjok and Korean-Americans felt that the retention of traditional Korean practices was important.

Education and Schooling

As they entered the educational system, the division between the private sphere of the home and the public sphere of dominant society became apparent. Because a majority of second- and third-generation Joseonjok grew up in Yanbian, most of them attended state-sponsored Joseonjok schools through elementary and middle school, although some completed their education in Chinese high schools. Because instruction in the Joseonjok schools was primarily conducted in Korean, most Joseonjok up through the third generation were fluent in Korean and Chinese, and for many first- and second-generation Joseonjok, Korean was their only language. Choi identifies the preservation of language as a key tool toward maintaining a strong ethnic identity. This is formalized in Yanbian where "the use of Korean as an official language...has been encouraged through education, publishing, and mass communication" (2001:126).

In contrast, for some Korean-Americans interviewed, their first experiences with the American school system were seminal moments in understanding the pressures of assimilating to life in the US. For Paula, a 24-year-old Korean-American, the shame of being assigned to ESL (English as a Second Language) classes in early elementary school became a motivation to consciously switch to using English both at school and at home.

> [My parents] would say that my first language was Korean, always Korean. And then what happened was I had to go to ESL. Because everything was in Korean, I couldn't comprehend English sometimes. Up until first grade, I was in ESL. My parents freaked out. So they were worried about me passing grades, so what they did when I was in second grade was pass an 'English-only' rule for the house.

While in formal schooling, all Korean-Americans adapted to the English-only environment relatively easily, but almost all talked about their parents' desires for them to learn Korean as well. For over half of the interviewees, this entailed a combination of different forms of education, from informal Saturday Korean schools often at the local Korean church or taking Korean language classes either in college or at Korean language schools in Seoul. Yet these efforts were not successful on the whole because they were not systematically enforced by the US government and were largely dependent on personal motivation or parental pressure. Overall, for all Korean-Americans I spoke with, the clear focus during childhood was excelling in the English-only space in school, while learning Korean held less importance, as evidenced by the overwhelming majority who self-evaluate their Korean reading and writing skill levels as very poor to high beginning.

This loss of fluency is increasingly part of the future Joseonjok see for themselves in China despite the Joseonjok school system. Recent economic development in China has created a push toward monolingualism. Chung ae attended Joseonjok schools through high school but believes this pattern will not hold in future generations of Joseonjok families. "In the past, most parents chose to send their children to Joseonjok schools. But in the end, if you want to attend college or work in a Chinese firm, then you need to be able to speak Chinese fluently...So going to a Joseonjok school is a slight disadvantage because you will not be completely fluent." For many third-generation Joseonjok, interest in attending Joseonjok schools has begun to wane, and the number of Joseonjok schools has continued to decline. One man spoke regretfully about his children's lack of interest in learning Korean, "Nowadays, when children play, they just use Chinese. They don't use Korean at all. It's not necessary to learn Korean [in China]. It's like the US, you don't need to learn Korean."

"Fobs" vs. "Twinkies": Korean-American Peers as Authorities

Families and schools are not the only arenas in which hybrid identities are regulated. Particularly as people reached adolescence and college-age, peer groups became more important "structures of authority" that monitored desirable expressions of hybrid identities. Focusing specifically on the Korean-American community, the labels "fob" and "Twinkie" were employed as a way to self-police each other into performing acceptable hybridized identities. In fact, all Korean-Americans negatively viewed straying into either extreme of being too Korean or too American, although where they drew the line differed across experiences. In over half of the interviews, the concept of "fob" came up in one form or another, which is a slang term for "fresh off the boat," referring to those people, in the words of one respondent, who "don't look like they are ever going to adapt to America; [they] can't speak English."

During adolescence and in the college years, one's social network became the primary basis for being labeled a "fob." While many Korean-Americans deliberately joined Korean-American student organizations in college or took courses related to Korean language and history in attempts to find other Korean-American friends, there was a tendency to guard against being seen as too "fobby," which referred to those who almost exclusively listened to Korean popular music (K-pop), watched Korean dramas, and even spoke mostly in Korean among each other or spoke with accented English. While initially, the term "fob" tended to refer to newer immigrants, its meaning has been modified by second-generation Korean-Americans. All the qualities of being a fob were seen as markers of foreignness, of one's inability to assimilate to dominant American culture.

However, being "too Americanized" was also held in contempt by the majority of interviewees, speaking to the importance of maintaining some connection to being Korean without assimilating completely. The labels that came up most frequently were "white-washed," "banana," and "Twinkie," all slang terms referring to being "yellow on the outside, white on the inside," by deliberately rejecting one's Korean heritage. In their study of identity in ethnic Chinese living in Singapore, Tong and Chan (2001) found that Chinese-educated respondents used the term "banana" as a pejorative term to refer to English-educated ethnic Chinese who were seen to have lost their roots to cultural assimilation.

A number of Korean-Americans whose primary social groups were non-Koreans talked about being seen as too assimilated. As Catherine explained, "From high school, I actually did not hang out with any Korean-Americans...They were very, very exclusive...The Korean-Americans at my school kind of looked down on me...They would call me Twinkie and that whole thing." The self-policing among Korean-American youth also led to a critique of Korean-Americans who didn't appear to have any Korean cultural capital. As Lydia, who inhabited mostly Korean-American social circles, put it, "Even among Korean-Americans, we say, 'Oh my god, he's such a Twinkie. Those people that don't know any Korean music, don't know what *bibimbap* (Korean dish consisting of rice, vegetables, and meat) is. That's being too American."

What emerged from the interviews were internal and external pressures on Korean-Americans at each stage of their lives, from their families, their friends, and themselves to enact normalized notions of "Koreanness" and illustrates the highly contested nature of hybrid identity construction within the "third space." In addition to the influence of specific actors, the idea of "time," particularly through memory, complicates how older and younger generations of Koreans envision hybridity in the US and China.

Fossilized Memory: Rooting "Koreanness" in Time

Maira (2002) refers to "fossilized" memory operating in the minds of Indian immigrant parents who resettle in New York but fix their memories of what is "Indian" at the time at which they immigrated. Likewise, what is labeled as "Korean" is largely based on the memories of the immigrant generation that are fixed in the time period in which they left. For the majority of Korean-American immigrants, the exodus, facilitated by the US Immigration Act of 1965, began during the early 1970s when South Korea had yet to enjoy the period of intense development and industrialization that has made it one of the largest economies in the world. Periods of hardship, poverty, lack of economic opportunity, and the static vision of Seoul as a "podunk city" loomed large in the collective memory of those Korean emigrants during this period and was often given as reasons for why the family came to the States. The "Korea" as envisioned by second-generation Korean-Americans was of an impoverished nation, as typified by Jessica's reaction upon moving to Seoul: "I thought it was going to be a lot more Third World, as embarrassing as that is. It's the 11th largest financial power in the world, but I didn't realize it was going to be this developed."

Because the immigration histories for Joseonjok took place in the early 1900s, before the establishment of South and North Korea, the term *"joseon"* refers to a Korea that is historically rooted, not geographically bounded. Joseonjok, which literally translates to "the people of Joseon," refers to the centuries in which the Korean peninsula was united during the Joseon Dynasty (1392–1910). During our interview, Kyeong soon, a Joseonjok woman in her early 20s, raised the question "aren't we all Joseonjok?" She argued that true Koreanness transcended the formation of nation-states and reached back to a historical context at the time of her family's out-migration for defining authenticity.

Authenticity was a theme that returned repeatedly in conversations with Joseonjok who were frustrated by the great degree of change in South Korea in terms of culture and language. With increased exposure to American cultural, political, and economic influences, English vernacular has become a growing part of Korean conversations, with English words such as "refrigerator," "phone," and "computer" replacing Korean words for the same objects. Instead, many Joseonjok interviewed thought that ethnic Korean communities in China kept the traditions and language "intact" and, in a sense, less corrupted by Western influences. Kyeong soon, a 32-year-old Joseonjok woman, observed, "Well, in the past, in my parents' generation, they kept the traditional customs intact from when their grandparents left Korea, but Korea has changed a lot, adapted things," implying that Joseonjok culture was more authentically Korean.

Myeong dae, a 31-year-old Joseonjok male, addressed the South Koreans' lack of knowledge of the "traditional" Chinese characters as additional evidence of the more authentic nature of Joseonjok identity. As he explained, "If you see South Koreans reading old books, they know less than me because I know all the characters (referring to "*hanja*," or Chinese characters). No matter what they say, Koreans don't know as much as me." While nearly 75 percent of the roots of Korean vocabulary come from Chinese characters, there has been a growing trend to replace many *hanja*-based words to Korean-based or English words. In South Korean schools, the curriculum has reduced instruction on the thousands of Chinese characters, so many young South Koreans have a limited knowledge of *hanja* characters compared to older generations. Joseonjok, both because of the ways in which traditional Korean language has been preserved and because of living in China, generally have a very thorough familiarity with Chinese characters that surpasses that of contemporary South Koreans.

In comparing Korean-American and Joseonjok ethnic Korean identities, hybridity is not assumed to be a uniform process, and there are important factors underlying Korean identities that are specific to the local context that will be explored in the next section. For Korean-Americans, the church played a key role in fusing religious and ethnic identities together and operated as a cornerstone for many Korean immigrant communities. For Joseonjok, the joint orientation of the Chinese state to both North and South Korea, rather than just the South, offered a distinctive twist to their understandings of Korean identity not found in the Korean-American sample.

Church, Religion, and the Korean Community: "It's hard to say what's Korean and what's Christian"

Devout religiosity and the Korean Christian church also played a large role in the conservative childhoods many Korean-Americans spoke about, to the point where, as Linda puts it, "It's hard to say what's Korean and what's Christian." Because the US takes a largely laissez-faire approach to ethnic preservation and diversity outside of English-only legislation, the church has functioned as a key institution in Korean communities, along with the family, to transmit traditional Korean values. Hurh and Kim (1990) found that rates of religious participation in Korean immigrant communities were very high across variables such as age, education, length of residence, gender, and socioeconomic status, as compared to other Asian immigrants such as Japanese or Chinese. They also noted that many of the 622 Korean immigrants they interviewed connected being Christian as a sign of being more westernized or Americanized. In addition, those identified as Christian were disproportionately from the urban, middle-class sector of South Korean population.

For many, being Christian and part of a Korean church was a significant part of their family lives and where they connected with Korean-American peers. Catherine grew up in New Jersey with her immediate family as well as her 11 aunts and uncles and numerous cousins in the same area. The closeness that her family had with the Korean community was also strengthened through church membership. As she said, "My cousins and I joined the same churches. Whenever you meet any...Korean-American from the New York area, there is undoubtedly a one-degree separation."

Chong argued that social marginalization as ethnic and racial minorities strengthened church participation in the Korean-American community she studied in Chicago. The church itself became a powerful transmitter of conservative religious values related to filial piety, obedience, and sexual conduct intertwined with core Korean values so that Korean Christianity was seen as an expression of ideal elements of religious and ethnic cultures blending to produce a superior type of Christian (1998:278). For Sang hee, "Korean Christianity" represented a strong link to the Korean immigrant community in Los Angeles and the Korean church was where her family devoted much of its time.

[W]hat I thought was Korean to them was Korean Christianity...We had to go to early morning prayer meetings at the church...I think Korean churches are more cohesive. They had so many gatherings. It's not like you go to church when you want to...Doing a lot of work at the church, working in the kitchen, teaching Sunday school, choir, I would say that is particular to Korean Christianity.

The Two Koreas: Orientation to North and South Korea

Rather than religion, the Chinese state played a key role in ethnic identity construction for Joseonjok, in this case, with the association of "Korea" with either North or South Korea. Linguistically, Joseonjok in interviews were careful to distinguish which Korea they were referring to by using *"han guk"* for South Korea, *"buk han"* or *"ee buk"* for North Korea, and *"joseon"* for themselves. Because a large number of Joseonjok have family members currently residing in North Korea or who originally migrated out of present-day North Korea, their orientation to the Korean peninsula includes both North and South Korea as well as parts of Manchuria. Presently, the Yanbian Autonomous Prefecture shares a border with North Korea, which has created a political situation in which North Korean refugees use China as the first destination in their migration projects.

Choi notes that during the 1950s and early 1960s, Joseonjok were more strongly influenced by North Korea. Because of the close political ties between the PRC (People's Republic of China) and North Korea and the legacy of the Cold War, "Koreans in China were encouraged to think of North Korea alone as their ancestral land and to follow North Korea in defining elements related to ethnic identity" (2001:131). Close to 85 percent of Joseonjok I interviewed had family members currently in North Korea, while fewer than 10 percent had family members currently residing in South Korea with whom they had contact. Unlike Korean-Americans, many Joseonjok, particularly those from Yanbian Prefecture, grew up with closer ties to North Korea. When I asked about her personal relationship with North Koreans, Hee Sook replied,

> My uncle lived in North Korea. When I was little, he came to visit us in China. In my house, everyone has gone to North Korea besides me...I used to chew North Korean gum, the things I ate were goods from North Korea, my book bag when I was in school was from North Korea.

However, with the political and economic rise of South Korea since the early 1980s, as well as the hosting of the1988 Olympic Games in Seoul, the status and perception of Koreans in China has increased as well. The Chinese government has relied on South Korea's economic development as a model for its own plan toward modernization, and "Chinese authorities implicitly encourage Koreans in China to visit their relatives in South Korea since the liberalization in policies regarding mutual visits of relatives in the mid-1980s"

(Choi 2001:132). Changes in the migration policies of both China and South Korea in the past two decades have significantly increased migration back and forth between the two countries. As Chul mu explained, "When I went to China last year, like I told you, when I gathered with my friends, almost 100 percent of them are somehow related to South Korea. If we don't talk about Korea, then we have nothing to talk about in Joseonjok society. I began to think that the fate of *dongpo* (ethnic Koreans living outside of the Korean peninsula) are left up to Korea. If it's not Korea, our ethnic Korean community in China and around the world will have a hard time standing up."

My conversations with Joseonjok made me conscious of my orientation solely to South Korea and my identity as a US citizen. I had always used "Korean" or *han guk* to refer to Korea or things Korean, with the assumption that Koreanness was rooted in South Korea. Upon reflection, as someone born and raised in the US, this is somewhat unsurprising given the legacy of the Korean War and the military and political support the US gave to South Korea as a key ally in the fight against the perceived threat of communism. My own parents' "fossilized memory" of North and South Korea contributed to pro-South Korean sympathies in our household as they told stories of their own families' escape from the North to the South. Furthermore in 2002, President Bush included North Korea as one of the "axis of evil" in his State of the Union Address.

Conclusion

> [T]he Third World grates against the First and bleeds. And before a scab forms it hemorrhages again, the lifeblood of two worlds merging to form a third country – a border culture. Borders are set up to define the places that are safe and unsafe, to distinguish *us* from *them*. A border is a dividing line, a narrow strip along a steep edge. A border line is a vague and undetermined place created by the residue of an unnatural boundary. It is in a constant state of transition. (Anzaldúa 1987:25, emphasis in original)

Anzaldúa (1987) refers to the "borderlands" as the location where *los atravesados* (cross-bred, hybrids) inhabit multiple borders that are both physical and cultural. Anzaldúa's borderlands are akin to Bhabha's concept of the "third space." A comparison of Korean-American and Joseonjok expressions of Korean hybridity is informative of the multiplicity of ethnic identity construction and how national and ethnic identities give rise to different ideas of what constitutes "Koreanness" in the US and China. The borders that hybrid ethnic Koreans inhabit every day separate national identities from ethnic identities but also bisect identities within their own communities – older from younger generations, family units from individuals, Korean-Americans from Joseonjok. The "borderlands" or "third space" is full of contradictions, and the ethnographic data for this chapter illustrates the highly contested meanings of being "Korean." Rather than a fixed formula combining Korean and Chinese culture or Korean and American culture into a seamless, compatible whole, hybridized Korean identities remain a constant negotiation between conflicting interests.

Chapter Sixteen

One Plus One Equals Three: Legal Hybridity in Aotearoa/New Zealand

Alex Frame and Paul Meredith

Although our title does not look like very good arithmetic, we hope to convince the reader that it is useful social theory for explaining what happens when two customary systems meet, and to suggest that it has relevance to the issues of legal pluralism. In particular, and based on our investigations into historical accounts of Maori customary legal concepts while engaged over the past decade at Te Matahauariki Research Institute at the University of Waikato, partly in the compilation of *Te Matapunenga: A Compendium of References to the Concepts and Institutions of Maori Customary Law*, we want to draw attention to the dynamic character of customary law and its capacity to absorb new elements and evolve in response to new conditions.

Our intention is to go beyond the shibboleth of "one law for all": that there should be only one legal system in each country and that every law should apply to everyone. This principle is usually unfavorably contrasted with "special laws" based on the status of a person, and any notion that the rules in a legal system might treat different categories of persons in different ways. Instead we invoke "legal hybridity," where law is seen both as a process and a relationship in a third space that no longer assumes rigid alternatives, but rather an organic and continuing interaction and adaptation. It offers a way of describing a productive and ambivalent space that engenders new possibilities that are not constrained by existing boundaries. Established cultural practices, norms, values, and identities that help shape the law have no "primordial unity or fixity." Here, we have drawn on Homi Bhabha's notions of hybridity and third space (1994) as well as Paul Meredith's own work (1999). Legal concepts and institutions are contestable, and the interweaving of the elements of two customary systems (and the attendant negotiation and renewal) create new hybrid concepts and norms.

We hypothesize that a similar process of hybridization might occur in the meeting of languages and the consequent production of new words, forms, and styles. We have found the analogy between language and customary law to be a fruitful one on other fronts, and we will bring that tool to bear on the question of what happens when two customary systems meet.

Our text is an adaptation of a paper jointly presented by the authors at a symposium titled "One Country, Two Laws" held in Auckland, New Zealand, on July 22, 2006. While the text is substantially revised and expanded, the authors have tried to retain a little of its character as an oral presentation.

History Warns against Dogmatism in Either Sense of the Question

In an address in 2005 to the Australasian Law Teachers' Conference at the University of Waikato, where the theme was "One Law for All?", the Chief Justice of New Zealand, Dame Sian Elias, said: "We forget some of our own legal history when we claim that it is a fundamental tenet of English and New Zealand law that there is no room for distinctions in law to recognise [sic] minority interests" (Elias 2005:5).

Dame Sian's judicial ancestor, the first Chief Justice of New Zealand, Sir William Martin, had commented many years earlier that "local and customary tribunals, and local and customary rules differing from those of the Common Law, have always been recognized in England. Our own civilization has grown up in this way" (Martin 1860:72).

The Treaty of Waitangi, signed in 1840 between Captain Hobson on behalf of the British Crown and by many Maori chiefs on behalf of their tribes, is the principal foundation for the subsequent constitutional relations between the indigenous Maori peoples of Aotearoa/New Zealand and the Crown. The Treaty contains three substantive articles: the first according powers of government to the Crown, the second guaranteeing the powers of the chiefs and the possessions and property of the tribes, and the third assuring Maori of full and equal rights of citizenship. Both the imperial authorities in London and the colonial authorities in New Zealand in the period after the Treaty of Waitangi recognized that Maori had developed "usages having the character and authority of law" (Lord John Russell, instructions to Hobson, December 9, 1840:24).

Furthermore, it was accepted by British authorities in the "Instructions" from London to the Governor in New Zealand that these usages might properly apply not only as between Maori but also, in designated areas, as between Maori and visitors (Colonial Office, Draft Instructions 1846, Chapter 14, quoted in Frame 1981:106–107), and that there was "no theoretical or practical difficulty in the maintenance, under the same Sovereign, of various codes of law, for the governance of different races of men" (Stanley to Fitzroy, February 10, 1844:173). Lord Stanley, the responsible British Minister, added examples: "In British India, in Ceylon, at the Cape of Good Hope, and in Canada, the aboriginal and the European inhabitants live together on these terms. Native laws and native customs, when not abhorrent from the universal and permanent laws of God, are respected by English legislatures and by English courts."

It was entirely consistent with these positions that Section 71 of the *New Zealand Constitution Act* 1852 of the British Parliament should provide that: "the laws, customs, and usages of the aboriginal inhabitants...should for the present be maintained for the government of themselves."

At the "Kohimarama Conference" in Auckland on Monday, July 16, 1860, called to discuss Maori concerns about the implementation of the Treaty of Waitangi, the Native Secretary, Donald McLean (known to Maori as *Te Makarini*), brought a message for the assembled Maori leaders from Governor Gore Browne. The Governor asked the leaders to consider some "rules" prepared by Sir William Martin for the administration of justice "between one native and another." When the Governor's message had been formally read, Te Makarini added this observation in the Maori language:

Kua mea etahi o nga rangatira kia kotahi tonu te ture. Ka tika ano tenei, otira, e kore pea e ata rite. E kore te tamaiti kia kaumatua i roto i te ra kotahi. Maha noa nga whakapaparanga e mahi ana te Ingarihi i taua ture i tino pai inaianei. Koia hoki e whakaaroa ai kia akona koutou ki nga wahi ngawari o te ture, kia tupu haere hoki to koutou matauranga; a kia waiho ia hei whakakapi mo nga ritenga kino o te Maori e mau tonu nei i nga kaumatua. He mea ata hurihuri marire enei ture na to koutou hoa na Te Matenga.

(English translation) Some of the chiefs have expressed a wish that there should be but one law. This is much to be desired by all but is not so easily attained. A child does not grow to a man's estate in a day. It took the English many generations before they brought their system of law to its present state. While such a difference exists in the usages and customs of the two races in this country, it is necessary that some of you should be gradually initiated into the elementary principles of law before you can appreciate it. With this object, and with a view of superseding some of the objectionable customs to which many of your old people still cling, your friend Dr. Martin has taken much pains to prepare these rules.

Evidently, at that time, Maori chiefs thought there should be "one law for all," while the Crown's representatives thought that would be impracticable. In recent times, some Maori have challenged the dogma that there must be one monolithic legal system. It seems that Maori and Government positions have changed diametrically over time. In Bob Dylan's phrase from his song "The Times They are a-Changin'," "the wheel is still in spin." Those who yesterday dismissed "one law for all" may tomorrow be its most fervent advocates, and vice versa.

It is true that this early acceptance of the viability of Maori customary law was subject to one repeated qualification – that some customary elements "repugnant to the principles of humanity" must fall by the wayside. It is interesting to note which elements were considered objectionable on this basis, with some exclusions being more comprehensible than others. Lord Russell's instructions to Governor Hobson stated emphatically that there could be no compromise on the eternal and universal laws of morality, which rendered it a duty on the part of the Government not to tolerate cannibalism, human sacrifice, and infanticide (Russell's Instructions to Hobson, December 9, 1840). The New Zealand Premier, Stafford, provided Governor Gore Browne with advice as to what were considered "objectionable customs" in 1857: "We advert particularly to such usages as those...of Taumau (or betrothal); of making

Tauas (hostile raiding parties) upon the innocent relatives of an offender; of punishing the imaginary crime of witchcraft; and of the Tapu (taboo or religious and legal restriction)"(Stafford to Gore Browne, May 6, 1857).

The confusion reigning among these "observers" of Maori custom is evident in their assessment of the central Maori concept of *tapu* (taboo or sacred). For Stafford in 1857, tapu was an "objectionable custom," but Lord Stanley at the Colonial Office in 1842 had, with apparent equanimity, suggested that tapu merited incorporation in the legal system (quoted in McLintock 1958: 393–394). Governor Grey himself functioned very adequately within the relevant customary principles as he journeyed with the Maori chief, Iwikau Te Heu Heu, through the North Island in the summer of 1849–50 (Frame 2002:44–47). For example, the Governor both grasped and supported the customary force of the '*rahui* or *tapu*,' under which the taking of eels or birds might be prohibited in certain places for some periods so that the resources might be controlled and protected. As to the punishing of the "imaginary crime" of witchcraft, we find Parliament itself enacting a few decades later the "Tohunga Supression Act," treating witchcraft as a very real crime. A Tohunga is an expert in any branch of knowledge, religious or secular, and a skilled practitioner of an art or craft. The 1907 legislation suppressing their activities was supported by both European and Maori Members of Parliament and by Maui Pomare, a future Maori Member of Parliament who was at that time a Maori District Health Officer. The initiative found favor with Maori Members of Parliament who were concerned with curtailing so-called "self-created Maori prophets" and perceived quackery in Maori communities. The influential Maori lawyer/politician Apirana Ngata, Member of Parliament for the East Coast, was among the supporters, although he added the reservation that Maori herbalist tohunga supplied a real need in their communities and lamented the failure of the medical profession to explore this field (Ngata 1907:520).

It would be easy to characterize these attitudes toward Maori custom as simple racism. However, a more charitable conclusion is perhaps that, until the appearance in 1861 of Sir Henry Maine's "Ancient Law" (Maine 1961), there was very limited awareness in imperial and colonial legal circles of comparative and historical methods for the study of legal institutions with a view to understanding their function and utility in their specific social contexts.

In the 19th century, editorials in Maori newspapers encouraged Maori to abandon "*makutu and tangata makutu*" (Anon. 1859b:4), being repugnant to both Christianity and English law, and the ignorant Maori law of tapu: "*me whakarere taua ritenga kuare o nga tupuna; kua puta nei te maramatanga*" (that ignorant custom of the ancestors should be abandoned, you have now been enlightened) (Anon. 1858:3). A more obscure objection was to the making and consumption of *kanga pirau* (fermented corn) and other fermented foods. This "modern customary practice" was deemed an offense pursuant to Chief Justice Martin's rules. Wiremu Patene of Ngai Te Rangi of Tauranga defended the practice: "*Kotahi hoki tenei ko te ture mo te kanga-kopiro, mo nga kai e pirau ana. Ko te kai pea tena e ora ai tetahi tangata. Ki te mahue i aia tana kai ka kino ia*" (I have another word to say. One of the rules relates to steeped corn and other putrid food; but perhaps that may be the favorite food of some one, and who, if deprived of it, may feel himself aggrieved) (Patene 1860). However, one anonymous commentator explained the rationale behind this objection, based on a concern for the health of the Maori:

> But one of the greatest causes of death and sickness is not from any English custom, nor is it from the customs of your forefathers, but it comes from a custom of your own making. It is not above thirty years since the Maories began to steep corn in water and when it had become rotten to eat it. Many of the middle-aged people remember when they first ate it. The practice began among the Ngapuhi people and gradually spread through the country, bringing with it swellings in the neck, hips, and sides, such as had never been before in this country. (Anon 1859a)

When Governor Browne came to instruct the European Resident Magistrate, F. D. Fenton, to draft a set of laws for Maori, he noted that: "The Natives... require a code of laws adapted to their present condition which shall *be made binding on both races* residing in native districts" (emphasis added). The Governor specified the matters to be dealt with:

> Adultery and criminal conversation;
> Trespass;
> Betrothal of women without consent of the parties concerned;
> The responsibility of relatives for offences [sic] committed by individuals without their knowledge or consent;
> Drunkenness and violence by Europeans;

Illegal squatting;

Use of that peculiar form of swearing considered so heinous by the Natives;

Prohibition of punishment for witchcraft;

Prohibition of Tapu, except in very special cases. (Gore Browne, Governor 1857:7)

Generally, however, Maori custom and law, if not repugnant to humanity, was to be tolerated temporarily as long as, in Chief Justice Martin's words, it "lies quietly side by side of our own and does not come into any sort of conflict or collision with it" (Martin 1860:72).

Accordingly, at a practical level, several hybrid regulations emerged. Governor Fitzroy introduced the *Native Exemption Ordinance 1844* in response to the concern that the English law pertaining to assault, larceny, and felony was irreconcilable with the Maori view of principle and propriety, and opposed to native custom. Why fines were payable to the Crown rather than given as compensation to the injured party was, in Maori eyes, inexplicable. The new Ordinance provided that in "mixed race" cases, convicted Maori thieves could pay up to four times the value of goods stolen in lieu of other punishment, the fine being used to compensate the victim and therefore fitting more closely to Maori concepts and values aimed at restoring balance. This policy was extended to assault cases by an amendment to the *Fines for Assault Ordinance 1845*. Robert Joseph has identified further ordinances that modified English law and its application to Maori to provide a more hybrid approach to accommodate Maori needs (Joseph 2002).

Accommodation between Maori custom and imported British law was both theoretically and administratively possible in the period 1840–1860. It was the onset of the *pakanga* – the wars in the 1860s between Maori tribes and imperial and colonial forces – that seems to have changed everything. Attitudes hardened on both sides, culminating in Chief Justice Prendergast's declaration in 1877 in the case *Wi Parata v. The Bishop of Wellington* that there was no such thing as Maori customary law and that New Zealand had been found "thinly peopled by barbarians without any form of law or civil government" (*Wi Parata*: 79). The Chief Justice dismissed the repeated legislative acknowledgments of Maori custom, and in particular that in the *Native Rights Act* 1865, with the observation that: "The Act speaks further on of the 'Ancient Custom and Usage of the Maori people,' as if some such body of customary law did in reality exist. But a phrase in a statute cannot call what is non-existent into being" (*Wi Parata*: 79).

The Dimension of Practicality

It is perhaps both a failing and a merit of the legal mind that it has a nagging tendency toward the problems of practicality. How will things actually work in the everyday world of administrative reality? It must be faced that the possibility of operating two or more systems of law concurrently, each with its own rules and administrative organs and processes, poses several problems at the practical level.

First, how would it be decided which of two or more systems applies in a particular case? Such questions will certainly arise, whether driven by parties hoping for the most favorable process ("forum shopping") or by jurisdictional rivalries between the respective tribunals. What happens if each system finds itself dealing with an aspect of a dispute that has been dealt with in the other system?

Second, what account would the respective tribunals take of the other's norms and decisions? Will there be mutual recognition? For all purposes, or only for some? How will the norms and decisions be "proved" in the recognizing tribunal?

These questions are not, of course, peculiar to Aotearoa/New Zealand. They arise in any legal system that faces what lawyers call "conflict of laws" issues. Some principles are required to help decide which rules apply to a particular case. We think that this practical dimension cannot be overlooked in the consideration of "legal pluralism." That seems to have been the primary reason for the abandonment in Europe of the Medieval multi-layered legal order accommodating church law (canon law), mercantile law, and manorial law, as well as the King's law, each with its own rules and courts.

It is for that very reason that we propose that the more promising answer to the question posed by legal pluralism is not assimilation, nor separatism, but *interaction* that produces something new. Hence our interest in legal hybridity, and a third space where customary systems can meet in a dynamic and evolving way. That interaction does not require anyone's permission – it is not within the control of politicians, but rather of the people in their everyday interactions, faced with the challenges of the "dialogues, confrontations, accommodations, risk-taking, and unplanned discoveries" (Greenwood and Wilson 2006:12). A cynical observer might wonder whether this accounts for the generally unfavorable view of custom held by legislators. Napoleon Bonaparte is the classic example: He abolished all French customary law with a stroke of his pen, replacing it with his famous Code, and had the achievement recorded in *bas relief* around his casket at Les Invalides in Paris.

A Common Law of Aotearoa/New Zealand?

Our recent task at Te Matahauariki Research Institute has been the completion, with our friend and colleague Richard Benton, of a work called *Te Matapunenga: A Compendium of References to the Concepts and Institutions of Maori Customary Law*. That compilation, which is in a substantially complete state as of December 2007, is an attempt to cull from archival and other materials authoritative statements on Maori customary legal concepts. The logical next step after *Te Matapunenga* would be a study of the extent to which the common law of Aotearoa/New Zealand, in theory based on the customs of the people as articulated by the courts, has been influenced by and has responded to Maori customary law, or what George Clarke, called the "Aboriginal Protector" in the 1840s, described as the "common or unwritten law" of Maori (Clarke 1844). Clarke proposed legalizing those native customs and usages that were not, in themselves, repugnant to humanity. This was to be achieved by an enactment establishing native courts to adjudicate in cases where natives only were concerned so as to administer justice according to "native customs and usages."

Leon Sheleff at Tel Aviv University argues that the incorporation of tribal law into modern legal systems is possible by means of the common law because "common law countries…continue to work within a legal culture that is still basically oriented to the flexible development of the law in which judges help make the law, and do so in terms of their understanding of an evolving society" (Sheleff 2000:82).

The foreshadowed study, starting from the oft-repeated axiom that "law reflects society," would analyze and describe, for the first time in a systematic way, the distinctive features and character that our common law is developing as our courts work in the unique and specific conditions of Aotearoa/New Zealand. The proposed research would suppose that if our custom is different from that of mid-nineteenth century England, then our common law ought to reflect that difference. If that turned out on inquiry not to be the case, then either the axiom is wrong, or something is inhibiting and retarding the healthy development of our common law.

The study might investigate the extent to which the evolution of a unique customary law in Aotearoa/New Zealand may find parallels in the evolution and interaction of our two main languages of Aotearoa/New Zealand – Maori and English. Following the work of the late Harry Orsman (1997), New Zealand English is now recognized and studied as a distinct form of English that has responded to, among other things, Maori culture. The evolution of Maori language under the reciprocal influence of the new arrivals has also been the subject of study to which we will later refer.

At the theoretical level, the research would bring two apparently disparate fields of inquiry into conjunction – law and language – and could illuminate the principles of development in each case. At the practical level, the study could provide a basis for discussion of the future path of our common law, which takes on particular significance with the creation in 2004 of the Supreme Court of New Zealand. That new Court replaces the Privy Council in London which had, many thought anomalously, been the final appellate court for New Zealand for more than 150 years, and will henceforth be responsible for authoritatively, exclusively, and finally declaring the common law of Aotearoa/New Zealand in accordance with Parliament's direction as to its purpose in section 3 of the *Supreme Court Act* 2003: "...to enable important legal matters, including legal matters relating to the Treaty of Waitangi, to be resolved with an understanding of New Zealand conditions, history, and traditions."

That command of Parliament emphasizes the point developed in *Grey and Iwikau* that the constitutional and evidentiary mechanisms already exist in our law for the incorporation of appropriate Maori customary elements. It is not structural change that is required for that process to unfold, but rather a change in the training and attitude of lawyers and judicial officers.

Cultural Arithmetic

What happens when two cultures encounter each other? Some observers appear to think that one of the cultures must inevitably prevail. These are the "assimilationists," and their central idea is borrowed from Darwin's observations about the "survival of the fittest." They suppose that one of the encountering cultures will prove to be so superior that it will eventually dominate and the other culture will be absorbed into it: **1+1=1**. That this was a prevalent ideology underlying even the most liberal of the colonial policies in New Zealand is undeniable. Accommodation of Maori custom and law was always to be *temporary* until more enlightened generations availed themselves of a self-evidently superior English law. An editorial in a government-sponsored Maori newspaper in 1857 advocated that:

> *He Ritenga ano o te Maori i mua, he Ture ano, a. e mau nei ano; a, he Ture ano to te Pakeha. Ma te Maori e ata whakaaro, ko tehea ranei e pai, hei ture whakaora mona…Waihoki, ko tenei, me he mea e tohunga ana te whakaaro, ka penatia nga ture o Ingarani; ka whaia ponotia kia wawe ia te whiwhi ki nga painga o aua Ture…ma te whai ture penei ana…ka kite ia i te noho tika, i te noho rangatira.*

> (English translation)…the Maori had, and still has, his old Customs and Laws, and the Pakeha [white man] has his. It is for the Maori to judge which are likely to serve him best…If he be wise, he will in likely manner endeavour as soon as possible to possess himself of the benefits of the English Laws…before he can become either civilized or prosperous. (Anon 1857:2)

Another group of observers take the arithmetic literally, to conclude that one plus one equals two. They say that when two cultures meet, the survival and health of each depends upon the maintenance of distance and independence. Hybrid derivations are viewed with suspicion and regarded as inauthentic and dangerous. In 1858 at the Paetai meeting to elect a Maori King, Hoani Papita, chief of the Ngati-Hinetu and Ngati-Apakura tribes, made an impassioned plea for independence and nationalism, using a whakatauki, or proverb: "Fresh water is lost when it mingles with salt water." He said, "Let us retain our lands and be independent of the Pakeha" (quoted in Cowan 1956:231). Those who advocate keeping races and their cultures apart might be viewed as "separationists" who see the arithmetic as **1+1=2**.

The idea explored in *Grey and Iwikau: A Journey into Custom* was that the encounter between two customary systems, whether of language or law, results in the generation of a third system. The two constituent parts are still there, intact in both theory and in fact, but a new element has been introduced.

The new element consists of, and is the product of, the interaction between the two and must now be added to the list of observable systems in its own right. This is an "interactive" model: 1+1=3.

An eloquent, and early, plea for that "third culture" resulting from the interaction of Maori and Pakeha traditions was that of Bishop Selwyn in his unsuccessful attempt to moderate the separatist tendencies to which the Maori "King Movement" had been driven in the 1860s by its determination to halt aggressive colonial policies and the alienation of further land to the government and the incoming settlers. At Peria in October 1862, the Bishop told the influential Maori political leader Wiremu Tamihana and the assembled tribes on the final day of the hui, or gathering:

> *Ehara ahau i te pakeha, ehara ahau i te tangata maori. He hawhekaihe ahau. Kau kai ahau i a koutou kai, kua moe ahau i roto i o koutou whare, kai tahi, korero tahi, haere tahi, inoi tahi, kai tahi i te Hapa Tapu. Koia ahau ka ki atu nei ki a koutou; he hawhekaihe ahau. E kore e taea taku hawhekaihetanga te unu. Kei roto hoki i toku tinana, i toku kiko, i oku uaua, i oku wheue, i taku mongamona. Ina hoki, he hawhekaihe katoa tatou.*

> (English translation) I am not a Pakeha, neither am I a Maori; I am a half-caste. I have eaten your food, and I have slept in your houses: we have eaten together, talked together, traveled, prayed together, and partaken of the Lord's Supper together; and therefore I tell you that I am a half-caste. My being a half-caste cannot be altered (or uprooted). It is in my body, in my flesh, in my sinews, in my bones, and in my marrow. We are all half-castes." (Selwyn, Bishop George Augustus 1862)

The conclusion of Claude Lévi-Strauss in the 1950s – one relevant to this study – was that, within certain limits, cultures thrive and prosper best when they encounter other cultures, and the *more different the cultures the better*. We have not overlooked that Lévi-Strauss came in time to be more sympathetic to cultural selfishness. In a speech to UNESCO in 1971, and perhaps to that organization's dismay, he expressed views more sympathetic to a "selfish" preoccupation with one's own culture (ethnocentrism) than he had done twenty years earlier in a work commissioned by the United Nations to combat racism:

> If...human societies exhibit a certain optimal diversity...we must recognize that, to a large extent, this diversity results from the desire of each culture to

resist the cultures surrounding it, to distinguish itself from them – in short to be itself. Cultures are not unaware of one another, they even borrow from one another on occasion; but, in order not to perish, they must in other connections remain somewhat impermeable toward one another. (Levi-Strauss 1985:71)

Wiktor Stockowski has recently provided an insightful discussion of the background and context of these apparently opposed positions (Stockowski 2007:7–51).

In the same spirit, some will object to the interaction of customary systems. One New Zealand writer on legal pluralism states: "As indigenous lawyer Moana Jackson lamentably opines, the ironical outcome of this otherwise laudable recognition of indigenous legal systems is the re-colonisation [sic] of peoples through the assimilation of their views via the language of legal pluralism" (Tie 1999:8).

We think that the writer probably meant to say that Moana Jackson's opinion was "lamenting" rather than "lamentable," and we have some sympathy for the concern expressed, as may be seen from our account elsewhere of the fate of Maori adoption custom (Frame and Meredith 2005). Nonetheless, we reiterate that the insulation of neighboring customary systems from interaction and change is not something that can be achieved by the edicts of legislators or by the strictures of philosophers.

Reflecting values and concepts in a legal system

Te Matahauariki Research Institute at the University of Waikato has the following as its mission statement: "To explore ways in which the best of the values and concepts of the founding cultures of Aotearoa/New Zealand might be reflected in its legal system."

These words plunge us into two big questions. The first is how the "best of the values and concepts" could be reflected in the legal system. The aspiration presupposes that a coherent and meaningful interaction between two different cultures is possible. It assumes that different cultures can have values and concepts with sufficient compatibility to be harnessed together, or to generate coherent and sufficiently faithful hybrid derivates.

The second question raised by the mission statement goes right to the heart of the matter. That monosyllable "best" – the "best" of the values and concepts that are to be reflected in the legal system of Aotearoa/New Zealand – drags us into the debate between "universalism" and "relativism." It assumes that some standard is both discoverable and workably applicable for assessing which concepts and values of each culture are meritorious, and which should be allowed to fall by the wayside.

What do the "relativists" say? A thumbnail sketch of the relativist position might suggest that the concepts and values found in a culture can only be understood in a manner relative to, and in the context of, that society. So, relativists say, you can't have universal values and standards against which cultures can meaningfully be judged. They conclude that it is not possible to say whether female circumcision in a particular culture is a good thing, or what should be thought of another culture that ceremonially sacrifices pigs using a traditional patu, or club. They say that these matters cannot be judged across cultures – each value is only *relative* to the culture in which it is found.

The critics of that position – the "universalists" – counter that relativists condemn themselves to moral paralysis and acquiescence in whatever practices may be adopted in other societies and cultures. So, the universalists say, their relativist opponents are compelled to accept that if it is the practice in a particular culture to torture criminal suspects, then no exterior judgment can be made against the practice and no general system of international norms can properly condemn it.

Both positions undoubtedly present uncomfortable implications, and the balance between them appears to depend on the illustrative examples chosen by each side. Relativists will tend to choose quaint and harmless ones, and universalists will seek out ones designed to shock.

We would suggest a partial answer to the dilemma, drawing on the work of American social anthropologist Clifford Geertz in an interesting work at the end of his long career, a book of essays called *Available Light* (2000). One of those essays is called "Anti anti-relativism." Geertz tries to take into account both positions and offers us this advice: You can't be morally paralyzed, but neither can you assume that your culture has got the best and final word on moral standards. Geertz thinks that there is a halfway house and writes: "The studying of other peoples' cultures involves discovering who they think they are, what they think they are doing, and to what end they think they are doing it. It involves learning how, as a being from elsewhere (with a world of one's own), to live with them" (2000:16, and see generally Frame and Seed-Pihama 2006).

The Language Analogy

Language is a system of rules or conventions just as customary law is. Each system generates both *prescriptive* and *descriptive* dimensions – what one *should* say or do, and what people *actually* say or do. Should we have "one language for all," or should we have "one country, several languages"? The question only has to be asked to be dismissed as idle. Linguistic pluralism is the inevitable consequence of the mingling of several cultures in a society. The more interesting question concerns the effect of the different languages on each other. Our hypothesis suggests that when Maori language encounters the English language, each will, over time, show change and adaptation. The original "pure" forms of each remain, both theoretically and in reality – they are stored in writings, stories, songs, and so on, and continue to be available. But a new Maori and a new English will also appear, showing mutually caused modifications and adaptations as a result of interaction.

Does the evidence we find about us support this hypothesis? Has "New Zealand English" been modified by Maori? Has modern Maori been modified by English? We suggest that the answer is affirmative in both cases, and at both the prescriptive and descriptive levels – what people should say and what people actually say.

Bernard Spolsky, born in New Zealand and currently Professor Emeritus of English at Bar-Ilan University in Israel, asserts such interchange is a continuation of a course of action that started two centuries ago, when the indigenous inhabitants (*tangata whenua*) of New Zealand and the European settlers began to negotiate an accommodation with each other, politically, socially, economically, culturally, and linguistically (Spolsky 2003).

As to the influence of the Maori language on New Zealand English, Harry Orsman's *The Dictionary of New Zealand English* (1997) shows the extent of borrowing and adaptation. Some words have consciously been taken up by speakers of New Zealand English: *mana* (status, prestige), *kai* (food), *tangi* (funeral), *korero* (talk), *waka* (canoe), *tapu* (sacred), and so on. Other words have insinuated themselves in disguised forms: puckeroo, meaning broken (Maori *pakaru*) (Orsman 1997:566); taiho, meaning wait or delay (Maori *taihoa*) (Orsman 1997:803); and the expression "eat one's toot," meaning to get acclimatized to local conditions (Maori *tutu*, a poisonous berry) (Orsman 1997:548). Other Maori words again have been consciously borrowed with the intention of evoking a Maori customary content. For example, Prime Minister Norman Kirk's labor government in the 1970s adopted the expression *ohu* (meaning a collective working party) to designate state-supported communes (Orsman 1997:548). John Macalister, a writer and teacher at Victoria University of Wellington in New Zealand, has also described the influence of Maori language on New Zealand English, particularly the names of flora and fauna and place names (2005). He observes that, while proper nouns of all types (often the names of plants and wildlife) still account for almost two-thirds of Maori words in New Zealand English, cultural terms now account for an increasing proportion of words of Maori origin (Macalister 2000, 2006). In 2005, Macalister published *A Dictionary of Maori Words in New Zealand English*, suggesting that the flow of Maori into English continues. Macalister found that the Maori presence in New Zealand English is not only evident in the use of "loanwords," but also in the creation of hybrids, giving them English nuances such as "maka-chilly" (based on *makariri* and "cold") – a tribute, Macalister says, to "New Zealanders' inventiveness with language" (2005:1).

Conversely, the influence of English on the Maori language has been most obvious through the use of transliterations both to designate new cultural things and concepts, and as alternatives to Maori words (Biggs 1968). Writing in 1949, Te Rangi Hiroa, better known in international anthropology as Sir Peter Buck, commented that "The coining of hybrid words was necessitated by English words which had no equivalent in Maori, and they were readily adopted in order that the people could express themselves in the current speech of the day" (Buck 1949:81–82). "Maorified words" borrowed from the English lexicon have become prolific, ranging from *kooti* (court), to *peeke* (bag), to *kuini* (queen), to *whutupaoro* (football). In what he claimed as a mere preliminary study, Terry Duval identified 2500 headwords in his dictionary of Maori "gainwords" that have their origin in language other than Maori (Duval 1996). Duval and Koenraad Kuiper have proposed a more comprehensive and complete study of Maori loanwords (Duval and Kuiper 2001:243–260).

Yet some have argued there are too many loanwords, and that they have been changing the language beyond recognition. In a Maori newspaper in

1903, Reweti Te Kohere lamented the use of transliterations, particularly where there was already an equivalent term in "pure Maori":

> *He tikanga tino he tenei. Na tenei tikanga ka poriro te ahua o to taua reo rangatira.*
> *Ko to matou reo ko to nga tamariki inaianei kua tangi ke, kahore i tino rite ki to te*
> *Maori...apopo ka rite to taua reo ki a taua ano ka awhekaihe awhekaihe tangata*
> *awhekaihe reo.*

> (English translation) This practice is very wrong. Because of this our noble language is being bastardised [sic]. Our language and that of our children today sound different, it doesn't sound Maori...in the future our language will be like us, half-caste – a half-caste people, a half-caste language. (Te Kohere 1903:3)

More recently, the Chief Executive of the Maori Language Commission, Haami Piripi, has expressed fears that English influences on the Maori language are "squeezing it out of shape" (Piripi 2005). The Maori Language Commission has sought to protect Maori from the onslaught of English by creating new terms for hundreds of modern concepts. The Maori linguist Peter Keegan has remarked that in the last 10 years 20,000 new words have been developed (Keegan 2004). Piripi and other cultural gatekeepers remind us that change is often a gradual process of negotiation around new and old signs of identity and innovative and traditional sites of collaboration and contestation.

Resistance to change in customary systems is difficult, and the resister is likely to be cast in the role of King Canute trying to drive back the tide. The Maori academic Koro Dewes, writing in 1964, and criticizing the many idealistic and sentimental discussions about the Maori language, concluded that it must be realized that Maori is a living language and must undergo change (Dewes 1964). Te Rangi Hiroa himself conceded that "what was wrong in the classical language of yesterday will become correct through usage in the current speech of tomorrow" (Buck 1949:82). The inevitability and speed of change in language is further emphasized by a report from a missionary in Tahiti in 1837 concerning the related Polynesian language of Tahiti:

> The content of the aboriginal language had changed in the thirty years he had resided in Tahiti, largely because of the increased influence of English-speaking foreigners. Ormond [the missionary] also believed that a standardized reference was needed before the aboriginal character of Tahitian was lost. (quoted in Mulhausler 1996:23)

The process may be gradual and unnoticed by those bringing it about. John McWhorter observes in his book *The Power of Babel* that: "People in France did not wake up one morning to find that the language they were speaking was now French instead of Latin...Latin evolved through 'Fratin' into French just as red evolves through purple into blue" (McWhorter 2002:35).

McWhorter's metaphor illustrates the same process as our proposed social arithmetic. If we take the color blue and mix it with yellow, we get green. We end up with three colors: the original two and now a third. The same writer tells us that no aspect of language is immune: "The truth is that everything about a language is eternally and inherently changeable. Not just the slang and the occasional cultural designation, but the very sound and meaning of basic words, and the word order and grammar" (McWhorter 2002:12).

We think that the interaction and reciprocal influences of customary legal concepts and institutions may be similarly wide-ranging. It is not just the content of rules, but the character, tone, and practical functioning of the institutions that support the rules that are likely to be affected.

Conclusion

We have tried to suggest that the co-existence of different systems of rules is not only possible but inevitable – and is playing out under our very noses. This is as true in the field of customary law as it is with language and other social customs. Moreover, we have proposed that the process has been under-way for quite a while and is worthy of study within several disciplines and, better still, by scholars and leaders from those disciplines in a collaborative undertaking.

There is, of course, a crucial corollary to our recommendation in the field of law: Artificial barriers should not be erected to obstruct the organic develop-ment we have tried to describe. In practical terms this means that our courts must be equipped and ready to investigate, articulate, and incorporate the concepts and values that are found to be emerging from the interactive social process.

"Respect other cultures and work to change your own" was the sound Lévi-Straussian advice. It reminds us that, whatever considerable treasures the ancestors have bequeathed to the present custodians in our several cultures, each culture has its peculiar problems, both structurally and in its response to modern circumstance – none is perfect. A question we would ask is whether it could be that the problems of Maori culture, as understood by itself, could only be solved by judicious borrowing from the newly arrived cultures, and that, conversely, the problems of those new cultures could only be solved by selective adaptations drawn from Maori and Polynesian cultures? Such a symbiotic relationship is often found in the natural world, and it may not be fanciful to suppose that it could have a place in the social world also.

We should end with two concrete examples of the interaction between Maori customary law and imported norms resulting in a third legal principle. Our first example involves the procedure of the Waitangi Tribunal. The Tribunal was first created in 1975 to hear and make recommendations on Maori grievances concerning alleged breaches of the Treaty of Waitangi by the state. It has, almost from its birth, conducted hearings on Marae (technically the courtyard in front of a Maori meeting-house, but now applied to the whole complex of surrounding buildings) in accordance with the Maori custom of the Marae. The Tribunal's empowering statute, *The Treaty of Waitangi Act 1975*, provides as follows:

> The Tribunal may regulate its procedure in such manner as it thinks fit, and in doing so may have regard to and adopt such aspects of *te kawa o te marae* as the Tribunal thinks appropriate in the particular case, but shall not deny any person the right to speak during the proceedings of the Tribunal on the ground of that person's sex. (Second Schedule, Clause 5(9))

Maori custom rules in that circumstance, but the proviso makes a concession to a fundamental freedom contained in domestic statute law and in binding international law. These intersections and interactions have produced a new rule.

Our second example concerns the law relating to whales. In 1910, the Chief Justice of New Zealand, Sir Robert Stout, a Shetland Islander knowledgeable in fishing matters, decided the case of *Baldick v. Jackson*. Jackson and his crew had killed and secured a whale in an apparently safe place. It later sank and was carried out into Cook Strait. Although Jackson continued to search for the whale carcass, Baldick found it and towed it to land, whereupon he claimed it.

Which of the parties had the superior right to the whale? Both principal issues identified by the Chief Justice are of interest to students of customary law in New Zealand. First, did an English statute from the time of Edward II appearing to claim whales as "Royal Fish" apply in New Zealand? Second, should Jackson's loss of control of his whale be treated as "abandonment" of his rights?

As to the first issue, Chief Justice Stout declared that the old English statute was "never applicable to the circumstances of the Colony" – the test that at the time determined whether English law applied in New Zealand. Whaling had been intensively practiced here both before and after the Treaty of Waitangi in 1840, and neither the Crown nor the Government of New Zealand had ever asserted the "royal prerogative" in relation to whales. The Chief Justice declared that the prerogative "is one not only that has never been claimed, but one that it would have been impossible to claim without claiming it against the Maoris, for they were accustomed to engage in whaling; and the Treaty of Waitangi assumed that their fishing was not to be interfered with" (Baldick v. Jackson: 344–345).

On the second issue, abandonment, the Chief Justice recognized that customary practice could vary among societies. In Greenland, it seemed that any loss of control of a fish made that fish a "lost fish," whether alive or dead. However, the evidence adduced by Jackson demonstrated that the *New Zealand* practice was otherwise: "If a fish is killed and put in what is believed a secure position, even though no boat belonging to the whaler who killed the whale is attached to the fish, still, that the fish having been killed by a whaler, it is deemed to be his property" (Baldick v. Jackson: 345).

Here is law being made by the customs of the people as declared by the Courts. The recognition of Maori customary rights in respect of stranded whales continues in modern times, as may be seen in various agreements and protocols entered into between tribes and the Department of Conservation to ensure cooperation in dealing with stranded whales, and to recognize the priority of the tribal claim to whale bone and teeth for carving and ornamental purposes.

Although we do not claim that these examples are as spectacular as some might wish, or that the "interactive channels" contemplated by our theory are as free-flowing in modern Aotearoa/New Zealand as might be desired, they do suggest that practical hybrid outcomes drawing from two or more rule-systems are both possible and workable, once attention shifts from the polarizing rigidities of 1+1=1 and 1+1=2 to the interactions of 1+1=3.

Chapter Seventeen

Occupying Third Space: Hybridity and Identity Matrices in the Multiracial Experience

David L. Brunsma and Daniel J. Delgado

Introduction: Hybridities in Theory, Culture, and Experience

Theories of contemporary social life, rooted primarily in critical constructivist, anthropological, feminist, and postcolonial inquiries, offer notable and valuable lenses through which to view and understand social organization, cultural systems, and identity in an era of globalization and empire. Concepts such as "liminality," "hybridity," "border," "creolization," and "mestizaje" have emerged from oppressive struggle to theorize as well as rhetorically acclaim a promising new era of human agency, democratic community, and cultural innovation amidst "hybridized webs of meaning" (Hannerz 1996, cf. Weber). Homi Bhabha's oft-cited statement on identity provides a glimpse into this theoretical regime:

> The move away from singularities of 'class' or 'gender' as primary conceptual and organizational categories has resulted in an awareness of the subject positions – of race, gender, generation, institutional location, geopolitical locale, sexual orientation – that inhabit any claim to identity in the modern world. What is theoretically innovative, and politically crucial, is the need

> to think beyond narratives of originary [sic] and initial subjectivities and to focus on those moments or processes that are produced in the articulation of cultural differences. These 'in-between' spaces provide the terrain for elaborating strategies of selfhood – singular or communal – that initiate new signs of identity, and innovative sites of collaboration, and contestation, in the act of defining the idea of society itself. (Bhabha 1994, 2)

What Bhabha describes here occurs in a "third space" delineated by processes that go by various names – creolization, hybridity, syncretism, mestizaje – and is highly heuristic for understanding both the human opportunities and constraints available in the 21st century. Both a location (and an anti-location) and a process (and an anti-process), third space offers a place to be at play in the fields of identity, traversing, so it seems, large swaths of historical constructions, political structures, social contracts (racial, gendered, classed, etc.), and cultural systems of meaning-making, in the emergent "space" for a new knowledge production system – a system grounded more in the people than in the meta-narratives proposed by modernism that founded the disciplines and dominant modes of knowledge production in the 19th and 20th centuries. It appears that the study of multiraciality and multiracial identity might benefit from such theoretical scaffolds.

Though these conceptual schemas and apparatuses are heuristic and pose potential threats to previous constructions so damaging to human agency, there is reason to be a bit skeptical of the uncritical usage of such notions to describe such a dizzying array of phenomena as to render the theories of hybridity and third space somewhat otherworldly, detached from lived experience, and potentially meaningless. Palmie (2006), following Boas (1966/1887), lays out a central problem in the study of hybridity and creolization by asking whether "[they are] meant to index a distinct class or group of objectively occurring phenomena that can be unambiguously distinguished from other 'noncreole,' 'uncreolized,' or 'creolizing' ones on the basis of specifiable criteria?" (434) or by postulating that perhaps we "come to realize that the distribution of phenomena characterized by x is so steadily approaching ubiquity that x has increasingly become essential (or at least typologically salient) to a historically specific group...of the late 20th and early 21st centuries" (437). These are strong critiques located at the level of conceptualization and operationalization, begging questions like: Is multiraciality (hybridity, mestizaje, in-betweeness) a unique feature of human experience in particular social circumstances and contexts, or is it merely representative of processes that all humans share but are unwilling to acknowledge?

Much of the theoretical literature on hybridity, following Bhabha, locates its problems at the level of culture and structure – broad macro processes rooted in sweeping histories, diasporas, and essentialist constructions, while providing space that leads to cultural syncretisms and new cultural, symbolic spaces where the old is blended to create the new (albeit still reliant on the old). This work has been useful for those studying world systems, globalization, postcolonial group formation, immigration, diaspora, etc., and, while the lived experience is implied in Bhabha and others' formulations of these ideas, the lived experience and the practice of embodied and socially structured human agency and identity work is assumed to follow similar paths. Of course, this is perhaps an ecological fallacy of sorts since theoretical formulations at one level do not necessarily follow similar processes at micro levels. Certainly cultural and social hybridity and third spaces are created in postmodernity and empire, but how actors work with(in) such material is an empirical question. Certainly multiraciality is working with dominant racial ideas and essentialisms, and certainly racially "hybrid" people have existed for a very long time, but how multiracial people invoke, deploy, and articulate such an identity, and for what ends, is a question for further study.

Closer to the notion of such an "experienced hybridity" are formulations of "mestizaje"/"mestiza" (Anzaldúa 1987) and possibly "creolization" (Cohen 2007). Mestizaje refers to an embodied and socially lived experience of a third space where tensions (us/them, inclusion/exclusion, pre-colonial/colonial/postcolonial, similarity/difference, etc.) are agentically, spiritually, symbolically, and culturally lived in a space of creative identity play and newness (also see Wade 2005). Creolization is similar in that it is a process of mixture and cultural innovation, but also collective and individual symbolic subversion within a kind of lived third space created via displacement and deterrioralization (see also DuBois' "double consciousness"); however, it has been used in a wide variety of ways in scholarship. In looking at such forms of hybridity and the occupation of such correlate third spaces by multiracial individuals, it should be noted that such theoretical notions can lead down very different paths: a blending of extant identities into a third, unique identity with potential for emancipatory action or a ideological, nationalistic, and collective sense of group pride and consciousness as a hybrid. Certainly, scholars of multiraciality, the multiracial movement, and multiracial identity have observed both tendencies.

Questions abound. Is multiracial identity a hybrid identity? Do multiracials exist in a third space? Are these concepts useful for understanding the identities, experiences, and futures of multiracial people? Or, do these concepts weakly veil racialized practice, history, culture, and material reality? Certainly a combination of two or more "races" is also the combination of the historical and contemporary contingencies of racialization and racism, but does occupying a third space, does deploying an identity from such a space, does this experienced hybridity lead to an emancipatory experience or a reinscription of essentialism within the consciousness of those in such a space? Multiracial people have been navigating spaces for a very long time – as have all people. Multiracials have developed their identities within a matrix of domination – as have all people. Recognizing the complexity of contemporary experience is the boon of these theories – negotiations (individual resolutions) might lead to marginalization and lack of unity, but collective communication, negotiation, and translation might bridge societies and indeed open new spaces. This chapter works with these theoretical notions and critically assesses their utility while presenting some intriguing initial data from a study of black-white multiracial young adults that may illustrate the lived reality of hybridity and the possibilities of occupying third space.

Research on Black-White Multiracial People

Previous scholarly work on multiracial identity in the past three decades has focused primarily on processes of racial identity formation of multiracial people. This body of research has highlighted that the racial identities of multiracial people are dynamic and structured in a matrix of experience – they are multifaceted. We know that multiracials' racial identities are: negotiated in social interaction (Brunsma and Rockquemore 2001, Rockquemore 1999, Rockquemore and Brunsma 2002a); generated in racialized experiences (Rockquemore and Brunsma 2002a, b; Rockquemore and Arend 2004); propagated in familial (Qian 2004, Rockquemore and Laszloffy 2005, Roth 2005) and institutional (Brunsma 2005; Harris and Sim 2002; Renn 2000, 2003) socialization; differentially embedded within racialized social spaces (Jaret and Reitzes 1999, Rockquemore and Brunsma 2002b, Wright et al. 2005); tied to appearance (Brunsma and Rockquemore 2001, Herman 2004, Rockquemore and Arend 2004); expressed through linguistic systems (Ali 2003, Wallace 2004) and frames of racial ideology (Bonilla-Silva 2004, Lewis 2001, Rockquemore and Laszloffy 2005); intersectionally coupled with gender (Gillem 2000, Phillips 2004, Rockquemore 2002, Rockquemore and Brunsma 2004), class (Brunsma 2005, Harris and Sim 2002, Herman 2004, Rockquemore and Brunsma 2002, Roth 2005, Twine 2005), and sexuality (Collins 2000, Mahtani 2007); parameterized to a degree by extant systems of classification (Brunsma 2006, Morning 2000, Qian 2004, Renn 2000, Roth 2005); and dynamic across the life course (Hitlin, et al. 2006) in all the variations of the above. After the years of research, we understand that multiracial identity is a constant process of "doing race" (Lewis 2003) or its interwoven process, "doing racial identity" – racial identity is both active and directed work.

We have certainly learned much across three decades; yet, an interesting epistemological pattern has emerged that ultimately limits our understanding of identity, race, and social experience for this particular group. The vast bulk of this work focuses on investigating multiracials' racial identities, or their racial self-understandings. While the racial identities of multiracials is important, offering us a more nuanced empirical and theoretical understanding of central social processes of racial hybridity, racialized double-consciousness, social marginality, identity work, etc., racial identity is not the only descriptor and locator of multiracials' experience. Multiracials, as all people, live a racialized experience (Mills 1997, Omi and Winant 1994); however, this experience is, like all experience, more complex – a multiracial who, at one temporal and spatial moment, identifies as "black" or "biracial" may not deploy this racial identity equally, consistently, or consciously across all areas of social life. Identities are more intersectional, balancing (or not) social, material, cultural, political, physical, and institutional realities among others. Recognizing that individuals exist in a matrix of domination (Collins 2000) requires an equally multifaceted notion of identity (as a matrix) and to understand the ways in which such identity matrices are used agentically by actors within the matrix of domination for a variety of different ends.

As "hybrids" (offensively, the mixture of two assumed pure "races"), these offspring of, in this case, a white parent and a black parent, a third, multiracial space is created. Our current knowledge of the social facts of multiracials' racial identity – its fluidity, its changing, its narrative, its negotiation, its flux, its contradictions, its active construction – mirrors the processes of contemporary identity more generally and highlights that these social facts are not essentially multiracial. This should encourage a move away from research on "multiracial identity" to a more complex view of the "identities of multiracials." The role of context, space, institutions, social structure, and agency all intertwine and inform these intra- and interpersonal identities. Research on "identity work" (Gubrium and Holstein 2003, Loseke and Cavendish 2001, Snow and Anderson 1987, Storrs 1999), "identity capital" (Cote 1996, 1997; Cote and Schwartz 2002), "cognitive maps" (Brubaker, Loveman, and Stamativ 2004; Zerubavel 1996, 1997), and "identity deployment" all echo such a notion of identity and are highly heuristic for the case of multiracials. Here we wish to move away from the either/or approach to understanding multiracial identity – either general identity processes of multiracials or racial identity processes of multiracials – and move toward a both/and approach that recognizes the fullness of multiracial experience by studying the identity matrices of these "hybrid" multiracials in a multiracial third space.

To reiterate, multiraciality, as a form of hybridity, is currently understood as a third space identity articulation. Research has found a consistency in the identity and biographical work that multiracials engage in to articulate this new racial identity; yet, scholars conceptualize racial identity as monolithic and the discussion ends there. We desire the problematization of racial identity through the concept of an "identity matrix" and ground the sociological processes of deploying an identity matrix through strategic and agentic processes in different social spaces: interactional, political, cultural, physical (embodiment), and institutional. Using data from 191 black-white multiracial young adults and follow-up in-depth interviews with 24 of these respondents, the concept of identity matrices is theoretically developed in this chapter. Black-white multiracials are a very useful case to study such an identity matrix. A more nuanced empirical look at the ways in which occupying this "racial third space" is differentially deployed across social, political, cultural, physical, and institutional spaces allows researchers to think more broadly about how third-space identities either do or do not provide agentic connections across various domains of social life.

Theoretical, Empirical, and Heuristic Work on Multifaceted Identities

Homi Bhabha's notions of hybridity and hybrid identities occur in what he calls a "third space," which is a space of transgression, of potential social change, of dialogue, and of creativity, where constructions and myths are challenged and new subjectivities and collectivities are allowed to emerge. According to Giroux, the "third space displaces the histories that constitute it, and sets up new structures of authority, new political initiatives" (1993:99). Such a view forms a cornerstone of the multiracial movement as they fight the system of racial classification in the US. At the same time, it describes the potential of the multiracial position. Such a position is akin to Victor Turner's (1964, 1969, 1974, 1982) notion of "liminality." For Turner, liminality refers to socio-cultural spaces and individuals within such spaces as "neither here nor there...betwixt and between the positions assigned and arrayed by law, custom, convention, and ceremonial" (Turner 1969:95). Liminal spaces within rituals, even interaction rituals (Collins 2006), are full of potential, "anti-structure," possibility, and "the liberation of human capacities of cognition, affect, volition, creativity, etc., from the normative constraints incumbent upon occupying a sequence of social statuses" (Turner 1982:44). The experience of multiracial people has always been one of liminality, in-betweeness, and hybridity – the "marginal man" (Park 1950), if you will – on the threshold. They have been historically, and currently are, in everyday interactions, actively connected and disconnected to extant structures. Turner's notion of liminality is highly relevant, for it recognizes both structure and agency in describing a state of emergence(y) where roles are in flux and, thus, heuristic for an identity that is influx and possibly emergent.

The work of James Cote (1996, 1997; Cote and Schwartz 2002) has been significant in theorizing the agency of identity deployment while simultaneously retaining a much more nuanced notion of structure. Identity, for Cote, is nested within the interrelationship between social structure (i.e., political, cultural, economic systems, etc.), interaction (patterns of behavior that illuminate the everyday contacts among people within institutions), and personality (i.e., social cognition, character, self, ego identity, etc.). For Cote, the social structure of the late-modern period demands identities that are "managed" – people must actively, reflexively, and strategically synchronize themselves into a community of "strangers" by meeting approval through the creation of the right impressions. The structure and process of the self is both "diffused" (lacking stable long-term commitments) and "discovered" (individuals are constantly discovering their identities through consumption and other-satisfaction). Cote (1996, 1997) states that individuals in late-modern life have two options: passivity (let the social river manipulate and articulate one's identity) or activity (strategize identity across various domains of existence in order to sustain some sense of meaning in one's own development). Cote's major contribution is the concept of "identity capital" in describing the process of navigating an identity – identity as a tool, selectively deployed in social life. The key, for individuals, is to form and sustain an identity that is practically and meaningfully situated in a social matrix that is in constant movement. Individuals, by investing in who they are, potentially reap future dividends in the "identity markets" of late-modern communities. To be an effective self in these various markets, one must create a set of identities that include a variety of social skills, behavioral repertoires, and cultural savvy to make up his or her identity toolkit.

As mentioned, the theory of mestizaje (or mestiza) has also been influential in thinking through multiracials' hybrid location and potential in third space. The work of Gloria Anzaldúa (1987) is highly relevant here. In *La Frontera*, she articulated a postcolonial feminist understanding of this position as challenging binaries, living with and utilizing tensions and contradictions, and ultimately fueling creative and innovative vision and forms of resistance. Wade highlights that there are two versions that can be detected in the work on mestizaje – "roots-hybridity" (when two become a unique third) and "routes-hybridity" (unpredictable diasporic movements) – and goes on to highlight that "people's experience of mestizaje are lived within a broader context wherein changing ideologies about the nation, its racialized components, and their relative value are disseminated" (2005:246). Multiracials in the US are experiencing and rhetorically articulating a "roots" hybridity, as their mestizaje is seen as a mosaic built from struggle and tensions from their socially, culturally, and historically constructed racialized poles.

Such frameworks recognize identity formation, navigation, and maintenance as an agentic and dynamic process replete with repertoires; strategies of action and deployment (see also Swidler 1986, Callero 2003, Storrs 1999).

They are helpful in looking beyond monolithic racial identity to consider the political, social, cultural, embodied, and formal identities of multiracials in lived third space. Such approaches give us a more palatable framework to recognize the interplay of structure and agency in the development of a multiracial identity matrix and its subsequent deployment across a matrix of experience. For instance, when a black political identity is deployed by a black-white multiracial individual, there may be a social or even a cultural objective as well: Identity can be seen as an active deployment from a larger pool of possibilities as identity capital in shifting identity markets. Identities are structured and strategic; identities are not singular entities, but multifaceted. Context/position may be extremely important for multiracial identity matrices, as are experiences of race. Where both the cognitive and structural interact to construct and maintain identities given contextual variability, differing opportunities for deployment present themselves. How are these identity matrices represented (see Morgan and Schwalbe 1990 for representational notions of social cognition), and how can empirical research illuminate this phenomenon? Do these "identity matrices" exist? What do they mean to these individuals?

Hybridity and the Identity Matrix: Social, Political, Cultural, Physical, and Formal Identities

There are, of course, a myriad of identities within any given identity matrix for individuals navigating their experience through this period of history, and no less is true of multiracials. Fundamentally, when one reads the literature on hybridity and third space, a critique of the literature on multiracial identity emerges: that the fullness of social experience for multiracials is not taken into consideration within the myopic focus on racial identity development. We know a great deal about the racial identity processes of multiracial people. Studies have moved through various normative paradigmatic assumptions (e.g., black-white multiracials would/should choose a black identity in the 70s, through a normative assumption of "multiraciality" for these folks throughout the 80s). We hope to move the conceptualization and theorization of multiracial identity in a more inclusive and more fully human notion of an "emergent" and becoming identity via the idea of an identity matrix. This contrasts with the static hybrid notion of identity, since such notions have not truly experientially captured the "third space" play at work in the everyday and everyspace in which multiracial people engage.

One of the most comprehensive understandings of multiracial identity comes from the work of Kerry Ann Rockquemore and David Brunsma (Brunsma 2005, 2006; Brunsma and Rockquemore 2001, 2002; Rockquemore 1999, 2002; Rockquemore and Brunsma 2001, 2002). In the past eight years we have worked toward a structural, symbolic interactionist, and critical race theory-rooted understanding of the racial self-understandings of multiracial adolescents and young adults. Grounded within a mixed-methods sociological study of black-white multiracials' racial self understandings, we found that multiracials understood themselves multifacetedly: as black, as biracial (either unvalidated or validated by others), as white, as "protean" (shifting via context), and as "transcendent" (no salient racial identity). Their typology was theoretically and empirically related to a variety of intersecting social conditions and experiences of these multiracials' lives: their social networks, feelings of closeness to blacks and whites, experiences of negative treatment from whites and blacks, social class, family structures, and, indeed, their appearance. This typology, the experience of multiraciality, and the social conditions that give rise to different racial understandings have been and are currently being tested by scholars of mixed-race individuals.

We already appreciate quite well how these black-white multiracials racially understand themselves, and that this is a crucial, if not core, dimension of their identity – one that is gendered, classed, and rooted in networks, interaction, and appearance. We understand, however, that the potential of their third space and the experienced hybridity is not currently captured by research on multiracials. Their hybridity has toyed with essentialism (while relying on them) and not truly articulated an experiential third space, which we call a matrix. Our interviews and survey data allow us to look at the variation (or not) of other aspects of their identities: social, political, cultural, physical, and formal. To begin to think about identity matrices, we wish to develop the social, political, cultural, physical/embodied, and institutional (formal) spaces and deployment of their racial identities across these. Grounded insight came from the biracials in the interview sample. We focus on six predominant ones: social identities, political identities, cultural identities, physical identities (embodiment), and formal/institutional identities, and particularly the role of racial identity in each of these five identities.

The Social Space of Multiracials' Identity Matrix

Of course, the vast majority of work on identity is fundamentally about social identity – identities are inherently social and are deployed socially across interactional space. That is, social identity here refers to how individuals understand themselves in social situations, how this component of identity is deployed in social interactions, and how social spaces bring together the opportunity for individuals to pull differentially from their matrix of identities to negotiate and construct who they are to others. Social identity refers to how individuals understand themselves in social situations, that is, their social identities are socially and interactionally mediated (Brunsma and Rockquemore 2001). Multiracials' identities are reflexive. As much as multiracials may choose their racial identities, these same identities are equally impacted by larger discourses about their appearance and presentation of self (Root 1990, Brunsma and Rockquemore 2001, Brunsma 2004, Khanna 2004). This means that within the identity matrix for multiracials we see that the social identity must be understood as contextually bound. To be sure, the context for multiracials, we were told, is initially defined by discourses about physical characteristics (racism and stereotypes) that constitute blackness, whiteness, and mixedness, but, by bringing the physical and the social together, individuals are given room for negotiating this physicality through discursive construction of who they are socially/interactionally.

The Political Space of Multiracials' Identity Matrix

In human matrices of identity, individuals also have varying political identities. Unlike social and physical/embodied identities, with their overt markers and seemingly omnirelevant symbols and meanings, a political identity lacks these markers and must be actively deployed – it is rarely an assumed given. Most research looks at political behaviors (Bobo 1997, Yancey and Emerson 2001), political attitude formation (Krysan 2000, Branton and Jones 2005) and, sometimes, political socialization and concomitant political identity formation. Given this research and the notion of identity, political identity refers to identity as it is influenced by the political structure of the United States, yet at the same time as it is influenced by the immediate social and cultural conditions in which it is deployed. Political identity and identity politics are constitutive of each other, one cannot exist without the other; however, for multiracial individuals, the categorical color lines become less visible. The respondents in this study had unique understandings of their political identities. However, again because of these individuals' liminal multiracial existence, they articulate a freedom to discursively construct a political identity as it jibes with their other contextually bounded identities. Given the two-party structure in the United States, we found interesting discursive linkages between their racial identities and their political identities/affiliations/behaviors – these were rooted in deeply entrenched, and problematic, historical constructions (i.e., "black equals democratic," "white equals republican"). Liminality, in this context, also allows for a potential discourse of "independence" and "focusing on the issues" (Forest 2001, Kuhn 2005).

The Cultural Space of Multiracials' Identity Matrix

There is no doubt that a significant and influential component of an individual's identity matrix is cultural identity – the salient meaning-making, cognitively and socially rooted mechanism for making sense out of one's position and available strategic options in society. It entails practices, preferences, ideologies, consumption, and imagery via linguistic styles, clothing symbology, music tastes, etc.; however, again, cultural identity need not imply overt markers of signaling to others. It too is often actively constructed in interaction and deployed differentially (Driedger 1974, Hall and DuGay 1996, Sussman 2000). Cultural identity, for multiracials, much like social identity, can be understood as being malleable due to its discursive construction within the racialized cultural structure – meanings attached to blackness, whiteness, and an emergent sense of multiraciality (Rockquemore and Laszloffy 2006). Cultural identity is a more agentic identity for multiracials, as we sees in various cultural practices and preferences such as food, clothing, and music. Because of their in-between status, these individuals must agentically construct their cultural identity; often this means that their cultural toolkits are, potentially, much more diverse than those of individuals who identify as only black or only white. Tanya Nedelcheva (2006) argues that identities are not bounded with regard to a person's race or ethnicity but rather constituted from an identity that is culturally linked to the contemporary social situation: "In order to build a cultural identity, there must be communication and interaction in a shared space of symbols and meanings" (83). She goes a step further and recognizes that identities, while being spatially bound, all exist within "the context of contemporary economic, political, and social conditions" (78). While thinking about the boundedness of cultural identity, we see that conceptualizing multiracials within an identity matrix, where culture is but one facet, is absolutely necessary to understand the complexities of contemporary identities (Campbell 2000).

The Physical Space of Multiracials' Identity Matrix

We are, first, embodied entities; however, our understandings of what being embodied (as men, as women, as multiracial, as children) means is what gives us a sense of who we are physically. This is, of course, existentially and ontologically crucial for the sustenance of other components of an identity matrix and how these may or may not interact and be deployed in social spaces. The body can do and be a multitude of things. For Bourdieu (1985), embodiment can be empowering, a site of resistance, and he views body as a form of physical capital, as symbolic bearer, or as a means of social and cultural positioning. In third space, the body is a site of creative interaction – the body recasts liminality and hybridity through performance while simultaneously offering "material evidence of oppression and conquest" (Hall 2007:12, see also Bolatagici 2004). Physical identity is the embodied experience of multiraciality described by individuals in the interviews. Physical identity and the experience of embodied multiraciality are largely felt. The individuals feel how they are interpreted and how they are understood, or rather, "how we experience the body as lived" (Gimlin 2007, also see Shilling 1993). A physical identity is not solely phenotypic, or linguistic, or stylistic, but also discursively constructed, constrained, and directed. Their physical identity is one that is perceived as multiracial (or not something else) by other people, which they describe as "you can tell," or the implicit "people treat me like I am biracial" – it underscores a contextual break from the normative interpretations of race as black or white and becomes liminality embodied.

The Institutional/Formal Space of Multiracials' Identity Matrix

The world is named and classified via structures of power, history, culture, institutional inertia, and it is ultimately functional for those in power (Bourdieu 1985; Foucault 1970; Zerubavel 1996, 1997). Such names and classifications often become formalized and institutionalized and form the parameters upon which identities can be formed – the normative, legitimate climate for identity formation. Bodies of different make-up choose between "male" and "female," while different bodies choose between "black," "white," "Asian," "Latino," etc. Dominant discourses about gender, sexuality, race, nation, etc., offer legitimate contours of identification, and this can and does affect identity formation. The importance of a formal identity, or rather an identity as it is deployed on various government forms, surveys, questionnaires, and other documents, is highlighted by the changes made in the 2000 US census, which read "check all that apply." For Brunsma and Rockquemore this means that race is no longer solely tied to one-drop rules and hypodescent, and there are significant variations in how multiracials identify in a post–2000 census environment (Rockquemore and Brunsma 2002a, 2002b; Brunsma and Rockquemore 2001, 2002; Brunsma 2004, 2005; Rockquemore 2006). In utilizing the notion of "identity matrix," one can examine how multiracial individuals utilize these racial identity options as they are contingent upon a specific discursive context. These options become viable strategies within a repertoire of identities (political, social, formal, physical, and cultural). The respondents were socialized into this structure of a pre-named world; however, they are, through formal identities, attempting to alter the world into which they were born. In feeling cornered, these individuals described being told that they must "pick something." Usually it was suggested that they pick black. This means that the liminal space that multiracials occupy can be directed by normative discourse: "You look black so you should bubble in black." Black-white multiracials provide a useful case to study third space and identity matrices. Do such matrices exist? Are there specific social conditions that give rise to certain identity matrices? Is racial identity the driving force behind these?

Occupying Third Space: The Identity Matrices of Multiracials

In order to investigate the validity of the idea of "identity matrices," we use data from the Survey of Biracial Experience. The contours of this data have been explicitly described in detail elsewhere (see Rockquemore and Brunsma 2002). Briefly, the data was collected in phases: 1) in-depth pilot interviews conducted with multiracial undergraduates at "Catholic University" in the Midwest were used largely to construct a survey; 2) the Survey of Biracial

Experience was produced and distributed in "Metro Community College" and "Urban University" in the Detroit metropolitan area (Midwestern sample); 3) purposive interviewing of selected survey respondents; 4) collecting survey data from Connecticut and Massachusetts (collectively referred to as our Eastern sample), and Alabama (Southern sample); and, 5) interviewing respondents in the Eastern and Southern samples.

In order to identify black-white multiracials for the project, researchers set the initial criterion as students who had one parent who self-identifies as "white" and one who self-identifies as "black." Across the Midwestern, Eastern, and Southern samples, a request for participation in the study was mailed to all students registered as "black or African-American," "Other," or those who left the race question blank. While these scholars continue to gather data, this methodology has, to date, resulted in a total sample of 231 black-white multiracial individuals from a wide variety of backgrounds. The majority of these cases (159) are from the Midwest, 41 are from the South, and 30 are from the East – representing the largest and (substantively and theoretically) useful dataset on black-white multiracials to date. These individuals vary quite widely in social class, skin tone, and even age. The survey data allows for the empirical verification of the identity matrices of black-white multiracials as well as investigation of the social conditions that give rise to certain matrices. These data allowed for the investigation of the identity matrices of multiracial individuals, these matrices' relationship with the racial identity of the respondents, and preliminary analysis of the social conditions related to the identity matrices. Two key variables are central to the analyses in this paper.

The central question that has formed the cornerstone of Rockquemore and Brunsma's work was embedded within the Survey of Biracial Experience: "How do you feel about your racial identity?" Respondents were asked which of the following seven statements best describes their racial identity: 1) I consider myself exclusively black (or African-American); 2) I sometimes consider myself black, sometimes my other race, and sometimes biracial depending on the circumstances; 3) I consider myself biracial, but I experience the world as a black person; 4) I consider myself exclusively as biracial (neither black nor white); 5) I consider myself exclusively as my other race (not black or biracial); 6) Race is meaningless, I do not believe in racial identities; or, 7) Other (fill in the blank). Responses were coded as follows: "1" and "5" represented the

singular identity (black or white), responses "3" and "4" represented the border identity (unvalidated or validated), response "2" represented the protean
identity, and response "6" represented the transcendent identity. Response
"7" or "Other" is used in some analyses and not in others. The typology has
been empirically substantiated, and it and its underlying theoretical material
have been utilized in several studies hence, including this one.

The truly central question for this chapter also appeared in the Survey of
Biracial Experience but has not been previously explored: "Individuals have
many different types of identities. How would you describe your identity
in the following contexts?" This general question was followed by five sub-
questions (or contexts): "social identity," "political identity," "cultural identity," "physical identity," and "formal identity," with possible responses of
"black," "biracial," "white," and "other." The responses varied quite amaz-
ingly, as we will see. In order to construct the identity matrix and to look
at patterns therein, we needed data that was complete for both the racial
identity question (black, white, biracial, protean, transcendent, etc.) and for
the other identity questions (physical, social, political, cultural, and formal).
Almost 200 (191) cases had complete data for the exploration of the identity
matrices.

Figure 1 shows the distribution of racial identities among these black-white
multiracials. One can see that the most prominent racial self-understanding
of these black-white multiracials is "biracial" (N=110, 57.6 percent of total),
with the majority (N=67, 60.9 percent of "biracials," 35.1 percent of total) of
these respondents experiencing no validation for that identity. Over 22 (22.5)
percent have experienced an interactionally validated sense of a biracial
identity. A good proportion of the sample (15.2 percent) do not utilize racial
notions in their self-understanding – they are the transcendents. Interestingly,
and contrary to dominant assumptions and discourse, 13.1 percent of these
black-white multiracials understand their racial identity as "black," while,
not surprisingly, only 2.6 percent understand themselves as "white." Some
multiracial people relish in their interactional and cultural savvy to be able to
shift across social spaces with ease: the proteans – we see 5.8 percent having
this type of identity. The remainder (5.8 percent) utilize the "Other" option
on the survey, usually highlighting ethnic, religious, or national identities as
the most important to them.

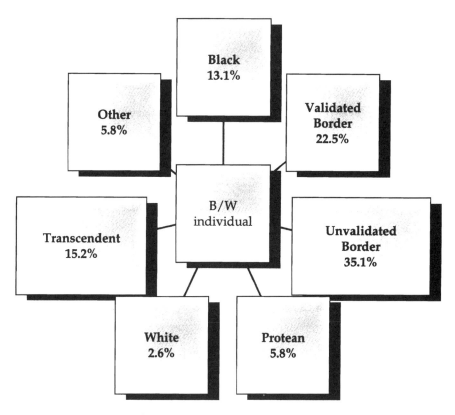

Figure 17.1. The Racial Identities of Black-White Multiracials.

Figure 2 shows the distribution of responses to the various identity questions on the Survey of Biracial Experience for these black-white multiracial people. The majority (51.8 percent) of respondents see themselves as deploying a biracial social identity, followed by a black social identity (36.6 percent), a white social identity (8.4 percent), and another type of social identity (3.1 percent). Concerning the political identity, again, the majority (48.7 percent) construct a biracial political identity, followed by a black political identity (30.9 percent), an "other" political identity (14.7 percent; this largely due to write-ins of "republican," "democrat," "independent," etc.), and only a few deploying a white political identity (5.8 percent).

Interestingly, multiraciality is highly resonant with these respondents' cultural identities – 58.6 percent understand their cultural identity as biracial, with a black cultural identity only salient to under a third of them (27.7

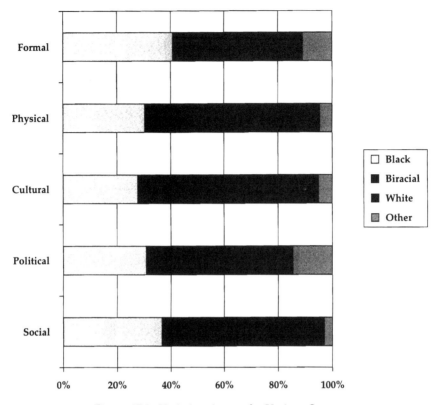

Figure 17.2. Variation Across the Various Spaces.

percent). Not surprisingly, the physical/embodied experience becomes very salient for these biracials' physical identities: 60.7 percent are multiracially embodied, 30.4 percent are black physically, and the rest are white or other (invoking gender). Finally, Figure 2 shows that while biracial (44.5 percent) and black (40.8 percent) are the typical institutional expression of their formal identities, 11 percent consider none of these, and only 3.7 percent formally indicate/identify as white. There are several things to note in this figure. First, the predominant response across these other types of identities is "biracial." Second, the predominance of "biracial" varies across the five dimensions of identity, from a high of 60.7 percent for physical identity, to a low of 44.5 percent for formal identity. Also, note the use of "other". This is instructive since it opens up further reflexive spaces for these multiracials and opens up analytic spaces for those of us studying these phenomena.

Hybridity, Human Experience, and Human Futures

Notions of hybridity, creolization, and, indeed, third space, emerged solidly from postcolonial theory. Let's not forget that postcolonial theory is primarily rooted in emancipation and resistance. As such, it should provide lenses that clarify the world, not simplify it. As Palmie explains, "creolization theory is ultimately a mere reflex of the very conditions it seeks to denounce and supersede – and so, once properly conceptualized, might itself be more profitably regarded as an object of, rather than a tool for, anthropological inquiry" (2006:448) in order to get closer to what Giroux believes possible:

> Identities are constantly being reworked and transformed within differences negotiated through the play of history, memory, language, and power...and how the discourses of difference can be used to rewrite the social contract between groups in ways that deepen and extend the possibility for a democratic community. (1993:98)

In order to promote such structures of deep democracy and participation, our notions of identity must also be quite responsive to the experience of identity formation, navigation, deployment, and maintenance across multiple social spaces in a matrix of human experience. This requires recognizing the dizzying diversity of lived identities without eliminating active, human action.

Since the explosion of work on multiraciality in the late- to mid–1990s (which has been somewhat tied to a multiracial movement), debates have consistently surrounded this work (see Brunsma 2006b, Spencer 2006). Embedded in this debate are attempts to lay political and cultural claims on multiracials based on their racial ancestry and their assumed racial identity (will they "stay" with black Americans? Will they "defect" and allow the arms of whiteness to envelop them? Will whiteness open its arms?). Identity politics to be sure; however, we do not know enough yet to engage meaningfully in these debates, for underlying the arguments are empirical questions, and social reality is hardly ever as neat as the discourse assumes it to be. To begin understanding the multiracial experience more fully, we need such theories of identity matrices across social, political, cultural, physical, and formal/institutional spaces. Once this is achieved, we can meaningfully add to both the debate and the scholarship of identity by analyzing the multiple components of a "multiracial" person by looking at the identities that constitute (only partially) a multiracial identity matrix – and perhaps help us understand

multiracial identity further and discuss the emergence of a multiracial consciousness upon which the identity politics have been assumed. But what
is more is that it will allow us to see the resemblance (instead of difference)
between these multiracial folks and those who "are not" multiracial.

It is clear that these black-white multiracials' identities are hybrid identities and that they exist in a space, which may be theorized as a third space
as Bhabha (1994) articulates it; however, not fully so. It is also clear that the
notion of an identity matrix is useful for understanding those who stand in
between and those whose space is exceptionally fluid because of this position.
As experience exists in a matrix, and as this matrix of experience is arrayed
along axes of various dominations (race, class, gender, etc.), histories, symbolic
structures, imaginations, constructions, etc., so do identities retain the play
across such spaces. The connection of two "cultures," "races," or "histories"
may theoretically set up a hybrid from whence identity play can emerge, or
it may theoretically encourage a third space from whence transgressional,
creative, and/or oppositional identities and individual/collective agents
may emerge. The reality is always much more complex than these theoretical constructs, as is seen in this brief theorization and empirical look at the
components of multiracial experience, and, therefore, identity components,
within multiracial identities for black-white multiracials.

So, is multiraciality (hybridity, mestizaje, in-betweeness) a unique feature
of human experience in particular social circumstances and contexts or is it
merely representative of processes that all humans share but are unwilling to
acknowledge? It is the case that hybridity, as a structure, provides potential
openings and provides a proverbial (and theoretical) third space; it provides
potentiality as histories and cultures collide and interact, etc. However, this
does not mean that the potential will be realized, nor that the potential will
be realized for the betterment of all people. In the case of multiracials in US,
one of the problems is individualism and other structural and ideological
structures in which such "third spaces" are embedded. Potential comes in
recognizing that it is not simply in the third space where people may realize their potential beyond the confines of restrictive constructions of racist,
patriarchal, and capitalist modernity. Instead, the necessary realization and
the theoretical work that needs to be done is that identities intersect across
multiple spaces, and therefore the potential in collective organizing is not
necessarily greater in third space, but it is greater in recognizing the multiplicity of identities and that ultimately we share more than we differ.

Identity matrices also allow us to begin to understand the potential of interracial or crossracial interactions, friendships, intimacies, and indeed solidarities, as multiracials may understand themselves socially as biracial, but politically as black, etc., allowing the variation in racial identity to emerge more clearly in all its multifacetedness. This, therefore, allows us to understand interaction on the micro level, but also perhaps as a more macro social movement membership and process. The matrices respond to a notion of the identities of multiracials, recognizing flexibility, whereas multiracial identity remains conceptually static and fixed – the many layers that make up our subjectivity providing explanations for variations in experience while also allowing for "hooks" that bring out our similarities rather than myopically focusing on our differences in identity and identification.

Author Biographies

JUDITH BLAU currently teaches at the University of North Carolina at Chapel Hill where she is the chair of the undergraduate Social and Economic Justice Minor. Her book, *Race in the Schools*, received the 2005 Oliver Cromwell Cox Award given by the American Sociological Association's Section on Race and Ethnic Minorities She published a trilogy on human rights with Alberto Moncada: *Human Rights: Beyond the Liberal Vision* (2005), *Justice in the United States: Human Rights and the US Constitution* (2006) and *Freedoms and Solidarities: In Pursuit of Human Rights* (2007); and is co-editor with Keri Iyall Smith of *Public Sociologies Reader*. She is the president of Sociologists without Borders-US and co-editor of its affiliated journal, *Societies without Borders*.

EMILY BROOKE BARKO. After receiving a BA in Sociology and Women's and Gender Studies from Bates College in Lewiston, ME, Barko is presently a MA candidate in the department of Sociology at Boston College in Chestnut Hill, MA. As an aspiring social psychologist, Barko's broad interests combine symbolic interactionism, mental health and illness, technologies of the body, critical race feminism, and medical and cultural sociology. In particular, Barko's current thesis work explores social constructions and social psychologies of recovery from anorexia nervosa as an impetus to understanding the phenomenology of recovery from the standpoint of the respondent.

ERIC BROWN received his Ph.D. from the University of California at Berkeley. He is currently an Assistant Professor of Sociology at the University of Missouri. His interests are in the areas of race and ethnic relations, urban sociology, social stratification, and social policy. He is currently engaged in research on "minority middle class formation." This work considers the roles of postindustrial labor market changes, government policies, and changing neighborhood patterns. One project looks at the African American professional middle class in the post-civil rights era. A second and related project examines the growth of a middle class among the Buraku people in Japan.

DAVID L. BRUNSMA is Associate Professor of Sociology at the University of Missouri in Columbia. He is author and coauthor of several books and articles, most notably: *Mixed Messages: Multiracial Identity in the 'Color-Blind' Era* (Lynne Rienner, 2006) and *The School Uniform Movement and What it Tells Us About American Education: A Symbolic Crusade* (Scarecrow, 2004). He continues to study the strategies and negotiated manifestations of racial identity in the post civil-rights era as illuminated by the interplay of social structural, cultural/symbolic, interactional, and biographical/narrative life structures. He is currently investigating human rights abuses in the United States, pedagogical strategies for teaching white students about race and racism, structural anti-racisms, and importing an epistemology of justice into the discipline of sociology. He is committed to investigating and initiating ways in which scholarship can be actively used to combat structural injustices. He lives in Columbia, MO with his wife Rachel and has three wonderful children: Karina, Thomas, and Henry.

RODERICK BUSH is an associate professor of Sociology at St. John's University in New York City. He is a recent Ph.D. after many years in the movement for Black liberation and social change. In 1984 his first book *The New Black Vote: Politics and Power in Four American Cities* was published by Synthesis Publications. His most recent book, *We Are Not What We Seem: Black Nationalism and Class Struggle in the American Century*, was published by NYU Press in 1999. Professor Bush is currently finishing a book entitled, *The End of White World Supremacy: Black Internationalism and the Problem of the Color Line* to be published by Temple University Press, and is working with Melanie E. L. Bush on a book entitled *Tensions in the "American" Dream: The Imperial Nation Confronts the Liberation of Nations* to be published by Temple University Press.

PATRICK GUN CUNINGHAME is a Sociology lecturer and elected RC30 (Sociology of Work) executive committee member. He was born in Ireland and grew up in Ireland, England and Scotland. His areas of specialization are cultural sociology, sociology of work, social movement theory, globalization theory, identity theory and American border theory. He received a Ph.D. in Sociology from Middlesex University, London, in 2002 with a thesis on Italian autonomous social movements of the 1970s. He has worked at the Universidad Autonoma de Ciudad Juarez since 2004, researching the relationship between globalization, the maquiladora export industry and transnational identities in the Ciudad Juarez-El Paso borderlands. He had worked previously at universities in Turin, Italy, London and Mexico City. Presently he is a Visiting Professor at the Universidad Autonoma Metropolitana in Mexico City, researching the role of social movements in the Mexican transition to democracy. He is fluent in Spanish and Italian.

FABIENNE DARLING-WOLF is an Assistant Professor of Journalism in the School of the Journalism and Theater at Temple University in Philadelphia. She also teaches and supervises graduate students in the school's Mass Media and Communication Doctoral Program. Darling-Wolf's research focuses on processes of mediated cultural influence and negotiation in a global context, paying particular attention to how such processes intersect with gendered, racial and ethnic identity formation. Because of Japan's longstanding engagement with cultural hybridity, much of her work has focused on the Japanese media environment. Originally from France, her research is also influenced, however, by the works of francophone scholars and aims at destabilizing essentializing dichotomies between various parts of the world, including those between "East" and "West."

DANIEL J. DELGADO currently is a graduate student at the University of Missouri – Columbia. His research largely is centered on how racial groups negotiate their identities, with a specific focus on Middle-class Latina/o people's identity negotiation in the Midwestern United States. Currently he is looking at how Latino/a bodies illuminate intersecting inequalities that impact their everyday lives.

ALEX FRAME LL.D. is a barrister and public law teacher, and advises extensively on constitutional questions in the South Pacific, and on Treaty of Waitangi matters in New Zealand. Most recently he has been Professor of Law at the University of Waikato, and Director of Te Matahauariki Research Institute engaged in a study of customary law. His biography of Sir John Salmond (1862–1924), *Salmond: Southern Jurist*, was published by Victoria University Press in 1995 and was awarded the E. H. McCormick Prize at the 1996 Montana Book Awards as well as the Law Foundation's J. F. Northey Prize for best legal publication in the same year. In 2002 Alex completed a study of the way in which our legal system might better reflect Maori customary law: *Grey and Iwikau – A Journey into Custom* was published by Victoria University Press in that year. His most recent book from the same publisher, Flying Boats: My Father's War in the Mediterranean, appeared in October 2007.

TRINIDAD GONZALES is a history instructor at South Texas College located in McAllen, Texas. His areas of research are Chicana/o, Latina/o and Borderland histories. In particular he examines issues related to identity and culture through an interdisciplinary approach. Gonzales has received several scholarships and awards including a Smithsonian Latino Predoctoral Fellow.

SHARLENE NAGY HESSE-BIBER, Ph.D., is Professor of Sociology and the Director of Women's Studies at Boston College in Chestnut Hill, Massachusetts. She has published widely on the impact of sociocultural factors on women's body image, including her book, *Am I Thin Enough Yet? The Cult of Thinness and the Commercialization of Identity* (Oxford, 1996), which was selected as one of Choice magazine's best academic books for 1996. She recently published *The Cult of Thinness* (Oxford, 2007). She is the coauthor of *Working Women in America: Split Dreams* (Oxford, 2005). She is coeditor of *Feminist Approaches to Theory and Methodology: An Interdisciplinary Reader* (Oxford, 1999), *Approaches to Qualitative Research: A Reader on Theory and Practice* (Oxford, 2004), and *Emergent Methods in Social Research* (Sage, 2006). She is also the coauthor of *The Practice of Qualitative Research* (Sage, 2006). She recently edited the *Handbook of Feminist Research Theory and Praxis* (Sage, 2007) which was selected as one of the Critics' Choice Award winners by the American Education Studies Association, and was also chosen as one of Choice Magazines's Outstanding Academic titles for 2007. She is co-editor of the forthcoming Handbook of Emergent Methods (Guilford, 2008). She contributed to the Handbook of Grounded Theory (Sage, 2008) and author of two forthcoming books, Mixed Methods for Social Researchers (Guilford, 2008) and The Handbook of Emergent Technologies for Social Research (Oxford, 2009). She is co-developer of the software program HyperRESEARCH, a computer-assisted program for analyzing qualitative data, and the new transcription tool HyperTRANSCRIBE. A fully functional free demo of these programs is available at www.researchware.com One will also find a free teaching edition for the programs on this site.

KERI E. IYALL SMITH's research explores the intersections between human rights doctrine, the state, and indigenous peoples in the context of a globalizing society. In this research, she is beginning to explore the study of indigenous peoples as public sociology. She has published articles on hybridity and world society, human rights, and teaching sociology. She is the author of *States and Indigenous Movements* (Routledge 2006) and co-editor, with Judith R. Blau, of *Public Sociologies Reader* (Rowman and Littlefield 2006). She is an assistant professor of Sociology at Suffolk University in Boston, MA. She holds a BA in Sociology from the University of Washington and an MA and Ph.D. in Sociology from the University of North Carolina at Chapel Hill. She is the Vice-President of Sociologists without Borders.

HELEN K. KIM is an assistant professor at Whitman College in Walla Walla, Washington. She earned her B.A. from the University of California at Berkeley, her M.A. from the University of Chicago, and her Ph.D. in social work and sociology from the University of Michigan. Her research interests include race and ethnicity, gender, second generation Asian Americans, and the body.

PATRICIA LEAVY is an Associate Professor of Sociology, Chairperson of the Sociology & Criminology Department, and the Founding Director of the Gender Studies Program at Stonehill College in Easton, MA. She is the author of *Iconic Events: Media, Politics, and Power in Retelling History* (2007) and *Method Meets Art: Arts-Based Research Practice* (2008). She is the coauthor of *Feminist Research Practice: A Primer* (2007) and *The Practice of Qualitative Research* (2006). She is co-editor of *Approaches to Qualitative Research: A Reader on Theory and Practice* (2003), *Emergent Methods in Social Research* (2006) and *The Handbook of Emergent Methods* (2008). She is the 2nd Vice President of the New England Sociological Association. She is regularly quoted in newspapers for her expertise in popular culture and gender and has appeared on CNN's *Glenn Beck Show* as well as *Lou Dobbs Tonight*.

HELENE K. LEE is a Ph.D. candidate in the Sociology Department at the University of California, Santa Barbara. She is working on completing her dissertation, *Bittersweet Homecomings: Korean Ethnic Identity Construction in Contemporary South Korea*, focusing on the connections between ethnic identity, nationality, gender and labor in the context of return migration.

PAUL MEREDITH was formerly a Research Fellow at Te Matahauariki Institute, University of Waikato, with a particular interest in Maori customary law. Paul is currently in the Office of the Pro-Vice Chancellor Maori at Victoria University of Wellington where he also recently taught in the History Department.

TESS HUIA MOEKE-MAXWELL (Ngai Tai ki Umupuia, Ngati Pukeko, Pakeha/European) is a senior researcher for a national Māori mental health workforce development organization in New Zealand. Her background is in social sciences and her Ph.D. was conferred in 2003. She also provides contract research to the mental health sector and is a registered counselor for the New Zealand Government's Accident Compensation Corporation (ACC). In this capacity, Tess provides clinical services to people who have experienced sexual violation. She currently lives in Wellington with her partner and has three adult children and six mokopuna (grandchildren). Tess has recently begun to write young adult fiction involving bi/multi racial Māori hybrid characters.

KEITH NURSE is Director of the Shridath Ramphal Centre for Internaional Trade Law, Policy and Services, University of the West Indies, Cavehill Campus, Barbados. He is a former member of academic staff at the Institute of International Relations, University of the West Indies, Trinidad and Tobago. Keith has published numerous scholarly articles on the global political economy of the clothing, banana, tourism, copyright and cultural/creative industries. He has also published on the impact of global restructuring on migration and diaspora, HIV/AIDS and security, and development assistance and capacity development. Recent publications include *Heritage Tourism in the Caribbean* (2007) and *The Cultural Industries in CARICOM* (2006). He is also the co-editor of *Caribbean Economies and Global Restructuring* (Ian Randle Publishers, 2002) and *Globalization, Diaspora and Caribbean Popular Culture* (Ian Randle Publishers, 2005) and co-author of *Windward Islands Bananas: Challenges and Options under the Single European Market* (Freidrich Ebert Stiftung, 1995).

BEDELIA NICOLA RICHARDS uses an ethnographic approach to explore race and ethnic inequality in education, the institutional and cultural contexts of schools and West Indian Immigrant Experiences. She is a Research Associate at Jobs for the Future (JFF) in Boston, MA where she contributes to the organization's work to create successful transitions for youth. As a member of JFFs *Early College High School Initiative*, she supports the needs of school developers through research on and documentation of selected school designs, practices, and student achievement outcomes. She is currently designing a project that uses the early college model to identify teaching practices that promote academic success in non-selective public schools where the majority of students come from low-income and minority families. Ms. Richards is also a Visiting Assistant Professor in the Education Department at Wellesley College. Prior to this, she held a number of teaching appointments at The Johns Hopkins University, where she recently earned her Ph.D. in Sociology. She holds a B.A. in sociology and spanish from Temple University.

SALVADOR VIDAL-ORTIZ (Ph.D., Sociology, The Graduate Center - City University of New York, 2005) is assistant professor of sociology at American University, in Washington, DC. His research interests include the participation of sexual minorities in Santería (an Afro-Cuban religious-cultural practice), racialized sexualities, transgender and transsexual studies, and Puerto Rican/Latino Studies in the US. His latest research interests incorporate US media portrayals in exploring the US American imaginary and perceptions of Santería. His recent work includes co-editing (with Karl Bryant) a Sexualities special issue on "Re-theorizing Homophobias." A book he co-edited with Nancy Naples, *The Sexuality of Migration: Border Crossings and Mexican Immigrant Men*, based on the research of late Lionel Cantú Jr., is forthcoming with NYU Press.

MELISSA F. WEINER's research examines the intersections of race, education and social protest. She is currently working on a book manuscript entitled *Racism, Resistance and Education: Jewish and Black Challenges to New York City's Public Schools* examining the ways in which education shapes racial identities and inequalities and efforts by marginalized groups to challenge these identities. Her articles have appeared in *Social Problems* and *The Sociological Quarterly*. She is an assistant professor at Quinnipiac University in Hamden, Connecticut where she teaches courses focusing on race/ethnicity, education, social movements, and popular culture. She holds a BS and a BA in Journalism and Sociology from Boston University and a Ph.D. in Sociology from the University of Minnesota.

References

Adler, Peter S. 1974. "Beyond Cultural Identity: Reflections on Cultural and Multi-cultural Man", in Larry A. Amaovar and Richard E. Porter, eds., *Intercultural Communication: A Reader*. Belmont, CA: Wadsworth Publishing, pp. 262–380.

Ahmad, Aijaz. 1995. "The politics of literary postcoloniality." *Race and Class* 36: 1–20.

Ahmed, Sara. 1999. "'She'll Wake Up One of These Days and Find She's Turned into a Nigger:' Passing through Hybridity." *Theory, Culture & Society* 16: 87–106.

Ahmed, Sara. 2004. *The Cultural Politics of Emotion*. New York: Routledge.

Alba, Richard. 1990. *Ethnic Identity: The Transformation of White America*. New Haven: Yale University Press.

Alba, Richard and Victor Nee. 1997. "Rethinking Assimilation for a New Era of Immigration." *International Migration Review* 31: 826–74.

Alexander, Jeffrey C. 2001. "Theorizing the 'Modes of Incorporation': Assimilation, Hyphenation, and Multiculturalism as Varieties of Civil Participation." *Sociological Theory* 19: 237–49.

Alexander, Jeffrey C. 2003. *The Meanings of Social Life: A Cultural Sociology*. New York: Oxford University Press.

Ali, Suki. 2003. *Mixed Race, Post-Race: Gender, New Ethnicities, and Cultural Practices*. Oxford, UK: Routledge.

Allen, Robert. 1970. *Black Awakening in Capitalist America*. Garden City, NY: Anchor Books.

Allen, Robert. 1976. "Racism and the Black Nation Thesis." *Socialist Revolution* 27: 145–150.

Allen, Robert. 2005. "Reassessing the Internal Colonialism Theory." *The Black Scholar* 35: 2–11.

Alvarez, Robert Jr. 1995. "The Mexican-U.S. Border: The Making of an Anthropology of Borderlands." *Annual Review of Anthropology* 24: 447–470.

Anderson, Benedict. 1991. *Imagined Communities: Reflections on the Origin and Spread of Nationalism, rev. ed.* New York: Verso.

Anderson, Benedict. 1998. "Nationalism, Identity, and the World-in-Motion", in Pheng Cheah and Bruce Robbins, eds., *Cosmopolitics*. Minneapolis, MN: University of Minnesota Press, pp. 17–33.

Andersen, Margaret L. 2005. "Thinking about women: A quarter century's view." *Gender & Society* 19: 437–455.

Ang, Ien. 2003. "Together in Difference: Beyond Diaspora, Into Hybridity." *Asian Studies Review* 27: 141–154.

Anon. 1857. "Maori Customs and English Laws." *The Maori Messenger: Te Karere Maori*, 15 August 1857 4: 1–2.

Anon. 1858. "Nga He o te Tapu." *Te Karere o Poneke*, 22 February 1858 1: 3.

Anon. 1859a. "Hints for the Maori People." *The Maori Messenger: Te Karere Maori*. 15 September 1859 6: 1–5.

Anon. 1859b. "Makutu in the Bay of Islands." *Te Karere Maori: The Maori Messenger*, 31 October 1859, 6: 1–5.

Anzaldúa, Gloria. 1987. *Borderlands/La Frontera: The New Mestiza, 2nd ed.* San Francisco, CA: Aunt Lute Books.

Appadurai, Arjun. 1996. *Modernity at Large.* Minneapolis, MN: University of Minnesota Press.

Augé, Marc. 1999. *An Anthropology for Contemporaneous Worlds.* Stanford, CA: Stanford University Press.

Aylsworth, Leon E. 1931. "The Passing of Alien Suffrage." *The American Political Science Review* 25: 114–116.

Awatere, Donna. 1984. *Maori sovereignty.* Auckland, New Zealand: Broadsheet Collective.

Bailey, Ronald. 1973. "Economic Aspects of the Black Internal Colony", in Frank Bonilla, and Robert Henriques Girling, eds., *Structures of Dependency.* Nairobi [E. Palo Alto], CA: distributed by Nairobi Bookstore, 161–188.

Bailey, Ronald and Guillermo Flores. 1973. "Internal Colonialism and Racial Minorities in the U.S.: An Overview", in Frank Bonilla, and Robert Henriques Girling, eds., *Structures of Dependency.* Nairobi [E. Palo Alto], CA: distributed by Nairobi Bookstore, pp. 149–159.

Bakhtin, Mikhail. 1981. *The Dialogic Imagination.* Austin, TX: University of Texas Press.

Bahktin, Mikhail. 1984. *Rabelais and his World.* trans., Helene Iswolsky. Bloomington, IN: Indiana University Press.

Balandier, George. 1966. "The Colonial Situation: A Theoretical Approach (1951)", in Immanuel Wallerstein ed., *Social Change: The Colonial Situation.* New York: John Wiley & Sons, pp. 34–61.

Baldick and Others v. Jackson, 1910, Vol. 30 New Zealand Law Reports, 343.

Balsamo, Anne. 1995. "Signal to noise: On the meaning of cyberpunk subculture", in Frank Biocca and Mark Levy eds., *Communication in the age of virtual reality.* Hillsdale, NJ:, Eribaum, pp. 347–368.

Banks, William M. 1998. *Black Intellectuals.* New York: Norton.

Barrett, James R. and David Roediger. 1997. "In-Between Peoples: Race, Nationality and the 'New Immigrant' Working Class." *Journal of American Ethnic History* 16: 3–44.

Bauman, Zygmunt. 2000. *Liquid Modernity.* Cambridge, England: Polity Press.

Belich, James. 1996. *Making Peoples: a history of New Zealanders: from Polynesian settlement to the end of the nineteenth century.* Auckland, New Zealand: Penguin Press.

Bell, Bernard W., Emily R. Grosholz, and James B. Stewart. 1996. "Introduction", in Bernard W. Bell, Emily R. Grosholz, and James B. Stewart, eds., *W. E. B. Du Bois on Race and Culture.* New York: Routledge, pp. 1–14.

Bennett, Lerone Jr. 1993. *The Shaping of Black America.* New York: Penguin Books.

Berland, Jody. 1992. "Angels Dancing: Cultural Technologies and the Production of Space", in Lawrence Grossberg, Cary Nelson, and Paula Treichler, eds., *Cultural Studies.* New York: Routledge, pp. 38–55.

Bernstein Sycamore, Matt. (Mattilda, A.K.A.). 2006. *Nobody passes: Rejecting the rules of gender and conformity*. Emeryville, CA: Seal Press.

Bhabha, Homi. 1990. "DissemiNation: time, narrative, and the margin of the modern nation", in Homi Bhabha ed., *Nation and Narration*. London, UK: Routledge, pp. 291–322.

Bhabha, Homi. 1990. "The third space: Interview with Homi Bhabha", Jonathan Rutherford, ed., *Identity: Community, culture, difference*. London: Lawrence and Wishart, pp. 207–22.

Bhabha, Homi. 1993. "Culture's in between." *Artform International* 32: 167–171.

Bhabha, Homi. 1994. *The Location of Culture*. Oxford: Routledge.

Biggs, Bruce. 1968. "The Maori Language Past and Present", in Erik Schwimmer, ed., *The Maori People in the Nineteen-Sixties*. Auckland, New Zealand: Longman Paul, pp. 65–85.

Blau, Judith R. and Charles Heying. 1996. "Historically Black Organizations in the Nonprofit Sector." *Nonprofit and Voluntary Sector Quarterly* 25: 540–44.

Blau, Judith R., Charles Heying, and Joseph R. Feinberg. 1996. "Second-Order Cultural Effects of Civil Rightson Southern Nonprofit Organizations." *Nonprofit and Voluntary Sector Quarterly* 25: 174–90.

Blau, Judith R. and Eric S. Brown. 2001. "Du Bois and Diasporic Identity: The *Veil* and *Unveiling* Project." *Sociological Theory* 19: 219–233.

Blau, Judith R., Mim Thomas, Beverly Newhouse, and Andrew Kavee. 1998. "Ethnic Buffer Institutions: The Immigrant Press." *Historical Social Research* 23: 20–37.

Blauner, Bob, Harold Cruse, Stephen Steinberg, et al. 1990. "Race and Class: A Discussion." *New Politics* 2: 12-58.

Blauner, Robert. 1972. *Racial Oppression in America*. New York: Harper and Row.

Bluestone, Barry. 1969. "Black Capitalism: The Path to Black Liberation?" *Review of Radical Political Economics* 1: 36–55.

Boas, Franz. 1966. 1887. "The Study of Geography", in Franz Boas, ed., *Race, Language and Culture*. New York, NY: The Free Press.

Bodnar, John. 1987. *The Transplanted: A History of Immigrants in Urban America*. Bloomington, IN: Indiana University Press.

Bolatagici, Torika. 2004. "Claiming the (N)either/(N)or of 'Third Space': (Re)presenting Hybrid Identity and the Embodiment of Mixed Race." *Journal of Intercultural Studies* 25: 75–85.

Bonilla-Silva, Eduardo. 2003. *Racism Without Racists: Color-Blind Racism and the Persistence of Racial Inequality in the United States*. Lanham, MD: Rowman and Littlefield Publishers.

Bordo, Susan. 1989. "Feminism, postmodernism, and gender skepticism", in Linda J. Nicholson, ed., *Feminism/Postmodernism*. New York: Routledge.

Bordo, Susan. 1989. "The body and the reproduction of femininity: A feminist appropriation of Foucault", in Alison M. Jaggar and Susan Bordo, eds., *Gender/Body/Knowledge*. New Brunswick, NJ: Rutgers University Press, pp. 13–33.

Borland, Katherine. 1996. "The India bonita of Monimbó: The politics of ethnic identity in the new Nicaragua", in Colleen Beverly Cohen, Richard Wilk, and Ballerino

Stoeltje, eds., *Beauty queens on the global stage: Gender, contests, and power*. New York: Routledge, pp. 75–88.

Bourdieu, Pierre. 1985. "The Social Space and the Gensis of Groups." *Theory and Society* 14: 723–744.

Bow, Leslie. 1995. "For every gesture of loyalty, there doesn't have to be a betrayal": Asian American criticism and the politics of loyalty", in Judith Roof and Robyn Wiegman eds., *Who can speak: Authority and critical identity*. Urbana, IL: University of Illinois Press, pp. 30–55.

Boxill, Bernard R. 1996. "Du Bois on Cultural Pluralism", in Bernard W. Bell, Emily Grosholz, and James B. Stewart, eds., *W. E. B. Du Bois on Race and Culture*. New York: Routledge, pp. 57–85.

Brea, Raphael and Jose Millet. 1995. "The African Presence in the Carnivals of Santiago de Cuba." *Journal of Caribbean Studies* 10: 30–49.

Brettell, Caroline B. 2003. "Bringing the City Back In: Cities as Contexts for Immigrant Incorporation", in Nancy Foner, ed., *American Arrivals: Anthropology Engages the New Immigration*. Santa Fe, New Mexico: School of American Research Press, pp. 163–196.

Britt, Lory and David Heise. 2000. "From shame to pride in identity politics", in Timothy J. Owens and Robert W. White, eds., *Self, Identity, and Social Movements*. Minneapolis, MN: University of Minnesota Press, pp. 252–268.

Broderick, Francis L. 1958. "German Influence on the Scholarship of W. E. B. Du Bois." *Phylon* 19: 367–71.

Brown, Mildred L. and Chloe Ann Rounsley. 1996. *True Selves: Understanding Transsexualism – For Families, Friends, Coworkers, and Helping Professionals*. San Francisco, CA: Jossey-Bass Publishers.

Brubaker, Rogers, Mara Loveman, and Peter Stamatov. 2004. "Ethnicity as Cognition." *Theory and Society* 33: 31–64.

Bruce, Dickson, Jr. 1992. "W. E. B. Du Bois and the Idea of *Double Consciousness*." *American Literature* 64: 229–309.

Brunsma, David L. 2005. "Interracial Families and the Racial Identification of Mixed-Race Children: Evidence from the Early Childhood Longitudinal Study." *Social Forces* 84: 1129–1155.

Brunsma, David L. (ed.). 2005. *Mixed Messages: Multiracial Identities in the "Color-Blind" Era*. Boulder, CO: Lynne Rienner Publishers.

Brunsma, David L. 2006. "Public Categories, Private Identities: Exploring Regional Differences in the Biracial Experience." *Social Science Research* 35: 555–576.

Brunsma, David L., and Kerry Ann Rockquemore. 2001. "The New Color Complex: Phenotype, Appearances, and (Bi)racial Identity." *Identity* 1: 225–246.

Brunsma, David L. and Kerry Ann Rockquemore. 2002. "What Does 'Black' Mean?: Exploring the Epistemological Stranglehold of Racial Classification." *Critical Sociology* 28: 101–121.

Bryant, Karl. Unpublished Manuscript. "Not just about Gender and Sexuality: Teaching intersex as a social justice issue." [Submitted to Teaching Sociology.]

Bryant, Karl. 2006. "Making Gender Identity Disorder of Childhood: Historical Lessons for Contemporary Debates." *Sexuality Research and Social Policy* 3: 23–39.

Bryant, Karl and Salvador Vidal-Ortiz. 2008. "Retheorizing Homophobias." *Sexualities* 11: 387–396.

Buck, Sir Peter (Te Rangihiroa). 1949. *The Coming of the Maori*. Christchurch, New Zealand: Whitcombe & Tombs Ltd.

Burawoy, Michael. 1974. "Race, Class and Colonialism." *Social and Economic Studies* 23: 521–50.

Burke, Phyllis. 1996. *Gender shock: Exploding the myths of male & female*. New York: Anchor Books.

Butler, Judith. 1990. *Gender trouble: Feminism and the subversion of identity*. New York: Routledge.

Butler, Judith. 1993. *Bodies that matter: On the discursive limits of "sex."* New York: Routledge.

Butler, Judith. 1994. "Against Proper Objects." *differences: a Journal of Feminist Cultural Studies* 6: 1–26.

Butler, Judith. 2006. "Undiagnosing Gender", in Paisley Currah, Richard M. Juang, and Shannon Price Minter, eds., *Transgender Rights*. Minneapolis, MN: University of Minnesota Press, pp. 274–298.

Butterfield, Sherri-Ann. P. 2001. Big Tings A Gwaan: Constructions of Racial and Ethnic Identity Among Second Generation West Indian Immigrants. Unpublished Ph.D. Dissertation, Department of Sociology, University of Michigan, Ann Arbor, MI.

Butterfield, Sherri-Ann. P. 2004. "We're Just 'Black': The Racial and Ethnic Identities of Second Generation West Indians in New York", in Philip Kasinitz, John H. Mollenkopf and Mary C. Waters, eds., *Becoming New Yorkers: Ethnographies of the New Second Generation*. New York: Russell Sage Foundation, pp. 288–312.

Byerman, Keith E. 1994. *Seizing the Word*. Athens, GA: University of Georgia Press.

Calderón, Roberto R. 1993. "Mexican Politics in the American Era, 1846–1900: Laredo, Texas." Ph.D. dissertation, Department of History, University of California at Los Angeles, Los Angeles, CA.

Campbell, Anne. 2000. "Cultural Identity as a Social Construct." *Intercultural Education* 11: 31–39.

Canclini, Néstor G. 2003. *Culturas híbridas: Estrategias para entrar y salir de la modernidad*. Mexico: Reprint Editorial Grijalbo.

Carmichael, Stokely and Charles Hamilton. 1967. *Black Power: The Politics of Liberation in America*. New York: Random House.

Castro, Juan E. 2001. "Richard Rodriguez in 'Borderland': The Ambiguity of Hybridity." *Aztlan* 26: 101–126.

Charmaz, Kathy 1995. "Grounded theory: Example of memo writing", in Jonathan A. Smith, Rom Harrre, and Luk Van Langenhove eds., *Rethinking Methods in Psychology*. London, UK: Sage Publications, pp. 27–49.

Cheru, Fantu. 2000. "The Local Dimensions of Global Reform", in Jan Nderveen Pieterse, ed., *Global Futures: Shaping Globalization*. London, UK: Zed Books, pp. 119–132.

Choi, Woo-Gil. 2001. "The Korean Minority in China: The Change of its Identity." *Development and Society* 30: 119–141.

Chong, Kelly. 1998. "What it Means to be Christian: The Role of Religion in the Construction of Ethnic Identity and Boundary Among Second-Generation Korean Americans." *Sociology of Religion* 59: 259–286.

Churchill, Ward and Jam Vander Wall. 1988. *Agents of Repression: The FBI's Secret Wars Against the Black Panther Party and the American Indian Movement*. Boston, MA: South End Press.

Clarke, George. 1844. *British Parliamentary Papers (New Zealand)*, Appendices 556.

Clerc, Susan 2000. "Estrogen brigades and 'big tits' threads: Media fandom on-line and off", in David Bell and Barbara M. Kennedy eds., *The cybercultures reader*. New York: Routledge, pp. 216–229.

Clifford, James. 1992. "Traveling Cultures", in Lawrence Grossberg, Cary Nelson, and Paula A. Treichler, eds., *Cultural Studies: Now and in the Future*. New York: Routledge, pp. 96–112.

Clifford, James. 1994. "Diasporas." *Cultural Anthropology* 9: 302–38.

Cohen, Abner. 1993. *Masquerade Politics: Explorations in the Structure of Urban Cultural Movements*. Berkeley, CA: University of California Press.

Cohen, Colleen Ballerino 1996. "Contestants in contested domain: Staging identities in the British Virgin Islands", in Colleen Ballerino Cohen, Richard Wilk, and Beverly Stoeltje eds., *Beauty queens on the global stage: Gender, contests, and power*. New York: Routledge, pp. 324–349.

Cohen, Robin. 1997. *Global Diasporas: An Introduction*. London, UK: University College London Press.

Cohen, Robin. 2007. "Creolization and Diaspora – the Cultural Politics of Divergence and Some Convergence", in Gloria Totoricaguena, ed., *Opportunity Structures in Diaspora Relations: Comprisons in Contemporary Multi-level Politics of Diaspora and Transnational Identity*. Reno, Nevada: Center for Basque Studies, University of Nevada Press.

Collins, Heeni. 1999. "Nga tangata awarua: The joys and pain of being both Maori and Pakeha", in M. Hutching, L. Evans, and J. Byrne, Wellington, eds., *Oral history in New Zealand*, vol. 11. New Zealand: National Oral History Association of New Zealand, pp. 1–5.

Collins, J. 2000. "Biracial-Bisexual Individuals: Identity Coming of Age." *International Journal of Sexuality and gender Issues* 5: 221.

Collins, Patricia Hill. 2000. *Black Feminist Thought: Knolwedge, Consciousness, and the Politics of Empowerment*. Oxford, UK: Routledge.

Collins, Randall. 2006. *Interaction Ritual Chains*. Princepton, NJ: University Press.

Colonial Office, "Draft Instructions" to the proposed 1846 Constitution, CO 881/1, XXXIII, National Archives, London.

Conzen, Kathleen Niels, David A. Gerber, Ewa Morawska, George E. Pozzetta, and Rudoph J. Vecoli. 1992. "The Invention of Ethnicity: A Perspective from the U.S.A." *Journal of American Ethnic History* 12: 3–41.

Cooley, Charles Horton. 1964. *Human Nature and the Social Order*. New York: Schocken.

Coombes, Annie E. and Avtar Brah. 2000. "Introduction: The conundrum of 'mixing'", in Avtar Brah and Annie E. Coombes, eds., *Hybridity and its discontents: Politics, science, culture.* New York: Routledge, pp. 1–16.

Corber, Robert J., and Stephen M. Valoochi, eds. 2003. *Queer Studies: An Interdisciplinary Reader.* Malden, MA: Blackwell Publishers.

Coser, Lewis A. 1971. *Masters of Sociological Theory.* New York: Harcourt Brace Jovanovich.

Côté, James E. 1996. "Sociological Perspectives on Identity Formation: The Culture-Identity Link and Identity Capital." *Journal of Adolescence* 19: 417–428.

Côté, James E. 1997. "An Empirical Test of the Identity Capital Model." *Journal of Adolescence* 20: 577–597.

Côté, James E. and Seth J. Schwartz. 2002. "Comparing Psychological and Sociological Approaches to Identity: Identity Status, Identity Capital, and the Individualization Process." *Journal of Adolescence* 25: 571–586.

Cowan, James. 1956. *The New Zealand Wars: A History of the Maori Campaigns and the Pioneering Period.* Wellington, New Zealand: R. E. Owen, Government Printer.

Cowley, John. 1996. *Carnival, Canboulay and Calypso: Traditions in the Making.* Cambridge, UK: Cambridge University Press.

Creighton, M. R. 1995. "Imaging the Other in Japanese advertising campaigns", in James G. Carrier ed., *Occidentalism: Images of the West.* New York: Oxford University Press, pp. 165–260.

Creswell, John W. and Vicki L. Plano-Clark. 2006. *Designing and Conducting Mixed Methods of Research.* Thousand Oaks, CA: Sage Publications.

Crozier, Michel, Samuel P. Huntington and Joji Watanuki. 1975. *The Crisis of Democracy: Report on the Governability of Democracies to the Trilateral Commission.* New York: New York University Press.

Cumings, Bruce. 1997. *Korea's Place in the Sun: A Modern History.* New York: W. W. Norton & Company.

Danky, James P., ed. 1999. *African-American Newspapers and Periodicals.* Cambridge, MA: Harvard University Press.

Darboe, Kebba. 2003. "New Immigrants in Minnesota: The Somali Immigrant Experience and Assimilation." *Journal of Developing Societies* 19: 458–72.

Darling-Wolf, Fabienne 2000. "Gender, beauty, and Western influence: Negotiated femininity in Japanese women's magazines", in Elizabeth Toth and Linda Aldoory eds., *The gender challenge to media: Diverse voices from the field.* Cresskill, NJ: Hampton, pp. 267–315.

Darling-Wolf, Fabienne 2004. "Sites of attractiveness: Japanese women and Westernized representations of feminine beauty." *Critical Studies in Media Communication* 21: 325–345.

Darling-Wolf, Fabienne 2006. "The men and women of *non-no*: Gender, race and hybridity in two Japanese magazines." *Critical Studies in Media Communication* 23: 181–199.

Das Gupta, Monisha. 1997 "What is Indian About You? A Gendered, Transnational Approach to Ethnicity." *Gender and Society* 11: 572–596.

de Beauvoir, Simone [1949]. 1989. *The second sex*. New York: Vintage books.

De Lauretis, Teresa 1987. *Technologies of gender: Essays on theory, film and fiction*. Bloomington, IN: Indiana University Press.

Denzin, Norman K., Lincoln, Yvonna S. and Linda Tuhiwai Smith. 2008. *Handbook of Critical and Indigenous Methodologies*. Thousand Oaks, CA: Sage.

Dewes, Koro. 1964. "Teaching Maori to Adults." *Te Ao Hou* 48: 46–48.

DeWind, Josh and Philip Kasinitz. 1997. "Everything Old is New Again? Processes and Theories of Immigrant Incorporation." *International Migration Review* 31: 1096–1111.

Dinnerstein, Leonard, and David M. Reimers. 1988. *Ethnic Americans*. New York: Harper and Row.

Drake, St. Clair, and Horace R. Cayton. [1945]. 1962. *Black Metropolis: A Study of Negro Life in a Northern City*. New York: Harper and Row.

Driedger, Leo. 1975. "In Search of Cultural Identity Factors: A Comparison of Ethnic Students." *Canadian Review of Sociology and Anthropology* 12: 150.

Du Bois, W. E. B. 1897. "Strivings of the Negro People." *Atlantic Monthly*, August pp. 194–98.

Du Bois, W. E. B. 1897. 1971. "The Conservation of Races", in Julius Lester ed., *The Seventh Son*, Vol. 1. New York: Random House, pp. 176–187.

Du Bois, W. E. B. 1903. *The Souls of Black Folk*. Chicago, IL: A. C. McClurg & Co. Cambridge, MA: Unviersity Press John Wilson and Son. Bartleby.com, 1999. www. bartleby.com/114/. (26 December 2001, 8 April 2003).

Du Bois, W. E. B. 1968. *The Autobiography of W. E. B. Du Bois*. New York: International Publishers.

Du Bois, W. E. B. 1903. "Of Our Spiritual Strivings." *The Souls of Black Folks*. Chicago, Illinois: A.C. McClurg & Co.

Du Bois, W. E. 1961. *The Souls of Black Folk*. Greenwich, CT: Fawcett Publications.

Dunn, Christopher. 2001. "Carnivals in Latin America and the Caribbean." http://www.africana.com.

Durdrah, Rajinder K. 2002. "British Bhangra Music and Disaporic South Asian Identity Information." *European Journal of Cultural Studies* 5: 363–383.

Durie, Mason. 1994a. *Māori cultural identity and its implications for mental health services*. Palmerston North, New Zealand: Massey University Press.

Durie, Mason. 1994b. *Whaiora: Māori health development*. Auckland, New Zealand: Oxford University Press.

Durie, Mason. 2001. *Mauri Ora: The dynamics of Māori health*. Auckland, New Zealand: Oxford University Press.

Durie, Mason. 2004. Indigeneity and the Promotion of Positive Mental Health. Paper Presented at the third World Conference for the Promotion of Mental Health and Prevention of Mental and Behavioural Disorders, Auckland, September 2004.

Duval, Terry. 1996. *A Preliminary Dictionary of Maori Gainwords*. Ph.D. dissertation, Department of Maori Studies, University of Canterbury.

Duval, Terry and Koenraad Kuiper. 2001. "Maori Dictionaries and Maori Loanwords." *International Journal of Lexicography* 12: 243–260.

Dwyer, Claire. 1999. "Veiled Meanings: young British Muslin women and the negotiation of difference." *Gender, Place, and Culture* 6: 5–26.

Edwards, Rosalind 1990. "Connecting method and epistemology: A White woman interviewing Black women." *Women's Studies International Forum* 13: 477–490.

Ekins, Richard & Dave King. 2006. *The transgender phenomenon*. London, UK: SAGE.

Elias, Rt. Hon. Dame Sian. 2005. "Equality Under Law." *Waikato Law Review* 13: 1–11.

Emery, Michael, and Edwin Emery. 1992. *The Press and America*. Englewood Cliffs, NJ: Prentice-Hall.

Enloe, Cynthia. 2004. *The curious feminist: Searching for women in an age of empire*. Berkeley, CA: University of California Press.

Espiritu, Yen Le. 2000. *Asian American Women and Men: Labor, Laws and Love*. New York: Altamira Press.

Etzioni, Amitai. 1995. "Old Chestnuts and New Spurs", in Amitai Etizionio, ed., *New Communitarian Thinking*. Charlottesville, VA: University Press of Virginia, pp. 52–70.

Ewen, Stuart. 1988. *All consuming images*. New York: Basic Books.

Feagin, Joe and Leslie H. Picca. 2007. *Two-Faced Racism: Whites in the Backstage and Frontstage*. New York: Routledge.

Foner, Nancy. 1997. "The Immigrant Family: Cultural Legacies and Cultural Changes." *International Migration Review* 31: 961–974.

Foner, Nancy. 2001. *Islands in the City: West Indian Migration to New York*. Berkeley, CA: University of California Press.

Fordham, Signithia. 1996. *Blacked Out*. Chicago, IL: University of Chicago Press.

Forest, Benjamin. 2001. "Mapping Democracy: Racial Identity and the Quandary of Political Representation." *Annals of the Association of American Geographers* 91: 143–166.

Foster, Rose. 1996. "The bilingual self: Duet in two voices." *Psychoanalytic Dialogues* 6: 97–98.

Foucault, Michel. 1970. *The Order of Things: An Archeology of the Human Sciences*. New York: Vintage Books.

Foucault, Michel. 1976. "Power as Knowledge", in Robert Hurley, trans., *The History of Sexuality, Vol. 1: An Introduction*. New York: Vintage Books, pp. 92–102.

Fausto-Sterling, Anne. 2000. *Sexing the Body: Gender, Politics, and the Construction of Sexuality*. New York: Basic Books.

Frame, Alex. 1981. "Colonising Attitudes Towards Maori Custom." *New Zealand Law Journal*. 1981:105–110.

Frame, Alex. 2002. *Grey and Iwikau – A Journey into Custom*. Wellington, New Zealand: Victoria University Press.

Frame, Alex and Paul Meredith. 2005. "Performance and Maori Customary Legal Process." *Journal of the Polynesian Society* 114: 135–155.

Frame, Alex and Joeliee Seed-Pihama. 2006. "Some Customary Legal Concepts in Maori Traditional Migration Accounts." *Revue Juridique Polynésienne* 12: 113–132.

Franco, Jesús, n.d. *El alma de la raza: narraciones históricas de episodios y la vida de los mexicanos residentes en los Estados Unidos del Norte America, la repatriación, la vida y origin de las comisiones honoríficas y de la cruz azul mexicana.* Compañia Editora "Lat Patria", El Paso, Texas.

Franklin, John Hope, and August Meier, eds. 1982. *Black Leaders of the Twentieth Century.* Urbana, IL: University of Illinois Press.

Frazier, E. Franklin. 1957. *The Negro in the United States.* Toronto, Canada: Collier-Macmillan.

Friedman, Susan. 1998. *Mappings: Feminism and the cultural geographies of encounter.* Princeton, NJ: Princeton University Press.

Friedman, Susan Stanford. 1995. "Beyond white and Other: Relationality and narratives of race in feminist discourse." *Signs* 21: 1–49.

Frye, Marilyn. 1983. *The politics of reality: Essays in feminist theory.* Freedom, CA: The Crossing Press.

Fuchs, Lawrence J. 1990. *The American Kaleidoscope: Race, Ethnicity and the Civic Culture.* Middletown, CT: Wesleyan University Press.

Fujieda, Mioko and Kumiko Fujimura-Fanselow 1995. "Women's studies: An overview", in Kumiko Fujimura-Fanselow and Atsuko Kameda eds., *Japanese women: New feminist perspectives on the past, present and future.* New York: The Feminist Press, pp. 15–180.

Gallaugher, Annemarie. 1995. "Constructing Caribbean Culture in Toronto: The Representation of Caribana", in Alvina Ruprecht and Cecilia Taiana eds., *The Reordering of Culture: Latin America, The Caribbean and Canada in the Hood.* Montreal, Canada: McGill-Queens University Press, pp. 397–408.

Gamson, Joshua. 1997. "Messages of Exclusion: Gender, Movements, and Symbolic Boundaries." *Gender & Society* 11: 178–99.

Gan, Jessi. 2007. "'Still at the back of the bus:' Sylvia Rivera's Struggle." *Centro: Journal of the Center for Puerto Rican Studies* 19: 124–139.

Gans, Herbert J. 1962. *The Urban Villagers: Group and Class in the Life of Italian Americans.* New York: Free Press.

Gans, Herbert J. 1979. *Deciding What's News.* New York: Pantheon.

Gans, Herbert J. 1979. "Symbolic Ethnicity: The Future of Ethnic groups and Cultures in America." *Ethnic and Racial Studies* 2: 1–20.

García-Canclini, Nestor. 1995. *Hybrid cultures: Strategies for entering and leaving modernity.* Minneapolis, MN: University of Minnesota Press.

Garrett, Robyne. 2004. "Negotiating a Physical Identity: Girls, Bodies and Physical Education." *Sport, Education and Society* 9: 223.

Geertz, Clifford. 2000. *Available Light: Anthropological Reflections on Philosophical Topics.* Princeton, NJ: Princeton University Press.

Gibson, Margaret A. 1988. *Accommodation without Assimilation*. Ithaca, NY: Cornell University Press.

Giddens, Anthony. 1999. *Modernity and self-identity: Self and society in the late modern age*. Cambridge, UK: Polity.

Gillem, Angela. 2000. "Beyond double jeopardy: Female, biracial and perceived to be Black", in Joan C. Chrisler, Carla Golden, & Patricia D. Rozee eds., *Lectures on the psychology of Women 2nd Edition*. Boston: McGraw-Hill, pp. 209–219.

Gillis, John R. 1994. *Commemorations: The Politics of National Identity*. Princeton, NJ: Princeton University Press.

Gilroy, Paul. 1993. *The Black Atlantic: Modernity and Double Consciousness*. Cambridge, MA: Harvard University Press.

Giroux, Henry A. 1993. "School For Scandal: Cultural Politics and the Pedagogy of Commercialization." *Transition* 59: 88–103.

Gandhi, Leela. 1998. *Postcolonial Theory*. New York: Columbia University Press.

Gleason, Philip. 1992. *Speaking of Diversity: Language and Ethnicity in Twentieth-Century America*. Baltimore, MD: Johns Hopkins University Press.

Goffman, Erving. 1959. *The presentation of self in everyday life*. New York: Doubleday Anchor Original.

González, Jovita. 1930a. "America Invades the Border Town." *Southwestern Review* 15: 469–477.

González, Jovita. 1930b. "Social Life in Cameron, Starr and Zapata Counties." M.A. thesis, University of Texas.

Gordon, Milton M. 1964. *Assimilation in American Life. The Role of Race, Religion, and National Origins*. New York: Oxford University Press.

Gore Browne, Governor Thomas. 1858. "Memorandum 28th April, 1857." *Appendices to the Journal of the House of Representatives*, E-5.

Gottlieb, Peter. 1991. "Rethinking the Great Migration", in Joe William Trotter, Jr., ed., *The Great Migration in Historical Perspective*. Bloomington, IN: Indiana University Press, pp. 68–82.

Greeley, Andrew M. 1974. *Ethnicity in the United States: A Preliminary Reconnaissance.* New York: Wiley.

Greenwood, Janika and Arnold Wilson. 2006. *Te Mauri Pakeaka: A Journey into the Third Space*. Auckland, New Zealand: Auckland University Press.

Grosfoguel, Ramon. 1999. " 'Cultural Racism' and Colonial Caribbean Migrants in the Core Zones of the Capitalist World-Economy." *Review* 22: 409–434.

Grossman, James R. 1989. *Land of Hope*. Chicago, IL: University of Chicago Press.

Grosz, Elizabeth. 1994. *Volatile Bodies: Toward a Corporeal Feminism*. Bloomington, IN: Indiana University Press.

Gubrium, Jaber and James Holstein. 2003. *Ways of Aging*. Hoboken, NJ: Wiley-Blackwell.

Gupta, Akhil and James Ferguson 1997. "Culture, Power, Place: Ethnography at the End of an Era", in Akhil Gupta and James Ferguson, eds., *Culture, Power, Place: Explorations in Critical Anthropology*. Durham, NC: Duke University Press, pp. 1–29.

Gutiérrez, David G. 1995. *Walls and Mirrors: Mexican Americans, Mexican Immigrants, and the Politics of Ethnicity*. Berkeley, CA: University of California Press.

Halberstam, Judith. 2005. *In a queer time and place: transgender bodies, subcultural lives*. New York: NYU Press.

Hale, Jacob C. 1998. "Consuming the Living, Dis(re)membering the Dead in the Butch/FTM Borderlands." *GLQ* 4: 311–348.

Hall, Maurice L. 2007. "The Postcolonial Caribbean as a Liminal Space: Authoring Other Modes of Contestation and Affirmation." *The Howard Journal of Communications* 18: 1–13.

Hall, Stuart. 1991. *Myths of Caribbean Identity*. Coventry, UK: University of Warwick, Centre for Caribbean Studies.

Hall, Stuart. 1992. "The Question of Cultural Identity", in Stuart Hall, David Held, and Ali McGrew, eds., *Modernity and Its Futures*. Cambridge, UK: Polity Press, pp. 273–326.

Hall, Stuart. 1992. "What is this 'Black' in Black Popular Culture?" in Gina Dent, ed., *Black Popular Culture*. Seattle, WA: Bay Press, pp. 21–37.

Hall, Stuart. 1996. "Minimal Selves", in Houston A. Baker, Jr., Manthia Diawara, and Ruth H. Lindeborg, eds., *Black British Cultural Studies: A Reader*. Chicago, IL: University of Chicago Press, pp. 16–60.

Hall, Stuart. 1997. "Caribbean Culture: Future Trends." *Caribbean Quarterly* 43: 25–34.

Hall, Stuart. 1997. "The Local and the Global: Globalization and Ethnicity", in Anthony D. King, ed., *Culture, Globalization and the World-System*. Minneapolis, MN: University of Minnesota Press, pp. 19–39.

Hall, Stuart and Paul DuGay. 1996. *Questions of Cultural Identity*. Thousand Oaks, CA: Sage Publications.

Hall, Stuart. 1997. *Representation: Cultural representations and signifying practices*. London, UK: Sage.

Handlin, Oscar. 1941. *Boston's Immigrants, 1790–1865: A Study in Acculturation*. Cambridge, MA: Harvard University Press.

Hannerz, Ulf. 1996. *Transnational Connections: Culture, People, Places*. New York: Routledge.

Haraway, Donna. 1991. *Simians, cyborgs, and women: The reinvention of nature*. New York: Routledge.

Harper, Phillip Brian. 1998. "Passing for What? Racial Masquerade and the demands of upward mobility." *Callaloo* 21: 381–397.

Harris, David R., & Sim, Jeremiah Joseph. 2002. "Who is multiracial? Assessing the complexity of lived race." *American Sociological Review* 67: 614–627.

Harrison, Bennett. 1974. "Ghetto Economic Development." *Journal of Economic Literature* 12: 1–37.

Hartstock, Nancy C. M. 2004. "The Feminist Standpoint: Developing the Ground for a Specifically Feminist Historical Materialism", in Sandra Harding, ed., *The Feminist Standpoint Theory Reader: Intellectual and Political Controversies*. New York: Routledge, pp. 35–54.

He, Jiancheng. 1990. "China's Policy on Nationalities," in Dae-Sook Suh and Edward Shultz, eds., *Koreans in China*. Papers of the Center for Korean Studies No. 16, pp. 1–20.

Heath, Shirley Brice. 1983. *Ways with Words*. New York: Cambridge University Press.

Hechter, Michael and Elizabeth Borland. 2001. "National Self-Determination: The Emergence of an Institutional Norm", in Michael Hecter and Karl-Dieter Opp, eds., *Social Norms*. New York: Russell Sage Foundation, pp. 186–233.

Hemmings, Clare. 2002. *Bisexual Spaces: A Geography of Sexuality and Gender*. New York: Routledge.

Henri, Florette. 1975. *Black Migration: Movement North*. Garden City, NY: Doubleday.

Henry, Frances. 1994. *The Caribbean diaspora in Toronto: learning to live with racism*. Toronto, Canada: University of Toronto Press.

Herman, Melissa 2004. "Forced to choose: Some determinants of racial identification in multiracial adolescents." *Child Development* 75: 730–748.

Hesse-Biber, Sharlene. 1996. *Am I thin enough yet?* New York: Oxford University Press.

Hesse-Biber, Sharlene and Patricia Leavy. 2006. *Emergent Methods in Social Research*. Thousand Oaks, CA: Sage.

Hill-Collins, Patricia 1991. "Black Feminist Thought in the Matrix of Domination", in Patricia Hill-Collins, eds., *Black Feminist Thought: Knowledge, Consciousness, and the Politics of Empowerment*. London, UK: HarperCollins.

Hind, Robert. 1984. "The Internal Colonialism Concept." *Comparative Studies in Society and History* 26: 543–568.

Hirsch, Arnold R. 2000. "Containment on the Home Front: Race and Federal Housing Policy From the New Deal to the Cold War." *Journal of Urban History* 26: 158–189.

Hitlin, Steven, J. Scott Brown, and Glen H. Elder, Jr. 2006. "Racial Self-Categorization in Adolescence: Multiracial Development and Social Pathways." *Child Development* 77: 1298–1308.

Ho, Christine and Keith Nurse. 2005. *Globalization, Diaspora and Caribbean Popular Culture*. Kingston, Jamaica: Ian Randle Press.

Holtwijk, Ineke. 2001. "Rio Carnival is all about Money, Publicity and Silicone." *Prince Claus Fund Journal* 7: 73–77.

Hooks, Bell. 1990. *Yearning: Race, gender, and cultural politics*. Boston, MA: South End Press.

Hurh, Won Moo & Kwang Chung Kim. 1990. "Religious Participation of Korean Immigrants in the United States." *Journal for the Scientific Study of Religion* 29: 19–34.

Iriye, A. 1967. *Across the Pacific: An inner history of American-East Asian relations*. New York: Harcourt Brace Jovanovich.

Irvine, Janice M. 1990. *Disorders of desire: Sex and gender in modern American sexology*. Philadelphia, PA: Temple University Press.

Irving, Dan. 2008. "Normalized Transgressions: Legitimizing the Transsexual Body as Productive." *Radical History Review* 100: 38–59.

Itzigson, Jose. 2001. "Living Transnational lives." *Diaspora* 10: 281–296.

Ivy, Marilyn. 1995. *Discourse of the vanishing: Modernity, phantasm, Japan*. Chicago, IL: The University of Chicago Press.

Iyall Smith, Keri E. and Leavy Patricia. 2008. Hybrid Identities: Theoretical and Empirical Examinations. Leiden, The Netherlands: Brill Publishers.

Iyengar, Shanto. 1996. "Framing Responsibility for Political Issues." *Annals of the American Academy of Political and Social Sciences* 546: 59–70.

Jacobs, Mark D. and Lyn Spillman. 2005. "Cultural sociology at the crossroads of the Discipline." *Poetics* 33: 1–14.

Jaggar, Allison. 1989. "Love and Knowledge: Emotion in Feminist Epistemology." *Inquiry* 32: 151–172.

James, C. L. R. 1980. *The Black Jacobins*. London, UK: Allison and Busby.

Jaret, Charles and Donald C. Reitzes. 1999. "The importance of racial-ethnic identity and social setting for Blacks, Whites, and multiracials." *Sociological Perspectives* 42: 711–737.

Jin, Shangzhen. 1990. "The Rights of Minority Nationalities in China: The Case of the Yanbian Korean Autonomous Prefecture", in Dae-Sook Suh and Edward Shultz, eds., *Koreans in China*. Papers of the Center for Korean Studies No. 16, pp. 31–43.

Johnson, Audreye. 1999. "The Black Experience." Unpublished paper, School of Social Work, University of North Carolina, Chapel Hill.

Johnson, Benjamin H. 2003. *Revolution in Texas: How a Forgotten Rebellion and Its Bloody Suppression Turned Mexicans into Americans*. New Haven, CT: Yale University Press.

Johnson, Carol. 2002. "Heteronormative Citizenship and the politics of passing." *Sexualities* 5: 317–336.

Johnson, Charlse. S. 1934. *Shadow of the Plantation*. Chicago, IL: University of Chicago Press.

Johnson, Daniel M., and Rex R. Campbell. 1981. *Black Migration in America*. Durham, NC: Duke University Press.

Johnson, Margaret. 2004. "Boldly Queer: Gender hybridity in Queer as Folk." *Quarterly Review of Film and Video* 21: 291–301.

Joseph, Robert. 2002. "The Government of Themselves." Te Matahauariki Institute Monograph. Hamilton: Te Matahauariki Institute.

Journal of Blacks in Higher Education. 2007. "Black Student College Graduate Rates Inch Higher But the Large Racial Gap Persists." Available at: http://www.jbhe .com/preview/winter07preview.html.

Journal of Blacks in Higher Education. 2007. " Black Women Students Far Outnumber Black Men at the Nations Highest-Ranked Universities." Available at: http://www .jbhe.com/news_views/51_gendergap_universities.html.

Kallen, Horace M. 1924. *Culture and Democracy in the United States: Studies in Group Psychology of the American Peoples*. New York: Boni and Liveright.

Kamara, Jemadari and Tony Menelik Van Der Meer. 2007. "On the Dialectics of Domestic Colonialism and the Role of Violence in Liberation: From Fratricide to Suicide." *Human Architecture: Journal of the Sociology of Self-Knowledge* V: 383–392.

Kasinitz, Phillip. 1992. *Caribbean New York: Black immigrants and the politics of race.* Ithaca, NY: Cornell University Press.

Kasinitz, Philip, Juan Battle and Ines Miyares. 2001. "Fade to black: children of West Indian immigrants in Southern Florida", in Ruben G. Rumbaut & Alejandro Portes, eds., *Ethnicities: children of immigrants in America.* Berkeley, CA: University of California Press, pp. 267–300.

Katz, Michael B. 2007. "Why Aren't U.S. Cities Burning?" *Dissent* 54: 23–29.

Katz, Michael B. 2008. "Why Don't American Cities Burn Very Often?" *Journal of Urban History* 34: 185–208.

Katznelson, Ira. 1981. *City Trenches: Urban Politics and the Patterning of Class in the United States.* Chicago, IL: University of Chicago Press.

Kazal, Russell A. 1995. "Revisiting Assimilation: The Rise, Fall, and Reappraisal of a Concept in American Ethnic History." *American Historical Review* 100: 427–71.

Kearney, Milo, Gómez Arguelles, Alfonso, González, Yolanda Z. 1989. *A Brief History of Education in Brownsville and Matamoros.* Brownsville, TX: The University of Texas-Pan American-Brownsville.

Keating, AnaLouise. 1996. *Women Reading Women Writing: Self-Invention in Paula Gunn Allen, Gloria Anzaldúa, and Audre Lorde.* Philadelphia, PA: Temple University Press.

Keegan, Peter. 2004. "Increasing Te Reo Maori Use with Maori-Medium Education." Education Gazette, New Zealand 83(8): online at http://www.edgazette.govt.nz/articles.php/show_articles.php?id=6633.

Kelsey, Jane. 1984. "Legal imperialism and the colonization of Aotearoa", in Paul Spoonley, C. Macpherson, David Pearson, and C. Sedgwick, eds., *Tauiwi: Racism and ethnicity in New Zealand.* Palmerston North, New Zealand: Dunmore Press, pp. 15–44.

Kessler, Suzanne and Wendy McKenna. 2000. "Who put the 'trans' in transgender? Gender theory and everyday life." *The International Journal of Transgenderism*, 4: July–September. http://www.symposion.com/ijt/gilbert/kessler.htm. Accessed on 28 February 2007.

Khanna, Nikki. 2004. "The Role of Reflected Appraisals in Racial Identity: The case of Multiracial Asians." *Social Psychology Quarterly* 67: 115–131.

Kilbourne, Jeanne. 2000. 'Killing Us Softly 3: Advertising's Image of Women', Videotape, Cambridge Documentary Films.

King, Dave. 2003. "Gender Migration: A Sociological Analysis (or The Leaving of Liverpool)." *Sexualities* 6: 173–194.

King, Martin Luther, Jr. 1967. *Where Do We Go From Here: Chaos or Community?* Boston, MA: Beacon Press.

Kinser, Samuel. 1990. *Carnival, American Style: Mardi Gras at New Orleans and Mobile.* Chicago, IL: The University of Chicago Press.

Kinshasa, Kuando Mbias. 1988. *Emigration vs. Assimilation: The Debate in the African American Press, 1827–1861.* Jefferson, NC: McFarland.

Kondo, Baba Zak. 1993. *Conspiracys: Unraveling the Assassination of Malcolm X.* Washington, D.C.: Nubia Press.

Kondo, D. 1997. *About face: Performing race in fashion and theater.* New York: Routledge.

Koo, Hagen and Eui-Young Yu. 1981. "Korean immigration to the United States: its demographic pattern and social implications for both societies." Papers of the East-West Population Institute. No. 74: pp. 1–30.

Kornweibel, Theodore, Jr. 1981. "From Great Migration to Great Depression", in Theodore Kornweibel, Jr., ed., *In Search of thePromised Land.* Port Washington, NY: Kennikat Press, pp. 131–139.

Kornweibel, Theodore. 1998. *Seeing Red: Federal Campaigns Against Black Militancy, 1919–1925.* Bloomington, IN: University of Indiana Press.

Kraidy, Marwan M. 2002. "Hybridity in cultural globalization." *Communication Theory* 12: 316–339.

Kraidy, Marwan. 2005. *Hybridity: Or the cultural logic of globalization.* Philadelphia, PA: Temple University Press.

Kuhn, Hans-Peter. 2005. "Gender-Related Aspects of Political Identity Formation in Adolescence: Theories, Concepts, Findings." *Journal for Sociology of Education and Socialization* 25: 399.

Kulick, Don. 1999. "Transgender and Language: A review of the Literature and Suggestions for the Future." *GLQ* 5: 605–22.

Kymlicka, Will. 1995. *Multicultural Citizenship.* Oxford, England: Oxford University Press.

Lamont, Michele. 2000. "Meaning-Making in Cultural Sociology: Broadening Our Agenda." *Contemporary Sociology* 29: 602–607.

Lawlor, C. 1993. "The World Turned Upside Down," *Hybrid* 3: 2–4.

Lee, Chae-Jin. 1986. *China's Korean Minority: The Politics of Ethnic Education.* Boulder, CO: Westview Press.

Lemann, Nicholas. 1991. *The Promised Land.* New York: Alfred A. Knopf.

Lemert, Charles. 1994. "A Classic from the Other Side of the *Veil.*" *Sociological Quarterly* 35: 383–96.

Lester, Julius. 1971. *The Seventh Son: The Thought and Writings of W. E. B. Du Bois.* Vol. 1. New York: Random House.

Lévi-Strauss, Claude. 1985. *The View from Afar,* trans. Joahcim Neugroschel and Phoebe Hoss. New York: Basic Books.

Lewis, Amanda. 2003. "Everyday Race-Making: Navigating Racial Boundaries in Schools." *American Behavioral Scientist* 47: 283–305.

Lewis, David Levering. 1993. *W. E. B. Du Bois: Biography of a Race, 1868–1919.* New York: Henry Holt.

Lieberson, Stanley. 1980. *A Piece of the Pie.* Berkeley, CA: University of California Press.

Lieberson, Stanley and Mary C. Waters. 1988. *From Many Strands: Ethnic and Racial Groups in Contemporary America.* New York: Sage Publications.

Lieberson, Stanley and Mary C. Waters. 1993. "The Ethnic Responses of Whites: What Causes Their Instability, Simplification, and Inconsistency?" *Social Forces* 72: 421–50.

Limón, José E. 1974. "El Primer Congreso Mexicanista de 1911: A Precursor to Contemporary Chicanismo." *Aztlán* 5: 85–117.

Lo, Ming-cheng M. 2002. *Doctors Within Borders: Profession, Ethnicity, and Modernity in Colonial Taiwan*. Berkeley: University of California Press.

Logan, Rayford W. 1965. *The Betrayal of the Negro*. London, England: Collier-Macmillan.

Lorber, Judith. 1994. Paradoxes of Gender. New Haven, CN: Yale University Press.

Loseke, Donileen R. and James C. Cavendish. 2001. "Producing Institutional Selves: Rhetorically Constructing the Dignity of Sexually Marginalized Catholics." *Social Psychology Quarterly* 64: 347–362.

Macalister, John. 2000. "The Changing Use of Maori Words in New Zealand English." *New Zealand English Journal* 14: 41–47.

Macalister, John. 2004. "Listening to Proper Nouns: Social Change and Maori Proper Noun Use in New Zealand English." *New Zealand English Journal* 18: 24–34.

Macalister, John. 2005. *A Dictionary of Maori Words in New Zealand English*. Melbourne, Australia: Oxford University Press.

Macalister, John. 2006. "The Maori presence in the New Zealand English lexicon, 1850–2000: Evidence from a corpus-based study." *English World-Wide* 27: 1–24.

MacIntyre, Alasdair. 1984. *After Virtue*. Notre Dame, IN: Notre Dame Press.

Mahtani, Minelle. 2007. "Tricking the Border Guards: Performaing Race." *Environment and Planning* 20: 425–440.

Maine, Sir Henry Sumner. 1861. *Ancient Law: Its Connection with the Early History of Society, and its Relation to Modern Ideas*. London, UK: John Murray.

Maines, David R. 2000. "The Social Construction of Meaning." *Contemporary Sociology* 29: 577–584.

Maira, Sunaina Marr. 2002. *Desis in the House: Indian American Youth Culture in New York City*. Philadelphia, PA: Temple University Press.

Malcolm X. 1971. *The End of White World Supremacy: Four Speeches*. New York: Merlin House.

Marable, Manning. 1986. *W. E. B. Du Bois: Black Radical Democrat*. Boston, MA: Twyne.

Marks, Carole. 1985. "Black Workers and the Great Migration North." *Phylon* 46: 148–61.

Marks, Carole. 1989. *Farewell – We're Good and Gone*. Bloomington, IN: Indiana University Press.

Martin, Chief Justice Sir William. 1860. "Remarks on the Administration of Justice among the Natives", Minutes of Evidence taken before the Waikato Committee, *Appendices to the Journals of the House of Representatives*, F-3.

Martin, Emily. 1992. *The woman in the body*. Boston, MA: Beacon Press.

Martinez, Diego Samper and Mirtha Buelvas Aldana. 1994. *Caribbean Carnival: An Exploration of the Barranquilla Carnival, Colombia*. Santafe de Bogota, Colombia: Diego Samper Ediciones.

Martinot, Steve. 2007. "Dual-State Character of U.S. Coloniality: Notes Toward Decolonization." *Human Architecture: Journal of the Sociology of Self* V: 371–382.

Masayuki, Suzuki. 1990. "The Korean National Liberation Movement in China and International Response", in Dae-Sook Suh and Edward Shultz, eds., *Koreans in China*. Papers of the Center for Korean Studies No. 16; pp. 115–143.

Mason-Schrock, Douglas. 1996. "Transsexuals' Narrative Construction of the True Self." *Social Psychology Quarterly* 59: 176–92.

Massey, Douglas S. 1995. "The new immigration and ethnicity in the United States". *Population and Development Review* 21: 631–652.

Massey, Doreen. 1985. "New Directions in Space", in Derek Gregory and John Urry, eds., *Social Relations and Spatial Structures*. New York: St. Martin's Press, pp. 9–19.

McDowell, Linda. 1999. *Gender, identity and place: Understanding feminist geographies*. Oxford, UK: Blackwell.

McVeigh, Brian J. 2000. *Wearing ideology: State, schooling and self-presentation in Japan*. New York: Berg.

McWhorter, John H. 2002. *The Power of Babel*. London, UK: William Heinemann.

Mead, George H. 1934. *Mind, Self, and Society*. Edited by Charles W. Morris. Chicago, IL: University of Chicago Press.

Mercer, Kobena. 1997. "Black Hair/Black Politics", in Ken Gelder and Sarah Thornton eds., *The Subcultures Reader*. London, England: Routledge, pp. 420–435.

Meredith, Paul. 1999. "Hybridity in the Third Space: Rethinking Bi-cultural Politics in Aotearoa/New Zealand." *He Pukenga Korero: A Journal of Māori Studies* 4: 12–16.

Meridith, Paul. 1999a. "Being 'half-caste': Cultural schizo or cultural lubricant?" *Tu Mai* 4: 24.

Meridith, Paul. 1999b. "Don't you like kina bey? Et, you're not a real Maori!" *Tu Mai* 3: 4–6.

Meridith, Paul. 1999c. "Hybridity in the third space: Rethinking bi-cultural politics in Aotearoa/New Zealand". *He Pukenga Korero* 4: 12–16.

Merleau-Ponty, Maurice. 1962. *Phenomenology of Perception*. Colin Smith (trans.). London, UK: Routledge and Kegan Paul.

Meyerowitz, Joanne. 2002. *How sex changed: A history of transsexuality in the United States*. Cambridge, MA and London, UK: Harvard University Press.

Mignolo, Walter D. 2007. "The De-Colonial Option and the Meaning of Identity in Politics," *Anales* N. E. (9/10): 43–72.

Mills, Charles. 1997. *The Racial Contract*. Ithaca, NY: Cornell University Press.

Mills, Wright C. 1959. *The Sociological Imagination*. New York: Grove Press Inc.

Ministry of Health. 2001. *New Zealand Health Strategy*. Wellington, New Zealand: Ministry of Health.

Ministry of Health. 2001. *New Zealand Disability Strategy*. Wellington, New Zealand: Ministry of Health.

Ministry of Health. 2002. *He Korowai Oranga: Māori Health Strategy*. Wellington, New Zealand: Ministry of Health.

Ministry of Health. 2002a. *Whakatātaka: Māori Health Action Plan 2002–2005*. Wellington, New Zealand: Ministry of Health.

Ministry of Health. 2002b. *Reducing Inequalities in Health*. Wellington, New Zealand: Ministry of Health.

Ministry of Health. 2006. *Whakatātaka: Māori Health Action Plan 2006–2011*. Wellington, New Zealand: Ministry of Health.

Mintz, Sidney. 1974. *Caribbean Transformations*. Baltimore, MD: John Hopkins University Press.

Mitchell, Reid. 1995. *All on a Mardi Gras Day: Episodes in the History of New Orleans Carnival*. Cambridge, MA: Harvard University Press.

Moeke-Maxwell, Tess. 2003. *Bringing home the body: Bi/multi racial Maori women's hybridity in Aotearoa/New Zealand*. Unpublished Ph.D., School of Education, University of Waikato, New Zealand.

Moeke-Maxwell, Tess. 2005. "Bi/Multiracial Maori Women's Hybridity in Aotearoa/ New Zealand." *Discourse: studies in the cultural politics of education* 26: 497–510.

Moeke-Maxwell, Tess. 2006. "Greenstone as Narrative Provocateur", in Judith McConaghy and Cathy McConaghy, eds., *Provocations and excitation in education*. New York: Peter Lang Publishers, pp. 95–118.

Mohanram, Radhika. 1999. *Black body: Women colonialism and space*. New South Wales, Australia: Allen and Unwin.

Mohanty, Chandra Talpade. 1991. "Introduction. Cartographies of Struggle: Third World Women and the Politics of Feminism", in Chandra Talpade Mohanty, Ann Russo and Lourdes Torres, eds., *Third World Women and the Politics of Feminism*. Bloomington, IN: University of Indiana Press, p. XX.

Monhanty, Chandra Talpade. 2003. *Feminism without borders: Decolonizing theory, practicing solidarity*. Durham, NC: Duke University Press.

Montejano, David. 1987. *Anglos and Mexicans in the Making of Texas, 1836–1986*. Austin, TX: University of Texas Press.

Morgan, David L. and Michael L. Schwalbe. 1990. "Mind and Self in Society: Linking Social Structure and Social Cognition." *Social Psychology Quarterly* 53: 148–164.

Morgan, Kathryn. 1991. "Women and the knife: Cosmetic surgery and the colonization of women's bodies." *Hypatia* 6: 25–53.

Morning, Ann. 2000. "Who is multiracial? Definitions and Decisions." *Sociological Imagination* 37: 209–229.

Moya, Jose C. 2005. "Immigrants and Associations: A Global and Historical Perspective." *Journal of Ethnic and Migration Studies* 31: 833–64.

Mulhausler, Peter. 1996. *Linguistic Ecology: Language Change and Linguistic Imperialism in the Pacific Region*. London, UK: Routledge.

Muñoz, José. 1999. *Disidentifications: Queers of Color and the Performance of Politics*. New York: NYU Press.

Murphy, Patrick D. and Marwan M. Kraidy. 2003. "International communication, ethnography, and the challenge of globalization." *Communication Theory* 13: 304–323.

Nedelcheva, Tanya. 2006. "Cultural Identity as an Everyday Life and Ideal." *Sociological Problems* 38: 76–88.

Nettleford, Rex. 1988. "Implications for Caribbean Development", in John W. Nunley and Judith Bettelheim, eds., *Caribbean Festival Arts*. London, UK: University of Washington Press.

Ngata, Apirana. 1907. *New Zealand Parliamentary Debates* 139: 520.

Nurse, Keith. 1999. "Globalization and Trinidad Carnival: Diaspora, Hybridity and Identity in Global Culture." *Cultural Studies* 13: 661–690.

Nurse, Keith. 2006. "Festival Tourism: Trinidad Carnival", in Chandi Jayawardena, ed. *Caribbean Tourism: More than Sun, Sea and Sand*. Kingston, Jamaica: Ian Randle, pp. 234–249.

Oak, Vishnu. 1948. *The Negro Newspaper*. Yellow Springs, OH: Antioch Press.

Oakley Brown, Mark A., J. Elisabeth Wells, and Kate M. Scott. 2006. *Te Rau Hinengaro: The New Zealand Mental Health Survey*. Wellington, New Zealand: Ministry of Health.

O'Dell, Jack H. 1966. "Colonialism and the Negro American Experience." *Freedomways* 6: 296–308.

O'Dell, Jack H. 1967. "A Special Variety of Colonialism," *Freedomways* 7: 7–15.

Ogbu, John U. 1978. *Minority Education and Caste*. New York: Academic Press.

Omi, Michael and Howard Winant. 1994. *Racial Formation in the United States: From the 1960s to the 1990s*. New York: Routledge.

Orange, Claudia. 1987. *The Treaty of Waitangi*. Wellington, New Zealand: Allen and Unwin.

O'Reilly, Kenneth. 1989. *Racial Matters: The FBI's Secret File on Black America, 1960–1972*. New York: Free Press.

O'Reilly, Kenneth. 1994. *Black Americas: The FBI Files*. New York: Carol and Graf Publishers.

Orozco, Cynthia E. 1992. "The Origins of the League of United Latin American Citizens (LULAC) and the Mexican American Civil Rights Movement in Texas with an Analysis of Women's Political Participation in a Gendered Context, 1910–1929." Ph.D. dissertation, Department of History, University of California Los Angeles.

Orsman, Harry, ed. 1997. *The Dictionary of New Zealand English*. Auckland, New Zealand: Oxford University Press.

Outlaw, Lucius. 1996. "'Conserve' Races? In Defense of W. E. B. Du Bois", in Bernard W. Bell, Emily R. Grosholz, and James B. Stewart, eds., *On Race and Culture*. New York: Routledge, pp. 15–38.

Owens Patton, Tracey, & Julie Snyder-Yuly. 2007. "Any four Black men will do: Rape, race, and the ultimate scapegoat." *Journal of Black Studies* 37: 859–895.

Oyserman, Daphna, Sakamoto, Izumi and Lauffer, Armand. 1998. "Cultural Accommodation: Hybridity and the Framing of Social Obligation." *Journal of Personality and Social Psychology* 74: 1606–1618.

Palmer, Ransford W. 1995. *Pilgrims from the Sun: West Indian Migration to America*. New York: Twayne Publishers.

Palmie, Stephan. 2006. "Creolization and Its Discontents." *Annual Review of Anthropology* 35: 433–456.

Parameswaran, Radhika. 1996. "Coverage of "bride burning" in the Dallas Observer: A cultural analysis of the 'Other.'" *Frontiers* 7: 69–100.

Parameswaran, Radhika. 2001. "Global media events in India: Contests over beauty, gender, and nation." *Journalism and communication monographs* 3: 51–105.

Parameswaran, Radhika. 2003. *Global queens, national celebrities: Tale of feminine triumph in post-liberalization India.* Association for Education in Journalism and Mass Communication, Kansas City, MO.

Parameswaran, Radhika. 2004. "Spectacles of gender and globalization: Mapping Miss World's media event space in the news." *The Communication Review* 7: 371–406.

Parameswaran, Radhika. 2005. "Global beauty queens in post-liberalization India." *Peace Review: A Journal of Social Justice* 17: 419–426.

Paredes, Américo. 1993. *Folklore and Culture on the Texas-Mexican Border.* Richard Bauman, ed. Austin, TX: University of Texas Press.

Park, Edward J. W. and John S. W. Park. 2005. *Probationary Americans: Contemporary Immigration Policies and the Shaping of Asian American Communities.* New York: Routledge.

Park, Kyeyoung. 1999. "'I Really Do Feel I'm 1.5!' The Construction of Self and Community by Young Korean Americans." *Amerasia Journal* 25: 139–163.

Park, Robert E. 1928. "Human Migration and the Marginal Man." *American Journal of Sociology* 33: 881–93.

Park, Robert E. 1950. *Race and Culture.* New York: Free Press.

Park, Robert E., and Ernest W. Burgess. [1921]. 1969. *Introduction to the Science of Sociology.* Chicago, IL: University of Chicago Press.

Patene, Wiremu. 1860. "Proceedings of the Kohimarama Conference." The Maori Messenger: Te Karere Maori, 31 July 1860 7: 3–62.

Pearson, David. 1990. *A dream deferred: The origins of ethnic conflict in New Zealand.* Wellington, New Zealand: Allen and Unwin.

Pearson, David. 1991. "Biculturalism and multiculturalism in comparative perspective", in Paul Spoonley, David Pearson and Cluny Macpherson, eds., *Nga take: Ethnic relations and racism in Aotearoa/New Zealand.* Wellington, New Zealand: Dunmore Press, pp. 194–215.

Perales, Alonso S. 1936. *En Defense de mi Raza.* Artes Graficas, San Antonio, Texas. *Primer Congreso Mexicanista Verificado en Laredo, Texas, EEUU de A. Los Dias 14 al 22 de Septiembre de 1911: Discursos y Conferencias Por La Raza Y Para La Raza.* Tipografia de N. Idar, Laredo, 1912.

Phillips, Layli. 2004. "Fitting in and feeling good: Patterns of self-evaluation and psychological stress among biracial adolescent girls." *Women & Therapy* 27: 217–236.

Piao, Changyu. 1990. "The History of Koreans in China and the Yanbian Korean Autonomous Prefecture", in Dae-Sook Suh and Edward Shultz, eds., *Koreans in China.* Papers of the Center for Korean Studies No. 16, pp. 44–77.

Pieterse, Jan Nederveen. 2000. "Shaping Globalization", in Jan Nederveen Pieterse, ed., *Global Futures: Shaping Globalization.* London, UK: Zed Books, pp. 1–19.

Pinkney, Alphonso. 1969. *Black Americans.* Englewood Cliffs, NJ: Prentice-Hall.

Piripi, Haami, quoted in Keenan, Elizabeth. 2005. "Kiwi Tongues at War", Time Pacific Magazine, online at http://www.time.com/time/magazine/article/ 0,9171,503050613–1069121,00.html.

Pitama, Suzanne and Paul Robertson, Fiona Cram, Matea Gillies, Tania Huria and Wendy Dallas-Katoa. 2007. "Meihana Model: A Clinical Assessment Framework." *New Zealand Journal of Psychology* 36: 118–125.

Portes, Alejandro and Ruben G. Rumbaut. 2001. *Legacies: the story of the immigrant second generation*. New York: Russell Sage Foundation.

Portes, Alejandro and Min Zhou. 1993. The new second generation: Segmented assimilation and its variants. *Annals of the American Academy of Political and Social Science* 530: 74–96.

Prashad, Vijay. 2000. *The Karma of Brown Folk*. Minneapolis, MN: University of Minnesota Press.

Price-Spratlen, Towsand. 1999. "Livin' for the City: African American Ethogenesis and Depression Era Migration." *Demography* 36: 553–68.

Qian, Zhenchao. 2004. "Options: Racial/ethnic identification of children of intermarried couples." *Social Science Quarterly* 85: 746–766.

Quijano, Anibal and Immanuel Wallerstein. 1992. "Americanity as a concept, or the Americas in the modern world-system." *International Social Science Journal* 134: 549–557.

Raskin, Jamin B. 1993. "Legal Aliens, Local Citizens: The Historical, Constitutional and Theoretical Meanings of Alien Suffrage." *University of Pennsylvania Law Review* 141: 1391–1470.

Renn, Kristen A. 2000. "Focus on students and student culture: Patterns of situational identity among biracial and multiracial college students." *The Review of Higher Education* 23: 399–420.

Renn, Kristen A. 2003. "Understanding the identities of mixed-race college students through a developmental ecology lens." *Journal of College Student Development* 44: 383–403.

Ribb, Richard. 2001. "José Tomás Canales and the Texas Rangers: Myth, Identity, and Power in South Texas, 1900–1920." Ph.D. dissertation, Department of American Studies, University of Texas, Austin, TX.

Richards, Bedelia Nicola. 2007. West Indian Roots and American Branches: Ethnicity, School Context and Academic Engagement Among Afro-Caribbean Students. Ph.D. dissertation, Department of Sociology, The Johns Hopkins University, Baltimore, MD.

Richardson, Diane. 2007. "Patterned Fluidities: (Re)Imagining the relationship between Gender and Sexuality." *Sociology* 41: 457–474.

Roberts, Kenneth D. 1997. "China's 'Tidal Wave' of Migrant Labor: What Can We Learn from Mexican Undocumented Migration to the United States?" *International Migration Review* 31: 249–293.

Robertson, Jennifer. 1998. *Takarazuka: Sexual politics and popular culture in modern Japan*. Berkeley, CA: University of California Press.

Robertson, Roland. 1992. *Globalization: Social Theory and Global Culture*. London, UK: Sage Publications.

Robertson, Roland. 1997. "Social Theory, Cultural Relativity and the Problem of Globality", in Anthony D. King, ed., *Culture, Globalization and the World-System*. Minneapolis, MN: University of Minnesota Press, pp. 69–90.

Rocha, Rodolfo. 1981. "The Influence of the Mexican Revolution on the Mexico-Texas Border, 1910–1916." Ph.D. dissertation, Department of History, Texas Tech University, Lubbock, TX.

Rockquemore, Kerry Ann. 2002. "Negotiating the color line: The gendered process of racial identity construction among Black/White biracial women." *Gender & Society* 16: 484–503.

Rockquemore, Kerry Ann and Patricia Arend. 2002. "Opting for White: Choice, fluidity, and Black identity construction in Post-Civil Rights America." *Race and Society* 5: 51–66.

Rockquemore, Kerry Ann and David L. Brunsma. 2001. *Beyond Black: Biracial Identity in America*. Thousands Oaks, CA: Sage Publication.

Rockquemore, Kerry Ann and David L. Brunsma. 2002. "Socially Embedded Identities: Theories, Typologies, and Processes of Racial Identity Among Biracials." *The Sociological Quarterly* 43: 335–356.

Rockquemore, Kerry Ann and Tracey Laszloffy, A. 2005. *Raising biracial children*. New York, NY: Altamira Press.

Rodriguez, Richard. 1982. *Hunger of Memory: The Education of Richard Rodriguez*. Boston, MA: David R. Godine.

Rogers, Reuel. 2001. "Black Like Who?: Afro-Caribbean Immigrants, African Americans, and the Politics of Group Identity", in Nancy Foner ed., *Islands in the City: West Indian Migration to New York*. Berkeley, CA: University of California Press, pp. 163–192.

Rohlehr, Gordon. 1990. *Calypso & Society in Pre-Independence Trinidad*. Port of Spain: Gordon Rohlehr.

Root, Maria P. 1990. "Disordered eating in women of color." *Sex Roles* 22: 525–535.

Root, Maria P. 1990. "Resolving 'Other' Status: Identity Development of Biracial Individuals." *Women and Therapy* 9: 185–205.

Roth, Wendy D. 2005. "The end of the one-drop rule? Labeling of multiracial children in Black intermarriages." *Sociological Forum* 20: 35–67.

Rubin, Gayle. "Thinking Sex: Notes for a Radical Theory of the Politics of Sexuality", in Henry Abelove, Michèle Aina Barale, and David M. Halperin, eds., *Lesbian and Gay Studies Reader*. New York: Routledge, pp. 3–44.

Rubin, Henry. 2003. *Self-Made Men: Identity and Embodiment among Transsexual Men*. Nashville, TN: Vanderbilt University Press.

Rumbaut, Rubén C. 1997. "Assimilation and Its Discontents: Between Rhetoric and Reality." *International Migration Review* 31: 923–60.

Rumbaut, Rubén C. 1994. "The Crucible Within: Ethnic Identity, Self-Esteem, and Segmented Assimilation among Children of Immigrants." *International Migration Review* 28: 748–94.

Russ, Joanna. 1985. *Magic Mommas, Trembling Sisters, Puritans, and Perverts: Feminist Essays*. Trumansberg, NY: Crossing Press.

Russell, Lord John. 1841. "Instructions to Governor Hobson of 9 December 1840." *British Parliamentary Papers (New Zealand)* 311: 24.

Sáenz, José de la Luz. 1933. *Los México-Americanos en la Gran Guerra y Su Contingente en Pro de la Democracia, La Humanidad y La Justicia.* Artes Gráficas, San Antonio, TX.

Safran, William. 1991. "Diasporas in Modern Societies: Myths of Homeland and Return." *Diaspora* 1: 83–99.

Sandos, James A. 1992. *Rebellion in the Borderlands: Anarchism and the Plan of San Diego, 1904–1923.* Norman, OK: University of Oklahoma Press.

San Miguel, Jr., Guadalupe. 2001. *"Let All of Them Take Heed": Mexican Americans and the Campaign for Educational Equality in Texas, 1910–1981.* College Station, TX: Texas A&M University Press.

Sanjek, Roger. 1996. "The Enduring Inequalities of Race", in Steven Gregory and Roger Sanjek, eds., *Race.* New Brunswick, NJ: Rutgers University Press, pp. 1–17.

Santiago-Vallès, Kelvin. 2003. "Some Notes On," Coloniality, And The Question Of History Among Puerto Ricans", in Carole Boyce Davies, ed., *Decolonizing the Academy: African Diaspora Studies.* Trenton, N.J. and Eritrea: Africa World Press, pp. 217–234.

Schiller, Herbert I. 1993. "The context of our work", in Kaarle Nordenstreng and Herbert I. Schiller, eds., *Beyond national sovereignty: International communication in the 1990's.* Norwood, NJ: Ablex, pp. 464–472.

Schilt, Kristen. 2006. "Just one of the guys? How Transmen Make Gender Visible at Work." *Gender & Society* 20: 465–490.

Schlossberg, Linda. 2001. "Introduction: Rites of Passing", in María Carla Sánchez and Linda Schlossberg, eds., *Passing: Identity and interpretation in sexuality, race, and religion.* New York: NYU Press, pp. 1–12.

Schmid, Andre. 2002. *Korea Between Empires 1895–1919.* New York: Columbia University Press.

Schwartz, Pepper and Virginia Rutter. 1998. *The Gender of Sexuality.* Thousand Oaks, CA: Pine Forge Press.

Scott, James. 1990. *Domination and the Arts of Resistance: Hidden Transcripts.* London, UK: Yale University Press.

Selwyn, Bishop George Augustus. 1863. "Speech at Peria, October 1862." *Appendices to the Journals of the House of Representatives* 1863, E-12: 9–12.

Sewell, Jr., William H. 2005. *Logics of History: Social Theory and Social Transformation.* Chicago, IL: The University of Chicago Press.

Shilling, Chris. 1993. *The Body and Social Theory.* London, UK: Sage Publications.

Shohat, Ella and Robert Stam. 1994. *Unthinking Eurocentrism: Multiculturalism and the Media.* London, UK: Routledge.

Simmel, Georg. [1922] 1955. "The Web of Group Affiliations", in Reinhard Bendix, trans. ed., *Conflict and the Web of Group Affiliations.* New York: Free Press, pp. 125–95.

Simmel, Georg. 1950. "The Stranger", in Kurt H. Wolf, ed. and trans., *The Sociology of Georg Simmel.* New York: The Free Press, pp. 402–408.

Simmel, Georg. 1950. *The Sociology of Georg Simmel.* Edited by Kurt Wolff. Glencoe, IL: Free Press.

Sinclair, Keith. 1986. *A destiny apart: New Zealander's search for national identity.* Wellington, New Zealand: Allen and Unwin.

Sloop, John M. 2004. *Disciplining Gender: Rhetorics of Sex Identity in Contemporary U.S. Culture.* Amherst, MA: University of Massachusetts Press.

Smith, Dorothy E. 1987. "Women's Perspective as a Radical Critique of Sociology", in Sandra Harding, ed., *Feminism and methodology.* Bloomington, IN: Indiana University Press, pp. 84–96.

Smith, Linda. 1998. *Decolonizing methodologies: Research and indigenous peoples.* New York: Zed Books.

Snow, David and Leon Anderson. 1987. "Identity Work Among the Homeless: The Verbal Construction and Avowal of Personal Identity." *American Journal of Sociology* 92: 1336–1371.

Solinger, Dorothy J. 1990. "Citizenship Issues in China's Internal Migration: Comparisons with Germany and Japan." *Political Science Quarterly* 114: 455–78.

Solinger, Dorothy J. 1995. "China's Urban Transients in the Transition from Socialism and the Collapse of the Communist 'Urban Public Goods Regime.'" *Comparative Politics* 27: 127–146.

Sollors, Werner. 1989. *The Invention of Ethnicity.* New York: Oxford University Press.

Soyer, Daniel. 1997. *Jewish Immigrant Associations and American Identity in New York, 1880–1939: Jewish Landsmanshaftn in American Culture.* Detroit, MI: Wayne State University Press.

Soysal, Yasemin Nuhoglu. 1994. *Limits of Citizenship.* Chicago, IL: University of Chicago Press.

Spolsky, Bernard. 2003. "Reassessing Maori Regeneration." *Language in Society* 32: 553–578.

Sprague, Joey and Mary Zimmerman. 1993. "Overcoming Dualisms: A Feminist Agenda for Sociological Method", in Paula England, ed., *Theory on Gender/Feminism on Theory.* New York: Aldine DeGruyter, pp. 225–279.

Spry, Tami. 2006. "Performing Autoethnography: An Embodied Methodological Praxis", in Sharlene Hesse-Biber and Patricia Leavy, eds., *Emergent Methods in Social Research.* Thousand Oaks, CA: Sage.

Stacey, Judith. 2004. "Cruising to Familyland: Hypergamy and Rainbow Kinship." *Current Sociology* 52: 181–197.

Stafford, Edward. 1858. "Stafford to Gore-Browne, May 6, 1857." *Appendices to the Journals of the House of Representatives, 1858, E-5.*

Stallybras, Peter and Allon White. 1986. *The Politics and Poetics of Transgression.* Ithaca, NY: Cornell University Press.

Stanley, Lord. 1958. "Memorandum of 23 August 1842", in Alexander H. McLintock, ed., *Crown Colony Government in New Zealand.* Wellington, New Zealand: Government Printer.

Stanley, Lord. 1844. "Lord Stanley to Governor Fitzroy, 10 February 1844, *British Parliamentary Papers (New Zealand)*, Vol. 2, Appendices (No. 4): 171.

Steinberg, Stephen. 1989. *The Ethnic Myth: Race, Ethnicity, and Class in America,* 2nd Ed. Boston, MA: Beacon Press.

Stice, Eric, Erika Schupak-Neuberg, Heather E. Shaw and Richard I. Stein. 1994. "Relation of media exposure to eating disorder symptomatology: An examination of mediating mechanisms." *Journal of Abnormal Psychology* 103: 836–840.

Stice, Eric and Heather E. Shaw. 1994. "Adverse effects of the media portrayed thin-ideal on women and linkages to bulimic symptomatology." *Journal of Social and Clinical Psychology* 13: 288–308.

Stockowski, Wiktor. 2007. "Racisme, antiracisme et cosmologie lévi-straussienne: un essai d'anthropologie reflexive." *L'Homme* 182: 7–51.

Stokes, Evelyn. 1999. *Wiremu Tamihana Tarapipipi Te Waharoa: a Study of his Life and Times.* Hamilton, New Zealand: University of Waikato.

Stone, John. 1996. "Internal Colonialism", in John Hutchinson and Anthony D. Smith, eds., *Ethnicity*. Oxford, UK: Oxford University Press, pp. 278–281.

Stone, Sandy. 1991. "The Empire Strikes Back: A Posttranssexual Manifesto", in Julia Epstein and Kristina Straub, eds., *Body Guards: The Cultural Politics of Gender Ambiguity*. New York: Routledge.

Storrs, Debbie. 1999. "Whiteness as Stigma: Essentialist Identity Work among Mixed-Race Women." *Symbolic Interaction* 22: 187–212.

Sugrue, Thomas J. 2003. "Revisiting the Second Ghetto." *Journal of Urban History* 29: 281–290.

Sussman, Nan M. 2000. "The Dynamic Nature of Cultural Identity Throughout Cultural Transitions: Why Home is Not So Sweet." *Personality and Social Psychology Review* 4: 355–373.

Tabb, William. 1970. *The Political Economy of the Black Ghetto.* New York: W. W. Norton.

Te Kohere, Reweti. 1903. "Te Reo Maori." *Te Pipiwharauroa: He Kupu Whakamarama* 70: 2–3.

Te Rau Matatini. (2006a). *Kia Puāwai Te Ararau: National Māori Mental Health Careers.* Palmerston North, New Zealand.

Te Rau Matatini. (2006b). *Recruitment and Promotion of Māori Mental Health Workforce Development Strategic Plan.* Palmerston North. New Zealand: Statistics New Zealand. 2001. Statistics New Zealand. Wellington. Statistics New Zealand. 2007. QuickStats About Māori. Statistics New Zealand, Wellington.

Terkessidis, Mark. 2000. "Global Culture in Germany or: How Repressed Women and Criminals Rescue Hybridity." *Communal/Plural* 8: 219–235.

Tie, Warwick. 1999. *Legal Pluralism: Toward a Multicultural Conception of Law.* Aldershot, UK: Dartmouth and Ashgate.

Thomas, William I. and Florian Znaniecki. 1918. *The Polish Peasant in Europe and America.* Boston, MA: Richard G. Badger.

Thompson, Janna. 1998. "Community Identity and World Citizenship", in Daniele Archibugi, David Held, and Martin Köhler, eds., *Re-imagining Political Community*. Stanford, CA: Stanford University Press, pp. 179–197.

Tinney, James S., and Justine J. Rector, eds. 1980. *Issues and Trends in Afro-American Journalism.* Lanham, MD: University Press of America.

Tolnay, Stewart. 1997. "The Great Migration and Changes in the Northern Black Family, 1940–1990." *SocialForces* 4: 1213–39.

Tomlinson, John 1999. *Globalization and culture*. Chicago, IL: The University of Chicago Press.

Tong, Chee-kiong and Kwok-bun Chan. 2001. "One Face, Many Masks: The Singularity and Plurality of Chinese Identity." *Diaspora* 10: 361–389.

Torres, Lourdes. 2007. "Boricua Lesbians: Sexuality, Nationality, and the Politics of Passing." *CENTRO: Journal of the Center for Puerto Rican Studies, Special Issue: Puerto Rican Queer Sexualities* 19: 230–249.

Towle, Evan B. and Lynn M. Morgan. 2002. "Romancing the Transgender Native: Rethinking the Use of the "Third Gender" concept." *GLQ: A Journal of Lesbian & Gay Studies* 4: 469–497.

Tricarico, Donald. 1984. "The 'New' Italian-American Ethnicity." *The Journal of Ethnic Studies* 12: 75–93.

Trotter, Joe William, ed. 1991. *The Great Migration in Historical Perspective*. Bloomington, IN: Indiana University Press.

Truett, Samuel and Elliott Young. 2004, eds. *Continental Crossroads: Remapping U.S.-Mexico Borderlands History*. Durham, NC: Duke University Press.

Turner, Victor. 1964. "Symbols in Ndembu Ritual", in Max Gluckman, ed., *Closed Systems and Open Minds*. Edinburgh, UK: Oliver and Boyd, pp. 20–51.

Turner, Victor. 1969. *The Ritual Process: Structure and Anti-Structure*. Chicago, IL: Aldine Publishing Co.

Turner, Victor. 1974. *Dramas, Fields and Metaphors: Symbolic Action in Human Society*. Chicago, IL: University of Chicago Press.

Twine, France Winddance. 1996. "Brown-Skinned White Girls: Class, Culture, and the Construction of White Identity in Suburban Communities." *Gender, Place, and Culture: A Journal of Feminist* 3: 205.

Urry, John. 2000. "The Sociology of Space and Place", in Judith R. Blau, ed., in *Blackwell Companion to Sociology*. Malden, MA: Blackwell Publishers, pp. 3–15.

U.S. Department of Education. 2006. "Minority Females as a Percent of Total College Enrollment, 1994–1996 to 2005–2006." Access statistical data at: http://www.collegeboard.com/highered/res/hel/hel.html.

Valoochi, Stephen M. 2005. "'Not yet queer enough:' the lessons of Queer Theory for the Sociology of Gender and Sexuality." *Gender & Society* 19: 750–770.

Vecoli, Rudoph. 1964. "*Contadini* in Chicago: A Critique of the 'Uprooted.'" *Journal of American History* 51: 404–16.

Vecoli, Rudoph. 1990. "From the Uprooted to the Transplanted: The Writing of American Immigration History, 1951–1989", in Valeria Gennaro Lerda, ed., *From 'Melting Pot' to Multiculturalism: The Evolution of Ethnic Relations in the United States and Canada*. Rome, Italy: Bulzoni Editore, pp. 25–54.

Vickerman, Milton. 2001. "Tweaking a Monolith: the West Indian Immigrant Encounter with "Blackness", in Nancy Foner, ed., *Islands in the City: West Indian Migration to New York*. Berkley, CA: University of California Press, pp. 237–256.

Vickerman, Milton. 2006. "Non-Hispanic West Indians in New York City", in Chrisopher Airriess and Ines Mirayes, eds., *Contemporary Ethnic Geographies in America*. Lanham, MD: Rowman and Littlefield.

Vidal-Ortiz, Salvador. 2002. "Queering Sexuality and Doing Gender: Transgender men's identification with gender and sexuality", in Patricia Gagné and Richard Tweksbury, eds., *Gendered Sexualities (Advances in Gender Research, Volume 6)*. New York: Elsevier Press, pp. 181–233.

Vidal-Ortiz, Salvador. 2004. "On Being a White Person of Color: Using Autoethnography to Understand Puerto Ricans' Racialization." *Qualitative Sociology* 27: 179–203.

Vidal-Ortiz, Salvador. 2008. "Transgender and Transsexual Studies: Sociology's Influence and Future Steps." *Sociology Compass*. 2: 433–450.

Vila, Pablo. 2000. *Crossing Borders/Reinforcing Borders: Social Categories, Metaphors, and Narrative Identities on the U.S.-Mexico Frontier*. Austin, TX: University of Texas Press.

Wade, Peter. 2005. "Rethinking Mestizaje: Ideology and Lived Experience." *Journal of Latin American Studies* 37: 239–257.

Waldinger, Roger. 1996. *Still the Promised City? African-Americans and New Immigrants in Post-Industrial New York*. Cambridge, MA: Harvard University Press.

Walker, Ranginui. 1987. *Nga tau tohetohe: Years of anger*. Auckland, New Zealand: Penguin Books.

Walker, Ranginui. 1990. *Ka whawhai tonu matou: Struggle without end*. Auckland, New Zealand: Penguin Books.

Wallace, Kendra. 2004. "Situating Multiethnic Identity: Contributions of Discourse Theory to the Study of Mixed-Heritage Students." *Journal of Language, Identity, and Education* 3: 195.

Wallerstein, Immanuel. 1974. *The Modern World-System*. San Diego, CA: Academic Press.

Wallerstein, Immanuel. 1979. *The Capitalist World Economy*. New York: Cambridge University Press.

Wallerstein, Immanuel. 1991. *Geopolitics and Geoculture: Essays on the Changing World-System*. New York: Cambridge University Press.

Wallerstein, Immanuel. 1991. "The Ideological Tensions of Capitalism: Universalism versus Racism and Sexism", in Etienne Balibar and Immanuel Wallerstein, eds., *Race, Nation, Class: Ambiguous Identities*. London, UK: Verso, pp. 29–36.

Waters, Mary C. 2001. *Black identities: West Indian immigrant dreams and American realities, (2nd ed.)*. Cambridge, MA: Harvard University Press.

Werlen, Benno. 1993. *Society, Action, and Space*. London, England: Routledge, MA.

West, Candance and Don H. Zimmerman. 1987. "Doing gender." *Gender and Society* 1: 125–151.

Whyte, William F. 1993. *Street Corner Society: The Social Structure of an Italian Slum, 4th Ed*. Chicago, IL: University of Chicago Press.

Wi Parata v. The Bishop of Wellington, 1877, 3 Jur. N.S. 72.

Wilcox, Annabelle. 2003. "Branding Teena: (Mis)Representations in the Media." *Sexualities* 6: 407–25.

William L. Yancey, Eugene P. Ericksen and Richard N. Juliani. 1976. "Emergent Ethnicity: A Review and Reformulation." *American Sociological Review* 41: 391–403.

Wilson, William Julius. 1987. *The Truly Disadvantaged*. Chicago, IL: University of Chicago Press.

Wright, Richard, Serin Houston, Mark Ellis, Stephen Holloway and Margaret Hudson. 2003. "Crossing Racial Lines: Geographies of Mixed-race Partnering and Multiraciality in the United States." *Progress in Human Geography* 27: 457–474.

Wu, Xiaogang and Donald Treiman. 2004. "The Household Registration System and Social Stratification in China: 1955–1996." *Demography* 41: 363–384.

Yancey, George. 2003. *Who is White? Latinos, Asians, and the New Black/Nonblack Divide*. Boulder, CO: Lynne Rienner Publishers.

Yang, Quanhe and Fei Guo. 1996. "Occupational Attainments of Rural to Urban Temporary Economic Migrants in China, 1985–1990." *International Migration Review* 30: 771–787.

Yeatman, Anna. 1995. "Interlocking oppressions", in Barbara Caine and Rosemary Pringle eds., *Transitions: New Australian feminisms*. New South Wales, Australia: Allen and Unwin, pp. 42–56.

Yegenoglu, M. 1998. *Colonial fantasies: Toward a feminist reading of Orientalism*. Cambridge, MA: Cambridge University Press.

Young, Robert. 1995. *Colonial Desire: Hybridity in Theory, Culture, and Race*. London, UK: Routledge.

Zamir, Shamoon. 1995. *Dark Voices: W. E. B. Du Bois and American Thought, 1888–1903*. Chicago, IL: University of Chicago Press.

Zamora, Emilio. 1993. *The World of the Mexican Worker in Texas*. College Station, TX: Texas A&M University Press.

Zephir, Flore. 2001. *Trends in ethnic identification among second generation Haitian immigrants in New York City*. Westport, CT: Bergin & Garvey.

Zerubavel, Eviatar. 1996. "Lumping and Splitting: Notes on Social Classification." *Sociological Forum* 11: 421–433.

Zerubavel, Eviatar. 2003. *Social Mindscapes: An Invitation to Cognitive Sociology*. Cambridge, MA: Harvard University Press.

Index

STUDIES IN CRITICAL SOCIAL SCIENCES

The Studies in Critical Social Science *book series, through the publication of original manuscripts and edited volumes, offers insights into the current reality by exploring the content and consequence of power relationships under capitalism, by considering the spaces of opposition and resistance to these changes, and by articulating capitalism with other systems of power and domination – for example race, gender, culture – that have been defining our new age.*

ISSN 1537-4234

1. LEVINE, Rhonda F. (ed.) *Enriching the Social Imagination.* How Radical Sociology Changed the Discipline. 2004. ISBN 90 04 13992 3
2. COATES, Rodney D. (ed.) *Race and Ethnicity.* Across Time, Space and Discipline. 2004. ISBN 90 04 13991 5
3. PODOBNIK, B. & T. REIFER (eds.) *Transforming Globalization.* Challenges and Opportunities in the Post 9/11 Era. 2005. ISBN 90 04 14583 4
4. PFOHL, S., A. VAN WAGENEN, P. AREND, A. BROOKS & D. LECKENBY (eds.) *Culture, Power, and History.* Studies in Critical Sociology. 2005. ISBN 90 04 14659 8
5. JORGENSON, Andrew & Edward KICK (eds.) *Globalization and the Environment.* 2006. ISBN 90 04 15132 X
6. GOLDSTEIN, Warren (ed.) *Marx, Critical Theory, and Religion.* A Critique of Rational Choice. 2006. ISBN 90 04 15238 5
7. DELLO BUONO, Richard A. & José BELL LARA (eds.) *Imperialism, Neoliberalism and Social Struggles in Latin America.* 2007. ISBN 90 04 15365 9
8. PAOLUCCI, Paul B. *Marx's Scientific Dialectics.* A Methodological Treatise for a New Century. 2007. ISBN 978 90 04 15860 3
9. OTT, Michael R. (ed.) *The Future of Religion.* Toward a Reconciled Society. 2007. ISBN 978 90 04 16014 9
10. ZAFIROVSKI, Milan. *Liberal Modernity and Its Adversaries.* Freedom, Liberalism and Anti-Liberalism in the 21st Century. 2007. ISBN 978 90 04 16052 1
11. WORRELL, Mark P. *Dialectic of Solidarity.* Labor, Antisemitism, and the Frankfurt School. 2008. ISBN 978 90 04 16886 2
12. IYALL SMITH, Keri E. & Patricia LEAVY (eds.) *Hybrid Identities.* Theoretical and Empirical Examinations. 2008. ISBN 978 90 04 17039 1